THE FORGOTTEN REALM

Endorsements for *The Forgotten Realm*

Elizabeth Landis's *The Forgotten Realm* is a great primer on government in America, explaining not just the federal government but also state, county, and city government and special districts. Understanding how the governments that have jurisdiction over you are organized and function is critical to responsible citizenship, and this book provides a good basic education in what you need to know.

Aaron Renn
Writer and social critic

The princely powers of American politics have for too long framed our system of governance to suit their own interests, focusing attention on the halls of power in Washington, D.C. They entice us to either join our voices to the amplified rage machine or withdraw in despair. Elizabeth Landis flips the machine on its head, inviting Christians to engage first, as our forefathers did, in community, in neighborliness, in local action, and in concern at the state level. Her step-by-step, bottom-up breakdown of the American system reveals that there are ample opportunities for Christians to engage responsibly and effectively in politics, not with rage but with mercy, bearing witness to our faith, and effecting the only kind of change that lasts, which is the change of the human heart.

Tony Woodlief
Author of *I, Citizen*

In writing this book, Landis did the hard but imperative work of making clear what is utterly opaque for most of us. As American Christians, we desperately need this book on civic engagement.

Benjamin R. Merkle
President of New Saint Andrews College

As a former mayor of Frankfort, Indiana, I can wholeheartedly attest that *The Forgotten Realm: Civics for American Christians* is exactly what our country needs. The book eloquently outlines how we, as a community of faith, can understand and engage with municipal government—an essential aspect of our democratic process.

Chris McBarnes
Indiana's youngest and Frankfort's only third-term elected mayor

A good book is one you enjoy upon first reading. A great book is one you pick back up again. Elizabeth Landis has produced such a book for those who have a sneaking suspicion that God's truth has been forgotten in the civil realm. We abdicate out of ignorance, but no one can plead ignorance after reading Landis's book. Written by a born-again Christian with a strong, conservative voice, this is a well-researched handbook that will help you explore how to faithfully steward your responsibilities as an American citizen and will inspire you to participate out of a love of God and neighbor. What is required is "an educated faith," says Landis. If you want to make a difference in your community, state, and country, Elizabeth Landis will show you how in *The Forgotten Realm.* Read this book once, and keep it accessible on a nearby shelf, because you'll be sure to pick it up again.

Quinton Cools
Vice President at TeenPact Leadership Schools

Now, more than ever, it is essential to stand up for our beliefs in the public sphere—but how can we do so effectively? This book provides a remarkably clear rationale paired with a practical "nuts-and-bolts" approach to fulfilling our duties as citizens.

Ben Hodge
California constituent of We the People

Elizabeth Landis has lived as a model of what an engaged Christian citizen should look like, both in the stands she takes and the grace with which she takes them. Her new volume is a useful guidebook for others to follow in the same work, where reinforcements are sorely needed.

Lincoln Davis Wilson
Senior Counsel for Alliance Defending Freedom

THE FORGOTTEN REALM

CIVICS FOR AMERICAN CHRISTIANS

ELIZABETH LANDIS

The Forgotten Realm: Civics for American Christians

Published by Roman Roads Press
Moscow, Idaho

RomanRoadsPress.com

General Editor: Daniel Foucachon
Editors: Aiden Anderson, Laura Baxter, Carissa Hale, John H. Wright
Interior Layout and Illustrations: Carissa Hale

For permissions or publishing inquiries, email info@romanroadspress.com

The Forgotten Realm: Civics for American Christians
Elizabeth Landis

ISBN 13: 978-1-963505-08-5
Version 1.1.0 November 2024

To my husband Greg Landis

and

To our children Caroline, George, Laurabeth with Dane,
Isabelle, and Jack

and

To our friend Chris Vawter who walked with us
into the wind

and

To the many people who have providentially
helped with this project

and

To Americans across our nation

CONTENTS

LIST OF FIGURES

7 National Government

8 Voting, Elections & Parties

Conclusion

FOREWORD

Miles Smith IV

When Abraham Lincoln ran for President in 1860, he remarked on his childhood poverty to journalists, calling it the short and simple annals of the poor. Poverty was his story. But he also mentioned the impact of his stepmother Sarah Bush Lincoln. She raised him as an adolescent and fired his love of reading, fostering his literary and (more importantly) his political imagination. Every initial lesson Lincoln learned, he received from his stepmother and his local community. He attended school only sporadically, so it was Lincoln's civic education—a homeschool education if there ever was one—that guided him and eventually made him one of our country's leaders.

Lincolnian politicians were in short order in 2024, and a healthy understanding of American civics and American politics are in even shorter order. A poll conducted by the University of Pennsylvania in 2023 noted that while two-thirds of Americans can name all three branches of the federal government, nearly twenty percent—one in five Americans—cannot name *any* of the federal branches. Kathleen Hall Jamieson, director of the nonpartisan Annenberg Public Policy Center, noted that "one is unlikely to cherish or work to protect freedoms one does not know one has and will have trouble holding elected and unelected leaders accountable if one does not understand the nature and prerogatives of each branch and the ways in which the power of each is kept in check." Understanding the government and how government works is vitally important for the maintenance of free republican societies.

Teaching civics, however, is an increasingly unpopular pursuit. Specific forms of ideological capture at major prestigious colleges and universities have relegated the idea of civics to the curricular backburner in exchange for ideologically driven classes focusing on race, class, and gender. Whatever value these new classes may offer pales in comparison to the necessity of teaching young Americans to be good citizens. Likewise our institutions, be they educational, political, or social, seem uninterested in either the civic foundations of the American union or the civics necessary to maintain healthy families, towns, states, and even countries. Indifference towards civics or even sometimes an outright antagonism towards the United States' civic foundations has occurred at the same time as the primary and secondary public school systems themselves have decayed through years of institutional ossification and poor policy choices, to say nothing of the rise of progressive and more extreme "woke" ideologies. There are few institutions willing to teach civics. The ones that do teach it often do so in ways that are antagonistic to republican liberties as codified in and guaranteed by the basic law of the United States, the Constitution.

The situation of civics in post-secondary education is not much better than in the public schools. Of the fifty most selective liberal arts colleges in the United States, only two—my employer and St John's College—make any substantive attempt at educating students on Western civilization and the United States' historical and political inheritance. These politics and history classes thrive in colleges where they are taught to students already possessing a healthy secondary civics education. It is hard to understand the power of Frederick Douglass's moral and unequivocally Christian plea for racial equality if you don't realize that Douglass understood the Declaration of Independence backward and forward. Civics drove the cultural and political life of the United States from its inception in 1776 right up to our own time, and we ignore it at our own risk.

Elizabeth Landis is a citizen, a wife, a mother, and an educator who is aware of the consequences of failures in civics education. Thankfully, she has chosen not to ignore the pressing question of how Americans, in particular American Christians, can reclaim teaching civics in a way that is ultimately ordered to the glory of God. *The Forgotten Realm: Civics for American Christians* is a reminder that our duties toward our families, our friends, and our fellow citizens require us to take our civic involvement seriously. Landis's work offers real wisdom, erudition, and humble counsel for the very real Christian citizens who do the steady and entirely nonsensational work of being parents to their children, friends to their neighbors, and fellow citizens to their countrymen.

The most refreshing aspect of *The Forgotten Realm* is its steady sobriety and its commitment to helping American Christians sustain civic institutions. In an era when conservative Christians are understandably frustrated, they also tend to embrace sensational and often unhealthy political screeds that sound more like revolutionary calls to burn down American civic life than they do calls to redeem and restore it. Landis isn't interested in iconoclasm or revolution. She wants to restore and sustain the best of American civics. *The Forgotten Realm* "is not a rally to put our hopes behind a candidate nor an attempt to whip up the far right. Instead, it is an appeal to walk humbly with the Lord God into the civic realm, which we seem to have forgotten, yet which is all around us."

Landis puts her money where her mouth is. The book you have in your hands is not a blueprint for national conquest by conservative Christians, and it is not a how-to manual to ensure your children will never be exposed to progressives or the left. It is a comprehensive guide to citizenship. Citizenship, Landis helpfully argues, is practiced at the local, state, and national levels. But all too many Christian works on citizenship focus only on national politics, leaving conservative Christians often entirely in the dark as to how their municipal or county governments work. Landis addresses local and state government comprehensively. There is, Landis rightfully notes, "great power in starting small." American Christians can learn government and effect change "incrementally beginning right where we live." American Christians seem to have no problem thinking about God in relation to the grand national institutions that few of them ever have a substantive relationship with—the army, Congress, the President, etc.—but how many Christians have ever considered that God might have them think about His doings in their local council-administrator county government or their mayor-council or council-manager city governments? Few, if any, books ever focus on these local governments that nonetheless are far more likely to affect the lives of Christians for good or evil than the federal government. The excesses of the Covid regime, for example, were impositions by city and county governments, not the national Congress.

A second helpful aspect of the work is Landis's irenic approach to her very real Christian commitments. This is a work for Christians—a Roman Catholic, a Baptist, and a Lutheran could all find it useful—without being a work that slips into unnecessary sectarianism. In a time when all too many understandably confused and worried Christians look to the church's spiritual mission to answer political questions, Landis offers a rightly ordered vision of Christian citizens doing the work of politics. In a time when debates over the relationship between church and state and between religion and the American republic are all the rage, Landis is one of the people who actually understands the mission of the church and the mission of civics and is capable of speaking to the relationship between them.

The Forgotten Realm is a carefully written, comprehensive, and humble call for American Christians to take up the mantle of citizenship that God has called them to. Landis reminds her readers that Christ taught His disciples to pray for His kingdom to come on earth as it is in heaven. With that long-range view in mind, American Christians "can afford to be patient and learn to serve in the civil arena with an eye of faith looking towards civic renewal and reformation." In a historical moment when institutional arson typifies American civic life, there is a desperate need for sober-minded and wise teachers who show American Christians how to stay at their civic posts and do the often-unglamorous work of civic life in their towns and counties. In Elizabeth Landis, American Christians have one such teacher.

Miles Smith IV
Hillsdale, Michigan
October 2024

PREFACE

This book is not a rally to put our hopes behind a candidate nor an attempt to whip up the far right. Instead, it is an appeal to walk humbly with the Lord God into the civil realm, which we seem to have forgotten, yet which is all around us. Our hope is in the Lord, not in our senators. The Lord gives justice to the oppressed. The Lord gives food to the hungry. The Lord gives freedom to the prisoners. Happy are we who have Him for our help. Why should we despair as we see our nation in ideological and partisan tatters? It seems that as we turn our gaze upon the public square and see all that there is to learn and do in our systems of governance, we should detect a mustard seed that will flourish as part of God's design in our lives, and we should have great hope.

Psalm 146

Praise the LORD!
Praise the LORD, O my soul!
2 While I live I will praise the LORD;
I will sing praises to my God while I have my being.
3 Do not put your trust in princes,
Nor in a son of man, in whom there is no help.
4 His spirit departs, he returns to his earth;

In that very day his plans perish.
5 Happy is he who has the God of Jacob for his help,
Whose hope is in the LORD his God,
6 Who made heaven and earth,
The sea, and all that is in them;
Who keeps truth forever,
7 Who executes justice for the oppressed,
Who gives food to the hungry.
The LORD gives freedom to the prisoners.
8 The LORD opens the eyes of the blind;
The LORD raises those who are bowed down;
The LORD loves the righteous.
9 The LORD watches over the strangers;
He relieves the fatherless and widow;
But the way of the wicked He turns upside down.
10 The LORD shall reign forever—
Your God, O Zion, to all generations.
Praise the LORD!

INTRODUCTION

As conservative American Christians, we are a politically frustrated people. Some of us survey the political landscape and throw in the towel. Some look for a political savior to appear. Others resort to anger or declare that Christians should have nothing to do with the political process. And a few muster the effort and finances to run for office often without much preparation for the real job if elected. But it doesn't have to be this way. We don't have to feel frustrated, defeated, angry, or unprepared. And we must not turn away. Our government was designed to be run by We the People.[1] Somewhere along the way, we lost that memo because we lost the instruction manual to the civil realm of American government. But the knowledge we lost was top-down knowledge. That loss resulted in somewhat of a chasm between the people and our government. There has been no clear path forged into the civil realm from the bottom upward until now.

Welcome to *The Forgotten Realm*—the realm of American civil government, tipped on its end and explained from the bottom (local) up (state then national) in a way that regular

1 More explanation of this term *We the People* is forthcoming in chapter 1, "The Realm of Civil Government and Dual Citizenship." For the sake of not opening a grammatical can of worms, I have chosen not to change the form *We the People* to *Us the People* when the sentence structure would otherwise require it.

people can understand. This book is specifically tailored for Christians and looks to Scripture—especially the Book of Proverbs—for guidance in navigating the systems of American government in a different manner from what is customarily done. There are many books already out there that analyze our current American plight philosophically or theoretically, but they offer very little practical hope or help. Their flabby solutions commonly reside in the final chapter and leave the reader without a feasible plan of action or sense of direction.

Greetings. I am Elizabeth Landis. I've pieced this forgotten realm together for you bit by bit. I must confess that I didn't know much about the civil realm myself until I was thrust headlong into it. I would like your point of entry to be more gentle, more measured, and more pleasant. That is, in part, why I wrote this book. The other part is that it has become a calling: if I can convey to you what I have learned, seen, heard, and experienced in the civil realm, I really believe that it can eventually renew our nation. This book represents my best efforts to understand our American system of governance. I bequeath it to you that you may take it and run forward to God's glory.

Regarding the book's organization, don't be deterred by all of the footnotes—this isn't a scholarly tome. The footnotes help readers who want more information. They represent how I stitched this realm together into a visible whole. You can dip down into them whenever and wherever you want to know more. If what is in the main text is enough for you, that's fine with me—chin up, stay on course, and don't jump ship because of the details swirling below the surface.

In order to get the most out of the resources listed in the footnotes, you will want to go to our website **CivilRealm.com**. Many of the footnotes contain online sources where more information can be found. This is indicated by the symbol 🔗. Our website provides a list of all of the resources used and a link to the corresponding web page.

Most of the chapters begin with a short story of someone engaging in the civil realm. As a companion to the footnotes, these true stories are meant to connect this realm to real life. Each story serves as a prelude to the chapter itself. Some of these stories are my own, and others come from friends and acquaintances who have had interactions with various levels of government in the civil realm. Wherever the stories are located, they are italicized to distinguish them as real-life examples.

Further, because this is a civics book, most of the chapters contain sections (sometimes lengthy) on the formation of government, the services it offers, how its law operates, and what its structure is. You will recognize a common repetition of legislative (making the law), executive (carrying out the law), and judicial (interpreting the law's meaning) branches throughout the book. This structure is not just a convenient categorization, rather it is a reflection of the U.S. Constitution's first three articles defining how public business is transacted at all levels of our nation's government.

Most chapters also feature a section containing **Other Things You Should Know**, the contents of which don't necessarily fit neatly elsewhere yet are very helpful to know. That section is generally followed by **Things You Can Do** which are simple, concrete action steps that you can take as you learn your way around the civil realm. It is not possible for one person to do all of them, but imagine the impact on American culture if all of us did just a few of them. This book is intended for all ages—young people through senior citizens. However, not all of the activities listed in **Things You Can Do** are appropriate for young people to do alone. Please exercise wise judgment in the application of the book's principles. The last section (informally and somewhat cheekily titled **So What?**) contains takeaways from the chapter to check your understanding. Underlined words are located in the Glossary at the back of the book. Also located in the back are appendices that contain expanded information on several topics for further reference.

Now for a cursory overview of each chapter:

Chapter 1: The Realm of Civil Government & Dual Citizenship

- The first discovery on the path is that there is a sphere of God's governing order that seemingly has been locked up tight. This sphere of governance goes by different names. I call it the civil realm. But you may not even know what civil realm means because we have forgotten about it for a long time.
- As American Christians, a people called to serve our Creator, it is generally clear to us that we should be active in our local churches. It is also clear that we should be faithful in raising our families. It is not as clear to us that we should be involved in the public governance of our cities, counties, special districts, states, and our nation. The current state of affairs reveals a distinct absence of Christian thought, kindness, leadership, and participation in the public square.

Chapter 2: Layers of Law—The Cornerstone Chapter

- This chapter presents the hierarchical framework of law as it exists in our nation in an accessible and understandable fashion. Here, we examine the layers of law (from the Scriptures to federal, state, and local law) that comprise the authority of governance that we live under as Americans. The contents consist of a top-down overview of authority as it exists in the law. The entire book is anchored in this chapter and expands from it. Thus, I refer to it as "The Cornerstone Chapter."

Chapter 3: City Government

- With this framework of law in view, I then invite the reader to dive down to the lower depths of the civil realm, the level most closely associated with where we live—the city. I call this approach the inverted model because rather than starting with the traditional model of presenting national government first, I begin with local government and build up from there to the White House, Capitol Hill, and the Supreme Court of the United States (SCOTUS).
- Here, we learn what the structure of city government can look like across the nation and how it works. The civil realm will remain forgotten unless we actually enter it and begin to engage as American citizens, so here is where I start the process of helping the reader step out and begin attending local government meetings.[2]
- As you begin to observe governance processes through the lens of your newly gained knowledge, you will see elected and appointed people who do it well and who do it poorly. Be patient and observe. Remember James 1:19–20: "So then, my beloved brethren, let every man be swift to hear, slow to speak, slow to wrath; for the wrath of man does not produce the righteousness of God." Public

2 In this book, the term *local government* means *city*, *county-equivalent*, and *special district governments*.

servants are people just like you and me. They did not have this book to learn from, but they did leap into public service—for better or worse.

Chapter 4: County-Equivalent Government

- This chapter distinguishes the county from the city: a distinction that is frequently blurred. Furthermore, some states use different names for a county, so this book uses the term *county equivalent.*
- Similar to the previous chapter, here we learn what the structure of county-equivalent government can look like across the nation and how each type generally works.
- We will also survey the landscape of other elected county-level offices along with the general services that counties provide. But we won't just learn **about** these systems of governance, we will learn to **engage with them as Christians**.

Chapter 5: Special Districts, Independent Cities, Townships & Regional Governments

- The structures of local government vary widely across the nation. Such variety presents a challenge when trying to understand how we may be governed. This chapter, though not entirely comprehensive, houses some of these lesser-known forms of government that exist among us. Lesser-known does not mean lesser in importance; there is much to unearth and begin to understand here.
- This is the first chapter since the "Layers of Law" chapter where we touch upon the lack of government accountability to We the People. As we

cover the layers of governance, you may notice that some areas lack direct representation such as local special districts (and later, some state and national agencies).

Chapter 6: State Government

- This book explains federalism—the principle that the U.S. Constitution[3] both outlines limited powers for the federal government **and** recognizes expansive powers of the states and the people. The principle of federalism beckons us into the civil realm at all levels but especially at the state level which is the focus of this chapter. Federalism points us to where We the People reside.
- Because the states have the freedom to manage their own governments, our states form a patchwork quilt of how the government operates. This book will help you find your place within the patchwork quilt and guide you to being loosely conversant there.

Chapter 7: National Government

- You wouldn't know it by the current size of the federal government or from the attention that it receives, but the Constitution outlines limited powers for the national level. Thanks in part to the news media, the national government customarily takes center stage in civics. In the inverted civics model, the national level has to wait until this chapter because there is so much to recover everywhere else.

---

3 Although written in shorthand as *Constitution* or *U.S. Constitution*, the document's full, official name is ***The Constitution of the United States***.

Chapter 8: Voting, Elections & Parties

- Here, we touch upon the topic of elections with the intent of helping the average reader be a registered, prepared voter in advance of each election.
- The reader will also learn where to verify results during and after an election. This information frees us from a dependency upon the media in order to know election outcomes.
- This is not a book about voting per se or about running for office as the primary solution to our governmental problems. The ballot box is not our savior, and I am not looking for us to feel smug if we have voted. Our duty as citizens goes much deeper than that. We have more significant groundwork to cover than trying to win an election. The civil realm does extend beyond the next election cycle.
- There is a lot of territory between your civic duty of voting and running for office—the territory that this book will explore. Until we learn how our cities, counties, special districts, and states function, we are merely being led by the nose at great expense. Knowing how these structures function is a strategic foundation for understanding elections.

Chapter 9: Christian Diplomacy

- In this chapter, we learn how our dual citizenship influences the civil realm. We learn how to navigate as Christians, and we learn how to navigate as Americans. Knowledge is power,[4] and we just

4 This quote is often attributed to Francis Bacon and reads in a parenthetical statement as such: "(for knowledge itself is a power whereby he knoweth)." Francis Bacon, *The Works of Francis Bacon, Lord Chancellor of England: A New Edition with a Life of the*

noted that we have much knowledge to recover in the civil realm before we pursue the powerful mantle of elected office. But knowledge alone is not enough to recover the forgotten realm, and elected office is not the sole future goal. The objective is much larger than that. We must interact with, communicate with, and care about our local communities. We need to seek the good of the city, the good of the county, the good of the special districts, the good of the state, and the good of the nation. That means caring about and graciously interacting with the people who live in our various geographical communities.

- The combination of knowledge of our American system of governance from the ground up, accompanied by faith in the Lord who placed us in this nation with His written Word, will guide us into all truth. Those two together will lead us into a new understanding of our country and our place in it. It will lead us to embrace and make time for a new era of citizen engagement where Christians become the model of grace.

Conclusion

- Finally, we see that the three realms of governance (family, church, and civil) converge in Christ. Each realm has its purpose and informs the other realms. This understanding propels us from a stance of complacency into one of interaction with the civil realm.

Author by Basil Montagu, vol. 1, comp. Basil Montagu (Philadelphia, PA: Carey & Hart, 1852), 71.

Miscellaneous other assumptions that undergird this book:

- In essence, this book is a call to American Christians to become educated, engaged citizens. It is not an endorsement of all of the processes and structures presented as they currently exist nor is it a textbook relegated to students. Rather, **this book is a survey of the landscape of American governance that will equip any reader to participate in the civil realm with understanding**.

- In life, we often know what to do and simply do not want to do it. Obedience is the missing part. In the civil realm, it can be just the reverse. **The missing key is actual knowledge.** Obedience is difficult, if not impossible, unless we know about the layers of the civil realm and have gained a knowledge base to act upon. We can't do what is right if we don't know what to do. We can't know **how** to think about our government if we don't know **what** to think about our government.

- I may occasionally refer to our elected representatives as dignitaries, rulers, or kings. I am not suggesting that there is an earthly king in charge of the nation. By way of reference, I make the scriptural application of all of these titles to our elected representatives of the people while they are in office because, as Americans, we have chosen these people to be our leaders. As Christians, we also know that God has raised them to their position to lead for a time. Remember the words from Daniel to King Nebuchadnezzar:

    Blessed be the name of God forever and ever,
    For wisdom and might are His.
    And He changes the times and the seasons;

> **He removes kings and raises up kings.**
> He gives wisdom to the wise
> And knowledge to those who
> have understanding.
> He reveals deep and secret things;
> He knows what is in the darkness,
> And light dwells with Him (Daniel 2:20–22).

If God raises up kings (governmental leaders), then we are to show those leaders respect. Showing respect does not negate our prayers for their salvation, nor does it preclude others from being raised up from among us to one day be set in places of leadership: "He removes kings and raises up kings." Whichever way we read it, God is the one who orchestrates the removal and the raising up. Typically, the Lord doesn't raise up leaders in a showy, sensational fashion. It's a lot more mundane. Mundane—like Joseph spending time in a pit or Daniel eating vegetables. Mundane—like learning about city governance models or the levels of code (written law) that drive those models.

- Further, with the above passage in mind, we will begin to think differently about our elected representatives. As we do so, the admonition that God gave to Moses in Exodus 22:28 should echo across time to us today: "You shall not revile God, nor curse a ruler of your people." Poignant words for us today who have become quite comfortable offering commentary regarding our rulers while settling for absentee citizenship. We have become living room spectators to the national political commentary rather than involved citizens interacting politically at the local, state, then national levels. Looming civic challenges confront us as Christians, and we need help making sense of them.

- That leads us to the question: Why do we need to do anything if God orchestrates our governing officials? Well, most of us believe in education. We believe that knowledge and understanding are gifts: "He gives wisdom to the wise, and knowledge to those who have understanding." And we are to act with those gifts. So we keep a foot anchored in the Scriptures and a foot anchored in this world. We read the Scriptures including a daily dose of the Proverbs, and we can pay attention to such things as the newspaper (which lists weekly meetings and public notices and puts a finger on the pulse of the community via letters to the editor) and local government websites. If we regard such information as a tool, not a poison, we have begun the process of entering the civil realm.

- You may want to start a civics notebook—a place to keep information and observations as you start to uncover the forgotten realm. You may want to use sticky notes to mark certain pages in this book (such as the page where the Glossary begins). Go ahead and turn down the corners of the pages that you plan to reference again and again (such as chapter 2, "Layers of Law—The Cornerstone Chapter"). Use a highlighter to mark the Scripture verses that you need to remember, meditate on, or memorize (such as 1 Corinthians 3:21–23). Do whatever it takes to make the information in these chapters resonate in your life. I didn't intend for this book to be a dry textbook. I pray that it becomes a well-worn manual.

- Lastly, offices at many levels of government can be changed by We the People through a bill in the state legislature to convert an office from an elected to an appointed position or vice versa. Further, the process of changing a system of local government, may also be conducted by a ballot initiative. Each state differs in its own procedures, but if an elected office in your part of the civil realm has changed and is inaccurately represented in this book, please reach out to us at **CivilRealm.com**. Thank you.

CHAPTER 1

The Realm of Civil Government & Dual Citizenship

We Christians don't know much about American civics. Many of us are not even sure what the word *civics* refers to. We are much more familiar with, say, the topic of economics than civics. Civics is a social science dealing with the rights and duties of citizens.[1] In other words, civics pertains to American civil government, the civil realm. For most of us, it has become the forgotten realm. Allow me to illustrate: Do you have a mayor? If so, what is your mayor's name? What is a county (or its equivalent)? How does that differ from a city? How does an idea become a city law? Or a state law? What gives the national government its power? Is America a true democracy? Whether by birth or by naturalization (the process of becoming a citizen), these are just a handful of the questions you inherited when you became an American. You own the questions, and you own the answers (even if you don't know what they are yet).

Unfortunately, for many reasons we are to our American citizenship what absentee landlords are to a rental property. Rarely spending a moment thinking about maintenance or repairs, we benefit from the cash flow and a paltry tax deduction, but that's about it. Day in and day out, we aren't pres-

1 *Merriam-Webster*, s.v. "civics."

ent to oversee our investment. As time passes, what was once a valued property becomes an eyesore. The roof is overrun with moss, the foundation is crumbling, and the fence fell down years ago. There are all the signs of neglect, the results of abdicating responsibility. This is the reality of the forgotten realm of civil government.

Imagine an American city, county, school board, or the nation itself. Imagine, as well, that you are in charge of the upkeep and maintenance of these institutions. What kind of citizen-owner would you be? Absent? Busy? Clueless? When we look at the results we're getting from any of the civil sectors we live under, we can know exactly what kind of citizen ownership has been happening. There is no mystery: The processes developed to run today's political spaces are generally conducted by elected representatives who do not operate on the principles of God's Word.

It is high time for a practical manual on American government written specifically for Christians. Hold the activism. Hold the platitudes. Hold the emphasis on voting and elections. Bring on what we have been missing for too long. Bring on how God parses out principles of governance. Bring on why the realms of governance matter. As Americans, we sense that we are nearing the brink of losing something great, but we're not sure what it is.

CHURCHY AND STATEY THINGS

The topics of church and state have taken a lot of heat over time. One of the first things that we have to put on the table is that we aren't exactly going to talk about religion and politics—that old taboo combination. We are talking about gospel and governance which can still be a flammable pair fraught with a tendency to go sideways pretty quickly. To define our terms, *gospel* in America means faith in Jesus Christ for the forgiveness of our sins. And *governance* in America means self-government carried out by We the People. Self-government brings us liberty as citizens of a nation. Faith in Jesus brings us liberty as members who belong to Him (2 Corinthians 3:17). So far so good. We'll leave it there for now, because the interaction of gospel and governance is best described by illustration, and that will come later in the book. Another thing to get out of the way is the misconception of the separation of church and state—a topic not located in the Constitution. Thomas Jefferson, in one of his letters, does refer to "the wall of separation," and this statement led to the notorious concept of the separation of church and state.[2] It is a short letter and well worth reading, as is the draft letter preceding it that Jefferson did not send. Both the letter and the draft are located in Appendix C.

You might be tempted to believe that you cannot be of God's kingdom and have a role in earthly governance. This is not true. In His sovereignty, God designs governments, just as He designed mankind. He calls people to follow Him, and He calls us to be leaders: "Follow Me, and I will make you fishers of men" (Matthew 4:19). God never prohibited people of faith from governing. He guided our Founders to design a government that does not overreach into church affairs. And that is what Jefferson was referring to by quoting the first amendment to the Constitution in his letter. Thus, God works through His people; He doesn't relegate us to some hands-off zone. Our job is to follow Him and excel in our work (Proverbs 22:29).

Finally, civic governance and heavenly faith should not be uncomfortable topics among Christian friends. However, wading into these topics also puts us in uncertain territory.

2 Thomas Jefferson, "Letter to the Danbury Baptists," *Library of Congress Information Bulletin*, June 1998, vol. 57, no. 6.

Many of us likely just don't understand the American governing process. It's an area of life that is easier to ignore than to find the time, energy, and direction to pursue. After all, is it really that important? Can't we just make a few sharp comments about Mr. President or the economy and be done with it? Well, no. We must do better than that.

In America, the governing process is how business affairs are conducted in order to take care of things and people. Governing or governance takes place in different realms, and, generally speaking, the Lord has established three realms that require governing: the family, the church, and the civil government (sometimes called the *state*). Each realm has its own governing rules and authority over our lives—parents govern their children, pastors and/or boards or hierarchies govern churches, and a combination of elected and appointed individuals govern America. These different groups require different governing structures, but they are all predicated on an assumed fourth realm—the realm of self-government. Without the realm of self-government, business-as-usual becomes unusual business, and we've seen a lot of unusual business lately.

Let's look at each of these three realms individually.

Family Realm

Genesis 1 contains the account of creation culminating in the miracle of God forming man and woman in His image and blessing them. In Genesis 2, the creation account of Adam and Eve continues, thus ordaining the realm of family government. Genesis 2:24 summarizes the essence of the family with this declaration: "Therefore a man shall leave his father and mother and be joined to his wife, and they shall become one flesh." Scripture emphasizes the concept of the family all over the place, but for quick snapshots, consider the Ten

GOVERNANCE STRUCTURE

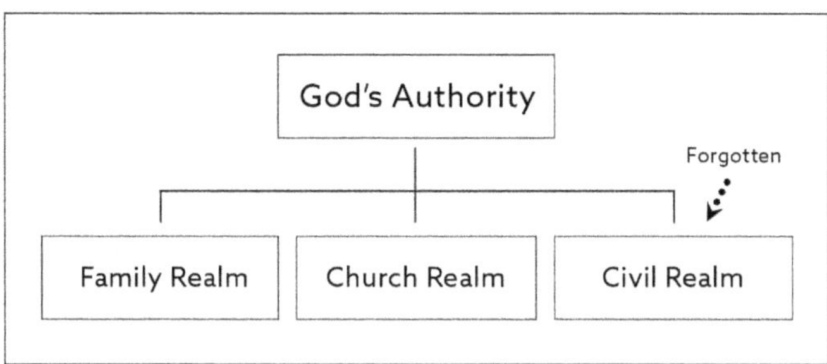

Figure 1.1

Commandments (found in Exodus 20 and Deuteronomy 5) and Ephesians 6:1–4.

Together, a husband and wife form a picture of Christ and the church living in communion with one another (Ephesians 5:31–32) which gives us a glimpse into the next realm. As Christ is head of the church, so the husband is the head of the wife and children. Note that Scripture sets forth certain laws or precepts for how the family should function within this picture. The wife is the husband's helper and simultaneously his glory; and the children live on after them as those who carry the baton into the future. Of course, within each family, there are house rules for how that specific home functions (such as who walks the dog and who does the dishes), but the biblical structure of family government is the same.

Church Realm

In the New Testament, the Apostle Paul describes the realm of church government along with its members and function when he says that God "gave some to be apostles, some prophets, some evangelists, and some pastors and teachers, for the equipping of the saints for the work of ministry, for the edifying of the body of Christ, till we all come to the unity of the faith and of the knowledge of the Son of God, to a perfect man, to the measure of the stature of the fullness of Christ" (Ephesians 4:11–13). Scripture sets forth laws that govern how the church should operate. Then, each local church decides what its specific ministries look like. Will the church gather on Sunday evenings? Will there be a weeknight service? What type of music characterizes the church? And so on.

Let me clarify two things in relation to the realms of family and church. Having one's family governance in order is a high priority among the realms. If you are married or have children, your responsibility to fulfill your role is paramount and should precede moving into action within the civil realm. Likewise, if vibrant participation in a local church is not part of your mode of life, this book about the civil realm is probably not where you should begin reading. Instead, you might want to start by finding your place within the church realm. A handbook like *The Complete Guide to Christian Denominations: Understanding the History, Beliefs, and Differences*[3] could be a good starting place.

Civil Realm

The realm of civil government is also described in the New Testament, where Paul commands every soul to be subject to the governing authorities. Then, he clearly sets forth the nature of those authorities: "For there is no authority except from God, and the authorities that exist are appointed by God" (Romans 13:1). The Lord appoints the civil realm, and

3 Ron Rhodes, *The Complete Guide to Christian Denominations: Understanding the History, Beliefs, and Differences* (Eugene, OR.: Harvest House Publishers, 2005).

what this realm looks and sounds like varies from nation to nation. Some countries are led by dictators, some by kings or queens through bloodlines, some by despots, some by parliaments or politburos—which impose laws upon their citizens. Whatever the form of government, Proverbs 29:2 succinctly states the bookends of citizen experience: "When the righteous are in authority, the people rejoice; / But when a wicked man rules, the people groan." When we hear fellow Christians groaning about their civil government, we can draw a simple conclusion about who is likely in power. At that point, we have two choices—continue groaning or do something about the situation. This book is a call to the latter.

In the United States, our civil realm is uniquely appointed as self-governance of We the People as established in our nation's Constitution. As inheritors within this realm, we elect individuals to represent our interests, choosing from among our rank-and-file selves. In the American civil realm, if we don't like the results we're getting from the representatives to whom we have delegated authority, we have the opportunity to replace them. We also have many other opportunities to effect change, but these opportunities are largely untapped and are part of uncovering the civil realm of government. We will explore such opportunities in each of the following chapters.

For Christians who are wary of the framework that I am setting forth, note that the divinely appointed civil realm is a lesser authority that exists under God Himself. For example, within the Roman Empire we see Jesus guiding with His Word as He admonishes His listeners (and us by extension) to "render to Caesar the things that are Caesar's" (Mark 12:17). The lesson here is that Jesus' followers are to perform their civic duty and pay their taxes. However, Jesus finishes by indicating that the civil realm is not supreme, admonishing them (us) to render "to God the things that are God's."

GOVERNANCE STRUCTURE IN THE UNITED STATES

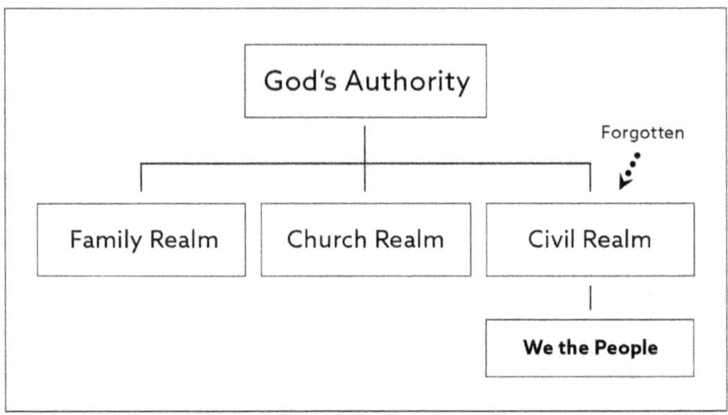

Figure 1.2

The Realm of Self-Government

Self-government is fundamental to all other types of government because if we are unable to control our own emotions, passions, desires, and tongues, how can we be qualified to oversee others' lives? To restate, if we can govern ourselves and our own passions, we are better positioned to consider governing others within the three realms. Self-control is, after all, a fruit of the Spirit, and the marked absence of it in public America today is a strong indicator of our nation's need for the Spirit.

There is an order to these things, and this theme of self-government is replete in Scripture. For example, Jesus tells us that a prerequisite to guiding others is to deal with ourselves first (Matthew 7:5). And Paul tells Timothy that a man must keep his own house in order (which can be reduced to keeping his own life in order) before he can take care of the church (1 Timothy 3:5). A reminder of this principle with a civic twist is that "He who is slow to anger is better than the mighty, / And he who rules his spirit than he who takes a city" (Proverbs 16:32). So one of the underlying premises of Scripture is that we must learn to govern ourselves. Because we are naturally rebellious and inherited that rebellion from Adam's fall in the Garden of Eden, the only real answer to self-government lies in the One who bridged the gap between our rebellion and God the Father. This One is our Redeemer Jesus Christ. He declares that He is "the way, the truth, and the life. No one comes to the Father except through [Him]" (John 14:6).

Regarding those who become aware of their rebelliousness and recognize their need for a Savior, He gives them the "right to become children of God, to those who believe in His name: who were born, not of blood, nor of the will of the flesh, nor of the will of man, but of God" (John 1:12–13). He gives us ability in areas where we had previously been unable. Because of the fruit of His Spirit in us, we are able to overcome old vices. Only then are we free to govern ourselves. Though we may stumble from time to time, overall, we move forward.

According to Glenn Sunshine, "virtue was an important word to the Founders. For centuries, it had been recognized that virtue was essential to the survival of a republic."[4] He goes on to state that in the absence of virtue, self-centeredness and all of its unpleasant cousins govern the civil decision-making process. Fast forward to today, and we can recognize some of those distant cousins among our leaders.

Poor governance is one result of Christians having retreated from the civil realm. In 1788, James Madison summed up the link between self-government and the need for controls upon ourselves. He said, "As there is a degree of depravity in mankind which requires a certain degree of circumspec-

4 Glenn Sunshine, *Slaying Leviathan: Limited Government and Resistance in the Christian Tradition* (Moscow, ID: Canon Press, 2020), 157.

tion and distrust, so there are other qualities in human nature which justify a certain portion of esteem and confidence. Republican government presupposes the existence of these qualities in a higher degree than any other form."[5]

God's grace transforms each of us who believe in Him from one who has no rule over his own spirit, like a city broken down without walls (Proverbs 25:28), to one who becomes the light of the world (Matthew 5:14). A city set on a hill that cannot be hidden. It is interesting to note that an individual who cannot manage himself is like a poorly run city, and an individual who follows Jesus is like an illuminated, well-run city. Individuals possessing the light and truth of God within themselves help populate and govern cities that possess light and truth within their borders. From a distance, we can look at some American cities today and conclude that light and truth are not within their borders. That's precisely why I am writing this book. Where the Spirit of the Lord is, there is liberty (2 Corinthians 3:17). Where the Spirit of the Lord is not, there is decay, suffering, and perversions of liberty akin to anarchy. Later I will ask you to look at your own city. Odds are good that you might not like what you find there. Liberty has become licentiousness.[6] There is a lot of work ahead of us.

Pictorial Description of the Three Realms

Having established the role of self-governance, we can now turn our attention back to the three main realms. In order to help you visualize the three realms and their purposes, let us picture them within what is known as Christendom. The word *Christendom* is not a common vocabulary word. It means the

5 James Madison, Alexander Hamilton, and John Jay, *The Federalist Papers*, no. 55, ed. Isaac Kramnick (London: Penguin Books, 1987), 339.

6 Sunshine, *Slaying Leviathan*, 157.

dominion that Christ purchased with His blood. In a smaller sense, Merriam-Webster defines it as the part of the world in which Christianity prevails. Within this context, the following pictorial description of the three realms may help us to have a clearer understanding of God's plan for governance over the various facets of our life on earth. If we think of Christendom as a town instead of a vast region, we can then consider the realm of the church as the cathedral at the center of the town.[7]

- The cathedral's ministry to its congregation is that of grace and peace. In other words, the church proclaims the redeeming truths of God's Word and administers the sacraments of baptism and communion.
- The civil authorities over the town—meaning those we have chosen to represent us in the civil governing realm—constitute the ministry of justice, and they promulgate or make the laws of the land known publicly and put them into force.
- The families of the town carry out the ministries of health, education, and welfare by providing for the needs of their members and for the needs of widows and orphans who are not set directly within families.

Of course, today the cathedral is no longer considered the strategic center of the town. Often, the local public high school gymnasium or football field assumes that role, and its message is not a proclamation of truth. The civil authorities oversee the center of town, the ministry of health, education, and welfare, as well as the creation and enforcement of public laws. We find ourselves in a situation of misordered priorities.

7 This metaphor is borrowed from New Saint Andrews College, *Thirty-Three Theses on Culture Shaping* (Moscow, ID: Canon Press, 2021), 3.

My goal is to help us as American Christians to see our plight and to do something about it.

Duties Within the Three Realms

As Christians, most of us would agree that the realms of church and family are legitimate spheres in which to devote ourselves.[8] Indeed, affiliating ourselves with a local church where we can worship God and fellowship weekly with other like-minded Christians should be fundamental to how we function in this life. The New Testament is replete with epistles penned to local churches which give us guidance on life within the ecclesiastical realm. In one of those letters, Timothy refers to the church as the house of God, the church

8 The term *spheres* can be attributed to Abraham Kuyper who loosely describes spheres and circles of life in his *Lectures on Calvinism* (Grand Rapids, MI: Eerdmans, 1987) and in his 1880 inaugural speech for the Free University of Amsterdam: James D. Bratt, ed., *Abraham Kuyper: A Centennial Reader* (Grand Rapids, MI: Eerdmans, 1998), 461.

Theologian Hans Boersma says that "Kuyper's theory of sphere sovereignty was primarily directed against the danger of the state as a great monster grabbing power and influence wherever it could. Kuyper saw such a Leviathan, which would take away all freedom from the individual, as the great danger of his time." Hans Boersma, "Sphere Sovereignty," *Clarion* 36, no. 21 (October 23, 1987): 462.

Likewise, Glenn Sunshine walks his reader through a historical survey of Christian resistance in his book *Slaying Leviathan* where he traces the term *Leviathan* to Thomas Hobbes's book on political theory by the same title. Hobbes argues "that the king had absolute authority in the kingdom." Thus, by definition, "a king could not violate laws or deprive people of their rights because all authority had been ceded to him by the people." Thomas Hobbes, *Leviathan*, (London: Penguin Classics, 2017), 2. Because we Americans are not governed under a monarchy or a dictatorship, we still do possess real control of our government (Sunshine, 174–5). We may not be able to slay the American Leviathan, but we can certainly begin the process of disempowering him. The tools (weapons) ready at our disposal to this end are God's life-giving Word (sword) and a thorough civic knowledge of all levels of our government. The former equips us spiritually and is appropriated through the triumphant blood of Christ with the ministry of His Holy Spirit. The latter equips us with knowledge and stands as the central missing piece in much Christian civic thought, writing, blogging, and podcasting today. Thus, as a Christian people, we can begin to move from a position characterized by a lack of involvement in government to one characterized by concern for the long game, attendance, observation, and involvement at meetings in session, and commenting when prudent and productive. All of which play a role in eventually redirecting policy by stewards who are found faithful over the government that we have been entrusted to oversee.

of the living God, and the pillar and ground of the truth (1 Timothy 3:15).

Along with being part of a local church, we should seek to raise godly families (or encourage others in this duty if we do not have children ourselves). In fact, leadership within the church should not even be a possibility if one cannot run his own household (1 Timothy 3:5). And running our homes in an orderly fashion should be the standard, not the exception. Granted, things teeter off balance from time to time, but, on the whole, we are to manage our families well and to God's glory. After all, He entrusted us with them.

Does the Civil Realm of Governance Really Matter?

This brings us to the third and largely forgotten realm of civil government. We have had significant trouble arriving at an agreement regarding this realm. Does it really matter that it is forgotten? Might engaging with it taint us? And here is the big question that we must ask ourselves: Is civil governance worthy of our time and attention? If it is, does Scripture give us any marching orders for how to proceed?

Obviously, we must always determine what we believe before we decide what to do—orthodoxy before orthopraxy. As Proverbs states, "The wisdom of the prudent is to understand his way, / But the folly of fools is deceit" (14:8). Rather than be deceived and assume that we already know things, we must wisely try to understand them. We can start now by contemplating whether or not Scripture sets forth the category of civil government as a legitimate realm over us. And if it does, how are we to approach interacting with it? Here are various biblical texts regarding God and the civil realm to help us begin.

Biblical Warrant for the Existence of the Civil Realm of Government

- **Christ created civil government** (Colossians 1:15–18):

  He is the image of the invisible God, the firstborn over all creation. For by Him all things were created that are in heaven and that are on earth, visible and invisible, whether thrones or dominions or principalities or powers. All things were created through Him and for Him. And He is before all things, and in Him all things consist. And He is the head of the body, the church, who is the beginning, the firstborn from the dead, that in all things He may have the preeminence.

- **The government is on His shoulder** (Isaiah 9:6–7):

  For unto us a Child is born,
  Unto us a Son is given;
  And the government will be upon His shoulder.
  And His name will be called
  Wonderful, Counselor, Mighty God,
  Everlasting Father, Prince of Peace.
  Of the increase of His government and peace
  There will be no end,
  Upon the throne of David and over His kingdom,
  To order it and establish it with judgment and justice
  From that time forward, even forever.
  The zeal of the LORD of hosts will perform this.

- **He establishes and curtails the authority of rulers** (Daniel 2:20–22):

  Blessed be the name of God forever and ever,
  For wisdom and might are His.
  And He changes the times and the seasons;
  He removes kings and raises up kings;
  He gives wisdom to the wise

And knowledge to those who have understanding.
He reveals deep and secret things;
He knows what is in the darkness,
And light dwells with Him.

- **He possesses all authority** (Matthew 28:18–20):

  All authority has been given to Me in heaven and on earth. Go therefore and make disciples of all the nations, baptizing them in the name of the Father and of the Son and of the Holy Spirit, teaching them to observe all things that I have commanded you; and lo, I am with you always, even to the end of the age.

- **He will receive honor and glory from the kings of the nations** (Revelation 21:23–26):

  The Lamb is its light. And the nations of those who are saved shall walk in its light, and the kings of the earth bring their glory and honor into it. Its gates shall not be shut at all by day (there shall be no night there). And they shall bring the glory and the honor of the nations into it.

Biblical Commands for Civic Life and Duty

- **Honor** (1 Peter 2:17):

  Honor all people. Love the brotherhood. Fear God. Honor the king.

- **Obey** (Romans 13:1, 5 and Titus 3:1–3):

  Let every soul be subject to the governing authorities. For there is no authority except from God, and the authorities that exist are appointed by God… Therefore you must be subject, not only because of wrath but also for conscience' sake.

> Remind them to be subject to rulers and authorities, to obey, to be ready for every good work, to speak evil of no one, to be peaceable, gentle, showing all humility to all men. For we ourselves were also once foolish, disobedient, deceived, serving various lusts and pleasures, living in malice and envy, hateful and hating one another.

- **Refrain from speaking evil** (Titus 3:2, quoted directly above, and Exodus 22:28):

> You shall not revile God, nor curse a ruler of your people.[9]

- **Do good** (Romans 13:3):

> For rulers are not a terror to good works, but to evil. Do you want to be unafraid of the authority? Do what is good, and you will have praise from the same.

- **Receive protection** (Romans 13:4):

> For he [the authority] is God's minister to you for good. But if you do evil, be afraid; for he does not bear the sword in vain; for he is God's minister, an avenger to execute wrath on him who practices evil.

- **Pay taxes** (Romans 13:6–7a):

> For because of this you also pay taxes, for they are God's ministers attending continually to this very thing. Render therefore to all their due: taxes to whom taxes are due, customs to whom customs…

---

9 This is an excellent short article on the topic: William MacDonald, "Thou Shalt Not Revile the Gods Nor Curse the Ruler of Thy People (Exodus 22:28)," *Bible Portal*, August 19, 2023. 🔗

- **Pray** (1 Timothy 2:1–4):

  Therefore I exhort first of all that supplications, prayers, intercessions, and giving of thanks be made for all men, for kings and all who are in authority, that we may lead a quiet and peaceable life in all godliness and reverence. For this is good and acceptable in the sight of God our Savior, who desires all men to be saved and to come to the knowledge of the truth.

- **Seek the LORD** (Proverbs 28:2, 4–5):

  Because of the transgression of a land,
  many are its princes;
  But by a man of understanding and knowledge
  Right will be prolonged.
  Those who forsake the law praise the wicked,
  But such as keep the law contend with them.
  Evil men do not understand justice,
  But those who seek the LORD understand all.

In addition to the above biblical commands, the Book of Proverbs serves as a handbook of scriptural wisdom applicable to the civil realm. You will see Proverbs sprinkled throughout this book serving as a guide for navigating the civil realm with wisdom. For further reference, there is also a list of selected Proverbs arranged topically located on the resources page at **CivilRealm.com**.

The Civil Realm Matters

We can ascertain from the above passages that God has designed earthly structures of governance for people on this planet. He has also given us clear directives for functioning within this sphere. They are the beginning of our marching orders for how to proceed into the civil realm. And because we do have marching orders, we can answer the question "Does the civil realm really matter?" with a resounding, "Yes!" It is among our duties on this earth and therefore well worth our time and attention.

DUAL CITIZENSHIP

Not only can we have a foot in all three realms (kind of like standing where Kansas, Missouri, and Oklahoma meet), but we are also citizens of two kingdoms: the heavenly kingdom and the earthly kingdom. After all, Jesus teaches us to pray that God's "will be done / On earth as it is in heaven" (Matthew 6:10). There is a link between heaven and earth. Eternity matters. This world matters.

Despite the fact that our U.S. minted currency proclaims "In God we trust," we are sternly informed that God and government are supposed to remain separate at all costs. Here is where we could get into a big kingdom-realm debate. But we won't. We've already established that the church has its government and the state (civil realm) has its government. Of course, self-control factors in, and the Spirit encompasses all. Yet, for us as American Christians, what is the glue that connects our faith and our government? It's dual citizenship—the powerful inheritance that we possess in two places at once.

As Christians, our primary citizenship is in heaven (Philippians 3:20–21). Christ secured this inheritance for His followers over two thousand years ago. Before He ascended to heaven to be seated at the right hand of the Father, He informed us that all authority was given to Him in heaven and on earth.

Because of Christ's intercessory work on our behalf (described in the self-government paragraphs above), we enjoy this royal inheritance. We did nothing to earn it, but we have things to do because of it.

Our second inheritance is citizenship in our nation. God sovereignly establishes the nations, and as Americans, we have citizenship in the United States of America. If we were born here or have parents who were, we did nothing to earn it. If we studied for our citizenship, we did earn it. Either way, our American citizenship defines a significant part of who we are and where our loyalties lie. Just as the Apostle Paul imitated Christ through his Roman citizenship (Acts 22:22–23:11) to God's glory, so we, too, can imitate Paul with our American citizenship. In 1 Corinthians 3:22–23, Paul tells us whether "the world or life or death, or things present or things to come—all are yours. And you are Christ's, and Christ is God's." We can make the most of our earthly status as American citizens because our marching orders in this life are closely tied to our marching orders in heaven.

We have looked at how we become citizens of heaven through Christ, so now let's look at the origins of our American citizenship.

The Origins of American Citizenship

Over two hundred years ago, our nation's Founders set forth a document declaring independence in light of a "history of repeated injuries and usurpations" perpetrated by King George III of England. This document was just that—the Declaration of Independence, adopted July 4, 1776. America's Founders secured a new beginning in self-governance with their lives, their fortunes, and their sacred honor in the war that followed the Declaration—the American Revolution, also known as the American War of Independence. This new nation was formed with a firm reliance on the protection of divine Providence.

After the war, some of the Founders, known as the Framers, then created (framed) the national constitution of the new regime. This second foundational document is the Constitution of the United States of America, signed eleven years later on September 17, 1787, and then ratified by the states. This document sets the governing parameters for the new nation, and its principles are reflected at every level of American government. The Constitution is the supreme governing document of the land, ordained and established not by a king, parliament, or legislature, but by the citizens of the United States.

The first words of the Constitution—*We the People*—declare that American government originates from its citizens. These three simple words serve as a powerful reminder that the true strength and legitimacy of the American experiment lie in the collective voice of each of us, the citizens of this great country. Note that, in this day of pronounced emphasis on pronouns, the Constitution is written for us as *We the People* not for yonder bureaucrats as *They the People.* This foundational principle underscores the idea that the authority and responsibilities of the government ultimately rest upon the shoulders of the individuals, as the Framers believed. We the People were and are best suited to govern and shape the destiny of the new nation—a nation where the citizens are encouraged and empowered to actively help shape the fabric of this constitutionally representative democratic society.

With these two documents in hand, we are now the possessors of the grand inheritance of the right to self-governance of our nation. Each of us has this right with our earthly American citizenship, and if you are in Christ, you also possess this inheritance through your citizenship in heaven. However, despite this dual citizenship, we are currently on the outside looking in. Right now, we can only peek through a keyhole into the forgotten civil realm where American self-governance takes place. We need help getting in because we, as American Christians, have effectively locked ourselves out for quite some time now. My purpose is not to upbraid us nor to assess how we arrived at this point of disengagement. I think that we can look around and see that we're not in a good spot. The point is that we can do something about it. There is hope, great hope. But there is also something in our way.

LOSS OF LIBERTY?

One of the obstacles that often blocks our view and hinders our path is our own comfort and complacency. Like the prodigal son, we have been given a great inheritance by God in the civil realm. Are we living in luxury while squandering that inheritance? On the whole, we live quite comfortable lives as American Christians. That is a blessing from God which we are to give thanks for lest it devolve into a curse (Deuteronomy 8:10–18). God also tells us in Matthew 6:24 that we cannot serve Him and money (this includes the comfort that money brings us).

Sometimes our prioritization of comfort leads to our loss of liberty. And we will tolerate losing our liberties, incrementally and slowly, with seemingly insignificant disruptions until it is pretty late in the game. But until it hurts badly enough, we may not be moved to action. That appears to be where we are now in America. I would like us to skip this comfort-swollen valley of civil inactivity and move forward into the civil realm with a firm grasp on the keys of civic knowledge and faith in God. The problem is that it's not comfortable to move into an unknown realm.

Approximately half a century ago, Christian philosopher Francis Schaeffer described man's overarching desire for personal peace and affluence as part of the downward trend of culture in his classic book *How Should We Then Live?* Regarding the civil realm, Schaeffer predicts, "I believe the majority of the silent majority, young and old, will sustain the loss of liberties without raising their voices as long as their own lifestyles are not threatened."[10] Schaeffer speaks the truth. I can testify to it. I had previously lived as part of the silent majority that Schaeffer mentions (though I would have denied it at the time) until my family's and my community's lifestyles were threatened. Then, I awoke from slumber and began the hard work of acquiring a hands-on political education. What I learned drove me to write this book. Schaeffer's hope for his generation was that they may "turn from that greatest of wickednesses, the placing of any created thing in the place of the Creator, and… get its feet out of the paths of death and may live."[11] That is my hope, too.

Schaeffer encouraged his readers (who were undoubtedly more civic-minded than this current generation) to speak out against authoritarian government. Since Schaeffer's time, in terms of civic knowledge, we have regressed in understanding our political processes. So for the civil realm, we generally know enough to be dangerous (meaning merely vocal and outspoken) because we have heard of our constitutional rights. But have we inquired, as in the two other realms, what our duties and responsibilities are? It can be quite an embarrassment to enter the governmental arena swinging our fists and exercising our rights if we don't understand what routinely transpires in the realm of civil government.

Here's a case-in-point to illustrate: Upon moving to a new city after having previously lived in a rural area, I decided to attend the meetings of my new local city council. After observing them for nearly two years, I found that there was much business conducted at those meetings that I did not understand, especially concerning budgetary matters. Then, the

---

10 Francis A. Schaeffer, *How Should We Then Live? The Rise and Decline of Western Thought and Culture* (Old Tappan, NJ: F. H. Revell Co, 1976), 227.

11 Schaeffer, *How Should We Then Live?*, 258.

COVID-19 pandemic garnered our city's attention. Our mayor and council responded with an emergency health masking and social distancing order. Just as Schaeffer had predicted, the conservative community's own lifestyles were threatened, and people came in force to testify before city council when the masking order was renewed. Although they were speaking out against authoritarian government, as Schaeffer encourages, they missed the larger picture at hand: that same night, the council passed a $96 million budget for a city with a mere population of just under 26,000 people. No one commented or testified concerning the authoritarian-sized governmental budget. Evidently, the taxes do not hurt our lifestyle enough yet. Sensational issues do, however, garner attention.

The day-to-day humdrum of local government escapes much of our notice. Over time, its processes have evaded our understanding. I hope to recover the forgotten realm of civil government and civic responsibility in the lives of Christians, connecting that realm to the commands that Christ gives us in the Great Commission as described in Matthew 28:19–20. Therein, He declares all authority to be His and subsequently gives us our marching orders. May we consider the civil realm to be worthy of our time and attention. May we invest ourselves in understanding the local, state, and national government processes. In so doing, may we bring the salt and light of the gospel to shine in the center of our cities, counties, states, and nation.

As a Christian, I look at civics in two ways. The first is as a scaffold for the gospel. The civil realm is full of people who may not have heard of Jesus Christ and His atonement for our sins. They have not seen His love in action in the lives of His people—because we haven't occupied those hallowed halls. We haven't taken the opportunity to get to know the civil-realm contingent. The second way I view civics is as a legal framework that supports the church realm because, in

America, our God-ordained civic freedom paves the way for our religious liberty. Consider Russia, China, and Cuba, where there is no government by We the People, and there is no liberty to openly serve at church. God's hands are not tied in those countries, but we have inherited a great blessing here that we should not brush aside. Note that this concept comes full circle, because God actually gives us our liberties, and our elegantly designed American system of governance exists because of those liberties.

My call to you is to see the forgotten realm and recognize that it is under the authority of Christ. He is the One who now sits at the right hand of the Father until His enemies are made His footstool. We are to pray that His kingdom comes and that His will be done on earth as it is in heaven. The civil realm of government falls under the umbrella of His authority. Government is not our savior, Christ is. However, it does sit upon His shoulder as a legitimate and very important part of His creation. Despite this reality, we have allowed others who are not His people (at least not His people *yet*) in large part to preside over this realm. As a result, we have a lot of work to do. Typically, that work is described in terms of voting or running for office. These two activities represent the common American default position for thinking we have fulfilled our civic duty. If we have voted or helped someone run for office or considered running for office ourselves, we think that the bases are covered. What else is there? What else are we supposed to do? In other words, as Francis Schaeffer so eloquently put it (based on Ezekiel 33:10), how should we then live?

The work that we have ahead of us is more foundational than elections. We must back up and figure out how our government functions. Who does what, when, where, and how? Most of us don't know, and because we feel embarrassed at our lack of civic knowledge, we tend to completely avoid the topic or overgeneralize it. But we are not to avoid or gloss over the unknown just because it is uncomfortable. We have not been given "a spirit of fear, but of power and of love and of a sound mind" (2 Timothy 1:7). I am convinced that because in Him we live and move and have our being, we should start right where we are rather than starting with what transpires in Washington, D.C.[12] One day, some of us will end up in D.C., but the best place to begin rightly ordering the civil realm of government is in our own backyard—our own town square.

Because our government is a structure by We the People, there can be great power in starting small. We can begin learning our systems of governance and effecting change incrementally beginning right where we live. I call this the mustard-seed approach to civics. We reap what we sow, and God delights in blessing small works. We can learn how government functions in the locale nearest us and move outward and upward from there. I will discuss this principle further in chapter 9, "Christian Diplomacy." For now, know that God, who inhabits eternity, made Himself small, finite, and in a limited body that was tied to the local in order to minister to the world—all mankind. We can follow His cue. We can focus on the local, where we dwell, in order to bring good to many. **But the purpose of this book is not to focus entirely on the local level; it is a call for us to begin at the local level and to proceed through all the levels of government, and in the process, find where God is calling each of us to minister in the civil realm.**

Unfortunately, there is not an abundance of local-government civics materials available because the models of government vary so much across this vast nation. As David Ber-

12 If you actually happen to live in the District of Columbia, you have my blessing to start at the national level because it is also your local level. In fact, the two levels intertwine because under the Home Rule Act of 1973, municipal (city) legislation in D.C. must be approved by Congress before it becomes law.

man points out in his book *Local Government and the States*, "the galaxy of local governments in the United States includes some 3,000 counties, 19,000 municipalities [cities] 16,000 town or township governments, 13,000 school districts, and 3,000 special districts."[13]

Christian-based civics materials generally take the approach that if we know the Constitution, the Founding Fathers, and the three branches,[14] then we have it covered. Secular government books typically begin there, as well, with the frequent addition of attention-getting political examples to encourage readers toward citizen activism. By the time both types of civics materials arrive at their last few chapters, they tend to gloss over the local arena. The resultant dismissal of local-government explanations for the city, county (or its equivalent), and special districts often occurs, and we graduate from courses or institutions without knowing how to engage in the public square. This knowledge remains a mystery to us.

My solution is to introduce the authority structure of the layers of law from the top down in order to give an overall picture of our American system. Then, I invert the standard civics model and begin with local government in order to give it the attention and priority that it deserves. Due to the aforementioned great variety of local government forms, I will encourage you to discover the local nuances of your own region online and then in person at public meetings.

Although Christians have neglected the civil realm, this neglect has happened, in part, because we have been so busy working in the realms of church and family. And, of course, the realms of church and family are extremely important. Back to Schaeffer's point, most of us go along in those two realms

---

13 David R. Berman, *Local Government and the States: Autonomy, Politics, and Policy*, 2nd. ed. (New York: Routledge, 2020), 12.

14 These are the legislative, executive, and judicial branches which will be covered in the next chapter.

until our civic toes get stepped on. It's amazing how toes affect eyes—when our toes smart from pressure, our eyes open, and we see more clearly. When we bump into an inconvenient law, or when a bureaucratic rule cramps our ability to do business, it smarts. As a result, we awaken to the existence of the civil realm.

My call to American Christians is, first, to wake up and see that the civil realm is there, and second, to view its order and complexity. I want us to understand the different levels of authority that we are under in the civil realm and the vastness of what needs tending there. I want to pique your interest in this area where you can serve the King, this realm where people need to know Him. And the civil realm is a legitimate arena in which we can be involved and serve the King—precisely because there is a higher law than the Constitution. We are under God's royal law first in all three realms of governance: church, family, and civil. Believing that God is sovereign in all three realms helps us to remember that we should not think in tight, little, box-like categories laden with exclusions. If, for example, you are a student, that doesn't mean you stop being a son, daughter, brother, or sister. As another example, hopefully you don't stop attending church when you begin attending college. Rather, it is healthy to participate in the family realm and the church realm during school.

I am here to encourage you to learn to participate in the civil realm more than you have before, even if you think that you do not have time to fit this sort of participation into your life. We are motivated to do so precisely because we have a King who bought us with His blood. He died and rose again so that we can live both now and in eternity. He told us to pray for His kingdom to come on earth as it is in heaven. With this long-range view in mind, we can afford to be patient and learn to serve in the civil arena with an eye of faith looking toward civic renewal and reformation.

When we first begin serving Him in the civil realm, it doesn't look like much. It starts with being present and observant. It starts with being faithful—a quality required in stewards. We do this because we desire to see the civil realm of government reformed. We do not desire a bloody revolution. Unlike other kings, our King purchased His territory and people with His own blood rather than purchasing His territory with other people's blood. He died for us so that we might have life and have it abundantly.

If we serve Him with all that we have in each realm, then there will be crossover among the realms. Take, for example, a person who attends church (the ecclesiastical realm) week after week. This person learns and internalizes God's truth when the Scriptures are preached there. If that person is a young mother, the more diligently she applies those truths at home, the more glory she brings to God in the home. As a result of her diligent obedience, she is blessed with obedient children. And our world is in awe of obedient children. Because her life and work are not a charade, she can take those children anywhere.

Further, because she is diligent in the realms of church and family, she can take her children on field trips in the civil realm to observe a city council meeting, to visit a county commissioners' meeting, or to tour the local fire or police station. And she shouldn't be surprised if the mayor calls one of her children up to the platform to "assist" with running the meeting. Here is a description of this type of lady:

> She watches over the ways of her household,
> And does not eat the bread of idleness.
> Her children rise up and call her blessed;
> Her husband also, and he praises her:
> "Many daughters have done well,
> But you excel them all."
> Charm is deceitful and beauty is passing,

> But a woman who fears the LORD, she shall be praised.
> Give her of the fruit of her hands,
> And let her own works praise her in the gates.
> (Proverbs 31:27–31)

Perhaps you are not a young mother. Maybe you are a college student or a member of the military, or perhaps you are retired or even already holding political office. Whoever you are and whatever your station, you can be an agent of change for good in your community by better understanding the civil realm and engaging in it as a follower of Christ.

As we navigate among the three realms, we should avoid conflating the operational rules that pertain to each realm. We can't take the rules that apply to the church realm and overlay them onto the civil realm or vice versa. For example, we would use different guidelines for electing a church officer than we would for electing a state senator. Recognizing who is in authority, who is subject to that authority, and what is the written source of that authority lends clarity to understanding the distinctives of each realm.

- In the realm of **family government**, the constituents are the children who are subject to their parents, with their father being the head. Of course, the family runs in accordance with God's Word.
- In the realm of **church government**, the constituents are the parishioners who are subject to God's Word first, then to the church structure as it is doctrinally laid out in each denomination and local body.
- And in the realm of **civil government**, the constituents are We the People. Not all of our citizens are aware that they exist under the authority of God's Word, but they do know that they dwell in America under the U.S. Constitution.

Our American nation is referred to as the Great Melting Pot—acknowledging the plurality of nationalities, cultures, and ethnicities of people arriving at our borders prior to becoming a nation, and every day since then. Unsurprisingly, new ideas and notions about self-governance emerge from all the folks in the melting pot, and ideally We the People discuss and debate the merits of the notions for potential further action. While we are debating notions, we're actually working with people. In this respect, the civil realm is no different from the family and church realms in that we need to be kind to one another (Romans 12:18 and 1 Corinthians 13).

In order for ideas and notions of self-governance to bear fruit, it takes accommodation to work with our fellow citizens. Accommodation doesn't mean compromising our core beliefs, but it may involve working with others toward a compromise of our preferences. As Americans, compromise has been with us since the beginning of our union as evidenced in our founding documents, including the U.S. Constitution.[15] The very document we cherish was nearly swept into the dustbin of history before it was even created due to the sheer pain and agony of human compromises suffered in its creation.

Achieving compromise means that we can concede a section of our agenda in order to ensure forward motion. It means the art of finding common ground without discarding our principles. Two steps forward, one step back. Rinse and repeat. That's the realistic approach to moving an agenda forward in the American civil realm. But before we move agendas anywhere, we need to learn the hierarchical structure of the authority of law in our American system of governance. That knowledge is waiting for you in the next chapter.

---

15 David Brian Robertson, *The Original Compromise: What the Constitution's Framers Were Really Thinking* (New York: Oxford University Press, 2013).

THINGS YOU CAN DO

After having read this chapter, here is a practical question designed to open your eyes to the civil realm near you: Can you locate or visualize the building(s) in the town where your local government meetings take place, or is it a faded image in your mind like the front cover of this book?

Drive to one of those buildings during banker's hours (9:00–4:00), maybe on your lunch hour. It might be named something like ____ City Hall or ____ County Courthouse.[16] Go inside and have a look around. This is your building, and you might not have even known it until today. If anyone asks what you are doing, you can reply, "I'm a citizen getting familiar with my local government." If your children are with you, try answering, "We're on a field trip."

While inside, notice the signs above or next to each door. If you don't know what they mean or what business is transacted there, by the time you finish this book, those signs should make sense to you. Today, they may just be words, and that is okay. It's a reminder that you are embarking on the process of uncovering the forgotten realm.

SO WHAT?

After having read this chapter and gained an understanding of the three realms of government (along with the understood realm of self-government), ask yourself if these realms are in order in your life. Is there an area within the family or church realm that you need to work on before proceeding further?

Almost every reader will have to rearrange family and church priorities in order to participate in the civil realm. If

16 For example, Columbus City Hall or Lincoln County Courthouse.

church activities are filling most nights of the week, you will have to consider forgoing something such as a book study, small group meeting, or choir to free up some time. At first, this is a hard concept to entertain, especially for people already in positions of church leadership, but it is vital if we are to recover the civil realm. Our best people are running businesses, schools, churches, and homes, but on the whole, we are not running our local, state, and national government. We must begin to think about the ramifications of our time investments. None of us can do everything, but all of us can do something. Perhaps it is time to diversify our portfolios.

Someone Like You

In this book, I will share brief stories of people who have discovered the civil realm and engaged there. These testimonials will serve as examples of what it can look like to put the material presented in each chapter into action. Reading through the book, you will see a variety of ways to enter and engage in the forgotten realm.

The following paragraph is the story of a young college-age man who had been accustomed to talking rowdy politics, yet who did not understand the civil realm itself. After he received the key to unlock the forgotten realm, he had less to banter about and much more to actually do and think about.

Thomas was raised in a conservative Christian home. When he came to college, he was quite vocal about his conservative political philosophy. Admittedly, he didn't begin to see the civil realm clearly until a friend questioned the value of being vocal with opinions without being able to practically apply them. Thomas started attending meetings of a civics club at his college. He decided to learn about the structure of the governing systems around him (city, county, etc.) and how to engage with people who might think very differently from himself politically. Soon thereafter, he began regularly attending his local city council meetings. Observing city governance in action caused Thomas to realize that decision-making is complicated, and a wooden application of political philosophy doesn't accomplish much. This experience caused a substantial shift in Thomas's approach as a Christian to the civil realm. He moved from being an idealist to being an informed, engaged member of his city—a citizen. Here is Thomas's take on entering the civil realm: "Come in first with the humility to learn how the game works before you try to improve it."[17]

17 Thanks to Thomas Carpenter for this contribution.

CHAPTER 2
Layers of Law—The Cornerstone Chapter

One fateful day, my invitation to the civil realm arrived via the local newspaper. In one of the early issues that my family received after subscribing, I read that a multinational corporation had begun conducting business in our county. As a result, the county needed to overhaul its local ordinance under the direction of its Area Plan Commission (commission is usually a code word for a board which is appointed rather than elected). This commission was preparing to redraft the language and standards of an ordinance (local law) that would subsequently be presented to the county's three commissioners for them to vote for or against. I sensed the seriousness of the issue and began attending these meetings as a concerned citizen. I knew none of the people at that first meeting and knew none of the legislative-drafting procedures.

At the time, I had concluded that this county ordinance was important, but I did not realize that the term ordinance is synonymous with the word law. I did not realize that this law, which was undergoing scrutinizing revision, lay almost at the bottom of the heap of the strata of laws governing my life. Yet, it was also closest to the hub where my family lived and conducted our daily lives.

———·———

As human beings first and as Americans second, multiple layers of authority exist under which we are governed. This chapter presents an overall top-down citizen's view of the American system of governance as established by law. It is a survey of the layers of authority that comprise our government. It is the cornerstone chapter upon which this entire book rests, and I will refer to it as such throughout the book.

In descending order, the layers of authority consist of universal law, national law, state law, special districts (tax-based law), county law, and city law. Many Americans do not realize that we live and move and have our being under the weight of at least five layers of law.[1] Of these layers, only the overarching universal law is perfect and exists without amendment or judicial reinterpretation.[2] So let's start there at the top and work our way down through the layers keeping in mind that the rule of law is the central theme in the civil realm. Please note that for the purposes of simplicity and clarity, I have chosen to present each layer of law separately. In reality, these layers mix and swirl together in complicated ways. Sometimes, they are referred to as a marbled layer cake.

GOD'S UNIVERSAL LAW

God is our Creator and first Lawgiver, and His universal law for mankind is contained in the Bible.[3] This law was enumer-

---

1 I would like to echo this statement from Stephen Elias: "CAUTION Sovereign Native American tribes have their own courts and laws. These essentially function outside the system we describe here, and are beyond the scope of this book." *Legal Research: How to Find & Understand the Law*, 19th ed. (Nolo, 2021), 6.

2 Although the scribes and Pharisees certainly tried to do so. See Matthew 12:1–2 and 24.

3 God's universal law was understood by Adam and Eve—they were to obey God's command not to eat from the tree of the knowledge of good and evil. They were to be fruitful and multiply, to fill the earth and subdue it. Cain and Abel knew that there was a standard for bringing a sacrifice to God. Cain knew that murder was wrong. Following that murder, God commanded Cain to be a perpetual wanderer upon the earth, yet he disobeyed and built a city. Noah knew God's universal standards, found grace in the eyes of the Lord, and received God's warning to build an ark to escape the coming judgment upon mankind whose wickedness was great in the earth. Noah knew about burnt offerings; he brought more than two of each type of clean animal aboard the ark in

ated to Moses by God in the book of Exodus (chapter 20) and restated in the book of Deuteronomy (chapter 5). It contains both ceremonial law (which found its fulfillment in Christ) and moral law, the backbone of which is known as the Ten Commandments. The law does not save an individual, but it does expose his or her sin and serve as a tutor to bring that person to Christ (Galatians 3:24). Once a person is redeemed by Christ, he or she is free and able to keep the moral law as summarized in the Ten Commandments. The Bible as a whole is referred to as the law of God. It is the highest law under which a Christian operates. It is the bedrock truth upon which the American judicial system is based. It is higher than what is commonly known to Americans as the highest law of the land (the U.S. Constitution).

God's law is universally true and sovereign over all; however, not all people are aware of its existence and preeminence. Far from bliss, ignorance of an existing law is not an acceptable excuse for breaking that law. Many of us have experienced this truth firsthand when a police officer stops us for violating the speed limit. It becomes painfully obvious that failure to notice a posted change in the speed limit is no excuse for not obeying the sign. The police officer may extend mercy and merely issue a verbal or written warning to us, or the officer may, as a law-enforcement officer, exert justice and issue a full traffic violation. That violation, then, may either require financial payment or be contested in a court of law where one's guilt may (or may not) be proven. A traffic violation is typically a straightforward violation of the law. As you read this chapter, though, I would like you to see that,

---

order to have animals for sacrifice (Genesis 7:2 and 8:20). Shem and Japheth knew about honoring their father (Genesis 9:23). In Abraham's day, both Pharaoh of Egypt (Genesis 12:18) and Abimelech king of Gerar (Genesis 20:5) knew that taking another man's wife was wrong. Each of these examples and many others predate the Mosaic Law, yet each of these examples illustrates either keeping or breaking God's law. Moreover, the letter of Paul the Apostle to the Romans tells us that "*since the creation of the world* His invisible attributes are clearly seen, being understood by the things that are made, even His eternal power and Godhead" (1:20, emphasis mine).

as Americans, we are under so many layers of national, state, county, and city law that it is virtually impossible not to break some form of the law on a fairly frequent basis. With that caveat in mind, let's continue at the top layer. We'll get back to the police later.

In the Scriptures, there are many synonyms for the word *law*, and they are all present in Psalm 119. In that psalm, law is referred to as testimonies, precepts, statutes, commandments, judgments, and ordinances. Remember these law-oriented words. They will continue to resurface as we survey the structure of government. All of these terms point to God's Word, which was given to us initially by the prophets, was fulfilled in Jesus, and was expounded upon by the apostles. God's Word is holy, entire, and complete. Our triune God reveals Himself through His written Word—through it, He exhorts us how to live, and by means of it, the Christian "receive[s] the instruction of wisdom, / Justice, judgment, and equity" (Proverbs 1:3). The Bible is universally true and governs all people; however, as illustrated in the traffic illustration above, not everyone is cognizant of that. Not all people know the link between legal words such as *statutes* and *ordinances* and the biblical source of those terms, as summarized in Psalm 119.

Before moving below this layer of God's universal law, it should be noted that the legal systems (laws) of Western civilization are based on God's law as set forth in the Bible, and that initially God, not human governments, gives rights to people. Thomas Jefferson points directly to this investiture in the Declaration of Independence: "We hold these truths to be self-evident, that all men are created equal, that they are endowed by their Creator with certain unalienable Rights, that among these are Life, Liberty and the pursuit of Happiness—That to secure these rights, Governments are instituted among Men, deriving their just powers from the Consent of the Governed." See Appendix A for the full Declaration of Independence.

NATIONAL (FEDERAL) LAW

The aforementioned Declaration of Independence (adopted July 4, 1776) declared the thirteen colonies to be free and independent states. These states proclaimed themselves to have powers such as the "full Power to levy War, conclude Peace, contract Alliances, establish Commerce, and to do all other Acts and Things which Independent States may of right do." And that which they declared, they were already in the process of doing. During the American War of Independence, the confederation of states (which had possessed a congress prior to the Declaration of Independence[4]) required a code of laws under which it must operate. The first stab at amassing a national governing document is known as the Articles of Confederation (agreed to by Congress in 1777 and ratified in 1781). There are eight articles in the Articles of Confederation, and these articles are a foreshadowing of the seven articles in the Constitution. (The term *article* means a paragraph division.) Codes of law at all levels of government are divided into articles and further divided into sections. These divisions exist so that laws can be located by reference points, and they function much the same as chapter and verse divisions function in the Bible.

The Constitution is the document that the people created after the war to authorize the exercise of representative self-governance, to set boundaries on that governance, and to draw a distinction between what the federal government does and what the state governments may/are allowed to do. Its role is to place limits on the federal government's power and to recognize the states wide breadth of authority. Although the Constitution is the highest American law, and although it

4 The First Continental Congress met in 1774, and Second Continental Congress met from 1775–1781.

is trumpeted by Americans collectively as well as individually, less than half of the populace claims to have read it. A Marquette University Law School national survey of over 1,400 respondents posed the question: "Have you personally ever read the entire Constitution, either in school or on your own?" Fifty-seven percent of the respondents reported having never read the entire Constitution.[5] Because civics no longer carries a high value in schools and because the Constitution is rarely on the bestseller list, the assumption can be made that many Americans like to tout knowledge of the document but few have ever waded through it.

For those among us who have never done so, a perusal of this document is in order. I have summarized it in the pages that follow for exactly that purpose. Use it as an introductory framework to help you understand the Constitution when you read the full document. Or feel free to pause here and read the whole thing now which is located in Appendix B. For those among us who have read it, what follows serves a quick refresher. I've included the full text of the Preamble—because it is beautifully concise and worthy of memorization—accompanied by a very brief overview of each Article (as well as a cursory review of Roman numerals included at no extra charge). When you encounter illustrations of different models or systems of government in chapters 3 and 4, note that they are designed upon the first three articles of the Constitution which follow.

5 "Marquette Law School Supreme Court Survey," Marquette University Law School Poll: A Comprehensive Look at the Wisconsin Vote.

"The survey was conducted Sept. 3–13, 2019, interviewing 1,423 adults nationwide, with a margin of error of +/-3.6 percentage points. Interviews were conducted by the National Opinion Research Center (NORC) using its AmeriSpeak Panel, a national probability sample, with interviews conducted online." "New Nationwide Marquette Law School Poll Finds Confidence in U.S. Supreme Court Overall, Though More Pronounced Among Conservatives," Marquette University News Center, October 21, 2019.

The Constitution of the United States of America—Ratified September 17, 1787

Preamble

"We the People of the United States, in Order to form a more perfect Union, establish Justice, insure domestic Tranquility, provide for the common defence, promote the general Welfare, and secure the Blessings of Liberty to ourselves and our Posterity, do ordain and establish this Constitution for the United States of America."[6]

Article I

Legislative Power: Congress, consisting of two houses—the Senate and the House of Representatives. Makes laws.

Article II

Executive Power: President, Vice President, cabinet, Electoral College. Executes or carries out the laws.

Article III

Judicial Power: Supreme Court, inferior (federal) courts. Reviews/evaluates the laws.

Article IV

States: Republican form of government, protection against invasion. States are equal to each other and should respect each other's laws and judicial decisions.

---

6 As an aid to memorizing, see "The Preamble" from *Schoolhouse Rock!* available on YouTube (see the links page at **CivilRealm.com** 🔗). Note that 'of the United States' is omitted in the lyrics. Lynn Ahrens, vocalist, composer, and writer, "The Preamble," *Schoolhouse Rock!: Special 30th Anniversary Edition*, directed by Tom Warburton (1975; Burbank, CA: Buena Vista Home Entertainment, 2002), DVD.

Article V

Supreme Law of the Land: Constitution and Amendments.

Article VI

The Constitution is the supreme law of the land. All other laws must be subordinate to the Constitution.

Article VII

Ratification by nine states (which took place September 17, 1787).[7]

(Note that there is no mention of local government in the Constitution. All forms of local government fall under the jurisdiction of the states.)

Have you ever thought about our American form of government and wondered who dreamed up the balance of power among the legislative, executive, and judicial branches? Do you even know what the legislative, executive, and judicial branches are? If not, that's okay; quickly take a peek back at Articles I through III which are highlighted in grayscale. Article I states that the legislative branch (or power) is Congress: the Senate and the House of Representatives. Article II states that the executive branch (or power) is the President. Article III tells us that the judicial branch (or power) is the Supreme Court. These are the three separate branches or powers of the U.S. government so that one branch does not exert too much power. This principle is known as the separation of powers, and it is reflected at every level of American government.

Have you ever wondered where the aforementioned Senate and the House of Representatives originated? Where is

7 Articles I through IV are further subdivided into Sections. Note that Section is a legal term meaning a subdivision of a law. So the Articles concerning Congress, the President, the Supreme Court, and the States have multiple Sections within them to further explain each concept.

THREE BRANCHES OF GOVERNMENT

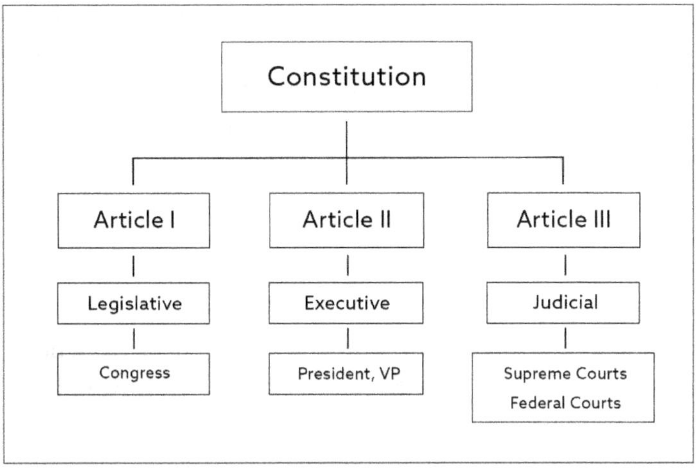

Figure 2.1

this information recorded? The answer to these questions lies in ancient history in the Roman Republic, the Roman Senate, the Greek idea of democracy, and the biblical principle of the fallen nature of mankind. Together, these elements constitute the foundation of the governing structure of our nation, and this structure is laid out succinctly in the Constitution. The Constitution is the law—not the only law that governs us, but it is the "supreme Law of the Land."[8] Unlike the universal highest law (the Bible), changes have been made over time to the Constitution in the form of amendments.

There are twenty-seven Amendments to the Constitution. A week and a day after the Constitution was ratified, Congress sent twelve proposed amendments to the States to adopt. Two were not immediately adopted, but the remaining

8 U.S. Const. art VI.

ten Amendments became the Bill of Rights.[9] They were ratified just shy of three years and three months later (December 15, 1791). I am summarizing them below because merely archiving them in an appendix at the back of this book would signify that they aren't important enough to warrant every reader's attention—only the attention of persnickety readers. Since the Bill of Rights plus the additional seventeen amendments comprise a sizable portion of the supreme law of the land, they deserve the textual real estate that they occupy in this book. After all, we are attempting to understand American civics. Again, note that the full version of the Constitution (including the Bill of Rights) is located in Appendix B. Also note that the Bill of Rights begins with a preamble, too.

Amendments to the Constitution of the United States of America

Amendments 1–10, Bill of Rights Ratified December 15, 1791

Preamble

"The Conventions of a number of the States, having at the time of their adopting the Constitution, expressed a desire, in order to prevent misconstruction or abuse of its powers, that further declaratory and restrictive clauses should be added: And as extending the ground of public confidence in the Government, will best ensure the beneficent ends of its institution..."[10]

9 Although I cannot endorse everything on this site, the following review of court rulings is enlightening: "Fifth Amendment—Right Against Self-Incrimination," Annenberg Classroom.

10 The remainder of the Preamble to the Bill of Rights cites the procedure of adoption which is "pursuant to the fifth Article of the original Constitution." The complete version of the Preamble to the Bill of Rights is included in Appendix B and can also be found at the U.S. National Archives and Records Administration website.

Amendment I

No national religion; no laws prohibiting free exercise of religion, freedom of speech, or of the press, or of the right to peaceably assemble or to petition the government for a redress of grievances.

Amendment II

The right of the people to keep and bear arms.

Amendment III

No soldier shall in time of peace or war be quartered in anyone's house without consent of the Owner but in a manner to be prescribed by law.

Amendment IV

The right of the people to be secure in their persons, houses, papers, and effects against unreasonable searches; no warrants without probable cause supported by oath/affirmation and particularly describing the place to be searched and the persons or things to be seized.

Amendment V

Capital offenses must be tried by a grand jury unless within the military, nor may a person be tried twice for the same offense (double jeopardy),[11] nor be a witness against oneself, nor be deprived of life, liberty, or property without due process of law, nor shall private property be taken for public use without just compensation.

11 "The principle of double jeopardy—which does not allow a defendant to be tried twice for the same charge—does not apply between the federal and state government. If, for example, the state brings a murder charge and does not get a conviction, it is possible for the federal government in some cases to file charges against the defendant if the act is also illegal under federal law." "Introduction to the Federal Court System," U.S. Department of Justice.

Amendment VI

The accused shall have a speedy, public trial in the state and district of the alleged crime with witnesses for and against and Assistance of counsel for his defense with the right to be informed of the nature of the pressed charges and evidence.

Amendment VII

The right of trial by jury in suits of common law exceeding twenty dollars, and no fact shall be reconsidered in another court except by rules of common law.

Amendment VIII

No excessive bail, nor excessive fines, nor cruel and unusual punishments.

Amendment IX

Rights other than those mentioned in the Constitution shall be retained by the people.

Amendment X

The powers not delegated to the United States or prohibited to the States by the Constitution belong to the States or the people.

Amendments 11–27

Amendment XI

Only specific lawsuits may come before the United States Judicial power: states are immune from certain lawsuits (ratified February 7, 1795).

Amendment XII

Modifies and clarifies the procedure for electing Vice Presidents and Presidents (ratified June 15, 1804).[12]

Amendment XIII

Neither slavery nor involuntary servitude (except for convicted criminal punishment) shall exist within the United States or places of its jurisdiction (ratified December 6, 1865).

Amendment XIV

Citizens (born or naturalized) in the United States have equal protection of the laws. No state shall make laws against them nor deprive them of life, liberty, or property without due process of law. Representation is based on the population of each state with special attention given to males twenty-one years of age. No person may hold elected office who has engaged in rebellion against the Constitution unless Congress votes to remove that disability. No public debt is to be assumed against the United States or any state for aid in rebellion against the United States (ratified July 9, 1868).

Amendment XV

The right to vote shall not be denied or abridged by the United States or by any state on account of race, color, or previous condition of servitude (ratified February 3, 1870).

---

12 The Electors shall meet in their states to vote by ballot for President and Vice President (they are the first and second string of the national executive branch) and shall send that sealed vote to the President of the Senate to open and count in the presence of Congress. (Congress refers to both the House of Representatives and the Senate. They make up the national legislative branch of government.) The winner shall have the greatest number of votes and the majority of the whole number of Electors. If there is not that majority, the House of Representatives shall choose the President immediately by ballot, each state having one vote and a quorum, meaning two-thirds of the states, must participate. The Senate shall choose the Vice-President following the quorum rules above. [*A choice must be made before March 4, or the Vice President shall act as President.*]

Amendment XVI

The Congress shall have power to lay and collect taxes on incomes (ratified February 3, 1913).

Amendment XVII

The Senate of the United States shall be composed of two Senators from each state, elected by the people thereof, for six years. Vacancies until the next election shall be temporarily appointed by the governor (ratified April 8, 1913).

Amendment XVIII

Intoxicating beverages prohibited (ratified January 16, 1919; repealed December 5, 1933).

Amendment XIX

Women's right to vote: the right of citizens of the United States to vote shall not be denied or abridged by the United States or by any state on account of sex (ratified August 18, 1920).

Amendment XX

Established start and end dates for presidential and congressional terms, and established succession plans for both in the event of a death (ratified January 23, 1933).[13]

---

13 The terms of the President and Vice President shall end at noon on January 20, and the terms of Senators and Representatives at noon on January 3, and the terms of their successors shall begin. The Congress shall assemble at least once every year and shall begin at noon on January 3. If the President-elect shall have died before his term begins, the Vice President shall become President. If by noon on January 3, a President shall not have been chosen, or if the President-elect shall have failed to qualify, then the Vice President-elect shall act as President until a President shall have qualified. If neither a President-elect nor a Vice President-elect shall have qualified, the Congress may by law declare who shall act as President until a President or Vice President shall have qualified. Congress may clarify what would happen if the House of Representatives must elect the President and one of the candidates from which it chooses dies, or if the Senate must elect the Vice President and one of the candidates from whom it may choose dies. Section 4 permits Congress to statutorily clarify what should occur if either the House of Representatives must elect the president and one of the candidates from

Amendment XXI

The eighteenth article of amendment to the Constitution is repealed; therefore, intoxicating beverages are once again legal (ratified December 5, 1933).

Amendment XXII

No person shall be elected to the office of the President more than twice. No person who has held the office for more than two years of a term to which someone else was elected shall be elected to the office of President more than once (ratified February 27, 1951).

Amendment XXIII

The District (of Columbia) constituting the seat of government of the United States (Washington, D.C.) shall appoint electors of President and Vice President as if it were a state but not more than the least populous state. They shall meet in the district and perform the duties of the twelfth amendment (ratified March 29, 1961).

Amendment XXIV

The right of citizens of the United States to vote in any primary or other election for President or Vice President, for electors for President or Vice President, or for Senator or Representative in Congress, shall not be denied by reason of failure to pay any tax (ratified January 23, 1964).

Amendment XXV

In the case of removal of the President from office or of his death or resignation, the Vice President shall become President. When there is a vacancy in the office of Vice President,

---

whom it may choose dies, and likewise for the Senate choosing a Vice President if one of the candidates dies.

the President shall nominate a Vice President who shall take office upon confirmation by a majority vote of both houses of Congress. The Vice President shall be acting President whenever the President transmits to the President *pro tempore* of the Senate and the Speaker of the House of Representatives his written declaration of his inability to discharge the duties of his office. If no inability exists, the President must transmit that in written form in the same process described above. He shall resume the duties of office unless the Vice President and a majority of either the principal officers of the executive department or of such other body as Congress may by law provide (ratified February 10, 1967).

Amendment XXVI

U.S. citizens eighteen years and older must not be denied the right to vote on account of age, and Congress shall have the power to enforce this article by appropriate legislation (ratified July 1, 1971).

Amendment XXVII

Varying the compensation for Senators and Representatives shall not take effect until an election of Representatives shall have taken place (ratified May 7, 1992).

That is an overview summary of the U.S. Constitution[14]—the highest law for Americans beneath the universal law set forth in the Bible. After adopting the Constitution and because of Article I of the Constitution, the nation's bicameral legislature began the process of enacting federal laws which are subject to the Constitution. Note that *bicameral* means *two houses* or

14 The Interactive Constitution at the **National Constitution Center** website allows the reader to display each article/section/amendment in the left sidebar along with legal commentary on that text displayed on the right in the main text box. See the links page at **CivilRealm.com**.

chambers and comes from the Latin prefix *bi*, meaning two, and *camera*, meaning chamber. These two chambers are the U.S. House of Representatives and the Senate. Further note that *legislature* at the federal level means Congress.

Before looking at how these laws are recorded and accessed, we should pause here and briefly summarize the basic duties of each branch of government. These duties are foundational to an understanding of American government, not just at the federal level. These branches are reflected at each level of our nation's government: city, county, and state. We will start with the legislative branch for two reasons: because the Constitution starts there (with Article I) and because understanding the law-making process helps us to more clearly identify areas of government overreach. The Founders attempted to prevent the growth of areas of government overreach into the lives of its citizens. Those areas, nonetheless, have grown to play a heavy role in our civic lives. In order to understand how we got here, we need to examine the law as a whole, starting with the systems the way they were originally designed and intended.

The Legislative Branch

The legislative branch, as Article I tells us, is called Congress. It consists of the Senate[15] and the House of Representatives,[16] and its primary function is making laws. A bill (the seedling of what could become a law) can originate in either chamber of Congress by a senator or a representative who is willing to

15 Each state elects two senators for a total of one hundred members of the Senate. Senators serve for six years and can be reelected indefinitely.

16 Each state elects representatives based on a ratio of its population to the U.S. population. The total number of elected representatives is set at 435. Representatives serve for two years and can be reelected indefinitely.

sponsor it.[17] We will talk later in chapter 6 about the difficult path a bill must take to become a law. Assuming that a bill passes both chambers, Congress sends the bill to the President for consideration. The President has the choice of approving the bill and signing it into law or vetoing it.[18] To veto means to prevent a legislature from enacting a measure so that it cannot become a law. In the case of a presidential veto, Congress can vote to override that veto, and the bill becomes law. But, if the President pocket vetoes a bill (does not sign it within ten days of receipt, Sundays excluded) and if Congress has adjourned, the veto cannot be overridden.[19] This system of passing a bill into law is intentionally complicated in order to prevent an onslaught of legislation.[20] And I have only listed the basic steps of the system without mentioning the immense amount of conversation, networking, lobbying, and pressure involved in each step.[21]

The compilation of these laws, known as the Statutes at Large, is a chronological list of the laws that is written exactly as they have been enacted and in the order that they have been approved.[22] The Statutes at Large contain the historical, legal, and chronological contents of laws that Congress has passed (and that the President did not veto). "The laws are

---

17 With the exception of bills for raising revenue which may only originate in the House (U.S. Const. art. I, § 7).

18 See "I'm Just a Bill," from *Schoolhouse Rock!* available on YouTube (see the links page at **CivilReam.com**). Jack Sheldon, vocalist, "I'm Just a Bill," by David Frishberg, *Schoolhouse Rock!: Special 30th Anniversary Edition*, directed by Tom Warburton (1976, Burbank, CA: Buena Vista Home Entertainment, 2002), DVD.

19 "How Laws Are Made," USA.gov.

20 "It will be of little avail to the people… if the laws be so voluminous that they cannot be read, or so incoherent that they cannot be understood." Madison, Hamilton, and Jay, *The Federalist Papers*, no. 62, 368.

21 Lee Drutman, *The Business of America is Lobbying: How Corporations Became Politicized and Politics Became More Corporate* (New York: Oxford University Press, 2015).

22 "How Our Laws Are Made," H.R. Res. 49, 110th Cong., 54, (2007), Congress.gov.

not arranged according to subject matter and do not reflect the present status of an earlier law that has been amended."[23]

After the laws are recorded as Statutes at Large, they are organized into the Code of Laws of the United States of America (also called the U.S. Code). The U.S. Code is simply the Statutes at Large rearranged topically in a useful manner for referencing. The topics are called titles, and there are fifty-four of them. Well, there are actually fifty-three because one is holding a "Reserved" space. These fifty-three titles are the official group of laws governing the land and are known as federal statutory law.[24] The Statutes at Large and the Code of Laws are **the direct result** of our U.S. Congress at work. In a moment, we will look at laws that are the indirect result of our U.S. Congress at work, but first, we must finish this overview of the three branches (also known as powers).

The Executive Branch

As defined in Article II, the executive branch consists of the President,[25] the Vice President, and the presidential cabinet. The Vice President is a member of the cabinet along with heads of the executive departments and other high-ranking government appointees.[26] The executive branch executes or carries out the laws passed by Congress and appoints heads of federal agencies to assist in that work.[27]

The President, in particular, wears five different "hats" while serving in office. The President acts as **chief executive** (administering government programs, including those in the

23 "How Our Laws Are Made," Congress.gov.

24 United States House of Representatives, "United States Code," Office of the Law Revision Counsel.

25 The President is elected to a four-year term and can be reelected only once. The Vice-President is also elected to a four-year term and can be reelected indefinitely.

26 "Branches of Government," USA.gov.

27 "The Executive Branch," The White House.

FEDERAL LAWS

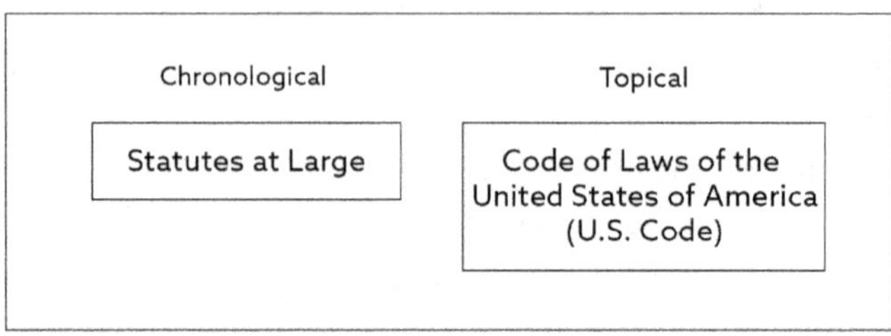

Figure 2.2

presidential cabinet, along with the power to exercise the right of legal pardon and appoint federal judges/justices[28] and ambassadors); **chief of state** (performing ceremonial duties and serving as a symbol of the country and delivering the annual State of the Union Address[29] to Congress and the American public); **commander-in-chief** (determining military strategy but not declaring war); **chief politician** (leading his/her party and supporting its candidates); and **chief diplomat** (writing treaties and recognizing new governments).[30]

The Judicial Branch

In Article III of the Constitution, we find that the judicial branch interprets the meaning of the law in a dual-court system where federal and state-level issues are treated separately.

28 In the federal system judges serve in lower federal courts, while justices serve in the Supreme Court.

29 The State of the Union Address is an annual speech given by the President to a joint session of Congress and to the American people with updates on the budget, economy, priorities, congressional proposals, agenda, accomplishments, etc.

30 William R. Sanford and Carl R. Green, *Basic Principles of American Government* (New York: Amsco School Publications, 1986), 153.

This system owes its existence to a larger concept called federalism. At first glance, this term has a dubious sound to it, but it is based squarely in the Tenth Amendment to the U.S. Constitution.[31] Federalism is an organizational system where power is distributed between a central authority and constituent (subordinate) units.[32] American federalism simply means that governmental powers are shared between the federal government and the state governments. Because of federalism, the American court system exists in two parallel tracks: the federal track and the state track. These two tracks do not intersect, but they may have areas of overlap. That is why there is the Supreme Court of the United States (SCOTUS) at the top of the federal system and a state supreme court at the top of each state system.[33] Both systems determine how written

31 "The powers not delegated to the United States by the Constitution, nor prohibited by it to the States, are reserved to the States respectively, or to the people."

32 Daniel Judah Elazar, *Exploring Federalism* (Tuscaloosa: University of Alabama Press, 1987), xii.

"There have been three critical federal experiments in the history of humanity to date. The Israelite tribal federation described in the Bible was the first... the establishment of a polity of tribes maintaining their liberties within the framework of a common constitution and law... The second was the Swiss Confederation. Seven hundred years ago it preserved liberty in medieval Europe. Later it fostered the principal liberating stream of the Protestant Reformation and survived to create a garden spot in the world, self-governed by free people. The third was the United States of America" (xii).

Elazar again: "Recurring expressions of the covenant or federal model are found in ancient Israel, whose people started out as rebels against the Pharaonic model; among the medieval rebels against the Holy Roman Empire; in the Reformation era among rebels against the Catholic hierarchy; among the early modern republicans who rebelled against either hierarchical or oligarchic regimes; and in authentic modern federal systems. Frontiersmen generally—people who have gone out to settle new areas where there were no established patterns of governance in which to fit and who, therefore have had to compact with one another to create governing institutions—are to be found among the most active covenanters and builders of federal institutions beyond that original covenant" (4–5).

33 "The Supreme Court of the United States is the highest court in the American judicial system, and has the power to decide appeals on all cases brought in federal court or those brought in state court but dealing with federal law. For example, if a First Amendment freedom of speech case was decided by the highest court of a state (usually the state supreme court), the case could be appealed to the federal Supreme Court. However, if that same case were decided entirely on a state law similar to the First Amendment, the Supreme Court of the United States would not be able to consider the case." "Introduction to the Federal Court System," U.S. Department of Justice.

law applies to our lives either as Americans (federal system) or as citizens of a particular state (state system) or to an overlap of both.[34] In the words of James Madison, "The federal and [s]tate governments are in fact but different agents and trustees of the people, constituted with different powers and designed for different purposes."[35]

This point is where many Americans' eyes glaze over. As far as I can tell, many of us simply do not understand the judicial branch with all of its different districts and levels. Although we don't broadcast it, we often tend to think thusly: "There is a glut of lawyers, and attorneys' services are very expensive. Therefore, it is generally best to stay out of trouble in order to sidestep the entire problem of the judicial system." To be sure, it is good advice to stay out of trouble, but it is also good advice to understand how the legal system is structured.

We will glance at both the federal and the state systems in this chapter for a general overview. After this chapter, we won't return to the federal judicial system again until chapter 7, when we consider national government. However, the state system will appear in the city, county, and state government chapters, respectively. Here's the reason why: The federal court system deals with questions of law as written in the

---

34 "Sometimes, the jurisdiction of state courts will overlap with that of federal courts, meaning that some cases can be brought in both courts. The plaintiff has the initial choice of bringing the case in state or federal court. However, if the plaintiff chooses state court, the defendant may sometimes choose to 'remove' to federal court.

Cases that are entirely based on state law may be brought in federal court under the court's 'diversity jurisdiction.' Diversity jurisdiction allows a plaintiff of one state to file a lawsuit in federal court when the defendant is located in a different state. The defendant can also seek to 'remove' from state court for the same reason. To bring a state law claim in federal court, all of the plaintiffs must be located in different states than all of the defendants, and the 'amount in controversy' must be more than $75,000. (Note: the rules for diversity jurisdiction are much more complicated than explained here.)" "Introduction to the Federal Court System," U.S. Department of Justice.

Criminal cases may not be brought under diversity jurisdiction. States may only bring criminal prosecutions in state courts, and the federal government may only bring criminal prosecutions in federal court.

35 Madison, Hamilton, and Jay, *The Federalist Papers*, no. 46, 297.

U.S. Constitution or the federal statutes or cases between two citizens of different states. This means federal courts have limited jurisdiction (the legal authority to hear a certain type of case). In contrast, the state judicial system handles cases dealing with questions of law regarding each state's constitution or statutes.[36]

Both systems operate in a similar three-tiered structure. From the bottom up, cases are initially heard in lower trial courts. At the federal level, trial courts are known as district courts. At the state level, trial courts are known by a variety of names. In both tracks, the second tier comes into play if a plaintiff[37] or a defendant[38] believes that the lower court decided a case in error. In such situations, an appeal can be made, and the case can be reviewed in an appellate court. If the verdict from the appellate court is considered to be in error, the case can be reviewed yet again at the third tier, known as the court of last resort. In the federal track, the court of last resort is the U.S. Supreme Court. In the state track, it is the state supreme court. This ability to appeal a lower court's decision is an internal check of power within the judicial branch of government. Another check is that court records, proceedings, and verdicts are generally available to the public, not kept secret.

Federal judges (and Supreme Court justices) are not elected by the people, rather each is appointed by the President and confirmed by the Senate. As such, the presiding President holds significant sway over the direction of the judicial system. The Supreme Court consists of one chief justice and eight associate justices appointed to serve for life or as long

36 Many times a case has both federal and state law, so the lawsuit can be in either federal or state court. "Introduction to the Federal Court System," U.S. Department of Justice.

37 The party or person who brings a lawsuit before a court.

38 The party or person against whom a lawsuit is brought before a court.

as they desire. In the state system, each state's law dictates whether its judges/justices are elected or appointed.

Having just clarified the similarities between the two judicial systems, let's continue with the federal track. In the federal court system, the first tier consists of the ninety-four district courts.[39] These are trial courts—where cases begin. The second tier includes the thirteen circuit courts.[40] These are known as first-level-of-appeal courts—where cases can be appealed. The third tier is the U.S. Supreme Court—where final federal decisions are made.[41] Supreme Court cases are mostly appellate in nature (meaning that they have previously been heard in lower-level courts),[42] with the purpose of declaring whether or not laws which have been passed are constitutional. Because there is no higher court than the U.S. Supreme Court, its decisions can only be overturned by rare constitutional amendment or by a subsequent ruling of the Supreme Court.[43]

Lower courts must follow precedent from higher courts which means they may not overturn a higher court's decision. They also must weigh historical court decisions in similar courts across the nation. This body of judicial precedent is known as common law or case law. It is law derived from prior judicial decisions instead of from legislative statutes. "American courts originally fashioned common law rules based on English common law until the American legal system was sufficiently mature to create common law rules either from

---

39 U.S. district courts also include specialty courts such as tariff court, tax court, administrative tribunals, customs court, and court of claims.

40 The number of district courts and circuit courts has increased over time in order to accommodate the caseload.

41 "Introduction to the Federal Court System," U.S. Department of Justice.

42 U.S. Const. art. III, § 2. The Supreme Court hears original trials for all cases affecting ambassadors and other public ministers and consuls, all cases of admiralty and maritime jurisdiction, controversies in which the U.S. is a party, and controversies between two or more states, or between a state and citizens of another state, or between citizens of different states. "The Judicial Branch," The White House.

43 "The Court and Constitutional Interpretation," Supreme Court of the United States.

STATE JUDICIAL SYSTEM

3rd Tier: State Supreme Court (court of last resort)

↑

2nd Tier: State Court of Appeals

↑

1st Tier: Trial Court

FEDERAL JUDICIAL SYSTEM

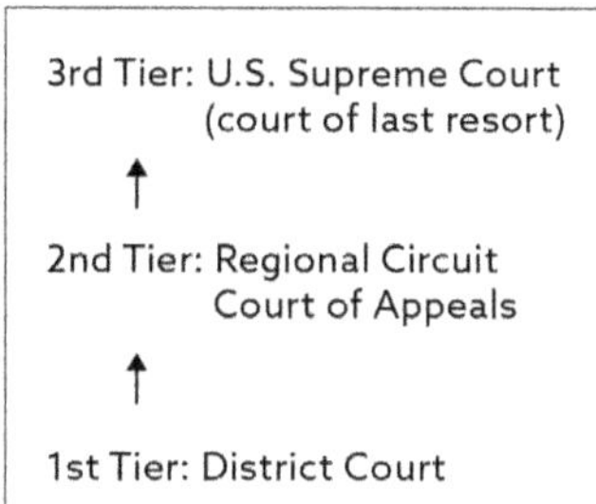

Figure 2.3

direct precedent or by analogy to comparable areas of decided law."[44] This principle is *stare decisis*—Latin for "to stand by things decided."[45] *Stare decisis* means that higher courts generally shouldn't change precedent.

On occasion, a court may decide not "to stand by things decided" and overturn a previous ruling.[46] For example, this situation occurred in the 1953 Supreme Court case of *Brown v. Board of Education of Topeka* when the court ruled in favor of Mr. Brown (and twelve other black families), thus allowing him to enroll his daughter (and the other families' children) in the local, nearby all-white public school rather than sending her to the farther away all-black school. In so doing, the Supreme Court overturned a prior ruling of the 1896 *Plessy v. Ferguson* case which stated that facilities could be racially sep-

44 *Wex Legal Dictionary and Encyclopedia*, s.v. "common law," Legal Information Institute, Cornell Law School.

45 *Wex Legal Dictionary and Encyclopedia*, s.v. "stare decisis," Legal Information Institute, Cornell Law School.

46 For a list of Supreme Court decisions overruled by subsequent decisions, see Constitution Annotated, "Table of Supreme Court Decisions Overruled by Subsequent Decisions."

arate as long as they were equal.[47] Over a half-century later, the Supreme Court no longer viewed the prior precedent of racial segregation to be constitutional and chose to chart the rare course of departing from *stare decisis* for compelling reasons, adhering to the principles of the Constitution. In 2022, the Supreme Court reversed its 1973 *Roe v. Wade* decision and its 1992 *Planned Parenthood v. Casey* decisions. Again, in 2024, the high court overruled *Chevron U.S.A., Inc. v. Natural Resources Defense Council, Inc.* Chevron was a 1984 decision that had required courts to defer to an administrative agency's interpretation of its own regulation(s). More on administrative agencies is forthcoming in the next section.

By this point in this chapter, it should be apparent that American government is centered on written law. Principally, God's Word gives us the overarching template of right and wrong. Then, the Constitution defines our federal governmental structures while protecting the rights of the states. National law is further created by Congress, enforced by the President, and interpreted by the judiciary, and it is the **direct result** of our U.S. Constitution and U.S. Congress at work.

The Fourth Branch?

Now for the **indirect** result of our U.S. Congress at work. Many Americans do not realize that there is an entire layer of laws not established by the Constitution nor directly passed by Congress. These indirect regulations are the work of federal regulatory agencies. Federal regulatory agencies do just what their name implies: create regulations, rules, procedures, orders, and decisions at the federal level which possess legal

47 *Wex Legal Dictionary and Encyclopedia*, s.v. "Brown v. Board of Education (1954)," Legal Information Institute, Cornell Law School.

effect.[48] The regulations that proceed from federal agencies are, in fact, known as law. Most of these agencies are the ideological grandchildren of Franklin Delano Roosevelt's New Deal programs that his administration created in an attempt to secure relief for Americans from the Great Depression of 1929–1939.[49]

Here are a few examples of today's agencies that possess quite recognizable names:

- EPA—The Environmental Protection Agency
- TSA—The Transportation Security Administration
- FDA—The Food and Drug Administration
- CDC—Centers for Disease Control and Prevention
- DOJ—Department of Justice

As mentioned above, the laws that these agencies create circumvent the constitutionally defined congressional process of creating law. How can that be? The Constitution explicitly establishes the right of Congress (composed of the House and Senate) to create laws. At various points throughout time, the Supreme Court has decided that Congress has the power to delegate some of its detail-oriented work to administrative agencies or programs.[50] To understand this concept, it helps to know that the term *agent* means one who is authorized to act for or in the place of another. Likewise, an agency is a group which is authorized to act for or in place of another group. Therefore agencies were created by Congress to act

48 "How Laws Are Made: The Administrative Agencies," Alexander Campbell King Law Library, University of Georgia School of Law.

49 A few of FDR's original agencies are still in existence today. Debbie Hadley, "7 New Deal Programs That Still Exist Today," ThoughtCo, updated September 2 , 2024.

50 For an extensive explanation of these rulings, see "Delegation of Legislative Power," Justia.

in its place in matters requiring professional expertise. And Congress grants them the authority that enables them to make rules and regulations that Americans must abide by.

Because these agencies produce rules and regulations, they themselves require some regulation. So in 1946, Congress passed the Administrative Procedure Act that governs the process by which federal agencies develop and issue regulations.[51] These rules and regulations are recorded daily in the Federal Register in chronological order of issue (much like the laws passed by Congress are recorded in the Statutes at Large in chronological order). Then, these rules and regulations are rearranged by topic into a codified version called the Code of Federal Regulations,[52] also known as C.F.R. (much like the U.S. Code is the topical rearrangement of laws that Congress has passed). These regulations constitute an entire body of law that many Americans are virtually unaware of.[53]

FEDERAL REGULATIONS

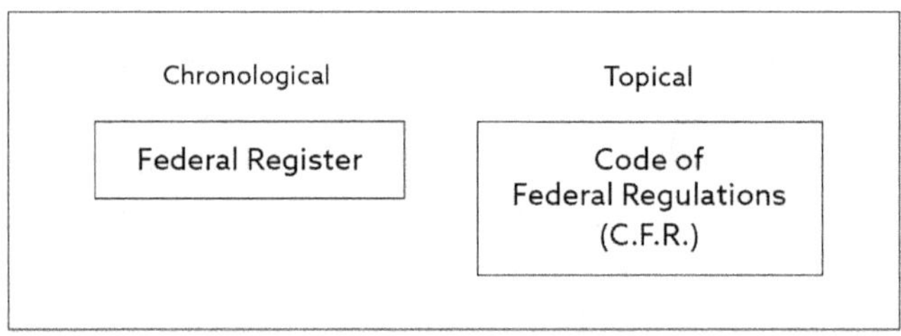

Figure 2.4

51 "Summary of the Administrative Procedure Act," U.S. Environmental Protection Agency.

52 "Federal Register Tutorial," U.S. National Archives and Records Administration.

53 The 2021 Code of Federal Regulations contains 245 volumes and 188,343 pages and is approximately four times the size of the 44,000-page United States Code of Laws. "Code of Federal Regulations," U.S. National Archives and Records Administration, accessed August 28, 2023.

See also Susan E. Dudley, "Milestones in the Evolution of the Administrative State," *Daedalus*, Summer 2021.

Administrative-agency law is a complicated business, and it has existed largely outside the American governing principle of checks and balances. The term *checks and balances* means that each of the three branches of government (legislative, executive, and judicial) has some degree of oversight in relation to the other two branches. This balance of power is reflected at every level of American government, which we will see in later chapters. At the federal level, for example, the President can veto legislation created by Congress and has the power to nominate heads of federal agencies. Congress can confirm or reject the President's nominees and can remove the President from office in exceptional circumstances. The justices on the Supreme Court, who are nominated by the President and confirmed by the Senate, can overturn unconstitutional laws.

In the absence of checks and balances, federal regulatory agencies themselves have been, in a very real sense, unregulated.[54] For example, the President cannot shut down agencies but can merely remove certain positions in these agencies. Congress may occasionally monitor agency actions through oversight hearings and legislative reforms. It is unlikely, but Congress could also pass a law to dissolve these agencies, or it could cease appropriating their federal funding. The judicial branch possesses the power to interpret these agencies' rulings, and until recently,[55] the courts have almost always deferred to the administrative agencies' interpretations of their

54 "The administrative state represents a new and pervasive form of rule, and a perversion of constitutional self-government. It has deep theoretical roots that were overlooked for a long time, roots inimical to the Constitution, thereby providing a lesson in the importance of understanding the principles of the Constitution. A chief feature of the administrative state is its relentless centralization, but with a reciprocal effect: its mandates, regulations, distorting funding mechanisms, and elitist professionalism have corrupted our political culture all the way back down to local government. It is the chief reason why Americans increasingly have contempt for government." Steven F. Hayward, "The Threat to Liberty: The administrative state and the end of constitutional government," *Claremont Review of Books*, Winter 2016/17.

55 Eric Katz, "Supreme Court ends judicial deference to federal agency expertise," Government Executive, June 28, 2024.

own rulings.[56] So some progress has been made. Yet these agencies' members are not elected, and thus are not accountable to voters at the ballot box.[57] The existence of this situation is far from ideal. I mention it not to sound the alarm but rather to inform my readers of the current state of affairs. Civic reformation begins with understanding the system as it currently exists and moves outward from there.

Determining which regulations are not lawful involves examining whether they comply with legal procedures and statutory authority. Federal agency regulations may be deemed unlawful if they exceed the authority granted to the agency by Congress, violate constitutional provisions, or fail to adhere to procedural requirements established by law. For instance, if Congress has not explicitly authorized an agency to regulate a certain area of activity, but the agency attempts to do so through a regulation, it would likely be deemed unlawful. An example of this would be if the Environmental Protection Agency (EPA) attempted to regulate firearms manufacturing. A regulation may also be struck down if an agency fails to follow proper procedures, such as providing notice and an opportunity for public comment. Or finally, if an agency enacted a regulation imposing content-based restrictions on political speech, it would likely conflict with constitutional provisions.

I mentioned earlier that although the Bible is not amended, all other forms of American law are subject to amendment or interpretation. The judicial branch possesses this power which is known as judicial review—the authority to assess the constitutionality of actions by the executive and legislative branches, including federal agencies. When challenged, federal courts have the authority to review agency regulations to ensure compliance. Parties aggrieved by a regulation, such as

56 Nicholas Mosvick, "How the Supreme Court Created Agency Deference," *Constitution Daily* (blog), National Constitution Center, June 25, 2021.

57 Maeve P. Carey, "An Overview of Federal Regulations and the Rulemaking Process," Congressional Research Service.

affected individuals, organizations, or states, may challenge its legality in court. Through judicial review, federal courts may find some regulations to be unlawful. Regulations found to be unlawful may be invalidated or struck down, requiring the agency to revise or rescind them. Judicial review will be discussed further in chapter 6, "State Government," but before we move on, let's look at an example of judicial review at the federal level.

Recall that during the COVID-19 pandemic, in airport terminals across the nation, travelers experienced an example of a federal agency rule being treated and considered as law. Loudspeaker announcements and freestanding signs in airports routinely proclaimed that passengers were required by federal law to wear face coverings. This proclamation, known colloquially as the Mask Mandate, was not federal law voted upon by Congress in the normally prescribed manner; rather, this "law" was a ruling by a federal agency known as the Centers for Disease Control (CDC). A Florida federal court finally declared that the "Mask Mandate exceeds the CDC's statutory authority (legal authority granted by Congress and defined in the federal statutes/Code of Laws) and violates the procedures required for agency rulemaking under the 1946 APA [Administrative Procedure Act]."[58]

As you can see, there is a great quantity of law in the federal law layer. The Constitution remains the foundational and supreme law of the U.S. government. The power of the legislative branch (Congress) is showcased in the nation's statutory law. Paralleling statutory law in organization but not in its directly constitutionally authorized power is the Code of Federal Regulations. The President is our chief executive and the most visible individual representing our federal government and casting a vision for national affairs. Lastly, the judicial branch interprets law largely (but not absolutely) in light

58 Health Freedom Defense Fund v. Biden, 599 F. Supp. 3d 1144 (M.D. Fla. 2022).

of prior precedent. As we will see below, this organization of law is repeated at the state level.

STATE LAW

Like the United States, each of the fifty states also possesses a written constitution. Each state's constitution is the highest law of that particular state, yet it remains subject to the U.S. Constitution. Quickly turn back to the Tenth Amendment, which is marked in grayscale. It declares that "the powers not delegated to the United States or prohibited to the States by the Constitution belong to the States or the people." This means that any rights not given to the federal government are reserved for the states (or for the people).

State constitutions appear to follow the model of the U.S. Constitution, but in reality, it is just the reverse. The early states' constitutions served as the models for our nation's constitution. As the thirteen colonies declared themselves states, they began the process of adopting their own constitutions. These documents actually served as both templates and inspiration for the federal document and demonstrate that the idea of a constitution is deeply rooted in the American psyche.[59] Remembering that the U.S. Constitution was ratified in 1787, you can see the footnote to look up the date that your own state's constitution was ratified.[60] Compare that date to the year that the current version in use was adopted using the resource in the following footnote.[61] You can also compare how long your state's constitution is (number of words) to

59 "The 1780 Constitution of the Commonwealth of Massachusetts, drafted by John Adams, is the world's oldest functioning written constitution. It served as a model for the United States Constitution, which was written in 1787 and became effective in 1789." "John Adams & the Massachusetts Constitution," Massachusetts Court System.

60 Wikipedia, s.v. "State constitution in the United States."

61 Ballotpedia, s.v. "State constitution."

other states' constitutions.[62] Some state constitutions are long and verbose (like Alabama's which is just over 340,000 words), while others are succinctly written (such as Vermont's which contains almost 8,300 words).[63]

State constitutions, being the supreme law of each state, all set out to describe how governing takes place in that state. Typically, constitutions have a preamble that articulates their purpose, a bill of rights for citizens of that state, and sections that discuss the state's procedures for voting and elections. Similarly, they describe the offices of state government (such as the executive office of the governor). Another constitutional purpose is to establish the state's power to tax and take on debt. Constitutions also outline the existence of local (county) government and contain a section detailing how they can be amended in order to remain relevant yet dependable.[64]

After the American territories (or colonies in the case of the original thirteen colonies) became states and ratified their constitutions, they established the forms of government set forth in each state's constitution consisting of legislative, executive, and judicial branches (which operate very similarly to the federal level described above). Once these branches of government were functioning, laws already in use within the colonies/territories were then ratified (adopted) by their state legislatures, and subsequent laws then began to accrue. Each state's laws originate in its legislature (legislative branch), then they are signed into official law by the governor (executive branch) and remain on the state books until they are nullified by the judicial branch or by further legislation from the legislature.[65] Similar to laws at the federal level, state laws are recorded in chronological order by date of passage in books

62 Ballotpedia, s.v. "State constitution."

63 "State Constitutions," USLegal.com.

64 "State Constitutions," USLegal.com.

65 We will learn in chapter 8 that in some states, laws may come into existence by ballot initiative and may be repealed by ballot referendum.

sometimes titled (Name-of-State) Session Laws that are published in separate volumes for each legislative term after a session has concluded.

STATE SESSION LAWS
(kept for historical records)

Laws listed in chronological order as they are made

- Alabama Laws
- Session Laws of Alaska
- Session Laws, Arizona
- Acts of Arkansas
- Statutes of California
- Session Laws of Colorado
- Connecticut Public & Special Acts
- Laws of Delaware
- Washington D.C.'s session laws have several names, and it is not a state
- Laws of Florida
- Georgia Laws
- Session Laws of Hawaii
- Idaho Session Laws
- Laws of Illinois
- Acts, Indiana
- Acts of the State of Iowa
- Session Laws of Kansas
- Acts of Kentucky
- State of Louisiana: Acts of the Legislature
- Laws of the State of Maine
- Laws of Maryland
- Acts & Resolves of Massachusetts
- Public and Local Acts of the Legislature of the State of Michigan
- Laws of Minnesota
- General Laws of Mississippi
- Session Laws of Missouri
- Laws of Montana
- Laws of Nebraska
- Statutes of Nevada
- Laws of the State of New Hampshire
- Laws of New Jersey
- Laws of the State of New Mexico
- Laws of New York
- Session Laws of North Carolina
- Laws of North Dakota
- State of Ohio: Legislative Acts Passed and Joint Resolutions Adopted
- Oklahoma Session Laws
- Oregon Laws and Resolutions
- Laws of Pennsylvania
- Public Laws of Rhode Island and Providence Plantations
- Acts and Joint Resolutions, South Carolina
- Session Laws of South Dakota
- Public Acts of the State of Tennessee
- General and Special Laws of the State of Texas
- Laws of Utah
- Acts and Resolves of Vermont
- Acts of the General Assembly of the Commonwealth of Virginia
- Session Laws of Washington
- Acts of the Legislature of West Virginia
- Wisconsin Session Laws
- Session Laws of Wyoming

Figure 2.5

These laws are then organized by subject (usually called titles, then subdivided—in some states—into articles, then subdivided into chapters, then subdivided into sections). Once the laws are organized in this fashion (or in some states, this organization is by name rather than by numbered titles), they are published in one volume per session as well as posted online by various names. If you have lived in various states, you may recall having heard or seen some of these names in the media.[66]

STATE CODES OF LAWS
(the version everyone uses)

Laws organized in order by topic

- Code of Alabama
- Alaska Statutes
- Arizona Revised Statutes
- Arkansas Code
- California Codes
- Colorado Revised Statutes
- Connecticut General Statutes
- Delaware Code
- D.C. Official Code (District of Clumbia-which is not a state and, in my opinion, should not be
- Florida Statutes
- Georgia Statutes
- Hawaii Revised Statutes
- Idaho Statutes
- Illinois Compiled Statutes
- Indiana Code
- Iowa Code
- Kansas Statutes Annotated
- Kentucky Revised Statutes
- Louisiana Laws
- Maine Revised Statutes
- Maryland Statutes
- General Laws of Massachusetts
- Michigan Compiled Laws
- Minnesota Code
- Mississippi Code
- Missouri Statutes
- Montana Code Annotated
- Nebraska Revised Statutes
- Nevada Revised Statutes
- New Hampshire Revised Statutes Annotated
- New Jersey Permanent Statutes
- New Mexico Statutes
- New York Statutes
- North Carolina General Statutes
- North Dakota Century Code
- Ohio Revised Code
- Oklahoma Statutes
- Oregon Revised Statutes
- Consolidated Statutes of Pennsylvania
- State of Rhode Island General Laws
- South Carolina Code of Laws
- South Dakota Codified Laws
- Tennessee Code
- Texas Statutes
- Utah Code
- Vermont Statutes
- Code of Virginia
- Revised Code of Washington
- West Virginia Code
- Wisconsin Statutes
- Wyoming Statutes

Figure 2.6

66 The information for Figure 2.5a is taken from Columbia Law Review, et al, *The Bluebook: A Uniform System of Citation*, 21st ed. (Cambridge, MA: Harvard Law Review Association, 2020), T1.3, 242–294.

The information for Figure 2.5b on the following page is from "Listing by jurisdiction," Legal Information Institute, Cornell Law School.

Just as there are regulatory agencies at the federal level that exist to assist the federal government in its ever-expanding governing of American life, there are also state-level regulatory agencies that exist for specific state purposes. These agencies produce rules which govern residents' lives in each state. Further, the agencies possess codes of rules with the power and effect of state (legislature-originated) law. Though these laws do not directly originate from the state legislatures, typically the legislatures pass laws (often referred to as enabling statutes) that direct the agencies to make administrative rules that serve their purposes. The names of the agency-based codes of regulations for each state and their codes with the force of state law can be found on the National Association of the Secretaries of State's Administrative Codes and Registers website.[67] Refer to Appendix D: Establishment & Enablement of State Agencies to see an example of how this process unfolds.

STATE REGULATIONS

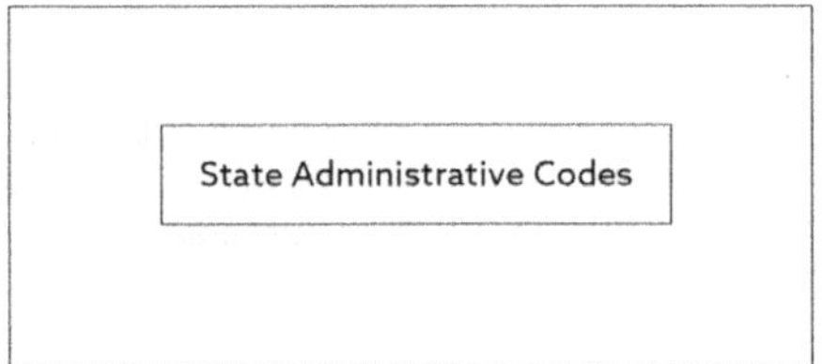

Figure 2.7

Before leaving the topic of law at the state level in this section, take note, once again, that the basic structure of state government is established in each state's constitution and then is further described in each state's code of laws. Thus, the state constitution serves to establish the law, and the state

67 National Association of Secretaries of State, "Administrative Rules—United States of America," Administrative Codes and Registers (ACR).

code of laws (statutes) serves to further describe and define the law. State agencies also churn out regulatory law (unnoticed by many Americans).

SPECIAL DISTRICT TAX-BASED LAW

Special districts are enabled by each state's legislature to provide single services[68] to a region of the state that the city or county equivalent[69] does not provide. Their only legal status pertains to the specific service they are created to provide. Generally speaking, special districts do not issue regulations, but they have the power to levy taxes or fees. And American citizens must comply with paying taxes.

COUNTY-EQUIVALENT LAW

The duties of county-equivalent government are set forth in state constitutions and state codes of law (also known as statutes or statutory law). A county equivalent primarily acts as an arm of the state government at the local level and refers to state law to carry out these duties.

Additionally, each county or its equivalent in a state typically has local ordinances (laws) that deal mainly, but not exclusively, with land-use issues. Some counties may have a charter to more clearly define their rights, powers, and privileges. Charters have typically been the domain of cities and will be further explained in the next section and in chapter 3.

---

68 There are rare occasions when a special district provides more than one service, such as the Central Florida Tourism Oversight District that manages Walt Disney World Resort. "Reedy Creek: The Facts You Need in 2024," Disney in Florida, February 1, 2024.

69 This book borrows the U.S. Census Bureau's term county equivalent to mean county or parish (Louisiana) or borough (Alaska) or regional council (Connecticut).

CITY LAW

Although in a few instances counties and cities merge together and govern as a unit, typically these entities govern separately, with one or more cities existing within a single county equivalent. These city governments can pass laws that are often called city codes of ordinances. Cities may also pass resolutions, but they expire at a stated point and are not as binding as ordinances.

Another aspect of city law is the city charter which is like a constitution for the city. Not all cities have a charter, but for those that do, as state constitutions mirror the U.S. Constitution,[70] so city constitutions mirror the state constitution. These city constitutions or charters "are the forgotten constitutions of our federal system. Scholars generally understand our democracy to be governed by federal and state constitutions, but there is a third, almost entirely ignored realm of constitutional law and practice that lives at the local-government level, embodied in the charters that govern cities, counties, and towns."[71] We will look further at city charters in the next chapter.[72]

And that brings us, for the purposes of this book, down through the basic layers of law that govern Americans. It should be noted that each lower layer is trumped by the authority of the layer over it. For example, a city ordinance cannot be contrary to or supersede a state law. However, a city can make laws that are stricter than state laws if the state has not reserved the right to make those laws, but a city law cannot be

---

70 Even though the colonial constitutions actually preceded and influenced the U.S. Constitution.

71 Nestor M. Davidson, "Local Constitutions," *Texas Law Review* 99, no. 5 (April 29, 2021).

72 Some counties are also incorporated and have charters. There is wide variety in local government structures across the nation, and this book merely treats overarching patterns.

GOVERNANCE STRUCTURE IN THE UNITED STATES IN TERMS OF LAW

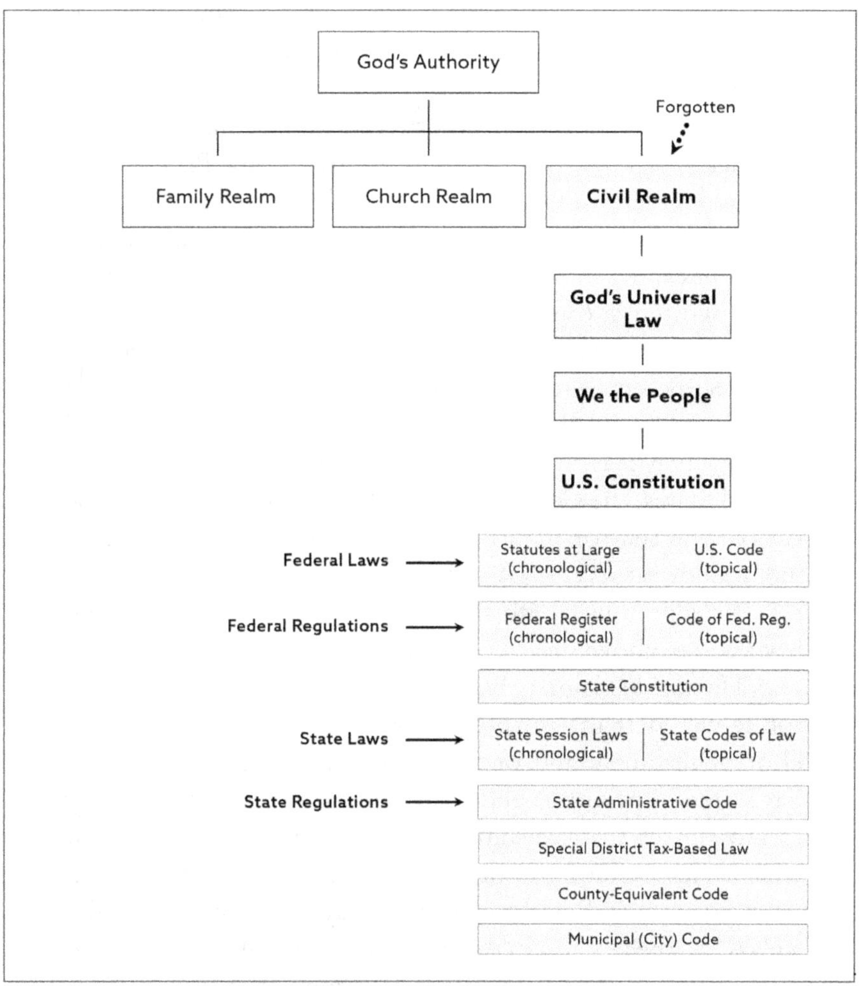

Figure 2.8

in conflict with the state law or the federal law without lawsuits following quickly behind. Further, city law generally only applies within the city limits.[73] If you live outside city limits, then only the county-equivalent law applies. Inside city limits, you must obey both in addition to state and federal laws.

The authority of the layers of law is on display during the ceremonial swearing-in of an officeholder. We have all seen a president-elect take the oath of office to become President of the United States (POTUS). An integral part of the ceremony is swearing to uphold the Constitution of the United States of America. We can observe our governing system's fidelity to the written law as elected officials assume their oath, not just at the national level, but also at the state, county, and city levels. Some time ago, I attended the first city council meeting of the new year where I live. Three new city councilors and one new mayor each swore to uphold the Constitution of the United States, the Constitution of the State of Idaho, and the laws of the State of Idaho. So at the city level (generally speaking, the lowest level of American government), officeholders acknowledge under oath that they will uphold the layers of law that are above them like an overarching umbrella.

Having explained this basic hierarchy of law from the top down, after this chapter, we will start at the smallest level of government and work upward. In this manner, we will have time to prioritize and focus on the levels that are closer to most of us than Washington, D.C. is. Because a lot of our civic understanding has been lost in recent decades, there is much to recover. Better to enter the fray late than never. Raise a glass "to the law and to the testimony!" (Isaiah 8:20) and join me in the next chapter to survey government at the city level.

73 With the exception of extra-territorial powers which will be explained in the next chapter.

OTHER THINGS YOU SHOULD KNOW

The United States Constitution is the world's longest-surviving written charter of government.[74] It has been in use since 1789 and has only been amended twenty-seven times. The model of self-governance and stability around the world, the Constitution was written to limit the power of the national government. It was written for the common man not for the bureaucrat. There are liberal contingents who want to tear down the Constitution because it was written by white males. Such contingents see life in terms of color and gender. We must do better than this. We must see life in terms of truth and grace.

We live in a constitutional republic (remember the summary of Article IV earlier in this chapter) where the government exists under the rules of the Constitution, and the governing members temporarily serve as representatives of the people. Our nation was not designed to support career politicians. It was never the intention of the Founding Fathers for We The People to elect public servants seeking careers. The intent was for many of the governed to serve for a time and then step down from elected office.

A constitutional republic differs from a pure democracy where the people govern themselves directly through the will of the majority. (Note that *demos* means "people" and *-cracy* means "form of government.") Direct democracy is not described in the U.S. Constitution. We do not each directly represent ourselves in policy-making (with the exception of some towns in New England and the ballot initiative—more on both of those topics later). Rather, the American constitutional system requires that we elect those who will represent us as they govern. Hence, I will frequently use the term

74 "Introduction," Constitution of the United States, United States Senate.

elected representatives of the people instead of the more commonly known term *elected officials* which sounds a little too official or officious and not quite representational.

The term *representative democracy* is also an acceptable term because it describes the people being governed by representatives. However, it is not as preferable as a constitutional republic, because it lacks the important reference to the Constitution. Perhaps the term *constitutional democracy* is closer to the point. Or better yet, *constitutional-representative democracy*. In reality, all of these limited-democracy terms make sense. Just be a tad leery of the term democracy used by itself.

THINGS YOU CAN DO

- Read the Constitution online[75] or in Appendix B.
- Look for resources on the Constitution such as Hillsdale College's Free Online Courses:[76]
    - Introduction to the Constitution
    - Constitution 101: The Meaning and History of the Constitution
    - Constitution 201: The Progressive Rejection of the Founding and the Rise of Bureaucratic Despotism
    - The Presidency and the Constitution
- Memorize the Preamble to the Constitution. It sets forth the scope of authority given to the government.

---

75 My favorite easy-to-read version can be located at **usgopo.com/constitution/**. Note that it does not contain the Preamble to the Bill of Rights which is located in Appendix B of this book and can also be found at the U.S. National Archives and Records Adminstration website: **archives.gov**.

76 Links to the courses can be found at **CivilRealm.com**.

- Order a pocket-size copy of the U.S. Constitution with the Declaration of Independence from the U.S. Government Printing Office.[77]

SO WHAT?

After having read this chapter, here are some questions to ask yourself:

- Do you believe that God ordains the governments on this earth?
- Do you understand authority—how one layer of law has authority over another?
- Do you see how all of the layers below the Constitution are dependent upon the Constitution?
- Can you see that the Constitution is special in how it relates to the people who are being governed?

77 Go to **bookstore.gpo.gov** and browse the website or search by stock #052-071-01591-4.

GOVERNANCE STRUCTURE IN THE UNITED STATES

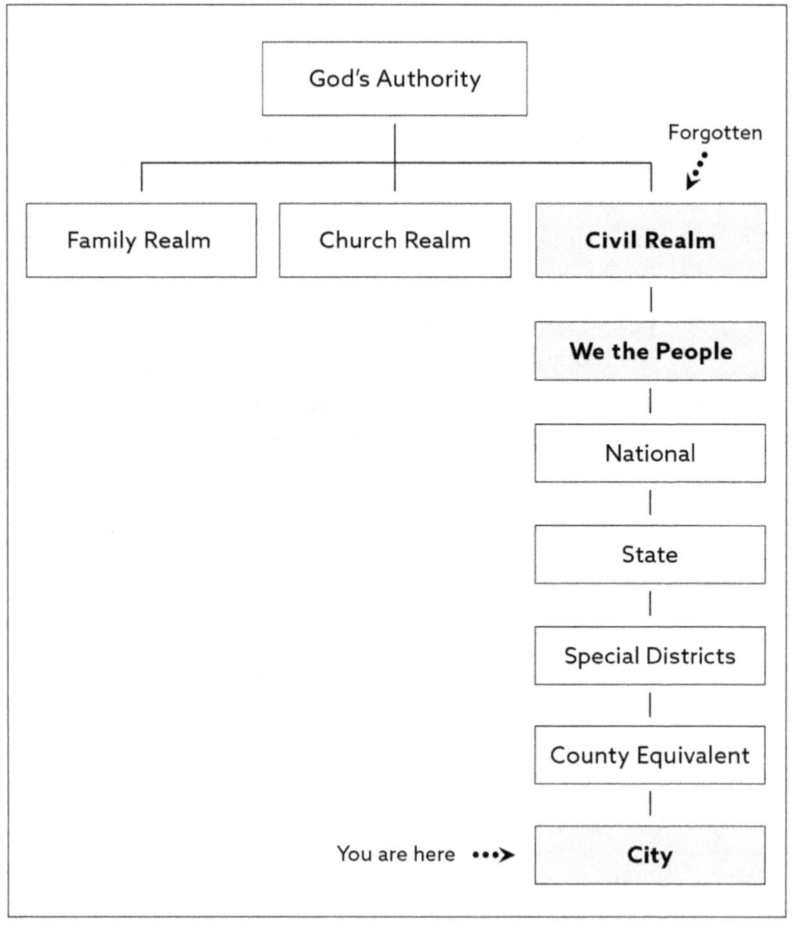

Figure 3.1

CHAPTER 3
City Government

It was a county issue, not a city issue, but I decided to go to the mayor—the head of the city—anyway. After all, this city was the county seat.[1] *I arrived on time for the meeting that I had requested with him. He opened the door to his office and invited me in. He was younger than I was (the youngest mayor elected in Indiana to date), so that was a plus. He was a Christian—another plus. But the conference table loomed large. Its dark wood gleamed. And the rolling chairs were grand, not to mention rather spacious. I perched on the front of the seat he had offered me. I was there to discuss a topic with him and wasn't exactly sure where to start. I gave a short review of my work on the issue up to this point, trying to be relevant. I made my case, relating the county issue to him as mayor. Finally, he said that he was looking for certain specific data, and no one had been able to provide it for him. I just happened to have the perfect article in my tote bag (homeschool moms like tote bags). Not only did the article possess the desired data, but providentially, I had also traced the data that the article quoted back to its original source, run the numbers, and verified the math. I had a photocopy of my pencil work on that as well. He reached out, took the article, looked me in the eye, and declared that it was the exact information he had been*

1 The term *county seat* generally means the capital city of the county and will be further explained in chapter 4, "County-Equivalent Government."

looking for, yet no one had been able to provide it. Later that week, I heard a radio broadcast clip where he was interviewed by public radio regarding his position on the county issue. He clarified that he is the mayor, the head of the city not the county. Nevertheless, the reporter pressed the issue, and Mr. Mayor was able to cite some poignant information.

We are starting with the city. Why? Most American government books begin at the national level with the Founding Fathers and then proceed to explain the three branches of federal government. They may offer a tip of the hat to state government generally, but because there are fifty different variations, the specifics of state government are left out. Local government receives a mere nod of acknowledgment because its variations are legion, and textbooks usually can't accommodate them.

The city-first approach to civics that I employ in this book will ensure that we do not run out of space, time, or energy to cover the smaller levels of government. As the story above illustrates, it is at the local level where Christians can begin to engage in the forgotten realm. That's where we can start learning to influence our leaders for good. Furthermore, laws at the local level are the ones that most closely affect our lives. Even in the Bible, it is in a city—the local level—where the gospel first went forth. Afterward, the good news radiated out from the city of Jerusalem to Judea to Samaria to the ends of the earth. Fast forward to our own day when, thanks to the media which can cover news from the ends of the earth, we all know about Mr. President at the national level, but few of us know Mr. Mayor at the local level. One gets all of the press while the other conducts business as usual and does so virtually unnoticed. We the People are able to comment on proceedings at the national level but are often unequipped to enter the local civil realm. The civil realm has become the forgotten realm.

THE INVERTED MODEL

This chapter begins the process of inverting the standard-textbook model. We will enter the civil realm at the local-grassroots[2] level, beginning with the city. **Even if you don't live in a city, please bear with me and read this chapter.** I want you to understand how the governance systems that We the People have created fit together regarding city-county relations, as the story above indicated. Your power as a citizen will be much richer if you understand the framework of self-governance and how you are connected to it. As a member of We the People, you will also be better able to assist your neighbor when he or she experiences a governance problem that you can help solve. Helping our neighbor in the civil realm is a spot-on application of our dual citizenship.

As we step into the smallest level (the city), I must give a disclaimer: Because the local levels of government vary so much across our nation and even within each state, you will need to make some adjustments to how I describe them in order to apply the prinicples to where you live. Rather than giving you an in-depth description of the particular city you currently live in, my goal is to provide you with an awareness of how each level of government functions and to propel you to look up your own city's government website on the internet. Along the way, you may also have to ferret out local characteristics or nuances which are exceptions to the general rule of thumb.

2 *Grassroots* means at the foundational level.

Here are some examples: Most often, multiple cities or towns[3] dwell within counties (which we will learn about in the next chapter).[4] However, sometimes a city may stretch over county boundaries.[5] But a city may not cross state boundaries because cities exist under the authority of states, and each state has its own laws.[6] Conversely, the small percentage of cities that are located outside of a county are known as independent cities (more on them in chapter 5) and are actually classified as primary administrative divisions of their states.[7] In Hawaii, however, there is no city government; only county and state government exist. Hawaii's county government is loosely based on a city mayor-council system of governance, so Hawaiians will still find much in this chapter that pertains. Because of the great variety across our nation, you will have

3 In this book, the terms *town* and *city* are used interchangeably. There is not an agreed-upon American definition of what constitutes a *town*. Particular geographic areas of the nation use the term *town* differently. In some places, a *town* is an unincorporated city without governmental powers (which I will explain in the following paragraphs). In other places, the term *town* is based on a specified population quota that is less than the requirement to be considered a *city*, but the town still has the ability to be incorporated. Connecticut, New Jersey, and Pennsylvania use the term *borough* to mean an incorporated municipality. Sometimes the term *village* also means an incorporated municipality. In Ohio, for example, a village means a small city—when a village exceeds 5,000 electors, it becomes a city. However, a village can also mean an unincorporated area in a larger city. Lastly, New York, Oregon, and Mississippi have hamlets; each state interprets *hamlet* differently, but none acts as an incorporated municipality. Austin Fernald, "The Difference between a Town and a City; plus Counties, Villages and More," *ZoningPoint* (blog), May 22, 2023.

4 "In most States, multi-county places are common; however in the New England States and the States of California, Montana, Nevada, and New Jersey, incorporated places do not cross county lines." U.S. Department of Commerce, Economics and Statistics Administration, Bureau of the Census, "Places," chap. 9 in *Geographic Areas Reference Manual (GARM)*, 9-9, issued November 1994.

5 "Cities 101—Types of Local US Governments," National League of Cities, December 13, 2016.

6 For example, Texarkana, Arkansas and Texarkana, Texas have different city governments. Thus, cities of the same name that might appear to be one are each distinct geographic entities. Also, Kansas City, Missouri and Kansas City, Kansas; Bristol, Tennessee and Bristol, Virginia. U.S. Department of Commerce, "Places," 9-9.

7 U.S. Department of Commerce, "States, Counties, and Statistically Equivalent Entities," chap. 4 in *Geographic Areas Reference Manual (GARM)*, 4-2.

to be a flexible, self-motivated reader to learn what the governance landscape looks like in your neck of the woods.

FORMATION

The authority for any city to exist comes from the state constitution and state laws which govern the state in which the city will be created. A city enjoys the privilege of existing due to the higher authority of state law. Likewise, state law defines and restricts the limits of city governance—what activities a city may or may not legally be involved in.

Municipal Corporations

A city is created when a group of people voluntarily gather together and decide to form a municipal corporation under the laws of the state in which they reside. Just look at an American map today, and it's clear that We the People have been extremely busy creating cities since foreign settlers first came ashore.[8] It may not be apparent, but we're still creating new cities. As an example, Erda, Utah, was incorporated as a city by a vote of the people in 2022. New cities today are almost without exception composed of regions which had already been populated and decided to incorporate.

What does it mean to incorporate? In most instances, states require a city to be formed as a corporation in order to conduct business. According to Merriam-Webster Dictionary, a corporation is a body (from the Latin word *corpus*) of people formed and authorized and recognized by (state) law to act as a single person and be legally endowed with various rights

8 For a list of the oldest city in each of the fifty states, see Alex Egoshin "The Oldest Cities in the U.S. Mapped," Vivid Maps, March 23, 2022.

and duties. For a city, the rights and duties of a business corporation include such self-governing powers as the ability to enter into contracts, to sue and be sued, and to own property. The term *municipal* is used as an adjective to mean city. Municipal park, municipal pool, or the municipal water supply are just a few examples. A municipal corporation parallels the way that a business corporation is authorized by the state to carry out various rights and duties. The following statement should now make more sense: a city is formed when a group of people voluntarily gather together and decide to form a municipal corporation.

A city, typically, has core operational functions that look just like a business (e.g., budgeting, accounts payable, accounts receivable, human resources, payroll, and such). The municipal corporation differs from the business corporation in that it is entirely public. The state authorizes the city's corporations status,[9] and in that sense, the city is an incorporated entity of the state, exercising local governing powers. All of this structure is under the authority of We the People as we have organized ourselves, or more accurately, as those people (who have gone before us) organized themselves. We are the next generation now inheriting the foundational fruit of their self-governance.

With this incorporated status, a city is authorized to enter into contracts, acquire and discard property, levy (impose) taxes, sue and be sued, enact ordinances (city laws), provide services, and exercise eminent domain (purchase private property for public use). Conversely, an unincorporated city or town does not have self-governing powers and is more like a neighborhood.[10] It relies upon a nearby local government

9 With the exception of Hawaii (also Puerto Rico, Guam, the Northern Mariana Islands, and Palau) which does not have incorporated places. U.S. Department of Commerce, "Places," 9-2.

10 Fernald, "The Difference between a Town and a City."

(such as the nearest city or county) to provide what services may be available.

City Charters

Many early and historically situated cities were established by charter. The concept of a charter is important practically as well as historically. Practically, a charter is a specific document which grants the rights, powers, and privileges to corporations as described above. We can think of a charter as a document used by any group, affiliated for any purpose, to nail down its mission, to articulate its rights and privileges, to identify the governing roles and authority within the group, and to lay out essential processes to support the group's efforts.

Historically, charters have been in use since the Middle Ages to define units of local organization. European monarchs "typically issued charters to towns, cities, guilds, merchant associations, universities, and religious institutions; such charters guaranteed certain privileges and immunities for those organizations while also sometimes specifying arrangements for the conduct of their internal affairs."[11] The most famous of these medieval charters was the Magna Carta (the Great Charter) of 1215 when King John of England granted certain rights to the English people.

But our focus is the United States of America, not England. Who issues our charters? Recall from the last chapter that our nation is a constitutional republic where the government exists under the rules of the U.S. Constitution, and the governing members temporarily serve as representatives of the people. In the same manner, municipal charters exist as city constitutions establishing how a city is designed to oper-

---

11 *Encyclopedia Britannica Online*, s.v. "charter (document)."

ate.[12] Some even have preambles[13] and outline the function of the local political process along with the city's mission, rights, privileges, governing roles, and authority. Other charters, similar to a bill of rights, "provide local protection for individual rights, many of which have no parallels in state or federal constitutional law."[14]

Generally speaking, the conglomeration of a state's laws which govern the structure and powers of a city can be referred to as the charter.[15] All state legislatures are authorized to issue city charters, but not every state legislature necessarily issues them or requires them for their state.[16] Forty-five states authorize cities to adopt (or allow states to grant) mu-

---

12 Sanford and Green, *Basic Principles of American Government*, 456.

13 Two sample preambles are as follows.

Preamble for St. Augustine Beach, Florida:

"We the people of the City of St. Augustine Beach, Florida, under the constitution and laws of the United States of America and the State of Florida, in order to provide the benefits of local government responsive to the will and values of our citizens, do hereby adopt this Charter to define the powers and structure of our government. By this action, we secure the benefits of home rule and affirm the values of representative democracy, professional management, strong political leadership, citizen participation, and regional cooperation. We believe in an open, responsive government that abides by the highest ethical standards, operates as a careful steward of the human, fiscal, and natural resources of our city; that allows for fair and equitable participation of all persons in the affairs of the city; that provides for transparency, accountability, and ethics in governance; that fosters fiscal responsibility; and that meets the needs of a healthy, progressive city. "St. Augustine Beach, Florida—Code of Ordinances / Charter Laws," Municode.

Preamble for Honolulu, Hawaii:

"We, the people of the City and County of Honolulu, accepting responsibility to seek to achieve in our time that righteousness by which the life of our land is preserved and to encourage and enable our people to participate in their governance, do hereby adopt this Charter of the City and County of Honolulu." "Revised Charter of the City & County of Honolulu 1973 (Amended 2017 Edition)," City and County of Honolulu, January 4, 2021, c.

14 Nestor M. Davidson, "Local Constitutions," *Texas Law Review* 99, no. 5 (April 29, 2021).

The Anchorage Bill of Rights, for example, sets forth rights such as "the right of immunity from official actions of the assembly taken after 12:00 midnight and before 7:00 a.m., actual time." Charter of Anchorage, Alaska, Art. II, § 5.

15 Charles R. Adrian, *State and Local Governments*, 2nd ed. (New York: McGraw-Hill, 1967), 125.

16 Ballotpedia, s.v. "Chartered Local Government."

nicipal charters. Five states—Alabama, Idaho, Illinois, Indiana, and Kentucky—do not.[17] In such cases, the state statutes and state constitution direct the form and structure of local governance. Note that when there is no specific charter, the city's history and establishment might be located in the city code of ordinances (laws).

Because state legislatures are protective of their own powers, they limit the rights or powers that cities enjoy.[18] The authority that states grant to municipalities in order to conduct their own affairs is known as discretionary power. There are four categories of discretionary power:

- structural authority (the power to choose the municipality's own organizational form of government. I will explain each system in the forthcoming **Structure** section of this chapter);
- functional authority (the power to govern locally in a narrow[19] or broad[20] manner regarding the functions a city performs);
- fiscal authority (the power to set tax rates, determine revenue sources, borrow funds, and such); and

17 Ballotpedia, s.v. "General Law Local Government."

Idaho has one city chartered under territorial law (before statehood). Illinois still has thirty-four chartered small towns and villages, and two hundred and nine cities have home-rule powers (explained later).

18 Sanford and Green, *Basic Principles of American Government*, 456.

19 Narrow powers of local governance were defined by two court cases decided by Judge John F. Dillon in 1868 and are known as Dillon's Rule which asserts that local "government may engage in an activity only if it is specifically sanctioned by the state government." Dillon's Rule was upheld by the U.S. Supreme Court in 1907 and 1923. As a result, local governing officials spent much time lobbying for bills to be passed at their statehouses granting local authority and against bills which restricted their authority. "Cities 101—Delegation of Power," National League of Cities.

20 Broad powers of local governance give a city more local authority to make decisions independent of the state legislature.

- personnel authority (the power to govern the number of municipal employees and their pay, rules, and employment conditions).[21]

The Special Charter

The special charter is the oldest form of city charter, but it offers the least local control because it is obtained through an act of the state legislature.[22] Likewise, amendments to the charter must also be passed by the legislature, which is an inconvenient process for city officeholders.[23] In some states, special charter cities can change rank by population following a state or national census.[24] Missouri and New Jersey are among states that still have a few special charter cities.[25]

The Optional Charter (General Law Charter)

In an optional charter, citizens vote directly from a selection of charter options[26] that are written by the state in order to meet specific city needs.[27] The number of charters to choose from can vary by state ranging from a couple of basic exam-

21 "Cities 101—Delegation of Power," National League of Cities.

22 Adrian, *State and Local Governments*, 127.

23 Nick Ragone, *The Everything American Government Book* (Avon, MA: Adams Media, 2004), 250.

24 Justia, "MO Rev Stat § 81.020 (2022)," US Law.

25 "Seven Missouri municipalities are still operating under special charters granted before 1875. They are Augusta, Carrollton, Chillicothe, La Grange, Liberty, Miami and Pleasant Hill. If the voters of these municipalities decide to relinquish their special charters, they will be governed by the appropriate sections of the statutes relevant to their population classification." John R. Ashcroft, "The Missouri Roster: A Directory of State, District, County and Federal Officials," 161.

Eleven cities in New Jersey are special charter cities. "Inventory of Municipal Forms of Government in New Jersey," New Jersey Legislative District Data Book, July 1, 2011, 13–14.

26 Ragone, *The Everything American Government Book*, 250.

27 Sanford and Green, *Basic Principles of American Government*, 456.

ples to a large number and variety.[28] The goal is to match a charter to a city's needs.[29] Each option represents a complete form or system of municipal government. New Jersey has optional charter cities, as does Tennessee.[30]

The Classified Charter

States which use the classified charter format actually classify cities by population and sometimes by form of government (mayor-council/council-manager)[31] and then issue city charters accordingly.[32] Cities are referred to by their classification and are permitted charter status based on their class ranking. The state of Washington serves as an example where cities and towns are classified according to their population typically at the time of their incorporation.[33]

The Home-Rule Charter

By far the most popular type of charter is the home-rule charter which grants power to a local municipal government to exercise self-government under the authority of the state constitution and state laws.[34]

---

28 Adrian, *State and Local Government*, 126. New Jersey offers fourteen options for its cities' charter choices.

29 Sanford and Green, *Basic Principles of American Government*, 456.

30 Under the New Jersey optional municipal charter law, there are four options of governmental systems: mayor-council, council-manager, small municipality, and the mayor-council administrator. "Inventory of Municipal Forms of Government in New Jersey," New Jersey Legislative District Data Book, 13–14.

See also "Types of Charters," University of Tennessee Municipal Technical Advisory Service (MTAS).

31 Adrian, *State and Local Government*, 126.

32 Sanford and Green, *Basic Principles of American Government*, 456.

33 "City and Town Classification," Municipal Research and Services Center.

34 Adrian, *State and Local Government*, 127.

With a home-rule charter, the residents of a city draft their own charter, and the voters approve it, which means that the local voters can amend their own charter.[35] The home-rule charter offers the most local control to municipal governments.[36] This type of charter allows residents to choose the form of city government that best addresses their needs.[37] "Local politicians (who wish to maximize their own autonomy from state control), good-government groups (which believe that efficiency and economy are furthered by local control of government), chambers of commerce (which have similar views), and other interests over the nation continue to press for home rule."[38] For a history of the development of home-rule in American municipalities and a glance at a possible future trajectory of home-rule overreach see the footnote.[39]

Home-rule is also an aid to local municipalities against federal and state dictates that intend to assume control over local property owners' rights.[40] This approach brings us to the Catholic principle of subsidiarity[41] which states that civil matters should be dealt with by the lowest level of government

---

35 Ragone, *The Everything American Government Book*, 250.

36 Adrian, *State and Local Government*, 127.

37 Sanford and Green, *Basic Principles of American Government*, 457.

38 Adrian, *State and Local Government*, 128.

39 I recommend David R. Berman's book, *Local Government and the States: Autonomy, Politics, and Policy*, 2nd. ed. (New York: Routledge, 2020), particularly the chapter titled "States, Cities, Home Rule: The Historical Perspective." Also see, Joshua A Douglas' article, "The Right to Vote under Local Law," *George Washington Law Review* 85, no. 4 (July 2017).

"Local democracy has always been important, but the ability of local governments to meet the needs of their communities in today's climate is insufficient… The time for a new, vigorous vision of home rule has arrived." Clarence E. Anthony, foreword to "Principles of Home Rule for the 21st Century.," National League of Cities, 2020.

40 Thomas C. Zambito, "NY created an agency to OK wind and solar projects quickly. Upstate towns aren't happy," *Journal News*, October 12, 2022, LoHud.

41 "Question 403: What is the principle of subsidiarity? The principle of subsidiarity states that a community of a higher order should not assume the task belonging to a community of a lower order and deprive it of its authority. It should rather support it in case of need." Pope Benedict XVI, *Compendium of the Catechism of the Catholic Church* (Vatican City: Libreria Editrice Vaticana, 2005), sec. 3.1.2.

in relation to them. Thus, the level of government closest to an issue is the level most suited to address it. This approach is known as governing by the lowest possible tier. Subsidiarity meshes well with the call to local civil engagement as well as with the inverted model of civics where more emphasis is placed upon the bottom-up approach to governing rather than the top-down approach. Admittedly, local governance can go awry from time to time; on those occasions, it can be judicious to appeal to a higher governing authority (such as the state), and subsidiarity allows for such a reversal.

SERVICES

When a city becomes incorporated under the general laws of the state by the people living within its boundaries, it performs functions that are exclusively local.[42] But what functions should a city be performing? How should the city pay for those services? The answer is: Whatever We the People have decided, and continue to decide, but those decisions must not conflict with the state constitution and the state code of laws.

Typically, a city can make ordinances (laws), collect taxes, and provide services such as water, sewer, trash, street maintenance, parks, fire, and police protection for its residents. These services fall under the term ***public works*** which means the ways that a city tends to its infrastructure. Public works can include the construction or maintenance of public water and sewer facilities, roads, bridges, docks, underpasses, viaducts, or public buildings and structures. In larger cities, these public works may be siloed into departments such as roads/ streets, water works, and sanitation. They could be privatized, but for the benefit of the public, they have been put under the administration of the city. As such, they are similar to agencies

42 Idaho Secretary of State, *Idaho Blue Book* (Caldwell, ID: Caxton Printers, 2021).

at higher levels of government and represent a domain that is in significant need of oversight by citizens like you and me.

A great place to begin surveying the scope of services and expenses is by viewing the city's annual budget along with its monthly financial statements which should all be available online. First, you have to locate the document somewhere on the city's website. Then you have to wade through the waters—it could be hundreds of pages in length. It helps to find out when the city's fiscal year begins and ends. A day-long budget workshop may be offered and open to the public to attend in advance of the new year's budget presentation. That may be an informative event to attend. However, there is no substitute for simply reading through the budget on your own. I suspect that one of the reasons our American public spending (at all levels of government) is so high is that, in general, we do not read and understand our budgets. The default position appears to be that it is easier for our legislative bodies to approve items within budgets and also to approve entire budgets rather than to dissect them in the light of day. What if citizens who are business-minded began to really examine and understand our public documents as they are posted on a monthly basis? **This one action alone could have a dramatic impact over time on our cities, counties, special districts, states, and our nation.**

Now, back to a general description of city services (that require line items in budgets). Generally, municipal services vary in terms of a city's size. Such services depend on the vision of individuals who create interest among other citizens to further expand those that exist or to adopt new ones. These new or expanded services rely on the willingness of voters to subject themselves to a tax increase for the privilege. The citizens of a small city

may want a city park, a city recreation program, and a sewer system to replace reliance on septic tanks. As a city grows

> larger, it may need an airport, an animal shelter, and subdivision regulations. When a city reaches about 100,000 people, it will often provide its citizens with a city-operated museum, zoo, convention center, college, and dozens of other programs which cities of fewer than 50,000 people seldom provide.[43]

Again, We the People decide what policy features and city services we prefer in the course of self-governance. Then, we have to persuade our fellow citizens whether (or not) those services are worth the taxes required to make them a reality.

As mentioned above, unincorporated towns do not provide municipal services, nor do they have their own government. Unincorporated towns are commonly known as suburbs or areas under the jurisdiction of the county. Residents in those areas generally pay privately (personally) for the water, septic, trash removal, and any other services that they receive. For libertarian types, moving to the suburbs or a rural area where privatization could be the norm is often a calming answer to avoiding government-subsidized services. Short of relocation, another alternative is to understand your system of government and begin the hard labor of informed reform.

Sometimes, rather than remaining privatized, some suburban areas are legally attached or joined to existing municipalities. This process of urban expansion is known as annexation. Each state's law outlines the requirements for annexation. Typically, state laws require approval by the city council/commission and a winning vote by the residents of the geographic area to be annexed.[44] Annexation increases the local municipality's tax base, but it also increases the demand for services.

43 Herbert Sydney Duncombe and Robert Weisel, *State and Local Government in Idaho and in the Nation* (Moscow, ID: University Press of Idaho, 1984), 122.

44 Duncombe and Weisel, *State and Local Government*, 115.

ACCOUNTABILITY

Public Office and Elected Representatives

At every level of government, our leaders serve in what is known as public office—a position of government leadership involving responsibility to the public characterized by both authority and service. Most of these leaders are elected, and some are appointed. The individuals who are accountable to you as a citizen are those who are elected to office. Therefore, the chain of command that matters to We the People is the elected chain of command.

One of the benefits We the People enjoy from governing ourselves is that we are able to decide, from time to time, on public service roles that we need to either create or eliminate regarding our civic affairs. Each role or office we create has a position title, a term or duration of time to fulfill, a description of authority and/or any limitations on that authority, and a basic job description with attendant responsibilities to the public being served. For most roles in public office, we elect from among ourselves individuals to fill and uphold those positions. As the end of an elected term approaches, the individual must decide whether or not to run for reelection. From school board to U.S. President, these are the elected representatives of We the People.

Our representatives are directly accountable to us because (theoretically) we can vote any one of these individuals out of public office if we don't like the results we're getting. Further, we can elect someone else who we think would do a better job of representing us. Alternatively, we can petition for a special recall[45] election (in states that allow for that) if waiting until the next election is not feasible. Of course, our power to

45 The procedure of removing an elected representative from office by a vote of the people. We will discuss this further in chapter 8, "Voting, Elections & Parties."

accomplish these endeavors exists in relation to our involvement with and investment in our local communities. More on that in the chapters on elections and Christian diplomacy.

Appointees to Vacated Elected Office

When an elected representative of the people resigns from elected office prior to the end of the term of service, there is usually a process by which a new representative can be appointed. This appointee usually assumes the complete mantle of his or her predecessor, and we no longer think of that person as an appointee. Technically, such individuals are fulfilling the role of elected representatives and remain fully accountable to We the People for the remainder of the term before the next election. Leading up to that election, that individual must decide whether or not to run for election (though that decision may appear as reelection to voters who had not been paying attention).

Paid Appointees to the Bureaucracy (Staff)

After elected public servants, there is a second layer of public service roles that exists at every level of government—those who are appointed as paid staff and thus not directly accountable to voters. These individuals are directly accountable to the elected representatives who appoint or hire them into the bureaucracy (non-elected government employees of administrative agencies). Often, they are referred to as staff or personnel—paid employees who oversee the operations of the government. These individuals are necessary to staff the governmental departments and to provide public services. They operate areas such as finance and human resources departments or legal and planning/zoning departments. Most personnel are hired employees who receive pay and benefits for their service. Their terms of employment are set either by the elected representative who makes each appointment or by ordinance.

Some staff members are only knowledgeable about the area in which they are assigned to work; they do not understand the larger picture of American governance or even the larger picture of the level in which they serve. Others (such as those in administration) are the experts who really know how to run the government because they do not come and go in the way that each new round of elected officeholders does. They are the real power brokers because they have a thorough understanding of the system. At the city level, the most powerful staff individual may be the city manager/administrator/supervisor with limited administrative authority yet with significant ability to guide and suggest (more on this position later in this chapter). Others are the clerk, the city attorney, and certain members of the various departments (administration, community development, public works, and so on). Another prominent figure is the oftentimes-appointed chief of police or the fire chief.

Volunteer Positions to Boards and Committees

Cities typically have boards or commissions to guide policy, create projects, and help with the workload. These commissions typically consist of concerned citizens who volunteer their time to serve their city in various advisory and sometimes very important policy-making capacities (as in a planning/zoning commission). They do so under appointment by an elected officeholder, such as the mayor, and under the city code of laws.

Accountability Summary

If you have an issue that pertains to the city (or any level of government, for that matter), it is critical to know that the public servants who serve you there are the elected officeholders. They should not be confused with the paid employees. There is no rule which prevents you as a citizen from speaking with a paid city employee. In many cases, they can be very helpful. However, it is important to know that their jobs exist to serve those in elected office. And those in elected office are the ones who directly represent you. You'll need to conduct a minimal amount of research for your city to understand which roles are elected, which are conducted by paid employees, and which are performed by appointed volunteers serving on boards and commissions. For example, the chief of police is typically an appointed position, though a few cities do elect their chief.[46] If you have a problem with the city police, you need to understand the elected official/appointed employee distinction. In any case, accountability starts and stops with the individuals we have elected to represent us. All of this structure takes place within the confines of the written code of law (described further in the next section).

Presently, we will look at the different structural models of city governance. It is helpful to know which model your city follows so that you can take your problem to the correct individual. In some cases this will be the mayor, and in others it will be the commissioner. If the elected mayor or commissioner cannot or will not help you, you have two options available: advance to the next level (in this case, the state) or consult another branch of government, such as the court system within the judicial branch (that is why we have a system of checks and balances—to prevent any of the other branches

46 The chief of police is an elected position in cities such as Santa Clara, California; San Angelo, Texas; Central, Louisiana; and other Louisiana cities.

from overreach). At the state level, you could talk to the governor or a member of the state legislature. We will learn more about those individuals in chapter 6, "State Government." The typical solution is to find a point of elected accountability and go there. The principle of elected representatives existing to serve We the People is true at all levels of government. If we don't like the results we're getting, we must determine the appropriate path forward.

At the same time, whether elected or appointed, American public service can be a thankless job. Day in and day out, public servants serve. While we're usually quick to denounce government bureaucracy, there are some true heroes of public service. One way to make an impact for Christ in the civil realm is simply to be kind to others. When you observe public servants who are doing their job well, thank them. They are accustomed to receiving complaints rather than compliments and may be quite shocked by the positive attention.

LAW

Cities conduct their business based on the city code of laws, commonly known as ordinances. The operations of the city are authorized and governed by its code of laws. The code is regularly updated by the city's governing body depending upon the form used in each geographical location across the nation. Reading the totality of your city's code can be tedious, but it can also be highly informative. This is a case where knowledge is power, so if you want to understand your city, it is well worth the time investment. State law requires that a city codify or compile its ordinances in a logical order. Their organization may be arranged by title, occasionally by article, then by chapter, and section. You can remember these subdivisions of law by the acronym TiCS (title, chapter, section) or by TACS (title, article, chapter, section).[47] All subdivisions of the code are numbered to aid in topical searches. For example, each title subject grouping should have a corresponding number. Within a title, each article or chapter will have a number. Then each section will have a number. Thus, searching through codes of law is similar to searching for a verse of Scripture in the Bible—the citation gives you all the information necessary to locate one verse situated within over a thousand pages of text.

Some city codes may be so large that you cannot realistically read all of the code, but you can familiarize yourself with the outline and groupings of law, and then cherry-pick individual topics to explore. While reading the code, you may discover information such as when your city was founded, what your city officials are paid, if it is legal to post private signs in public places, and so on. You may have already looked at your city's code of laws on your city's government website in the last chapter. If not, this is a great time to do so. Try referencing a public feature of your city that you might already be interested in such as parks and recreation or noise regulations or powers of the mayor. See what you can discover about how your city functions. Further laws pertaining to cities within a state can be located in the state code of laws which was briefly mentioned in the previous chapter and will be taken up again in chapter 6.

Municipalities also have what is known as police power which means the authority of a government to exercise control over people or property within its jurisdiction to accomplish a public goal (usually regarding the protection of the public's health, safety and welfare). In fact, any level of government that makes rules and enforces them is appropri-

47 I pass out Tic Tac mints to my civics club members to serve as a mnemonic device.

ating police power.[48] Possessing police power doesn't necessarily mean that the police department punishes infractions (though it could mean that). It denotes the power to enforce rules such as following land-use plans and zoning laws, necessitating business licenses (such as in real estate, restaurant, or beauty professions), or even setting speed limits.

If you live outside city limits, it is important to know that the cities throughout the nation may have "extra-territorial powers—that is, powers beyond their borders."[49] These powers include planning, zoning, emergency health orders, and police pursuits of criminals. A common example of extra-territorial powers is the residential garbage removal service. The largest incorporated city in a region may be the primary voice at the negotiation table with sanitation vendors. The outcome of such negotiations is usually straightforward: Residents will have their trash picked up once per week, and the cost will vary depending on the size of the receptacle. But, who is a resident? Assuming that elected representatives from outlying communities are negotiating well with the elected representatives of a bigger city, and vice versa, residents of outlying areas may benefit from the city's trash collection services. But residents may have no say if negotiations happen in a city with extra-territorial powers.

Before purchasing land as a homeowner outside city limits, it is important to check and see what jurisdiction the city might have over your property. If you live in an extra-territorial area, elected officeholders in the city may be able to make decisions with ramifications that affect you even though you cannot vote in the city elections. As new regimes come and go in the city, different priorities will take precedence accompanied by a variety of changes. (It is possible that problems

48 California Senate Local Government Committee, *What's So Special About Special Districts? A Citizen's Guide to Special Districts in California*, 4th ed.(October 2010), 3.

49 Duncombe and Weisel, *State and Local Government*, 116.

arising from such situations could be taken care of at the state level of government.)

ACCOUNTABILITY
(WHO IS ACCOUNTABLE TO WHOM)

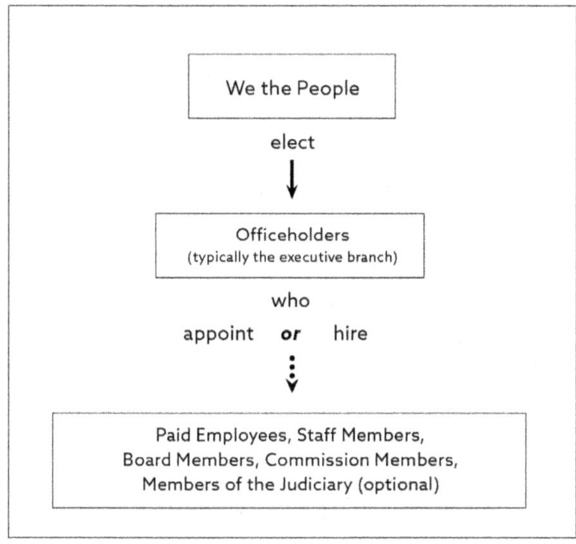

Figure 3.2

KEY

↓ = elect

⇣ = appoint(s)/hire(s)

GOVERNANCE STRUCTURE

Legislative and Executive Branches

Because of the nature of local systems (meaning models or forms) of government, the three branches are not as distinct as they are at the state and federal levels. The legislative branch still mirrors Congress as the governing body that can pass laws, and the executive branch still mirrors the President or the governor as the agent who executes or carries out the law. The difference is that they function much more closely together at the local level. You will see that closeness illustrated in some of the visual diagrams that depict each system of governance. The judicial branch will appear on each diagram, but we will not discuss it until later in the chapter. Lastly, the diagrams are purposely simplistic in order to illustrate the core units of governance within each system. Later, I will encourage you to locate your own city's much more complicated organizational chart.

Cities are not all governed in the same manner across the nation or even within a state.[50] Therefore, it is useful to be acquainted with the five general forms or systems of city government across the United States. When reading the descriptions in this book and pairing that information with your own city's website, you can determine what system of governance you live under. Also, if your city has a charter, the system of governance below may define a significant component of the charter.

The five general forms of city government are as follows:

- commission
- council-manager
- mayor-council

50 Kentucky has three forms of city government across the state. "Form of Government," Kentucky League of Cities.

- (open) town meeting
- representative town meeting

These forms differ regarding the distribution of power between elected representatives and professionals (whether appointed or hired). They also differ in how much power a council has in relation to the mayor. Note that these forms are generalizations for each type of city government due to the myriad of variations on each theme that exists across the nation. Also, you will see that the first three of the city models listed above recur in the next chapter on county government with slightly different names. The last two town-meeting models are particular to the New England states and by extension to parts of the East and Midwest.

Legislative

In all of these forms, the focus is on policy-making at the city level (we will see the same process reflected at various other levels of government). Because of this hierarchy of law, the local municipal legislative body or branch has the power to enact ordinances (laws) and resolutions (policies).[51] And it must do so in accordance with state law. Within this authorized scope, the legislative body can do the following:

- enact a city budget
- define roles, powers, compensation, benefits, and working conditions of city officeholders (elected representatives of the people) and employees
- impose fines and penalties for violation of city ordinances

51 "Knowing Your Roles: City and Town Governments," *MRSC Insight* (blog), Municipal Research and Services Center, January 10, 2024.

- enter into contracts
- acquire, sell, convey, or dispose of property
- provide municipal services
- set the rates/fees for those services
- impose taxes
- own/operate municipal utilities
- approve claims against the city
- grant franchises for the use of public ways
- license businesses
- enact municipal governance procedures[52]

Executive

The executive branch executes or carries out the laws passed by the legislative body and appoints heads of departments. Thus, the function of the executive branch at the municipal level is to oversee city departments, bureaus, or commissions and to carry policies approved by the legislative branch.[53]

Terminology Review

Before looking at each of these five models, it would be helpful to recall the following terms from chapter 2, "Layers of Law":

- A **constitutional republic** exists under the written rules of a constitution or charter where its governing members serve as elected representatives of the people for a specific duration of time or term of office.

52 "Knowing Your Roles," *MRSC Insight.*

53 "Cities 101—Mayoral Powers," National League of Cities, December 13, 2016.

- A **pure democracy** exists where the people govern themselves directly through the will of the majority.
- A **representative democracy** exists as the will of the people where the people elect representatives to represent them.

Commission System

The commission system originated in Galveston, Texas in 1901 as a response to the significant loss of life and property following the Galveston hurricane.[54] Once championed by progressives, today this system only exists in approximately twelve percent of American cities.[55] Voters elect individual commissioners to a small governing board. The commission collectively sits as the city council—the legislative body of local municipal government.[56] Each commissioner has individual executive power over one aspect of the municipality, such as fire, police, finance, or public works (water, sanitation, roads).[57] One commissioner is appointed as ceremonial mayor or chairman and presides over meetings. All decisions require a majority vote by the commissioners.[58] There is neither an elected executive nor an appointed official to oversee the commission. No large cities are remaining in the U.S. that operate under this system,[59] and it is considered to have served as a precursor to the more progressive council-man-

54 Bradley R. Rice, "Commission Form of City Government," *Handbook of Texas Online*, 1952.

55 "Municipal Form of Government (2018–19)," International County-City Management Association (ICMA), July 2, 2019.

56 "Municipal Form of Government (2018–19)," ICMA.

57 Christopher A. Simon, Brent S. Steel, and Nicholas P. Lovrich, "Municipal commission government," sec. 7.I.III in *State and Local Government and Politics: Prospects for Sustainability* (Corvallis: Oregon State University, 2019).

58 Sanford and Green, *Basic Principles of American Government*, 459.

59 Portland, Oregon had been a large city utilizing this model of governance, but it no longer does so. "Portland voters approve charter reform, city launches transition," City of Portland, November 9, 2022.

ager form of city government.[60] Note: Do not confuse this commission-system form of city governance with appointed boards which are also called commissions. Appointed boards and commissions can exist as a subset of almost any form of governance and their members are often volunteers.

COMMISSION SYSTEM

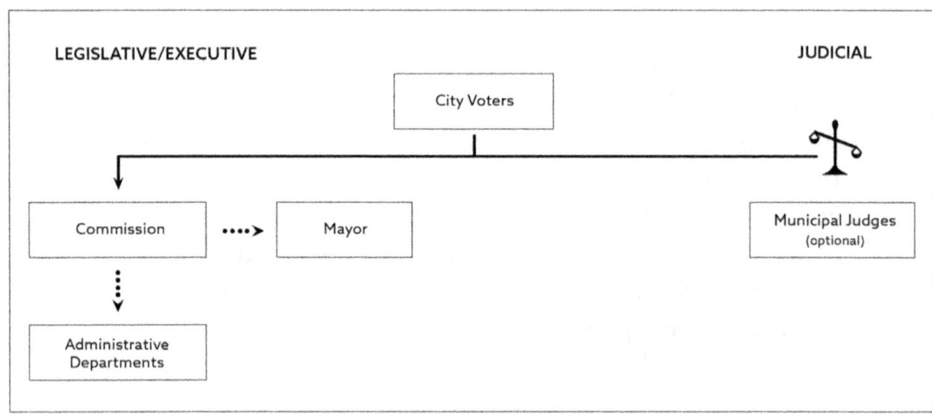

Figure 3.3

KEY

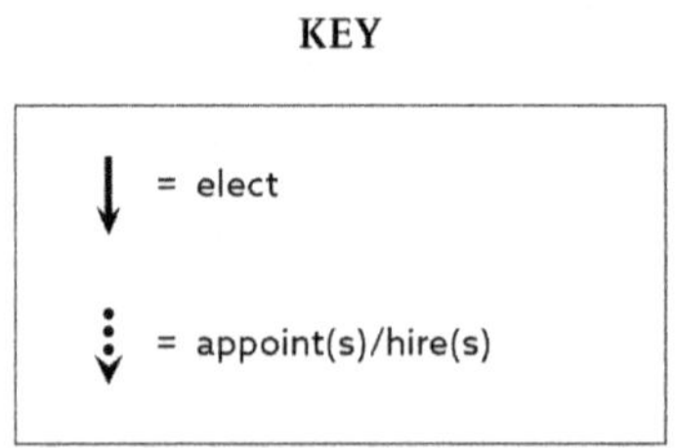

60 Rice, "Commission Form of City Government," *Handbook of Texas Online.*

Council-Manager System

This model is the most common form of municipal government with approximately forty percent of U.S. cities implementing it.[61] The council-manager system consists of three elements: a strong council, a weak mayor, and a city manager who is appointed by the council.[62] As a result, this system is sometimes known as the weak mayor model of city government because the mayor has weak powers, possesses no veto power,[63] and serves merely ceremonially.[64] The elected council members (elected at large, meaning across the entire city not across districts of the city, or by district depending upon the city's code) vote among themselves to select a mayor from among their ranks to serve on a rotating basis.[65] In some cities, the mayor is chosen by the electorate which strengthens the mayoral office in the public eye (unless the public understands this system of governance).

The council itself is powerful—it serves as the legislative body which makes policies, sets the budget, and hires a non-elected professional city manager to serve as (but not actually be) the city's executive. It also has executive authority to terminate the hired manager. As a paid staff member, the manager is thought to be more professional and less prone to political pressure than an elected executive[66] who has reelection concerns to consider. This appointee carries out the daily ad-

61 "Municipal Form of Government (2018–19)," ICMA.

62 Sanford and Green, *Basic Principles of American Government*, 459.

63 National Civic League, *Model City Charter*, 8th ed., Second Printing (Denver, CO: National Civic League Press, 2011), 29.

64 Adrian, *State and Local Government*, 225.

65 "The city should provide extra compensation for the mayor because, in addition to regular responsibilities as a council member, the mayor has intergovernmental, ceremonial, and city related promotional responsibilities." National Civic League, *Model City Charter*, 12.

66 Simon, Steel, and Lovrich, "City managers as executives," sec. 7.I.IV in *State and Local Government and Politics.*

ministrative operations of the city. As a professional, this person can devote time and effort to understanding and encouraging the implementation of policy rather than concentrating on pleasing the public. Note that without a directly elected executive, there is a weakened check on the legislative council.

COUNCIL-MANAGER SYSTEM I

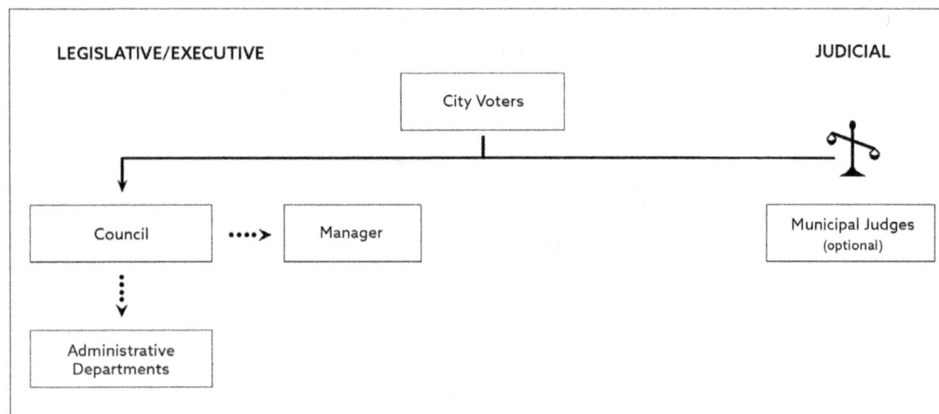

Figure 3.4a

KEY

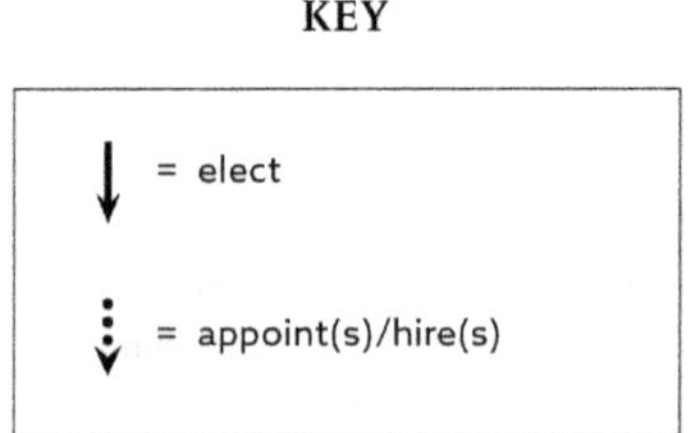

COUNCIL-MANAGER SYSTEM II

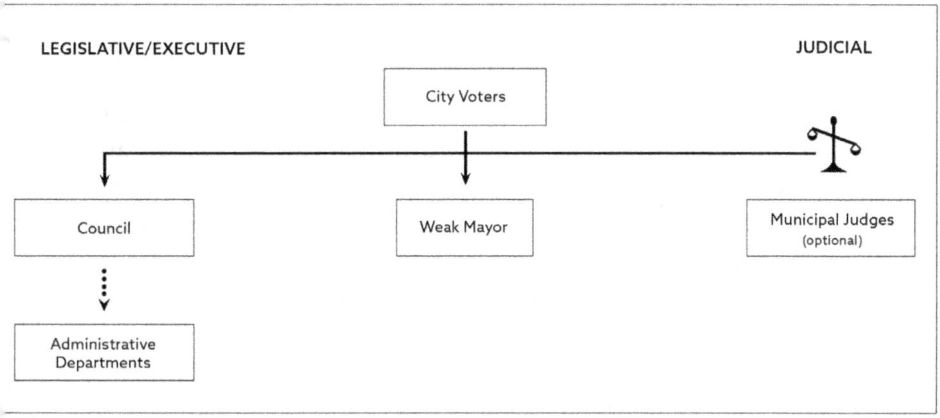

LEGISLATIVE/EXECUTIVE

JUDICIAL

City Voters

Council

Weak Mayor

Municipal Judges (optional)

Administrative Departments

Figure 3.4b

Mayor-Council System

The mayor-council system (also called the strong-mayor model) is the second most common form of city government and is implemented in approximately thirty-eight percent of U.S. cities.[67] It is also used for governing Hawaiian counties. It features a separation of powers similar to that at the state and federal levels. The mayor is elected by the city at large, and the council members are elected either at large or by voters in each of the city's geographic council districts. Together, these members serve as the municipal legislative body[68] (referred to as the council) which has the authority to override advisory decisions proposed by boards and commissions and to pass ordinances and resolutions.

67 "Municipal Form of Government (2018–19)," ICMA.

68 Sanford and Green, *Basic Principles of American Government*, 457.

The mayor serves as the full-time paid chief executive who administers the daily municipal affairs, makes administrative staff appointments, enforces the city's ordinances, and has budgetary authority. The publicly-elected mayor of the mayor-council system is generally the executive and administrative head of the city who ensures that municipal laws are enforced and that city policies are carried out.[69] The mayor supervises the day-to-day operations of the city, including hiring and firing of employees, appointing members to boards and commissions (subject to approval by the legislative body),[70] enforcing contracts, approving bonds, bringing lawsuits (again, with council approval), presiding over meetings, voting only as a tie-breaker, calling special meetings, planning or proposing a budget, making proclamations, making emergency orders, performing ceremonial duties and presenting the annual State of the City Address.[71] Further, the mayor has the power to veto an ordinance that the council passes, but the council can override that veto with a majority vote.[72]

Additionally, the mayor often appoints the chief of police, who is a municipal employee sworn to the service of the city.[73] Interestingly, the chief of police may report back to the city manager/administrator/supervisor who is another appointed staff member.

69 "Knowing Your Roles," *MRSC Insight.*

70 "Knowing Your Roles," *MRSC Insight.* Note: except for town councils.

71 "Knowing Your Roles," *MRSC Insight.*

72 Duncombe and Weisel, *State and Local Government,* 119–120.

73 "Chiefs of Police usually are municipal employees who owe their allegiance to a city. Oftentimes, Chiefs are appointed by the Mayor of a city; or, they may be appointed by or subject to the confirmation of a Police Commission." National Sheriffs' Association, "FAQ: Question 6."

MAYOR-COUNCIL SYSTEM

LEGISLATIVE
EXECUTIVE
JUDICIAL

City Voters

Council
Strong Mayor
Municipal Judges (optional)

Administrative Departments
Administrator

Figure 3.5

KEY

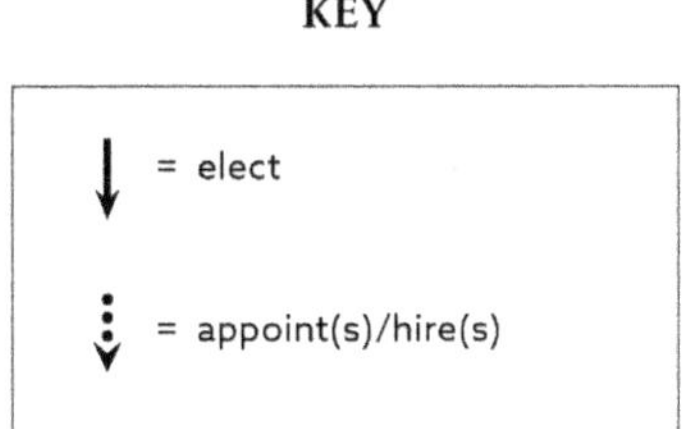

Town Meeting (sometimes called <u>Open Town Meeting</u>)

Found in each of the six New England states of Massachusetts, New Hampshire, Vermont, Maine, Connecticut, and Rhode Island, this system of municipal government is designed for towns with fewer than 6,000 inhabitants,[74] though there is no population cap requiring a change in governance

74 "Without a direct counterpart in most other U.S. states, New England towns are conceptually similar to civil townships in other states, but are incorporated, possessing powers like cities in other states. New England towns are often governed by town meeting. Virtually all corporate municipalities in New England are based on the town

structure.[75] The term *town meeting* can refer to the meeting itself, or it can refer to the legislative body (the council).[76] The legislative body consists of all eligible voters in the town.[77] Together, they pass the local statutes (also called by-laws or ordinances), vote on the budget, and choose a board (in the past called selectmen, now often called select board).[78] The elected select board fulfills the chief executive function[79] and may enforce the approved policies or may appoint a town manager to do so.[80] There may be an additional elected office of clerk or constable,[81] but these are not executive offices.[82]

Open town meeting government[83] was established by the Puritans in the early 1600s to make decisions on local issues.[84]

---

model; statutory forms based on the concept of a compact populated place, which is prevalent elsewhere in the U.S., are uncommon." Familypedia, s.v. "New England town."

75 "Massachusetts law still provides that no town with a population of less than 12,000 may adopt a city form of government and no town with a population of less than 6,000 may adopt a representative town meeting form of government." Jean McCarthy, "Why Become a City?," *City and Town*, Massachusetts Department of Revenue Division of Local Services (MDR) 12, no. 9 (November 1999): 1.

"Decisions about which form of government to adopt—including whether to be a city or a town—are made by local voters. Under the Massachusetts Constitution, a municipality must have at least 12,000 people to adopt a city form of government, but there's no upper limit on the size of a town." John Ouellette, "Local Government 101," Massachusetts Municipal Association.

76 Ouellette, "Local Government 101," Massachusetts Municiapl Association.

77 "A New England Tradition," *The Recorder*, posted May 3, 2015, YouTube video, 1:29.

78 "Municipal Form of Government (2018–19)," ICMA.

79 "In local government, town meeting serves the legislative function, the Select Board serves the executive function, and various boards and committees serve the judicial function." Rebecca Townsend and Carmin C. Reiss, "An Enduring System of Local Deliberative Democracy: The 21st Century Legal and Normative Structure of Massachusetts Town Meeting," *Journal of Deliberative Democracy* 18, no. 1 (June 1, 2022): sec. 3.3.

80 "Municipal Form of Government (2018–19)," ICMA.

81 A town or township's officer responsible for peacekeeping and minor judicial duties. *Merriam-Webster*, s.v. "constable."

82 "Town and Township Government in the United States," National Association of Towns and Townships, 3.

83 For a visual foray into town meetinghouses, see Paul Wainwright, "A Space for Faith: The Colonial Meeting Houses of New England," posted by 4x5guy, February 22, 2010, YouTube video, 3:35.

84 Participedia, s.v. "New England or 'Open' Town Meetings."

It is known as the purest form of democracy because the citizens serve directly as legislators, thus representing themselves as the governing leaders. This form of government is practiced today in 9.6% of the nation's municipalities.[85]

(OPEN) TOWN MEETING

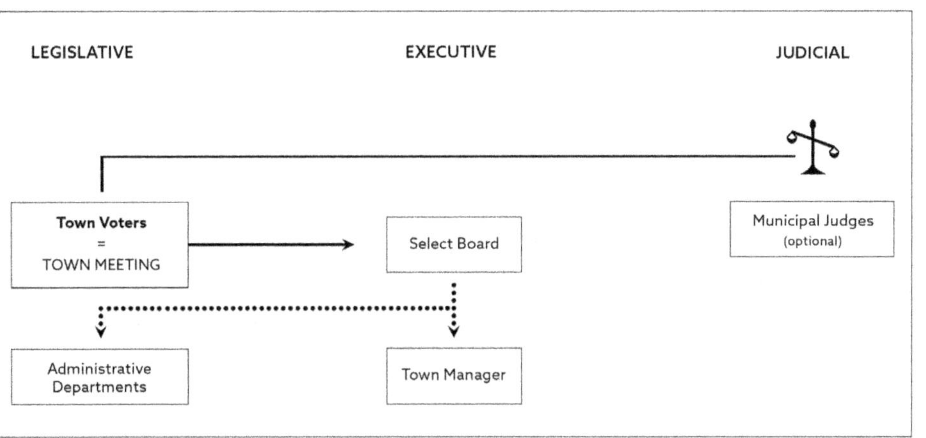

Figure 3.6

KEY

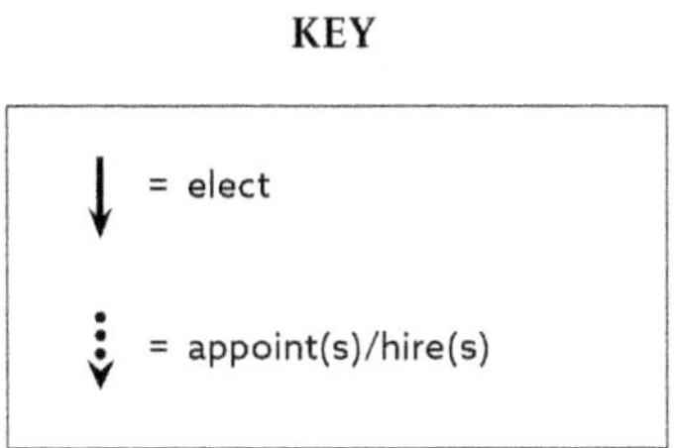

85 "Municipal Form of Government (2018–19)," ICMA.

Representative Town Meeting (sometimes called Limited Town Meeting)

The representative town meeting also originates in New England and is a variation of the open town meeting model of pure democracy. As the name suggests, this system of governance is representative democracy where voters elect those to represent them in order to vote as a select board on town meeting business. It should be noted that all residents may participate in pre-vote debates, but only the elected representatives may actually vote on the issues.[86] "The voting members are elected from and represent a certain precinct or area of the town."[87] Sources state that this form of government exists in less than 1% of towns.[88] However, it is also implemented in twenty states in the Northeast and Midwest[89] under the name of town or township[90] government and often predates statehood in each area.[91] "Because there is typically no separately elected executive, the board also performs a number of executive functions, such as enforcing ordinances, approving expenditures, and hiring employees."[92]

---

86 "Municipal Form of Government (2018–19)," ICMA.

87 Ballotpedia, s.v. "Representative town meeting."

88 "Municipal Form of Government," ICMA, and "Cities 101—Forms of Municipal Government," National League of Cities.

89 Connecticut, Illinois, Indiana, Kansas, Maine, Massachusetts, Michigan, Minnesota, Missouri, Nebraska, New Hampshire, New Jersey, New York, North Dakota, Ohio, Pennsylvania, Rhode Island, South Dakota, Vermont, and Wisconsin all have town or township government. "Town and Township Government in the United States," National Association of Towns and Townships, 2.

Louisiana has towns (and villages), but it has no township form of government.

90 In some states, townships function as municipalities which is why townships are listed here with towns; in other states, they function similar to but not the same as counties (this will be discussed in more detail later in chapter 5, "Special Districts, Independent Cities, Townships, and Regional Governments"). See also, Austin Fernald, "The Difference between a Town and a City," *Zoning Point* (blog).

91 "Townships in the U.S.," Michigan Townships Association.

92 "Town and Township Government in the United States," National Association of Towns and Townships, 2–3.

REPRESENTATIVE TOWN MEETING

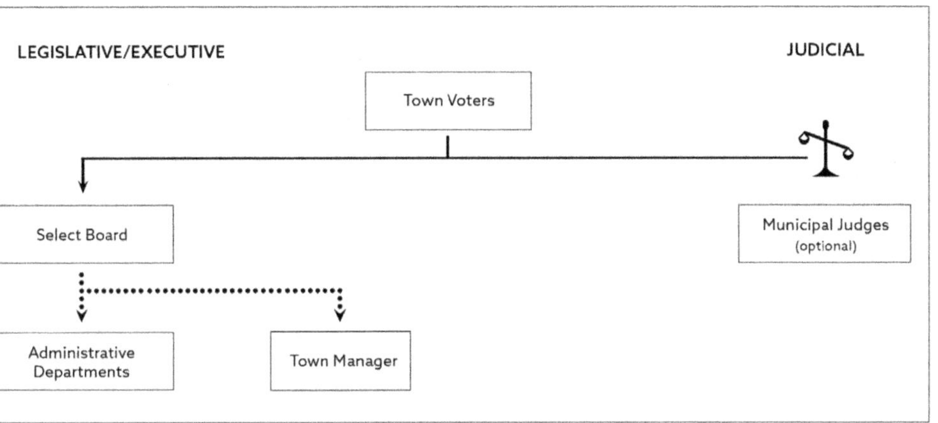

Figure 3.7

KEY

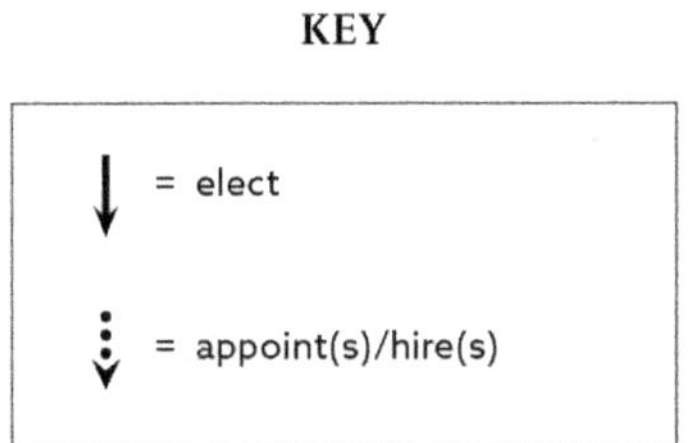

Through examining the five forms of city government, we've been able to look at the mechanics of how cities work in more detail. Cities that have consolidated with their outlying county will be covered in the next chapter on county government. I strongly encourage you to spend time exploring your own city's government website. As you read the information contained there, compare it to these five models.

REVIEW OF SYSTEMS OF CITY GOVERNANCE

1. Commission
2. Council-Manager
3. Mayor-Council
4. (Open) Town Meeting
5. Representative Town Meeting

Figure 3.8

City Manager/Administrator/Supervisor

Now that the systems (models) of city government have been outlined, it is worth circling back to the city manager/administrator/supervisor introduced earlier in this chapter under the heading **Paid Appointees to the Bureaucracy (Staff)**. This person is one of the most significant players on the municipal team. In the case of a city following the council-manager system of government, or even in the mayor-council system, and to some extent in the town meeting model, it is important to know how vital a hired city administrator is to the inner workings of the city.

This individual reports directly to the council and serves at its pleasure, being the chief administrative officer (in a business sense) of the city. As such, this staff member performs work in advance of the official meetings (by preparing the city budget and city reports), attends the meetings (along with the city attorney and city clerk), offers instruction on precedent and procedures during those meetings, and follows up later by ensuring that city ordinances are being implemented.[93] Though this person is the principal administrator (play-

93 Duncombe and Weisel, *State and Local Government*, 121.

ing a crucial role in forming municipal policy), most likely, there is a subordinate fleet of others who head departments, boards, or commissions.

The city administrator "is likely to know his particular governmental activity better than the chief executive or the legislators."[94] When testifying before the council, this person excels at telling the councilors "what he wants them to know and often demonstrating great skill at withholding information unfavorable to his point of view."[95] All the while, he or she serves as a living reference source who ensures that parliamentary procedure[96] is followed. (We will touch more upon parliamentary procedure toward the end of the chapter.)

GOVERNANCE STRUCTURE

Judicial Branch

The judicial system was described generally in the previous chapter where we learned that all fifty states have entry-level trial courts operated by the state. However, thirty states[97] have municipal courts which are created and operated by cities and towns and are not always subject to the state judicial system. These city-run courts may be called by various names such as town, summary, justice, mayor, or police courts, and they generally hear cases involving violations of their city's laws

94 Adrian, *State and Local Government*, 312.

95 Adrian, *State and Local Government*, 312.

96 Parliamentary procedure is a series of formal rules that define how a public meeting is to be conducted.

97 Those states are Alabama, Arizona, Arkansas, Colorado, Delaware, Georgia, Indiana, Kansas, Louisiana, Michigan, Mississippi, Missouri, Montana, Nevada, New Jersey, New Mexico, New York, North Dakota, Ohio, Oklahoma, Oregon, Rhode Island, South Carolina, Tennessee, Texas, Utah, Washington, West Virginia, Wisconsin, Wyoming. Alexandra Natapoff, "Criminal Municipal Courts," *Harvard Law Review* 134, no. 3 (January 2021).

(these violations are known as misdemeanors which we will learn about later).

Because municipal courts almost exclusively hear cases dealing with local ordinances which govern the city, they are courts of limited jurisdiction—hearing cases only of a particular subject matter.[98] Some common examples of municipal code violations are traffic charges, public intoxication, disorderly conduct, assault charges, theft, possession of drugs, driving under the influence, tobacco/alcohol possession by minors, reckless damage/destruction, breaking fish/game laws, and boating or parks/forests regulations.[99] Occasionally, these courts hear civil cases pertaining to small sums of money or loss.

But it is difficult to categorize these courts because "each municipal court has its own processes and procedures. What is 'standard' in one municipal court can be completely different than in another municipal court."[100] Strangely municipal court judges may not be required to be attorneys. Further, they might be appointed by the city council or the mayor. Sometimes the judge is the mayor. In some municipal courts, there is no attorney to prosecute the offender, so the arresting police officer may serve in that role. This situation illustrates the lack of separation of powers as we learned about in the previous chapter. Additionally, they are not courts of record (meaning they are not required to keep written records of their proceedings), and their verdicts are rarely appealed to the state court system which operates upon records. Therefore, an appeal from a municipal court ruling must start fresh in a first-tier state trial court.

---

98 *Wex Legal Dictionary and Encyclopedia*, s.v. "limited jurisdiction," Legal Information Institute, Cornell Law School, last updated June 2020.

99 "What Kind of Offenses Are Handled in Municipal Court?," AskTheLawyers, April 26, 2020.

100 "What Is the Difference between Municipal Court, District Court, and Federal Court?," Roth Davies LLC.

Very little information has been available about the municipal court system until the landmark article by Alexandra Natapoff entitled "Criminal Municipal Courts" published by *Harvard Law Review*. Information not otherwise footnoted in this section is derived from it. Learn more at Natapoff's website **municipalcourts.org**.

OTHER THINGS YOU SHOULD KNOW

Service and Grace

We as Christians have a duty to serve Christ in the civil realm because, after all, it belongs to Him. As Psalm 24:1 states, "The earth is the LORD's, and all its fullness, / The world and those who dwell therein." And whatever we do, we are to do all to His glory (1 Corinthians 10:31). Further, as the Apostle Paul says, we are to be the fragrance of Christ to those who walk among us (2 Corinthians 2:14), and we are to be tenderhearted, forgiving one another even as God in Christ forgave us (Ephesians 4:32). For, where would we be without His grace extended to us? That question often dials the civil realm back into perspective.

As we enter the city level of the civil realm, we are to extend this same grace to others—who may be very different from ourselves. We may be irritated by them and want to voice our feelings on the spot. Or in an email. Or in a letter to the editor. Or on social media. However, my challenge to you is to treat others the way that you would like to be treated. Jesus says that is the second greatest commandment. We can only behave this way by His grace; it is not in our human nature to do so. It is not compromising our position to treat others in the manner which the Lord commands; it is obedience. Often being likable is confused with pandering to others for their approval. I suppose that could be the case, but that is not the sort of likableness I intend. I am referring to obeying the second greatest commandment (Matthew 22:39).

As noted in the Introduction, do not be exasperated while observing the governance processes for the area in which you live. From the lens of your newly gained civic knowledge, you will see those in the civil realm who conduct themselves well and those who conduct themselves poorly in terms of what they know and how they act. You will see people appear on the governance stage in these roles: elected, appointed (both paid and volunteer), office staff, and citizen (both engaged and activist). You will see Democrats and Republicans. You will see so-called nonpartisans who are obviously partisan.[101]

Again, do not be exasperated by what you see. We all bring assumptions and expectations into the civil realm that can range from the prideful ("These people are idiots" or "All bureaucrats are worthless") to the discouraged ("I must be the only one who doesn't really understand how all of this works"). Rather than camping on your assumptions (wherever they are on the spectrum of opinion), be patient and observe. Remember James 1:19–20: "So then, my beloved brethren, let every man be swift to hear, slow to speak, slow to wrath; for the wrath of man does not produce the righteousness of God." Those in the civil realm are people just like you and me. They may not have had a book like this to learn from, but they did make a leap into civic service—for better or worse. Our job is to learn to work with these people or learn to go around them. Navigating this well requires wisdom and isn't necessarily easy (compare Proverbs 26:4 with Proverbs 26:5).

Further, because we have forgotten the civil realm, we tend to forget that even there, we all need Jesus. Some of us need to get to know Him, confess our sins to Him, and allow Him to change us. Those of us who think we know Him but have a judgmental attitude need to do likewise. His

101 Partisan means belonging to or affiliating with a political party.

grace is greater than our sin, and He works with each of us individually. All of that is going on simultaneously while we engage with the civil realm. There are two ways to look at our role in the civil realm: one is hard-nosed policy—pushing our agenda to the forefront. The second is bringing the wisdom, patience, and grace of Christ into the civil realm by pursuing the long game. This latter process is hard to describe because I haven't seen it done very often. But our job is to do the right thing in the right way with the souls of others in mind as we proceed. This approach doesn't mean that we are weak-spined. To navigate the civil realm in this way actually requires an extra-strong spine to counter wrong in a way that wins the affection/loyalty of the opposition or of those in the middle ground whenever possible.

In the Assessment section of Figure 3.9, the average person is way over to the left in terms of knowledge. That's why we need this book. We want to move from the left column toward the right column. We cannot make others move from the left column toward the right column. We can only accept them where they are, but recognizing where they are on the spectrum helps to eliminate our shock factor. The point of the chart is to help our words and actions be seasoned with grace rather than exasperation, knowing that "wisdom strengthens the wise / More than ten rulers of the city" (Ecclesiastes 7:19).

Public Documents

On a city website, in addition to the city code of laws, you will find crucial documents such as the city's

- annual budget (shows all of the incoming revenue and outgoing expenditures for the year, organizational charts for city authority structure, and much more);

THE TYPES OF PEOPLE YOU WILL MEET IN THE CIVIL REALM

Roles/Positions

☐ Democrat	☐ Nonpartisan	☐ Republican
☐ Citizen	☐ City Volunteer	☐ City Staff (hired)
	☐ Elected	

Assessment

(Examine this list to determine how to work with and guide people in the civil realm)

Negative ⟶	Positive
Isolated knowledge/expertise	Breadth of knowledge/expertise
Incompetent	Competent
Arrogant	Approachable
Not engaged	Engaged
Not informed	Informed
Vague/verbose	Direct/clear communicator
Inarticulate	Articulate
Non-critical thinker	Critical thinker
Inexperienced in the role	Experienced in the role
Sneaky	Transparent

Figure 3.9*

*Many thanks to John H. Wright for creating this chart.

- comprehensive plan[102] (shows the goals of the city and serves as the foundational land-use planning and zoning document required by state statute);
- strategic plan (provides the shorter-term implementation of the comprehensive plan);

102 Planopedia, "What Are Comprehensive Plans?," Planetizen.

- vision statement[103] (expresses present to distant future ambition of what the city wants to be); and
- mission statement (expresses current purpose and current key objectives to accomplish the vision).

Reading these documents will help you thoroughly understand the city's emphases. It will also set you apart as a knowledgeable, concerned citizen. Even if you do not understand all of the data, you will still know how and where to access the data when local issues, questions, and controversies arise. There is highly useful information embedded in these documents (such as flow charts of the layers of city supervision/heads of departments). This material is part of the wealth of knowledge we must mine in order to speak intelligently concerning city-related issues and to encourage or guide elected city officeholders and appointed city staff.

Parliamentary Procedure

Almost without exception, the entire framework for any local, public meeting in America is based on the book *Robert's Rules of Order.*[104] It is **the** resource for understanding the order of business for a public meeting and how business is transacted within the structure of a meeting—which is called parliamentary procedure. *Robert's Rules of Order* allows groups of people to have a reasonably measured approach to processing what can be dozens, or hundreds, or thousands of decisions—depending on the size of the municipality or district—in an efficient and orderly manner.

103 Almas Tazein, "Vision and Mission of Award-Winning Cities, Municipalities, and Local Governments around the World," *Best Practice Improvement Resource* (blog), November 22, 2021.

104 Henry M. Robert III, Daniel H. Honemann, and Thomas J. Balch, *Robert's Rules of Order Newly Revised*, 12th ed. (New York: PublicAffairs, 2020).

I highly recommend purchasing a copy of *Robert's Rules of Order Newly Revised in Brief*[105] which is a shortened version of the original book. It is a remarkably clear guide designed to help you run (or understand) a meeting. If you read it, you will have a much better idea of what is taking place within local government. You will understand what a quorum[106] is, how a meeting is called to order, who is allowed to speak and when, how votes are taken on issues, and so on. The whole book is quite helpful, but Part II titled "So You're Going to a Meeting" is particularly poignant. Modern-day people are not generally trained in parliamentarian skills, and when they are elected to public office they are often at a loss as to how the system works. You, on the other hand, will be considerably ahead.

Open Meetings/Closed Meetings

Public meetings—which is to say any meeting where elected or appointed individuals within the civil realm make decisions about policy, spending, or priorities—are generally considered to be open to the public. What the term *open* means can vary slightly from state to state, but every state has laws mandating that all government business (business of We the People) at every level of government must be conducted publicly. In other words, the public must have access to open meetings. These laws can be referred to by terms such as *sunshine* or *open-government laws*; their purpose is to hold those who govern accountable to the public. Sunshine laws help shine light on what could be shady business.

The opposite of open meetings also exists—and for a purpose which happens to be legal. These meetings may be referred to as closed meetings or executive sessions and liter-

105 Henry M. Robert III, Daniel H. Honemann, and Thomas J. Balch, *Robert's Rules of Order Newly Revised In Brief*, 3rd ed., (New York: PublicAffairs, 2020).

106 A *quorum* is the minimum number of members of an assembly that must be present to make a meeting valid.

ally happen behind closed doors. Each state's open-meeting law will also specify a limited list of topics that qualify for such privacy, known as closed-meeting laws. It makes sense, for example, that if a legislative body is going to make a hiring decision, and there will be discussion containing personal details of prospective hires that aren't publicly known or accessible, then those details should remain private. However, the actual debate and vote by the legislative body on the question of which candidate to hire must occur publicly in the open portion of the meeting.

You will want to research and have, at the very least, a basic understanding of your state's laws regarding open and closed meetings. And, to the extent that you are able, you should seek to hone your understanding even further. While these laws can no longer be considered a new development, people do come and go in elected roles, and thus knowledge about open meetings can ebb and flow. Having this knowledge will build confidence in your citizenship duties.

Let's conclude this topic with an observation that shouldn't surprise you: The average elected representative doesn't like the heat of public accountability. Likely, you may find that there are individuals in any public office near you who are simply determined to force their agenda and make decisions in violation of open meeting laws. The question then becomes, what do you do? As we learned earlier, identifying and notifying elected representatives higher up the ladder is a good place to start as is checking with another branch of government.

Chambers of Commerce

If you become active in your city's affairs, you are likely to come across a local chamber of commerce.[107]

107 A chamber of commerce is an affiliation of businesses that lends local support in favor of interests of its members. While not a government entity, a chamber

THINGS YOU CAN DO

Spend time getting to know your city's website.

Find the names and faces of the following:

- your elected representatives (mayor, councilors, or commissioners)
- the appointed board or commission members (especially planning/zoning boards)
- some of the city staff

Locate the following:

- when and where the public meetings take place
- the next meeting's agenda (upcoming business posted in advance of the meeting)
- the last meeting's minutes (a record of business completed at the prior meeting)
- the annual budget (should contain city organizational charts and much valuable information)
- the comprehensive and/or strategic plan
- the vision and/or mission statement
- the city code

---

networks with government to better serve its members. According to Aaron Renn's "A Field Guide to Chambers of Commerce," chambers exist for mutual business support (making introductions, giving discount perks), civic improvement (running business improvement districts), and lobbying (local, state, or federal government). There are four types of chambers of commerce: 1) U.S. Chamber of Commerce in Washington, D.C.—a big business organization that lobbies, 2) state chambers—generally having a conservative agenda, 3) city/metro/regional chambers—generally having a progressive agenda and do civic development activities/operate business development districts, 4) local/neighborhood chambers—generally dealing with mainstream issues: how to attract people to the community, to street festivals, by banners on city signs. Renn summarizes that all chambers of commerce hate social conservative policies thinking that such policies are bad for business. He recommends that Christians not abandon chambers but work with them for the good of the community. Aaron Renn, "A Field Guide to Chambers of Commerce," *The Aaron Renn Show*, posted January 31, 2022, YouTube video, 26:58.

Compare your city (or town's) organizational chart to the chart in this book.

Quite likely, you will find this chart within the city's annual budget. If you are unable to locate either the budget or the organizational chart, call your city and ask for help.

Familiarize yourself with *Robert's Rules of Order*.

Earlier, I mentioned purchasing a copy of *Robert's Rules of Order Newly Revised in Brief*. It is also very helpful to watch some YouTube videos that demonstrate how to use *Robert's Rules* before you attend a public meeting. You do not need to become an expert at this point; the goal is to begin the process of gaining some fluency in parliamentary procedure so that you understand the mechanics of a public meeting.

Attend some of your city's live meetings.

It will take a bit of doing to ascertain which meeting(s) you should attend. In the beginning, it may be pretty confusing. Just dive in, attend some meetings, survey the meeting landscape, and gain experience. Expect that you will occasionally show up to find that the meeting has been canceled or rescheduled.[108] An agenda for the meeting should be posted several days ahead of the actual meeting, and it should be online. Print it and bring it along. If you are unable to do so, there should be a copy of the agenda available at the meeting. Further details for each agenda item may also be available online. In my city, this is called the Agenda Packet, which may

108 Meetings that fall on a national holiday are typically rescheduled for the following day. Likewise, if the government holiday falls on a Sunday, the following Monday is typically considered a national holiday.

be several hundred pages long, so plan ahead on how you will access such documents if you're going digital.

There is value in visiting each of your city's boards or commissions, as these groups are the citizen think tanks that forward policy information and recommendations to the policy-making council, but you should be mindful of a great temptation when visiting. Because some boards and commissions entrench themselves in work that ranges from superfluous to unbiblical, it is paramount to maintain your decorum. There may be no shortage of shocking issues which cause dishonor or disrespect for various reasons. In some moments, it may feel like you're facing a tidal wave of ungodliness. Current issues (especially when attended by inaccurate assumptions, questionable data, and/or lack of procedural understanding) can cause anger to well up within the human breast. My charge to you is this: Don't jump ship. Resist the overwhelming desire to react in the moment. Recall the chart (Figure 3.9) a few pages earlier in this chapter. Then, observe, take note, and (most importantly) verify the elected chain of command so that you know where the actual point of accountability is. If prudent, follow up with one (or all) of the appropriate elected representatives who are present at a later time. It is advisable to remain a silent observer until you understand the structure of the governmental system and can gracefully navigate within it.[109] Taking a step back to see yourself and the city in a larger context is quite helpful here. Remember Proverbs 25:28: "Whoever has no rule over his own spirit / Is like a city broken down, without walls."

Pray for your leaders' souls.

In the New Testament, Timothy urges us "that supplications, prayers, intercessions, and giving of thanks be made for all

109 Based on the concept of "Do not say, 'I will recompense evil'; / Wait for the LORD, and He will save you" Proverbs 20:21–22.

men, for kings and all who are in authority, that we may lead a quiet and peaceable life in all godliness and reverence" (1 Timothy 2:1–2). And in the Old Testament, God's people who were carried away from Jerusalem to Babylon were explicitly told to "build houses and dwell in them; plant gardens and eat their fruit... And seek the peace of the city where I have caused you to be carried away captive, and pray to the LORD for it; for in its peace you will have peace" (Jeremiah 29:5–7). We are to seek the peace of the city and pray to the Lord for it. In his book, *The Meaning of the City*, Jacques Ellul states, "We are not first asked to preach and convert Babylon, but rather to pray. Involved in a battle for Sodom, our duty is to pray for the good of the city."[110] Ellul continues, "As servants of the Word, we must for its sake accept working with what revolts us, hurts us, and breaks our human hearts, for blind refusal is a disservice to the Word of God, and this Word declares forgiveness with judgment, not a judgment without pardon. And the life of the city is dependent on such an attitude."[111] So we pray for our city leaders by name—or with them in person.[112]

Introduce yourself.

Eventually, after you have become comfortable observing the meetings, introduce yourself to your elected representatives and to any nearby staff. The smaller the meetings, the more conspicuous you will be, and those who run the meeting may seek you out before you present yourself to them. That's okay. Greet them and show appreciation for their service to the community. Overall, theirs is a thankless job—they hear from complainers

110 Jacques Ellul, *The Meaning of the City* (Grand Rapids, MI: William B. Eerdmans, 1993), 75.

111 Ellul, *The Meaning of the City*, 76.

112 Richard Bledsoe, *Metropolitan Manifesto: On Being the Counselor to the King in a Pluralistic Empire* (Monroe, LA: Theopolis Books, 2015).

on a regular basis. So a new, patient, optimistic face is a breath of fresh air to most elected representatives of the people.

Look for city events in the newspaper (if your city still uses one).

The local newspaper has been called obsolete. However, it often contains a lot of helpful information, such as upcoming public meetings, notices of public hearings, police reports, and letters to the editor—all of which are hard to find in one place on social media. Much like Albus Dumbledore from the Harry Potter books, I learn a lot from reading the local paper. When asked how he is privy to certain information, Dumbledore replies, "You see, I read the Muggle newspapers, unlike most of my Ministry friends."[113] Even if you are not a Harry Potter fan, Dumbledore speaks the truth here. In the Introduction of this book, I mentioned being unwittingly drawn into the civil realm. God used an article in the local newspaper to catch my attention and cause me to attend a local, public meeting regarding the issue at hand. My life has never been the same since.

Consider touring some of your city's public works facilities.

It is easy to take municipal services for granted and be agitated about the cost of those services without understanding the complicated nature of providing them to all residents. Once, my daughter organized a tour of our city's wastewater treatment plant for our family members because we did not know what happened after water went down the drain. Come to find out, the process of treating raw wastewater and turning it into

---

113 J. K. Rowling, *Harry Potter and the Goblet of Fire* (New York: Arthur A. Levine Books, 2000), 602.

reusable water is quite complex. We gained an appreciation not only for the process but also for the water reclamation facility supervisor.

Consider pursuing a Maser of Public Administration (M.P.A.) degree.

An M.P.A. is a graduate-level degree that can be earned online in one to two years and gives students experience in running local government. After reading this book and attending public meetings, if you have an interest in public administration (such as being a city manager/administrator/supervisor), this degree may be worth considering.

Respect and invest in your leaders.

There is a difference between speaking the truth about someone's actions or political platform and speaking evil against that person. In the civil realm, it can be commonplace to revile those whom God has set over us in authority. Sometimes we can get pretty comfortable with badmouthing others as part of the spectator sport that politics has become in our time. But we are strictly warned in multiple places not to do so. The admonition found in 2 Peter 2:10 is sobering because it describes rebellious people as those who "are not afraid to speak evil of dignitaries." Exodus 22:28 tells us, "You shall not revile God, nor curse a ruler of your people." Acts 23:5 phrases it as, "You shall not speak evil of a ruler of your people." Titus widens the court to include all people when he writes the command, "speak evil of no one" (Titus 3:2). Lastly, Jude equates those who speak evil of dignitaries with those who defile the flesh and reject authority (Jude 1:8). He then briefly describes a fascinating interchange in verses 9–10.

Municipal public servants' jobs are more complicated than we may have initially thought. In my city, for instance, the councilors meet two afternoons per month to do the preliminary council business. Then, they meet two evenings per month to conduct the regular council meetings. Sometimes, after that meeting, they adjourn and reconvene in executive session (without ordinary citizens present). Then, they are each responsible for attending several monthly commissions and boards as *ex-officio* members and report back to the city council. Note that *ex officio* is Latin and means "because of the office." If a board always has a position for, say, a mayor, then the person who serves as mayor also serves as an *ex-officio* member of that board—because of his or her office. All of the previously mentioned duties are in addition to daily tasks such as answering emails and interacting with the public. The job is a lot of work for not a lot of pay in many cases.

As time passes, and you gain some experience with city operations, be open to the idea of meeting one or more of your leaders for coffee. Or even more radical, invite them to your home for dinner (be sure to inquire about any food allergies or preferences in advance). Let them have a glimpse into the life of one of their Christian constituents. This is an opportunity to develop a relationship, so avoid hot topics that will cause immediate division, and find common ground to discuss (such as length of time as a resident here, daytime or moonlighting work, family members, hobbies, and so on). This is a fine time to share your faith in Christ and explain the gospel as the motivation for the things that you do in life: being free from God's wrath and the fear of appeasing Him, we are set free to do good.

If you are knowledgeable about a particular issue that is before your city's leaders, schedule time to meet with each of them individually to share your viewpoint with them. They may not have previously heard the perspective that you hold. If you disagree with them, do not look at them as the enemy. Rather, look at them as fellow human beings who have taken on added responsibility as citizens.[114] The more serious or complicated the issue, the more critical it is to bring along documentation to prove your point(s) systematically yet efficiently. If this type of data-informed presentation is done with a calm, generous spirit, it can be compelling.

We often make the mistake of assuming that the person in elected office is corrupt without considering who has been speaking into his or her ear. It is easy to underestimate the influence of a counselor. Consider the malleability of King Ahasuerus from the Book of Esther.[115] When Ahasuerus listened to the counsel of Haman, he decreed to annihilate the Jewish people; when he listened to Esther, he decreed to preserve and protect them. Of course, Esther's role as counselor came at the risk of her own life, so this is not an easy business. But it is a fruitful business. Look at the results in Esther's day: "Then many of the people of the land became Jews, because fear of the Jews fell upon them" (Esther 8:17). We know from Proverbs 21:1 that "the king's heart is in the hand of the LORD, / Like the rivers of water; / He turns it wherever He wishes." But have we considered our role in the

---

114 Robert L. Morlan, "Local Governments—The Cities," chap. 14 in *The Fifty States and Their Local Governments*, ed. James W. Fesler (New York: Alfred A. Knopf, 1967), 494. Regarding the insider (politician) and the outsider (layperson), Morlan says this:

> The 'outsider' possesses the great luxury of free criticism and of considering an issue solely from his own standpoint. As a consequence, he often finds it virtually impossible to conceive how anyone but a fool could think differently. But the man behind the council table does not have this luxury. He has an obligation to look at all sides and to consider all implications of a question. More than that, his responsibility does not terminate with the conclusion of argument—he must vote. He must vote knowing that the issue is not black and white, knowing that there is justice in many of the contentions of the other side, aware that all the facts may not yet be known, conscious of his own fallibility, wishing often that a decision could be postponed, and certain that many people will be unhappy with the outcome. Yet vote he must, and on his vote may ride the decision (494).

115 Keep in mind that Ahasuerus was an absolute monarch and that absolute power corrupts. There is no system of checks and balances in such a system. Here, we focus on the impact that a leader's counselors have.

divine bending of the king's heart—in ministering to our leaders? And have we considered the outcome—many people of the land turning to God?

At the beginning of this chapter, I described a meeting with the mayor. I hope that story brings you encouragement. I didn't realize it at the time, but many of our local leaders don't have aides to conduct research for them, and there is no way that they can educate themselves thoroughly on every issue. Their jobs are quite complex. There is a real need for us to come alongside our elected representatives and tactfully inform them regarding our viewpoints.[116] This sort of investment is a way to influence our communities for good, to begin taking back the public square for Christ, and to seek the peace of the city.

In summary, our work is not in vain in the Lord. The book of Proverbs gives us many pointers on how to conduct ourselves with elected leaders, some of which we will cover in chapter 9, "Christian Diplomacy." For now, may this text greatly encourage you: "By the blessing of the upright the city is exalted, / But it is overthrown by the mouth of the wicked" (Proverbs 11:11). Meanwhile, as we enter the civil realm and begin to act upon these local needs, we yearn for something better, something perfect. We can't help but wonder if we should be doing such menial and earthly things as soiling our hands in city government, learning about charters, models of city governance, the municipal judicial system, or boards and commissions. We look at the staff that it takes to serve the elected officeholders; we consider the built-in nature of parliamentary procedure; we observe the prevailing worldview of those among us; and we hardly know what to make of it all. Take heart, we are in good company with Abraham who lived in tents, trained an army, raised the seedling of a new

---

116 You may be able to find resources to assist you from organizations such as **strongtowns.org**.

generation, and "waited for the city which has foundations, whose builder and maker *is* God" (Hebrews 11:10).

SO WHAT?

After having read this chapter, here are some questions to ask yourself:

- Do you understand that cities are under the authority of the state in which they are located?
- Do you understand that cities typically dwell geographically within counties?
- Do you understand that the way cities are run could vary even within a state (because the authority granted for choosing the city model comes from the state constitution)?
- Does it make sense that knowing your local model of city government helps you understand which elected representative(s) of the people represent you? You can go to that person with problems, but more powerfully, you can invest in that person without having your hand out asking for more goods, services, or favors. Generally speaking, such representatives are accustomed to being treated poorly rather than kindly.
- Do you see that far beyond voting or running for office, Christians have a vast opportunity to influence city government and the lives of others?
- If you walk through city hall, is there a building directory listing the various departments? Are the department names beginning to make sense to you?
- Do you understand that *Robert's Rules of Order* is the invisible structure behind the local-governance meeting process?

GOVERNANCE STRUCTURE IN THE UNITED STATES

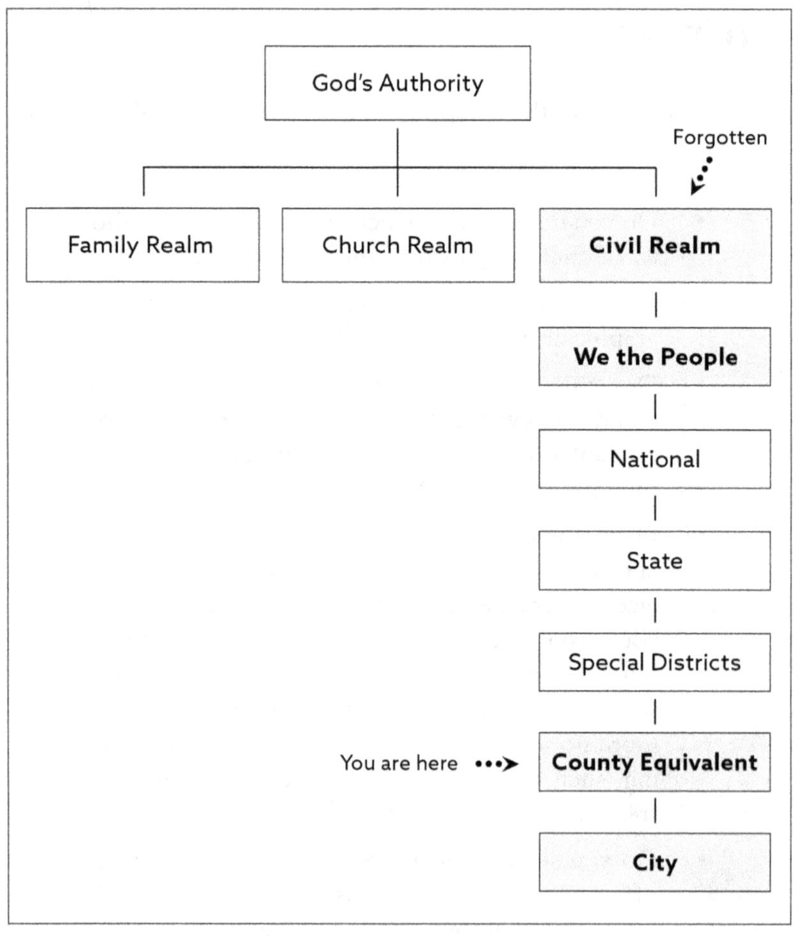

Figure 4.1

CHAPTER 4
County-Equivalent Government

Note: Even if your state doesn't use the term *county*, don't skip this chapter. It contains information that will help you better understand where you live.

When a local county issue caught Susan's attention, she was a homeschool mom of five children (ranging from infant to age eight). Susan didn't know exactly what local government was, but she did know that ignoring an emerging local energy issue was not an option: By appearances, a private company was trying to corner the market on green energy in her county with little to no regard for private property rights—and she was compelled to get to the bottom of the issue.

This journey began by regularly filing her little tribe into a row of seats in the county commissioners' meeting, to learn about local government. "We always went together to the meetings," Susan recollected, where the baby often fell asleep, and the toddler was savvy enough to sit still in exchange for a post-meeting ice cream. Susan described some parts of the meetings as being over their heads, but other parts were well within their ability to understand.

Eventually, Susan decided to campaign for county council.[1] *She and her family went door-to-door on the local campaign trail,*

---

1 County council is a fiscal body that exists in 89 of Indiana's 92 counties to approve the finances for the legislative body. "Unravelling local government: County commissioners vs. county council," *IndyStar*, April 22, 2016.

learned about voting and voter contact strategies, and all while continuing to learn about local government. Susan did not win her first campaign for office, but she was elected to the office on her second attempt!

Susan's husband, an integral part of this process, found it strikingly memorable the day he checked the box for his wife on his voter ballot. Family and civic life continued fruitfully, and during Susan's term serving as county councilor, child number six came along. Susan's takeaway from this journey: "Good people have been complicit for too long in allowing others to run our government."[2]

FORMATION

Our nation severed ties with England in the eighteenth century, but much of our American heritage is rooted in English tradition prior to our country's existence. The county is a case in point. In England, the term *shire* precedes the term *county* and appears to date back to Alfred the Great (A.D. 871–899).[3] In brief, the shire was co-administered by an alderman and a shire-reeve (sheriff). Vestiges of those offices continue to exist in America today. After France invaded England in 1066, the French word *county* came to dwell alongside the Old English word *shire* (bringing with it the connotation of French royalty). In English history, the county existed as "the principal subdivision of the country for political, administrative, judicial, and cultural purposes."[4] Looking ahead to this side of the pond, the first American colony—the Virginia Colony later called

2 Thanks to Susan Huhn for this contribution.

3 *Encyclopedia Britannica Online*, s.v. "Shire."

4 *Encyclopedia Britannica Online*, s.v. "county (division of government)."

Jamestown—was founded in 1607. By 1634, it contained the eight original New World shires (later called counties).[5]

This backward glance reveals that counties are one of America's oldest forms of government[6] which generally spread across the newly developing continent. The counties in the colonies including and south of Virginia were each governed by an appointed (not elected) sheriff and several justices of the peace.[7] The colonies north of Virginia chose not to appoint but rather to elect their county governing leaders. Due to the widespread presence of towns and cities, those counties had fewer responsibilities and were the administrative agents of the crown.[8] Later, after the American Revolution (1775–1783), counties became administrative agents of the states in which they resided. This is because, as you may recall from chapter 2, "Layers of Law," the U.S. Constitution does not mention local government. Rather, the constitutional system features federalism where powers belong either to the national government or, as the Tenth Amendment declares, to the states or to the people.[9] That means state law—not federal law—closely defines the workings of county government. Therefore, each state establishes the ability of local government to exist and does so through charter via its state constitution and the laws of its state legislature.[10] Each state legislature also sets the geographic boundaries for its counties and provides rules for revising those boundaries if necessary.

5 *Encyclopedia Virginia*, "Virginia Counties 1634–1640."

6 "Counties Matter: Stronger Counties Stronger America," National Association of Counties (NACo), February 2019, 2.

7 "States with the Most Counties 2024," World Population Review.

Justices of the peace are part of the judicial system that predates the Constitution. They can serve as judges in the municipal court system that we learned about in the previous chapter.

8 "States with the Most Counties 2024," World Population Review.

9 We often neglect the "or to the people" part of the Tenth Amendment.

10 "Counties Matter," NACo, 2.

Historically, counties were designed as local outposts of state government. In times past, and even today in larger states, it was complicated to make the trek to the state capitol, from which the state manages its own business operations. Thus, counties perform a wide variety of local duties on behalf of the state including road construction and maintenance, law enforcement, judicial courts, property assessment for taxes (and their collection), and consistent elections.[11] Other county duties include levying taxes, borrowing money, making appropriations, setting salaries for county employees, licensing and regulating businesses, and maintaining county property (such as the courthouse, jail, hospital, and so on).[12] "Counties still perform these functions, as well as a growing list of other functions, under the supervision of various elected and appointed officials."[13] As such, counties are considered much more an arm of state government than cities are. The relationship between county and state is much closer than the relationship between city and state. Remember from the previous chapter that cities are municipal corporations created voluntarily by a group of citizens.

Counties are quasi-corporations (not full corporations thus not fully incorporated) because they are not created by the voluntary decision of the people who compose them.[14] Rather, they are created as local extensions of the state. Counties are "intergovernmental partners implementing federal and state policies at the local level often under strict rules and funding constraints."[15] Today, there are over three thousand

---

11 "County Elected and Appointed Officials," Municipal Research and Services Center of Washington (MRSC).

12 Clarence B. Carson, *Basic American Government* (Wadley, AL: American Textbook Committee, 1993), 312–313.

13 "County Elected and Appointed Officials," MRSC.

14 *Wex Legal Dictionary and Encyclopedia*, s.v. "quasi-corporation," Legal Information Institute, Cornell Law School.

15 "Federal Policies Matter to County Government," National Association of Counties (NACo), posted September 22, 2015, YouTube video, 5:57.

counties in the United States.[16] None of them are precisely the same; they differ in structure and in the services that they deliver to their communities.

Before considering the general structure of the forms of county government, it is helpful to clarify a few misconceptions surrounding counties. Sometimes, people think that city government is for city dwellers, and county government is for country dwellers. That is not really the case. Cities usually reside within county limits.[17] Typically counties are the next larger level or region of government after the city. Generally speaking, we can consider the county as a mid-sized unit of local government that administers functions delegated to it by the state.[18] The confusing part is that sometimes the county provides a service for all its residents—think of the county vehicle licensing office. However, if some services are provided to residents of the incorporated city, which is geographically located within the county, then the county does not duplicate that service to its rural residents. For example, residents of an incorporated city within a county have city law enforcement—the city police department. But residents of rural and unincorporated areas have county law enforcement—usually the county sheriff's department.[19] This principle of non-duplication of services helps to conserve finances and manpower for local governments.

Let's look at a law-enforcement example: Imagine you've had just about enough of reading this civics book. You slam it down, jump in your car, and speed away in an uproar while remaining within city limits. You see flashing lights and are stopped by a city police officer—typically in a dark blue uni-

---

16 A beautiful animated map of the nation's counties is here—see if you can locate your county. Carmen Ang, "Animated Map: The History of U.S. Counties," Visual Capitalist, published July 31, 2020.

17 Except for independent cities which are not considered part of the county.

18 Nick Ragone, *The Everything American Government Book*, 247.

19 Though Alaska does not have sheriffs—it has state troopers.

form. You think, "Ah, I must still be within the city limits." If you don't reach full speeding frenzy until you are outside the city limits but still within the county, you could be pulled over by your county sheriff or deputy sheriff. You think, "Ah, that probably explains why his uniform is a lighter brown, not dark blue." If, however, you happen to be fuming mad and exceeding the speed limit on a state highway, a state trooper could pull you over. One law enforcement officer is not above another. They simply have different jurisdictions. Officers can exercise their powers outside their territorial jurisdiction, but there are limits on the reasons to do so.[20] (This touches on the concept of extra-territorial powers mentioned in the previous chapter.) By now, you should not be surprised that those limits are set by the state's legislature and are found in the state's code of laws. I hope this book doesn't propel you into such a speeding frenzy, but if it does, and when you're being pulled over, at least you'll understand jurisdictional structure. How you respond to the officer and what you say (in this situation or in other types of situations) is a separate topic to pay close attention to.[21]

While addressing some general concepts about county government, I should mention that not all states have counties, but most do. The term that the U.S. Census Bureau uses for areas of the nation that function more or less as counties but are not counties in name is county equivalent[22]—hence, the title of this chapter. Due to the wide liberty given to the states by the U.S. Constitution, our nation is a patchwork quilt

---

20 John McCurley, "Police Jurisdiction: Where Can Officers Make Arrests?" Lawyers.com.

21 James J. Duane, *You Have the Right to Remain Innocent: What Police Officers Tell Their Children about the Fifth Amendment* (New York: Little A, 2016) and Sam Kamin and Zachary Shiffler, "Obvious But Not Clear: The Right to Refuse to Cooperate with the Police during a Terry Stop," *American University Law Review* 69, no. 3 (2020).

22 "Substantial Changes to Counties and County Equivalent Entities: 1970–Present," U.S. Census Bureau.

of governmental variety. Therefore, when you see the term *county*, consider it to also mean *county equivalent.*

Since one of the purposes of this book is to prepare you to engage with local government wherever you live in the United States while simultaneously giving you an overview of the nation as a whole, it is helpful to know which states do not use the county system or use variations of it. For example, Connecticut and Rhode Island have counties that are geographic regions in name but do not function governmentally as such. They simply do not have functioning counties.[23] This is likely because their state capitols are just not that far away from any of the state borders. County outposts are not essential the way they are in larger states. Connecticut does, however, have nine planning regions that have been adopted by the Census Bureau as county-equivalent geographic units[24] called Regional Councils of Government (COG).[25] Rhode Island simply has cities and towns, not counties.

Adding to this national patchwork quilt, Louisiana refers to counties as parishes, hearkening back to remnants of its Roman Catholic heritage under its prior rule by France and Spain,[26] and Alaska refers to them as boroughs.[27] These are

---

23 Sandra M. Stevenson, *Understanding Local Government*, 2nd ed, The Understanding Series (Newark, NJ: LexisNexis, 2009), 3.

24 "Governor Lamont Announces U.S. Census Bureau Approves Proposal for Connecticut's Planning Regions To Become County Equivalents," The Office of Governor Ned Lamont, CT.gov, June 6, 202.

25 Global Site Plans—The Grid, "Connecticut Since the Abolition of County Government in 1959," Smart Cities Dive.

26 "Louisiana was officially Roman Catholic under both France and Spain's rule. The boundaries dividing the territories generally coincided with church parishes. In 1807, the territorial legislature officially adopted the ecclesiastical term. Through each change in her history, Louisiana never deviated and the primary civil divisions have been officially known as parishes ever since." "Why Is Louisiana the Only State to Have Parishes and Not Counties?," Vermilion Parish Tourist Commission.

27 "The State of Alaska's Constitution, Article X, Section 2, provides that two forms of local government, cities and organized boroughs, form the basic structure of Alaska's Municipal Government. Both cities and boroughs are municipal corporations and political subdivisions of the State of Alaska. Alaska's Constitution also requires that

not to be confused with New York City's five boroughs which are like smaller cities within a metropolis. Nor are they to be confused with New Jersey's,[28] Pennsylvania's,[29] or even Connecticut's[30] boroughs which are smaller than cities, or Virginia's boroughs which resulted from consolidation.[31]

All of the above is part of the nation's patchwork quilt—you might even call it a crazy quilt. It does, indeed, seem kind of crazy. And here is just one more variation for your consideration: If you live in Hawaii, you will have county government without city government. Each county does, however, contain elements of city government such as a charter and a mayor.

Because we have already covered city government and are in the process of understanding county government, another term to be familiar with is *county seat*. I mentioned it in the prior chapter's opening story, but what is it? The county seat is the city which is the administrative center of the county where services such as the county courthouse are located. In a sense, it could be considered the county's capital city, and it is often (but not always) the most populous city in the county. Typically, only one city is known as the seat even though other cities may sit geographically within the county, but of course, exceptions can exist to almost every rule. Some counties have

---

the entire state be divided into organized or unorganized boroughs, based on standards such as natural geographic boundaries, economic viability, and common interests. For the most part, organized boroughs were formed in those areas where economies were better developed. The large portion of the state that has not incorporated as an organized borough is designated the unorganized borough." The Great State of Alaska—Department of Commerce, Community, and Economic Development, Introduction to "Municipal Government Structure in Alaska," revised October 2, 2018.

28 "New Jersey," U.S. Census Bureau.

29 "Pennsylvania," U.S. Census Bureau.
See also Irina Zhorov, "Explainer: Cities, boroughs, and townships, oh my! Pa. municipalities clarified," WHYY, April 4, 2016.

30 "Connecticut," U.S. Census Bureau.

31 Virginia Law, "Code of Virginia, Article 2: Consolidation of Certain Counties, Cities and Towns, § 15.2–3534: Optional provisions of consolidation agreement," Legislative Information System.

more than one county seat, and at least one county has none.[32] To determine what local government quirks are specific to your area, check your county (or parish or borough or planning region) government website.

Although counties are generally larger geographic entities than cities are, they lack the broad powers of self-government that cities typically enjoy. As administrative subunits of the state, counties experience more overall legislative control by the state than cities do. Because of this status, possessing a charter is not a defining characteristic of county government. However, there is a modern trend toward counties adopting home-rule charters[33] which represents "more often an attitude toward local government than it is a legal injunction against legislative action"[34] by a state toward a county. According to the National Association of Counties, home-rule authority provides more flexibility and control concerning the governmental structure, function, and financial power of county government.[35]

SERVICES

County equivalents act as an arm of the state by providing many services to their residents. They perform these functions operating under the state constitution and according to state statute. In a moment, we will learn about various systems or models of governance that counties also operate under in order to perform services to their residents. For now, here is a

32 "Arlington County does not have a county seat, while Harrison County, Mississippi, has two: Gulfport and Biloxi." "County," National Geographic. 🔗

33 Ballotpedia, s.v. "Home Rule."

34 Charles R. Adrian, *State and Local Governments*, 128.

35 "Counties Matter," NACo. 🔗
For a graphic of which counties operate under home rule see "2017 County Authority," NACo found on the links page at **CivilRealm.com**. 🔗

list that will illustrate the great variety of services that may be available in a county:

- Issuing marriage and driver's licenses
- Removing and recycling garbage
- Providing parks and recreational facilities along with attendant programs
- Educating children
- Supplying police and fire protection
- Prosecuting criminals
- Conducting elections on behalf of the state election office
- Organizing public transportation
- Administering health services (such as vaccinations) and facilities (hospitals)
- Administering behavioral and mental health services
- Administering nursing homes
- Administering veterans services
- Organizing programs such as 4-H and the annual county fair on behalf of the state land-grant university

LAW

Now for a quick brush with the law as it pertains to the county. In chapter 2, "The Cornerstone Chapter," we learned that county law generally deals with land, agricultural, and building issues that occur outside of incorporated municipalities located within the county. Typically, a county will have a planning and zoning board to help plan and make allowance for variances within this written code.

Now is an excellent time to look at the county code of laws that regulates your area. This body of laws may be relatively manageable in size, and you can read it in an hour or so. Or, it may be quite sizable, and in that case, you should apply our mnemonic device TiCS or TACS (see previous chapter) and stay mainly at the title level. There will be another reminder at the end of the chapter to locate and read your county code of laws.

The penalty for an infraction of county code is civil rather than criminal in nature and would result in a fine rather than jail or incarceration. Thus, a county sheriff (the county law enforcement representative whose role will be explained later in this chapter) would make arrests based on state law rather than county law. Infractions of local land regulations are considered civil in nature, and the penalty for breaking those should not be incarceration but rather a fine. The county itself is an arm of the state; as such, the county enforces state law and its structures are rooted in and abide by state law.

GOVERNANCE STRUCTURE

Legislative and Executive (part-one) Branches

In the previous chapter, we surveyed five forms of city government. Now we find ourselves in the county—the next larger geographical and political region with similar models of governance sporting slightly different names. These systems or forms of county government are primarily legislative in nature. The work of the legislative branch largely comprises the delivery of the types of services mentioned above by the county (an arm of the state) to its residents. Legislative-function work involves enacting ordinances or resolutions, adopting budgets, setting policies and tax rates, approving appointments, and overriding vetoes (if applicable).[36] What we will call executive part-one branch function is achieved by the oversight in some capacity of a single chief executive, administrative executive, or county manager (depending on the type of system being used). The duties of this part-one executive include such work as exercising the veto (elected executive), preparing budgets, appointing heads and members of county boards and commissions, signing deeds or contracts, and managing county properties.[37] This primary (or part-one) executive function exists in all of the systems except in the pure commission model.[38] We will consider part two of the executive branch (row officers) after covering the different governmental systems. As in the previous chapter, these offices are illustrated with diagrams that include the judges that represent the judicial branch. An explanation of this third branch will follow our discussion of the four systems.

Usually, there are only three general forms of county government across the United States, but I have included a fourth in this chapter. They are 1) the commission system, 2) the council-administrator system, 3) the council-elected executive system, and 4) the consolidated city-county system. These first three models of county government correspond nicely to the first three models of city government presented in the previous chapter.

---

36 Frank J. Coppa, *County Government: A Guide to Efficient and Accountable Government* (Westport, CT: Praeger Publishers, 2000), 8.

37 Coppa, *County Government*, 8.

38 "Home Rule Charter, Article 3 The Executive Branch," Clark County Council, Clark County, Washington.

Commission System

When we looked at how city government works, we learned that the commission system is the least common form of city government. The opposite is true for the county—the commission system is America's most widely used model of county government. Approximately two-thirds of the counties in the United States have this form of local government.[39]

The members of the commission system are often referred to as the board of county commissioners or sometimes the board of supervisors.[40] These boards are comprised of three to five members, and, typically, these commissioners are elected to their legislative-branch position. Although one of these members may be appointed as president or chairman of the board, one commissioner is not more important than another. Together, they have the power to pass legislation (adopt budgets and make ordinances/enact regulations) by a two-thirds or a three-fifths majority (meaning that two of the three commissioners—or three of the five—must vote the same way to enact county business). They also have the power to execute or carry out policy (set policy direction and appoint county administrative department heads). Thus, the board acts as the legislative and executive branches of the county and has been known as the plural executive form of government.[41] The board also serves in a quasi-judicial function by hearing and rendering verdicts on such matters as

---

39 Ragone, *The Everything American Government Book*, 248.

40 Elected members of governing bodies in Louisiana are called parish police jurors. "What is a Police Jury and its duties?," Assumption Parish Police Jury Louisiana.

Until 2020, New Jersey's county elected members were called chosen freeholders. Now they are called county commissioners. "Governor Murphy Signs Legislation to Eliminate the Title of 'Freeholder' from Public Office: County Governments will replace 'Chosen Freeholder' with 'County Commissioner,'" State of New Jersey, August 21, 2020.

41 "County Forms of Government: Commission Form," Municipal Research Services Center (MRSC).

property-value protests, taxation-cancellation or planning and zoning requests, and indigent issues.[42] The county board of commissioners may appoint an administrator vested with a range of authority in order to assist with the commissioners' business at hand.

COMMISSION SYSTEM

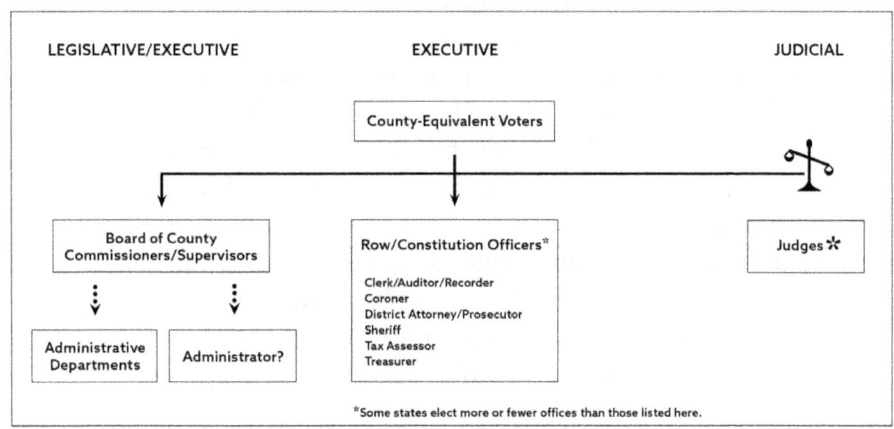

Figure 4.2

KEY

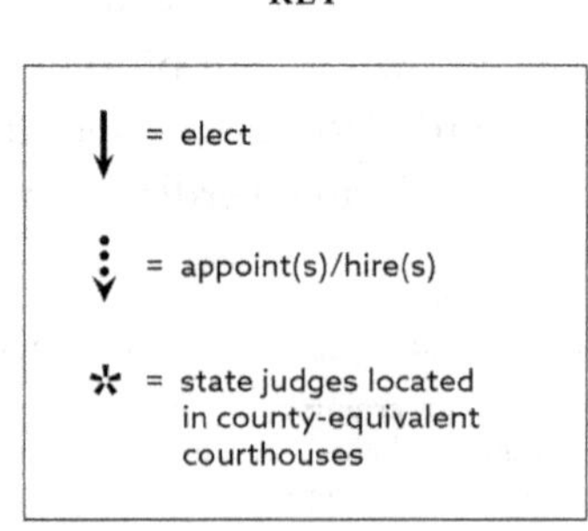

42 "Commissioners," Latah County Idaho.

Council-Administrator System

In the council-administrator system of county government, the elected county council serves as the legislative branch. The council hires an administrator to help serve the county in both administrative and policy-making capacities. As explained below, this person can have a broad range of appointed executive power. The purpose of this form of county government is to "separate policy-making and administrative functions."[43]

Note that this model is very much akin to the council-manager form of city government described in the prior chapter, where the elected board hires or appoints a professional manager to serve as the principal administrator.[44] This person's responsibilities can range from being merely appointed and symbolic to wielding such power as drafting the budget, overseeing construction, or appointing department heads.[45] At the weak end of this range is a hired county administrative assistant, lacking formal powers, who offers advice to the council and performs administrative tasks on its behalf.[46] In the mid-range of responsibility is the chief administrative officer, an executive appointed by the council. This person can oversee interdepartmental policies but can neither appoint nor fire heads of the county departments.[47] In the purest, strongest version, "the county manager exercises broad executive power, including setting the legislative agenda, developing the county budget, appointing department heads, and hiring county staff."[48] Even the strongest administrator is not

43 Coppa, *County Government*, 8.

44 Duncombe and Weisel, *State and Local Government in Idaho and the Nation*, 133.

45 Ragone, *The Everything American Government Book*, 248.

46 David R. Berman, ed., *County Governments in an Era of Change* (Westport, CT: Greenwood Press, 1993), 23.

47 Berman, *County Governments in an Era of Change*, 23.

48 Berman, *County Governments in an Era of Change*, 23.

comparatively as powerful as the city manager is within the city system. This is due to the presence of elected row officers (explained later) who serve as additional elected executives.[49]

COUNCIL-ADMINISTRATOR SYSTEM

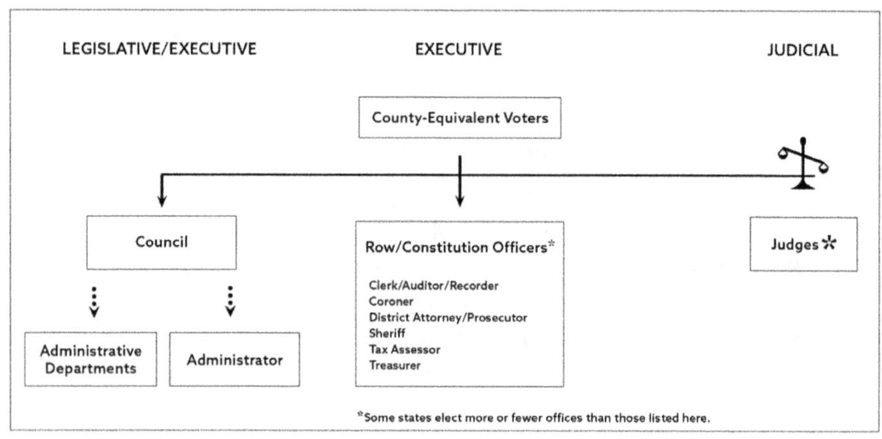

Figure 4.3

KEY

↓	= elect
⋮↓	= appoint(s)/hire(s)
✲	= state judges located in county-equivalent courthouses

49 Berman, *County Governments in an Era of Change*, 23.

Council-Elected Executive System

The council-elected executive system of governance for the county can be likened to the mayor-council model for the city that we learned about in the last chapter. The chief executive is elected separately from the council members and, thus, is totally independent of the council (unlike the council-administrator system).[50] This person serves as the head of the executive branch of county government (much like the state governor does) and appoints an administrator to serve as head over the administrative departments.[51] The council serves as the legislative branch.[52] Inherent in this design is the American separation of powers principle, where the executive branch (individual) is elected separately from the legislative branch (council). The executive, as the chief administrative officer, typically holds the power both to veto ordinances (despite the possibility of an override) and to hire or fire heads of county departments.[53]

According to the *Model County Charter Revised Edition*,[54] county commissioners or county council members in the above three systems are elected in one of five alternative methods. Each election method is based on an at-large model (residents of the entire county vote for their candidate of choice), a district model (voters and candidates must reside in corresponding districts), a combination of these two models, or by proportional representation (members are elected in order of popular vote).[55]

---

50 Ragone, *The Everything American Government Book*, 248.

51 Coppa, *County Government*, 8, 10.

52 Duncombe and Weisel, *State and Local Government*, 133.

53 Coppa, *County Government*, 8.

54 National Civic League, *Model County Charter*, 12. 🔗

55 National Civic League, *Model County Charter*, 12–13, (condensed):
Alternative I: Election At Large
Members are elected by the voters of the county at large.

COUNCIL-ELECTED EXECUTIVE SYSTEM

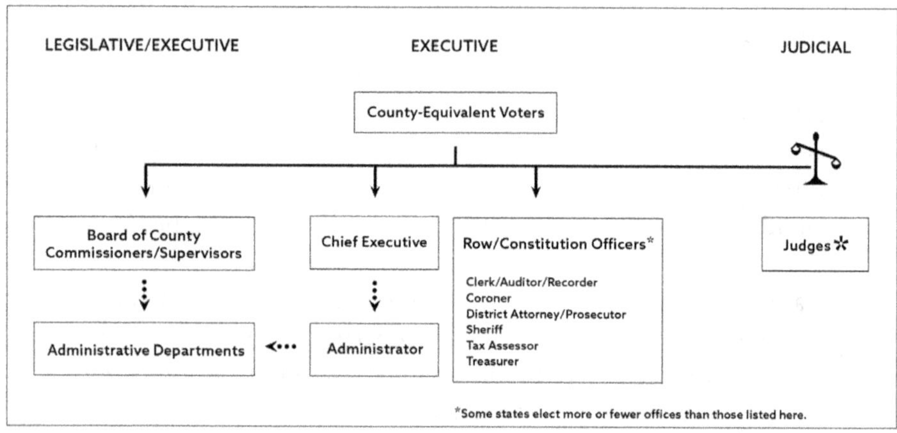

Figure 4.4

KEY

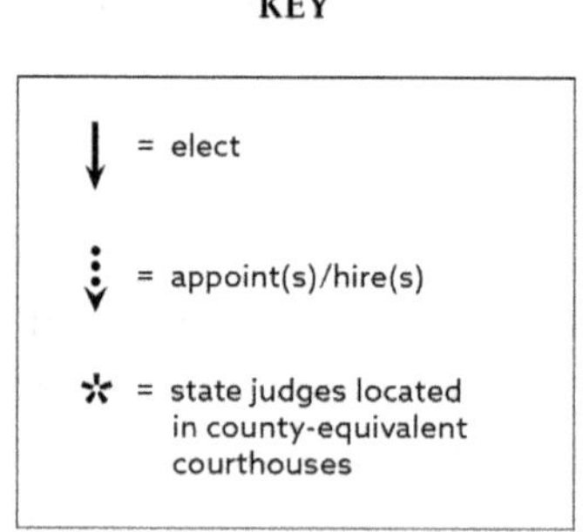

Alternative II: Election At Large with District Residency Requirement
Not more than one member shall reside in each of the districts.
All shall be nominated and elected by the voters of the county at large.
Alternative III: Mixed At-Large and Single Member District System
Members shall be nominated and elected by the voters of the county at large.
Members shall be nominated and elected by the voters of each of the council districts.
Alternative IV: Single-Member District System
One council member shall be nominated and elected by the voters in each of the council districts.

Consolidated City-County System

When a city becomes large enough to join formally with the county government, this merger is called the consolidated city-county system. This combined governing body performs both city and county responsibilities, as the name implies, and operates as a unified jurisdiction.[56] Often, the city is dissolved as a separate corporate entity and merged into the county.[57]

One of this model's benefits is preventing the duplication and overlap of city and county services. The common form of governance consists of "a single chief executive and a multi-district council with a few at-large seats. The executive, or mayor, has veto power, while the council has both legislative and fiscal functions."[58] Indianapolis-Marion County, located in my former home state, is an example of the city-county system, and it occurred by requirement of the state legislature without a popular vote from the affected localities.[59]

For a listing of city-county consolidations across the nation, see the **Ballotpedia** website.[60]

Alternative V: (Proportional Representation)

Members elected by the registered voters of the county at large.

The Council shall be elected by proportional representation by the method of the single transferable vote.

56 Austin Fernald, "The Difference between a Town and a City; plus Counties, Villages and More."

57 "City-County Consolidation in North Carolina," UNC School of Government, 2024.

58 "City-County Consolidations," National League of Cities, September 4, 2013.

59 Berman, *County Governments in an Era of Change*, 137.

60 Ballotpedia, s.v. "Consolidated Government."

CONSOLIDATED CITY-COUNTY SYSTEM

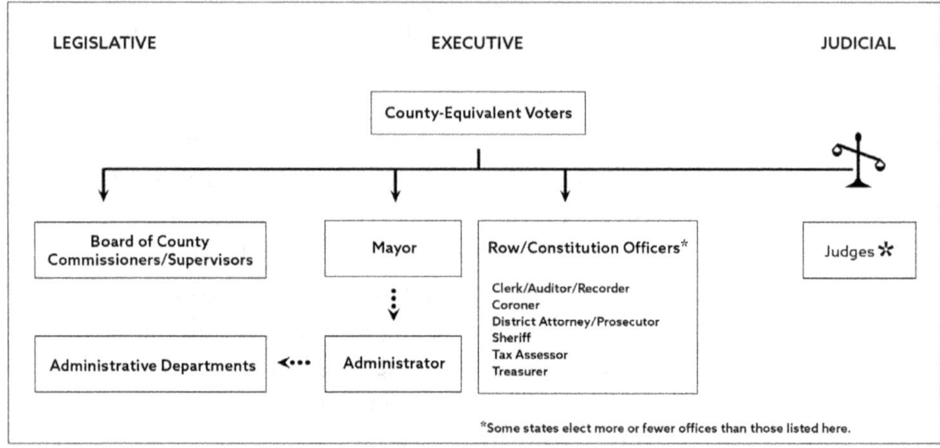

Figure 4.5

KEY

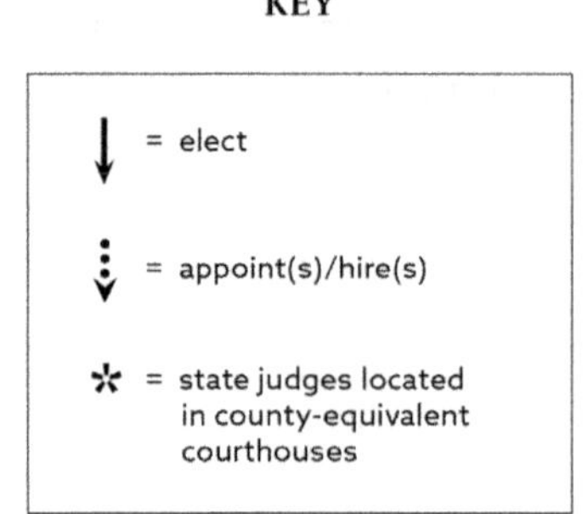

COMPARISON

SYSTEMS OF CITY GOVERNANCE	SYSTEMS OF COUNTY GOVERNANCE
Commission	Commission
Council-Manager	Council-Administrator
Mayor-Council	Council-Elected Executive
(Open) Town Meeting	Consolidated City-County
Representative Town Meeting	

Figure 4.6

Parliamentary Procedure, Staff, Boards & Commissions

As we learned in the previous chapter, the public meetings for any of these four systems of county governance should run under the parliamentary procedural guidelines of *Robert's Rules of Order*. There also should be a clerk present to take the minutes of the meeting and most likely an appointed county attorney present to ensure that business takes place in a legally sanctioned fashion.

All of the above county-equivalent governmental systems appoint boards or commissions that extend the county's work of We the People into different areas of expertise. Counties may have such entities as a parks and recreation commission to supervise local county parks, a community guardians board to aid with the elderly or shut-ins, or a historic preservation board to maintain architectural continuity across the past.

The two most essential commissions for any county, in terms of land use, are the planning commission and the zoning board. The planning commission members review and recommend changes to the county comprehensive plan and the land use ordinance (county code of laws). The zoning board members serve in a quasi-judicial role by conducting public hearings for applications, often requesting variances under the land use ordinance. These latter two boards are very powerful, and attending their meetings is an excellent point of entry into understanding county government.[61]

The appointed members of any of these boards are usually concerned citizens who volunteer their time to serve, and who, as a result, may become trusted and respected individuals in their communities. Sadly, the converse may also be true. Some board members may perform poorly or selfishly (for example, engaging in a conflict of interest rather than recusing themselves from an agenda item from which they might profit personally) and not expect anyone to care or notice. Recall Figure 3.9 in the previous chapter that describes the type of people you will encounter in the civil realm.

GOVERNANCE STRUCTURE

Executive Branch (part two): Row or Constitutional Officers

The councilors and commissioners who form the legislative branch are not the only elected officeholders in a county. The other elected county-level officeholders (who also typically work at the county courthouse or an annex location) complete the executive branch. The number of these part-two-executive-branch officeholders ranges from four to ten (and varies by each state's law), and the state constitution or statute endows them to execute (carry out) services to those who live

61 Lydia Lo, "Who Zones? Mapping Land-Use Authority across the US," *Urban Wire* (blog), Urban Institute, December 9, 2019.

within the county's borders.[62] Funding for the many functions that the county performs is provided by the county's property taxes, federal and state funds (some of which proceed from the state or county sales tax, if applicable), fees, and fines. County employee salaries are set by the county's legislative body (council or commission).

Initially, these officers were listed in a row on the election ballot, so sometimes they are known as row officers.[63] Other times, they are known as constitutional officers because the origin of their power is anchored in the state constitution. Since they represent the executive branch, they can appoint deputies and other hired assistants to serve under them.[64] Typically, these elected officers are the county clerk, the county tax assessor, the county treasurer, the county coroner, the county sheriff, the county prosecutor (and possibly the public defender[65]), the county engineer, and the county surveyor. We will look at each of these offices in more detail momentarily, but note that this list of elected officeholders is an overview and an approximation. As we recall from the "Layers of Law" chapter, each state's code of laws (statutes) determines which elected offices exist in the state's counties. Look online for your state's constitution and for your state's code of laws to determine exactly which row officers your state vests with authority as elected representatives to serve the people. Following the name of each office, the elected representatives' duties will be enumerated there.

62 Lo, "Who Zones?"

63 "Row Officers," Montgomery County Pennsylvania.

64 Thus, deputy sheriffs, deputy prosecutors, deputy treasurers, deputy coroners, and such are assistants appointed by the elected sheriff or prosecutor or treasurer or coroner, etc.

65 Public defenders are elected in San Francisco, Florida, Tennessee, and Nebraska. Andrew Howard, "The Public's Defender: Analyzing the Impact of Electing Public Defenders," *Columbia Human Rights Law Review Online*, April 15, 2020.

Clerk

The clerk is not an elected executive office in all states.[66] In some states, this position may be appointed or may not even exist. The clerk may also be referred to as the auditor or the recorder (remember CAR as a mnemonic device). In the states that feature this office, the clerk maintains all official records for county residents from the cradle to the grave. These records include birth certificates, auto licenses (if they are not issued through the sheriff's office), business licenses, marriage licenses, deeds, and death certificates. Not only does the clerk's office maintain these personal/public records, but it also maintains "records of all governing body transactions including resolutions and ordinances."[67] In less populated counties, the clerk may additionally serve as the clerk of court with deputy court clerks managing civil and criminal cases presided over by the trial-level judges. This office may also oversee elections as an arm of the state—in such counties, the clerk works under the direction of the secretary of state's office. We will learn about the secretary of state's role in elections in chapter 6 on state government and in chapter 8 on elections.

Tax Assessor

The tax assessor does just that—assesses the value of properties in the county (based on evaluations throughout the county) to determine the property tax for each one. The property

66 According to the National Association of Counties, the following states elect their county clerks: Alabama, Arkansas, Colorado, Delaware, Idaho, Illinois, Indiana, Michigan, Missouri, Mississippi, Montana, Nebraska, Nevada, New Jersey, New Mexico, Oklahoma, Tennessee, Texas, Utah, Vermont, Washington, West Virginia, Wisconsin, and Wyoming. The states of California and New York can decide whether to elect or to appoint their clerk, and in the remaining states, the office of county clerk may not exist. Jacqueline J. Byers,"Role of the County Clerk," National Association of Counties (NACo), November 2008.

67 Byers, "Role of the County Clerk."

assessments are to be conducted uniformly throughout the state at market value and then recorded on a roll that becomes the source data for producing property tax bills.[68] These rolls are to be updated on a regular basis based on state statute.[69] Pure county assessors assess property values—they neither issue tax bills nor collect taxes. However, some states combine the assessor with the role of the tax collector and/or with some of the duties of the clerk.[70]

Treasurer

The treasurer is an elected office in thirty-four states[71] and is vested with the authority to collect all money due to the county treasury (including property taxes), disperse funds according to law, invest surplus funds and act as the chief liaison between the county and its depository banks, institute actions against any delinquent parties, keep accurate records of all monies received and dispersed, provide annual fiscal accounting, act as the county banker, and collect money from other county departments.[72] In some states, the treasurer is

68 Here is a ranking of real estate property taxes by state: John S. Kiernan, "Property Taxes by State (2024)," WalletHub, February 20, 2024.

69 "Assessor," Idaho County.

70 Such as Texas where the tax assessor also processes motor vehicle title transfers, issues motor vehicle registration and licenses (and may do the same for boats), registers voters, and may conduct elections! "County Tax Assessor-Collector," Texas Association of Counties.

71 The following states constitutionally elect a treasurer for each county: Alabama, Arizona, Arkansas, Colorado, Georgia, Iowa, Idaho, Illinois, Indiana, Kansas, Massachusetts, Maine, Michigan, Minnesota, Missouri, Montana, Nebraska, Nevada, New Hampshire, New Mexico, North Dakota, Ohio, Oklahoma, Oregon, Pennsylvania, South Carolina, South Dakota, Texas, Utah, Virginia, Vermont, Washington, Wisconsin, and Wyoming. "The position is appointed in Alaska, Hawaii and North Carolina and can be either elected or appointed in California and New York. In West Virginia, following the old Anglo-Saxon governmental form, the Sheriff remains the chief tax collector to this day in the combined role of Sheriff-Treasurer." Jacqueline J. Byers, "County Treasurer: Keeper of the Dollar$," National Association of Counties (NACo), November 2008.

72 Byers, "County Treasurer."

"responsible for collecting not only the money due to the county, but also any funds owed to the municipalities within its borders, the school system, the state, and any other taxing entities within the county."[73] We will learn about special taxing districts in chapter 5, "Special Districts, Independent Cities, Townships & Regional Governments."

Coroner

The coroner is an elected position in some states and is responsible for investigating and certifying "the cause and manner of the death of persons who die within the county under circumstances that are sudden, unexpected, unnatural, suspicious, or violent."[74] Few states require the coroner to be a physician; more likely, state law stipulates training in death investigation.[75] If the coroner has difficulty arriving at a conclusion as to the cause of death, this person will enlist the aid of others (including law enforcement or other investigators). Occasionally, the coroner will summon a jury for assistance in reaching a conclusion. "For example, if there is a question of whether a person was accidentally shot, murdered, or committed suicide, a coroner's jury may be called to render a decision."[76] In at least one county, the coroner serves as the first backup to fill the role of sheriff should the sheriff become incapacitated. Check your county website to see if your area has a coroner and if that is an elected or appointed office that represents the people.

---

73 Byers, "County Treasurer."

74 Note that in this state (Ohio), the coroner must be a licensed physician. "What Is a Coroner?" Franklin County Forensic Science Center.

75 The following states require coroners to be licensed physicians: Kansas, Louisiana, Minnesota, and Ohio. "Coroner and Medical Examiner Laws," CDC.

76 Carson, *Basic American Government*, 314.

Sheriff

The sheriff is an elected position in most states[77] and provides law enforcement to areas of the county that are outside incorporated towns. In other words, sheriffs "provide virtually the only law enforcement outside city limits,"[78] and are "generally (but not always) the highest, usually elected, law-enforcement officer of a county."[79] Note that the county prosecutor, discussed in the next section, is also known as the top law enforcement official for the county. Like all row officers and all persons elected to public office, sheriffs swear to uphold their state constitution as well as the U.S. Constitution. Sheriffs and their deputies perform various duties within their counties, such as keeping the peace and enforcing state law. The sheriff's office is often in charge of the jail, 911 emergencies, and search and rescue services. In some states it is also in control of the vehicle licensing section of the county branch of motor vehicles. The sheriff is an officer of the county court. As such, either the sheriff or a deputy sheriff must be present at all times the court is in session. Further duties include serving summonses, warrants, and subpoenas,[80] in addition to confining those who await trial and those who have been convicted

77 Sheriffs are not elected in Alaska, Connecticut, or Hawaii. "Office of Sheriff State-by-State Elections Information," National Sheriffs' Association.

"The Alaska State Troopers are primarily a rural police department. Alaska does not have counties, sheriff's offices or deputies. The Alaska State Troopers provide complete law enforcement services for areas outside of the traditional 'city limits' of most Alaska cities." "State Troopers—Recruitment," The Great State of Alaska—Department of Public Safety.

In Connecticut, sheriffs were replaced with a privatized state marshal system in 2000. "Marshal Commission, State: FAQs," CT.gov.

In Hawaii, there are not sheriffs, but deputy sheriffs do serve in the Sheriff's Division of the Hawaii Department of Public Safety. "Department of Law Enforcement," State of Hawaii.

78 Carson, *Basic American Government*, 313.

79 "FAQ," National Sheriffs' Association.

80 A summons is a written document requesting a person to appear before a judge, a warrant is a written document authorizing a person's arrest, and a subpoena is a written document requesting a person to attend a trial for the purpose of providing evidence.

until their transportation to prison.[81] As a final point, recall that, typically, a sheriff differs from a chief of police in that the former is elected and serves the county while the latter is appointed and serves the city.

Prosecutor/District Attorney

The county prosecutor (also commonly known as the district attorney or prosecuting attorney)[82] is often known as the top law enforcement official for the county in the criminal justice system.[83] This person serves as the intermediary between the sheriff (or police) and the judicial branch by deciding what offenses should be charged, who they should be charged against, and finally by presenting the case in court.[84] This office is supposed to prosecute all crimes that occur within the county.[85] Further, it represents the state in criminal judicial proceedings (because state law not county law defines what criminal offenses are).[86] Due to this tremendous discretion, "the prosecutor has more control over life, liberty, and reputation than any other person" in the county.[87] Additionally, as

---

81 Carson, *Basic American Government*, 314.

82 A few other states refer to this office by other names: state's attorney in Illinois, state attorney in Florida (note the elimination of the possessive), commonwealth's attorney in Virginia, and county attorney in Montana, Arizona, and Minnesota. This position differs from the staff attorney appointed to give the county legal counsel.

83 Angela J. Davis, "Prosecutors as the Most Powerful Actor in the Criminal Justice System," Race, Racism and the Law, February 7, 2014.

84 David Alan Sklansky, "The Nature and Function of Prosecutorial Power," *Journal of Criminal Law and Criminology* 106, no. 3 (Summer 2016): 504.

85 Note that felonies are more serious crimes with longer sentences and can result in loss of rights to vote, possess firearms, or hold public office. Felonies often involve a twelve-person jury. Misdemeanors are less serious offenses punishable by less than one year of incarceration. Misdemeanors can involve a smaller (six-person) jury. Also note that there are rogue prosecutors who refuse to uphold state law.

86 *Wex Legal Dictionary and Encyclopedia*, s.v. "District Attorney (DA)," Legal Information Institute, Cornell Law School.

87 Robert H. Jackson, "The Federal Prosecutor," *Journal of Criminal Law and Criminology* 31, no. 1 (Summer 1940): 3. Note that prosecutors have the same type of powers at the county, state, and federal levels.

an attorney elected to the executive branch of government, in some states, the prosecutor can serve as legal advisor to the elected county officeholders. However, there may also be an appointed staff attorney who fills this function and may attend public meetings.

Public Defender

As the name implies, the public defender serves to legally defend clients from the public who are unable to afford private attorney fees and are "at risk of losing their liberty if convicted."[88] Every county in the nation (with several exceptions) appoints rather than elects its public defender.[89] In California, the combined city/county of San Francisco stands alone in the state as having an elected public defender.[90] In Tennessee, all counties except one—Shelby County—elect their public defenders.[91] Some parts of Nebraska elect a public defender, but large parts of the state do not.[92] A public defender is elected in each of Florida's twenty judicial circuits[93] (a judicial circuit can encompass several counties).

Surveyor and Engineer

There are other administrators central to county government who are not typically elected. Two examples are the coun-

---

88 Lenore T. Adkins, "What does a public defender do in the U.S.?" ShareAmerica, September 17, 2020.

89 Andrew Howard, "The Public's Defender," 63n.

90 "The exact reason San Francisco chose when it was first established in 1921 to elect its Public Defender, unlike every other county in the state, is unknown." Howard, "The Public's Defender," 21n.

91 Howard, "The Public's Defender," 67n.

92 Howard, "The Public's Defender," 67n.
Today, 38 of the current 93 counties in the state have elected Public Defenders, and those offices oversee all of the largest population areas. "Nebraska," Gideon at 50.

93 "Public Defender," State of Florida—Fourteenth Judicial Circuit.

ty surveyor and the county engineer. The surveyor maintains county land survey records, including property boundary lines. The county engineer is responsible for designing and constructing the county infrastructure (building projects within the county often including roads and bridges). Certain other county officers, such as highway commissioners, health directors, and welfare superintendents could serve as further examples of appointed public servants.[94]

GOVERNANCE STRUCTURE

Judicial Branch

As mentioned earlier, there are two tracks in the American judicial system that run mostly parallel to each other: the state and the federal. The state track deals with violations of the state constitution or state laws, and the federal track deals with violations of the U.S. Constitution or federal laws. Because county government is an arm of state government, the county judicial system primarily prosecutes violations of state law. Summarizing the county level of the judicial system is very difficult because each state's system, courts, and names of courts vary so greatly across the nation.[95] However, all the states follow the process outlined below.

- With the exception of muncipal courts (which were explained in the previous chapter), the first or beginning level of courts are trial courts. Note that there can be several different types of these

94 *Encyclopedia Britannica,* s.v. "County, United States."

95 For a brief overview of the nation's judicial processes, **USLegal.com** produces a "State-by-State Summary of Judicial Selection" on its website.

entry-level courts (criminal,[96] civil,[97] juvenile,[98] tax tribunal,[99] probate[100]).

- At the intermediate level, there are courts of appeal. In courts of appeal, a lower court's decision can be reviewed by a higher court. Appeals courts are the next resort when it appears possible that the trial court's decision was made in error.
- The court of last resort dealing with state-related laws is the state supreme court. Armed with that general overview of the state system, you should find the interactive State Court Structures chart at the Court Statistics Project website to be helpful. Go to **courtstatistics.org** and look for "State Court Structures." A second useful online resource is **Ballotpedia**'s "Judicial selection in the states."

STATE JUDICIAL SYSTEM

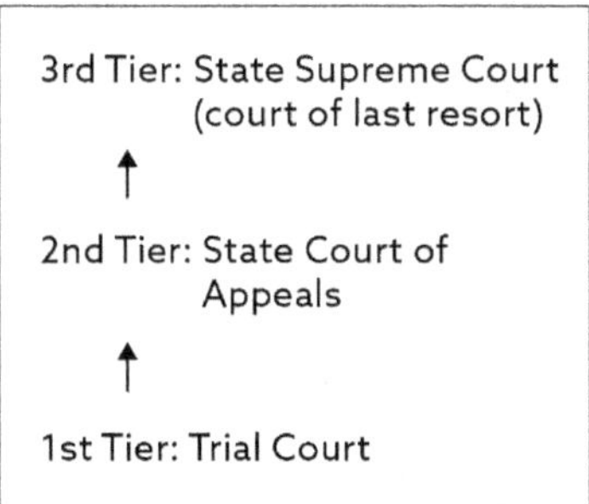

Figure 4.7

96 For violation of state law.

97 For alleged wrongdoing against another person or entity.

98 For violation of state law by minors.

99 For state tax violations.

100 For paying creditors of a deceased person and distributing assets to beneficiaries.

Recall that we discussed at the beginning of this chapter that the county code of laws (especially for rural counties) is primarily, but not wholly, land-use based. Breaking those laws would likely result in a fine rather than a prosecutable offense. Due to counties and codes of local government varying so much, there may be geographical areas that prosecute violations of county law more aggressively than others.

Courts hear cases depending on the type of law that was broken. Let's make a hypothetical situation personal. Say I receive a summons to court, and I am very confused as to the reason. You might give me the following accurate explanation:

> To determine what court you are going to be in, it largely depends on what law the government alleges that you have broken. If the government alleges you have broken a federal law you end up in federal court; if the government alleges you broke a state law you end up in district court; if the government alleges you broke a city law you will always begin in municipal court. Each of these courts has limited jurisdiction and can only hear certain cases. In some instances their jurisdiction overlaps and your case may be able to be heard in more than one court.[101]

Lastly, in terms of the ballot and within the judicial branch, there may also be individuals running for or seeking reselection[102] for the office of judge on the local ballot. Since judges are not row officers, it can be surprising to find them listed on an election ballot. And not all judges are elected; some are ap-

---

101 "What Is the Difference between Municipal Court, District Court, and Federal Court?" Roth Davies Trial Lawyers.

102 Yes, reselection. According to the Missouri Plan, it "works like this: citizens and lawyers, working as a team, serve on nominating commissions to select the best three candidates to fill an open judgeship. The governor then appoints one of those candidates to the position. Then, at the general election following their first 12 months on the bench and at the end of each term, each judge must stand before the voters in a retention election." "How the Missouri Plan Works," Your Missouri Judges.

pointed.[103] Note also that at the time of their installment, elected representatives of We the People at any level of government swear to uphold the U.S. Constitution as well as the state constitution and laws of the state in which they are elected.

OTHER THINGS YOU SHOULD KNOW

Now, I'd like to bring us back to Susan from the opening of this chapter.

Remember Susan's takeaway from her civic journey, "Good people have been too complicit for too long in allowing others to run our government." She is right, and she is the second elected county officeholder to have told me that. These two officeholders were not aware of one another or even in the same county, and yet their takeaways were the same. This is a warning call from those who have served and know from the inside.

Let me quickly tell you about the other gentleman who gave me the same message. At the beginning of my journey into civics, I attended a meeting at the local public library auditorium where residents could testify before the county area plan commission (the planning division that recommends changes in land-use laws for the legislators to consider). Afterward, a nice-looking older gentleman shook my hand and thanked me for speaking. I inquired who he was, and he responded, "I'm your county commissioner." Ouch. That was humbling. I realized I was standing at the foot of a vast learning-curve mountain. I had not been able to find a good civics curriculum up to that point, and now I was living in one.

Later that year, just before his elected term drew to a close, I scheduled a meeting with Mr. Commissioner in order to ask him to

---

103 "State-by-State Summary of Judicial Selection," USLegal.

review a presentation that I would give directly afterward to a continuing commissioner. I had never given an informational presentation to an elected officeholder before and was eager for Mr. Commissioner's feedback. However, the meeting did not unfold at all in the manner that I had imagined. He was taken aback when he saw my notebook of meeting records, newspaper articles, and scholarly studies. He said that we need more people like me in the county. People who care about what's going on. Specifically, and I remember his exact words, he said, "Good people don't run for office." He said that good people—as he called them—are too busy raising families, serving in their churches, and working at their professions. Those things take their time. That leaves the less-than-stellar people wide open to run our communities. It is a problem that he did not know how to solve. He talked about that issue during our scheduled meeting for almost an hour. In a sense, what he told me was more helpful than any feedback he could have given me about my presentation. I certainly have remembered it.

Since that time, I have not run for office. I have been too busy observing how our American system of governance works. I have realized that few people actually understand it, but lots of people like to talk as if they do. And I am not convinced that the place to start is sounding a clarion call for good people to run for office. Running for office is an obvious eventual destination, but too many people think that it is the first solution. I disagree. The first solution is to learn how our governing systems work by study and by observation. You are already reading this book and have probably already begun to familiarize yourself with your local government websites. Now, I would like to encourage you to begin observing local county meetings in person or watching them live-streamed or recorded. If you attend in person, you will glean much more of the larger situation at hand than what you would receive exclusively through the eyes of the camera. If anything noteworthy happens, mark it down and remember it for the next time. There's no telling what information you may come across in your observations. Noting the time (on the clock) makes it much easier to find that event when viewing a video recording of the meeting and makes it easier to share that information with others.

THINGS YOU CAN DO

Spend time getting to know your county's website and locate the following:

- your elected representatives (commissioners or councilors)
- the appointed board or commission members
- the planning and zoning boards ("power" boards where significant preliminary decisions are made then presented to the legislative body)
- some of the county staff
- when and where the public meetings take place
- the next meeting's agenda
- the last meeting's minutes
- the annual budget (analyze it line by line and year compared to year)
- the comprehensive and/or strategic plan
- the vision and/or mission statement
- the county code

Attend some of your county's live meetings.

In the last state where I lived, our county commissioner meetings occurred at set times. I attended them every first and third Monday morning of the month. Yes, Monday mornings. Of course, this was the same morning that the trash had to be put out at the end of our quarter-mile driveway, and I had to organize our homeschool for a new week. After the feat of simply getting there, I sat in the back of the meetings and took notes regarding the goings-on. Eventually, I knew who ran the county landfill, who the county engineer was, who the county clerk was, and so on. The courthouse became quite a familiar place to me.

In my new state of residence, I have been watching my city for years. Eventually, I decided to add county governance into the mix. However, this county's commissioners have meetings scheduled throughout the day every Monday and Wednesday, in addition to special meetings on other days—as well as evenings. It has taken me a while to decide how to jump into this county's processes.

I have come at it from around the edges: a special meeting here, another there. The meeting agendas are posted on the county website, and I signed up to receive email reminders when the specific agendas are posted. But the regular meetings posed a problem: I found that the day-long meetings alternate between open-session meetings and executive-session meetings. That translated to me having to sit on a bench outside the closed doors of the chamber until the executive session was over and someone with authority opened the chamber doors allowing readmittance.

I cleared a Monday morning (yes, Monday morning again) to observe this type of regular meeting routine. Our state legislators attended and gave presentations to the county commissioners during the first hour (remember, the county is the arm of the state—there is a close relationship between the two levels of government). At the conclusion, the legislators left and the meeting adjourned to an executive session (or closed meeting).[104]

Ousted to the bench in the hallway, I waited. Fifteen minutes later, the doors reopened, and a lady informed me, "You may

104 Described in the previous chapter.

come back in." So I resumed my seat along the back wall. One of the county commissioners, who obviously had not been paying attention, turned around, rather alarmed, and asked me, "Were you here for that?" He immediately fired another question, "What is your name?" My mere presence at the meeting made this county commissioner uncomfortable.

Accountability is not always comfortable but checks and balances are part of the American system. Observing our local government in action is one way for We the People to place a check on it. Once we realize that, as Christians, we have forgotten one of God's institutions—the realm of civil government, particularly at the local level—we will begin to see a plethora of ways to influence our government for good in the future. Engaging with your county government may not look like much today or tomorrow, but one day it will look like a whole lot. Our job is to be faithful today and trust God with the results. "Moreover it is required in stewards that one be found faithful" (1 Corinthians 4:2).

As when you observed city government, it will, again, take a bit of doing to ascertain which meeting(s) you should attend at the county-equivalent level of government. But it is well worth the time and effort. And if possible, follow Susan's lead and bring your children along.

Pray for your leaders' souls.

Scripture encourages several venues for prayer. Jesus tells us to pray in our closet with the door closed. As a church (corporate body of believers), we are to pray for our leaders. And we are encouraged to pray for one another as needs arise. All of these have their place. At home and at church, you can pray for the elected representatives of We the People by name who serve at the county level of government. This includes the row officers and the judges. Now you know who they are and what they do.

Even though we are not to parade our righteousness on the street corner, you may consider praying with individuals who enter and exit the county courthouse.

One day, I was standing outside the courthouse trying to decide how to best proceed on an issue when two gentlemen approached me, gave me their business card, and informed me that they were pastors. Part of their ministry was to stand on the courthouse greenspace and pray for people who approach and depart from the courthouse, realizing that these may be people who have great needs and who are potentially in serious legal or family trouble.

These pastors asked if they could pray for me and what they could pray for. They were rather astonished to hear that my request was for the county commissioners inside the building in whose hands very important decisions for the county rested. I asked these two pastors to pray for the commissioners' souls and consciences. Of course, we had an encouraging conversation because we were both engaged in a spiritual battle for the residents of our county. If you are a pastor or church leader, consider conducting a similar prayer ministry on the grounds of your county courthouse.

Introduce yourself.

As described in the previous chapter, when the time is right, introduce yourself to your elected representatives and staff. Remember to express congratulations for their recent election or appreciation for their work. Do not be false, but whether you are addressing a political friend or foe, find a kind word to speak.

Look for county events in the newspaper.

Don't discount the value of the newspaper. As I mentioned earlier, it was through the newspaper that I first entered the civil realm. It was through the newspaper that I knew where there would be a Veteran's Day gathering that honored those who have served our nation from our county. And it was through the newspaper that I knew to attend a service honoring our local sheriff who received an award bestowed upon him by our district's U.S. senator.[105]

Consider touring some of your county's public works facilities.

Schedule a visit to your county's landfill. See what goes on there. Often, common hearsay doesn't describe the true picture. Or schedule a visit to other departments within a county equivalent such as the road/highway department (for the building of new roads and bridges or for grading/maintaining roads or for snow plowing) or the new building permitting or inspecting departments.

Invest in your leaders.

Above, I described meeting with Mr. Commissioner in preparation to meet with other commissioners regarding a decisive issue facing our county. Elected representatives are not sup-

105 "Crapo Honors Latah County Sheriff With Spirit of Idaho Award," Mike Crapo U.S. Senator for Idaho, September 5, 2019.

posed to meet together in groups to discuss public business outside of public meetings (according to state law—which could vary by state). That principle dictates that if you intend to discuss or apprise them of an issue, you will need to meet with them individually or possibly in groups smaller than a quorum. (A quorum is the minimum number of members of an assembly that must be present to make a meeting valid.) Of course, this takes time, but it can be worth the investment.

Often citizens are not aware of issues regarding the county, or they gripe to their leaders via email. Presenting a third alternative of appreciation coupled with objective data-driven guidance can be a breath of fresh air to elected leaders. They are much more accustomed to apathy or its opposite—vitriolic venting. Follow up your meeting by sending a handwritten thank you note or possibly an email with attachments of any documents that you might have promised to send. You are investing in your elected officials, and the tougher the issues at hand, the harder you work to invest. Hopefully, though, your introductory investments can be gentle. And of course, trust God to richly bless your endeavors.

Serve as a volunteer member of a county commission or as a poll worker.

County-equivalent governments can have all manner of appointed committees, boards, advisory councils, and commissions, including volunteer election poll workers. Just like at the city level of local government, these groups are a great place to begin serving and understanding how principles of governance operate. You don't have to agree with or condone all of the aspects of an appointed group in order to gain experience in local government. Those who understand processes are in a better position to bring about reform.

SO WHAT?

After having read this chapter, here are some questions to ask yourself:

- Do you understand that some states have county equivalents (which are similar to counties yet called by different names) and that two states don't have counties at all?
- Do you understand that county equivalents are extensions of the state in which they are located?
- Do you understand that cities dwell within county-equivalent borders?
- Do you understand that despite some local variation, typically one city serves as the county seat?
- If you walk through your county courthouse or one of your county-equivalent buildings, is there a directory sign listing the various departments? Are the department names beginning to be more understandable?
- Similarly, do you now recognize any of the department signs located by various office doors?
- Does it make sense that there might be two sets of executives in the county system: part one who serves along with the legislative branch and part two who are the constitutional or row officers?
- Do you understand that the planning and zoning commissions make crucial preliminary decisions that are presented to the legislative branch?
- Do you see that Christians have a vast opportunity to influence county government which, in turn, influences the lives of others living in the county?

GOVERNANCE STRUCTURE IN THE UNITED STATES

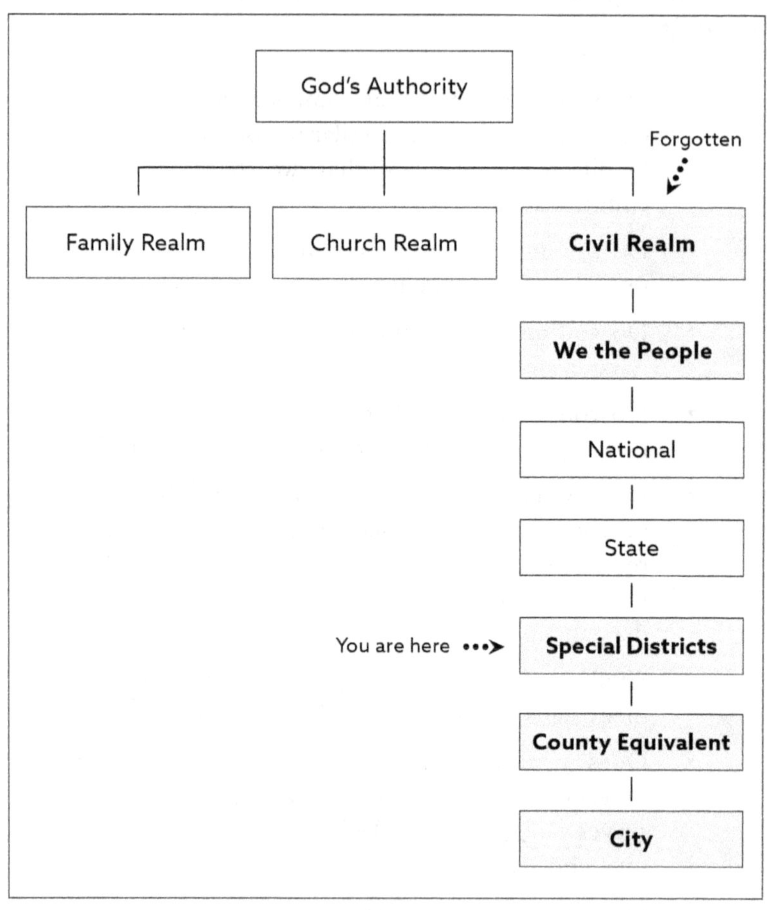

Figure 5.1

CHAPTER 5

Special Districts, Independent Cities, Townships & Regional Governments

My grandfather was a township trustee and had first run for the position long before I was alive. As my uncle recounts, when the other potential candidates found out Grandpa was running, no one would run against him. They would have been wasting their time because he was seen in the community as being extremely fair, extremely honest, and extremely smart. He had also served for many years as a school board member.

The township trustee position that Grandpa held still consists of a three-member board elected in odd-numbered years, with each member serving a four-year term. That board of three trustees is actually the government for that township operating under its state statutes. The trustees approve an annual budget and operate within it. They are responsible for the roads, the zoning, the cemeteries, waste disposal, fire protection, and police protection—in conjunction with the county sheriff.

Grandpa passed away long ago, but recently my uncle wanted to make a change to the family property which required a visit to the county courthouse. When the man at the courthouse found out about his relationship to my grandfather, my uncle suddenly became a guest of honor there. The courthouse gentleman said the zoning laws Grandpa and the other two trustees wrote from scratch were outstanding. He said Grandpa was as smart and as fair as anyone could be. Those three men then became known as the first zoning board after they wrote the framework for the county's land use. Due to Grandpa's legacy, my uncle exclaimed, "That guy at the courthouse was incredibly kind to me."

This is a story with roots going back decades. It shows the importance of investing in one's place—one's locale. But what about those of us who are called to uproot and move to a new locale? One where our roots don't go way back. What then?

Fast forward from decades ago to today and meet Cody—a homeschool dad. He and his wife have four children. Because of his homeschooling experience, Cody was encouraged by local legislators to run for a seat on the public school board in Connecticut. He campaigned, was elected, and served as a board member. Later, Cody and his family were called to move to a new state in the West. Again, Cody decided to run for the local public school board in his new hometown. This time people asked, "Why would a homeschool dad run for school board?" Cody's answer shows an understanding not only of the civil realm but of the nature of We the People: "Homeschool-educated children and public-school-educated children will have to work together in the same community both today on the playground and tomorrow in the marketplace. I want them to live peaceable lives. I want them both to know real American history, not revisionist American history, because they are all Americans."[1]

Special districts, townships, and regional governments cover some middle ground between the county and the state. Whether you have deep roots in your locality, or you are recently transplanted to a new part of the nation, how you approach local

1 Thanks to Cody Barr for this contribution.

governance is up to you. Consider this chapter to be another personal invitation to become informed and get involved.

Local government is the quintessential patchwork quilt of American independence. Full of variety and exceptions across the country, not all local government falls into the tidy categories of city or county-equivalent levels. Therefore, this chapter will serve as a catch-all for parts of government that typically remain almost invisible and inexplicable to the average American citizen. So numerous are the variations that even within this catch-all, I am aware that I will not catch it all—there will be examples that escape my notice. Thus, the drumbeat of looking up your own local government websites continues to sound in this book.

SPECIAL DISTRICTS

Not Judicial Nor Legislative Districts

The term *district* appears all over the place in governance. In order for a people to govern, they need to be grouped into various geographical categories. Often these groupings are referred to as districts. There are districts for the legislative and judicial branches of government at both the state and federal levels. You might live in Legislative District Six or the Ninth Federal Judicial District. You also live in the jurisdiction of one or more special districts, but they are usually unnumbered districts both in terms of how we refer to them and how they are listed on the election ballot.

Single-Theme Local Governments

Special districts (sometimes called taxing districts,[2] ad hoc districts,[3] community improvement districts,[4] or special services areas) are local governments formed by communities in order to provide some public service within defined boundaries.[5] These are single-theme[6] local governments that most of us know very little about. **They are formed in order to provide services that the city or county does not provide.** However, their boundaries are very specific and may cross over city and county lines which can add to their effectiveness and/or almost certainly to their complexity.

As governing entities of We the People, special districts have the power to do such things as enter contracts, hold property, hire employees, issue debt, levy taxes, charge fees, and sue or be sued. They do so as unincorporated governments called quasi-corporations typically without possessing police powers.[7] Here, the term *quasi-corporation* means an unincorporated entity enabled by state law, with no legal status apart from the single service it is designed to provide while possessing the ability to act independently of the state.[8] Such districts serve the needs of local regions and commonly perform isolated duties such as maintaining roads or cemeteries.

Because they are taxing districts, perhaps the best way to tell what districts your residence/address belongs to is by

---

2 Byron S. Matthews, *Local Government: How to Get Into It, How to Administer It Effectively* (Chicago, IL: Nelson-Hall, 1970), 15.

3 Matthews, *Local Government*, 15.

4 Kelly Phillips Erb, "Disney Sues Florida Gov. Ron DeSantis Over Control Of Special District, Alleging Retaliation," Forbes, April 26, 2023.

5 "Cal. Gov. Code § 82048.5," Casetext.

6 Very rarely, special districts may feature more than one service.

7 California Senate Local Government Committee, *What's So Special about Special Districts?*, 2.

8 Dylan G. Rassier et al., "Quasi-Corporations and Institutional Sectors in the U.S. National Accounts," Bureau of Economic Analysis and United States Department of Commerce, July 2016, p. 2.

looking at your local annual property tax statement. If you rent your residence, rather than own it, you will not receive a property tax bill. In that case, ask your county treasurer's office for a list of the local taxing districts that affect the address where you live. On that statement, you should find a brief list of local special districts that provide services that are funded by your tax dollars. There may also be a list available through your local election office or your state controller's office. The list that you locate could contain any district, such as the following in the column on the right[9] (the left column lists all types of governing districts).

ALL DISTRICTS

City (Council) District No. __
(optional-varies by city)

County (Commissioner) District No. __
(optional-varies by county)

Special Districts
(usually unnumbered)

State Legislative District No. __
(slight changes after census redistricting)

State Judicial District No. __

US Congressional District No. __
(slight changes after census redistricting)

US Judicial District No.__

SPECIAL DISTRICTS

Abatement
Airport
Ambulance
Aquifer Recharge
Auditorium
Business Improvement
Capital Crimes Defense Program
Cemetery
Drainage
Economic Development
Fair Board
Fire Protection
Flood Control
Grazing District
Ground Water
Highway
Hospital
Infrastructure
Irrigation
Intermodal Commerce Authority
Junior (or Community) College
Levy
Library
LID (local improvement district)
Port
Recreation
Recreational Water and Sewer
Road
School District
Soil Conservation
TV Translator
Urban Renewal
Water
Water Conservation
Watershed
Water and Sewer
Weather Modification

Figure 5.2

9 As defined for Census Bureau statistics on governments, the term *special district governments* excludes school district governments. They are defined as a separate governmental type because some public schools are administered by systems that are agencies of the county, city, or state government. However, for the purposes of this introductory book, school districts are included as special districts. U.S. Census Bureau, *Individual State Descriptions: 2022 Census of Governments,* April 30, 2024), 5.

Each special district provides a specific service to the community within its jurisdiction and is governed by a board that is either elected by We the People or appointed by a state, county, municipality, or township that comprises the special district. A well-known example of a special district that could have elected members is the local school district board (though some sources do not consider school districts to be true examples of special districts because they receive state funding).[10] The school district board then appoints a superintendent to oversee the school system.[11] School districts are usually under the authority of the state board of public education in addition to state laws (and public education is even established in the state constitution), whereas typical special districts do not have an authority-enforcement structure over them. So, school boards are a special kind of special district.[12]

As mentioned above, special districts rely upon tax revenue (usually property tax, rarely sales tax), service charges, grants, or borrowed money to carry out their services. As quasi-corporations, they have the authority (via a vote of the people) to impose and levy these fees or to receive these grants.[13] Because of this legal status, special districts are considered financially independent of other multi-purpose local govern-

---

10 California Senate Local Government Committee, *What's So Special about Special Districts?*, 5. See also Duncombe and Weisel, *State and Local Government in Idaho and in the Nation*, 144.

11 Nick Ragone, *The Everything American Government Book*, 253.

12 School boards direct how schools are run. In recent history, people involved in private education often took no interest in the local public schools. Large segments of the population (homeschoolers and private schoolers) have ignored what goes on in the local public schools thinking that it has no bearing on our lives. The problem with this approach is that the public school is churning out individuals who profoundly affect the community we live in and are using our tax dollars to do it. If we don't like identity politics changing our local society, then we should take an interest in who is on our school boards and who is teaching our community's children. Whether we want to ignore it or not, these people have huge influence on the civil realm. Further, influence on the school boards can have a salvific effect on the next generation's souls.

13 Sometimes when special districts levy fees targeted toward those who use their service, they are known as enterprise districts. California Senate Local Government Committee, *What's So Special about Special Districts?*, 6.

ments. Within this status of financial independence, there are two types of special districts: dependent and independent. Dependent districts rely upon another existing local government to govern them (such as the local board of county commissioners).[14] In this sense, the county commissioners would also serve as *ex-officio* members of the specific special district board. Independent districts have board members who are typically elected by We the People but can also include board members who are appointed by another local government's representative to serve for fixed terms.[15]

Legislative and Executive Functions of Special Districts

The boards of these single-purpose local government entities fulfill the legislative function by creating policy and establishing regulations in order to administer the special local service that the district provides.[16] The executive function is also carried out by these single-purpose local government boards as they oversee the delivery of the special service.[17] It is worth noting a similarity here between special districts at the local level and administrative agencies at the state and federal levels (mentioned in that cornerstone chapter, "Layers of Law"). The boards of dependent (or independent but term-appointed) special districts are not directly accountable to the electorate (the voters). As such, special districts are susceptible to corruption[18] because they do not have as many inherent checks and balances.

---

14 Simon, Steel, and Lovrich, *State and Local Government and Politics: Prospects for Sustainability*, sec. 6.E.I.

15 Simon, Steel, and Lovrich, *State and Local Government and Politics*, sec. 6.E.I.

16 Simon, Steel, and Lovrich, *State and Local Government and Politics*, sec. 7.H.

17 Simon, Steel, and Lovrich, *State and Local Government and Politics*, sec. 7.H.

18 Jeremy L. Hall and Michael W. Hail, "Special Districts," Center for the Study of Federalism Encyclopedia, last updated 2006.

Furthermore, special districts remain largely invisible to most of us who partake of the services that they provide. Because I was never taught the inverted model of civics, I never discovered the topic of local government, which means that I did not comprehend the existence of special districts. Years ago, my first indication that such an entity existed was when I stopped at a soil and water conservation information booth at my local county fair. Shortly afterward, I noticed that the soil and water conservation district maintained its own office building in a rural area of my county. It had all the appearance of a government office but was not located with the other county offices. Hmmm.

Perhaps you observed the following scenario in your own town or city. After COVID-19 hit our nation, my local public library remained closed longer than other city and county offices. Under the guiding directive known as following the money trail, I began to look into its funding source. I realized that it, too, is a special district and creates its own policies—which also makes sense because libraries operate under a largely autonomous, almost invisible board. Some of us may only be familiar with the library director, who may occasionally make the news, but most of us do not know that it is the library board that not only appoints the director of the library but annually reviews that person's job performance in order to maintain a standard of accountability. As with city and county-equivalent government, it is important to identify the chain of authority. Those who are elected by We the People are directly accountable to We the People. Those who serve in appointed positions do so at the request of those who have been elected and are directly accountable to them, not to We the People.

For those of us recently discovering the forgotten realm, the invisibility of special districts can smack of clandestine cloaked power at worst or unaccountable power at best. Take heart and look on the bright side. Now you know about special districts, and because they are forms of local government, they provide an excellent means of directly observing and participating in the governance of the areas closest to your home. And there is no lack of them. As of 2021, there were 38,542 special district local governments in the United States.[19]

The following quote describes the type of individuals who are adept at running special districts and serves as a motivation to the rest of us to consider engaging at this level as Cody did:

> The people active in the establishment, management, and operation of special districts are frequent participants in contemporary local meetings relating to sustainability. These people have demonstrated particular skill at local-level adaptation to change in the past, and they will likely be among the leading voices heard regarding policies needed to address the challenges of global climate change and related problems facing our state and local governments in the years ahead.[20]

There should be room at the special districts tables across the nation for individuals who represent a variety of viewpoints that may challenge prevailing opinions (such as global climate change). The beginning step is realizing that special districts exist. A subsequent step is visiting a special district meeting and even visiting it regularly in order to be a better-informed citizen. This step could and should be followed by individuals campaigning for seats on special district boards or seeking appointments to them.

---

19 America Counts, "From Municipalities to Special Districts, Official Count of Every Type of Local Government in 2017 Census of Governments," U.S. Census Bureau, October 29, 2019.

20 Simon, Steel, and Lovrich, *State and Local Government and Politics*, sec. 7.H.

INDEPENDENT CITIES

Independent cities were briefly mentioned in chapter 3, "City Government." However, because this chapter features several concepts that do not fit neatly into the city, county, and state progression, it is worth briefly revisiting independent cities here. There are forty-one independent cities in the nation. Thirty-eight are in Virginia, and the other three are Baltimore, Maryland; St. Louis, Missouri; and Carson City, Nevada.[21] The United States Census Bureau classifies them as county equivalents for the purpose of statistical conversion.[22] Their governing powers are similar to that of the consolidated city-county system of government that we learned about in the previous chapter. However, the independent city exists as its name implies—it is either independent of (legally separated from) a county, or it replaces a county that altogether ceased to exist.[23] Most independent cities are in Virginia (thirty-eight are in that state as described in the Virginia Constitution).[24] In Virginia, there is a tug-of-war between counties, cities, and towns. One solution to this financial tension is the independent city.[25]

---

21 Wikipedia, s.v. " Independent city (United States)."

Baltimore City: "As a governmental unit, the City separated from Baltimore County in 1851, and has been considered on a par with county jurisdictions since the adoption of the Maryland Constitution of 1851." Maryland State Archives, "Baltimore City, Maryland," Maryland Manual On-Line: A Guide to Maryland and Its Government, April 19, 2024.

Saint Louis: "St. Louis's current boundaries were established in 1876, when voters approved separation from St Louis County and establishment of a home rule charter. St. Louis was the nation's first home rule city, but unlike most, it was separated from any county." STLOUIS-MO.GOV, "A Brief History of Saint Louis," City of St. Louis.

Carson City: "In 1969, the county was abolished, and its territory was merged with Carson City to form the Consolidated Municipality of Carson City." "City Facts," Carson City, Nevada.

22 "Terms and Definitions," U.S. Census Bureau.

23 Older, more complete definition here: U.S. Department of Commerce, Economics and Statistics Administration, and Bureau of the Census, "Places," chap. 9 in *Geographic Areas Reference Manual*, November 1994. Newer, less complete definition here: "Independent City Definition," U.S. Census Bureau.

24 Virg. Const. art VII, §1.

25 "Virginia Cities That Have 'Disappeared'—and Why," Virginia Places.

TOWNSHIPS

I am placing townships in this chapter rather than in the county-equivalent chapter because they represent so much variety across the nation.[26] The U.S. Census Bureau considers towns and townships to be minor civil divisions of the county (MCDs), and there are two types of townships: survey townships and civil townships.[27] A survey township is ideally a six-mile by six-mile square plot of land[28] and is referred to by a number based on the Public Land Survey System (PLSS).[29] A civil township is based on the survey township and serves not as a geographic unit but as a political subdivision of a county. It "is a type of local government that is in a gray area between counties and municipalities."[30] Twenty states have counties which are subdivided into civil townships.[31] Their state laws each outline the responsibilities and the specific form of the township government.

In most states of the Northeast and Midwest, a township is defined as a rural subdivision of a county having the status of a unit of local government with varying governmental powers. Township government is defined somewhat differently by the different states which possess it.[32] In New England states, where counties either do not exist or serve minimal functions (such as performing judicial activities and

26 "Terms and Definitions," U.S. Census Bureau.

27 "Public Land Survey System (PLSS)," Thomson Reuters Practical Law.

28 "But natural and man-made boundaries (e.g., rivers and county lines), as well as annexation, and sparse population densities have caused some variation. In most states town and township governments generally have jurisdiction over a distinct geographic area, outside of cities and villages." "Town and Township Government in the United States," National Association of Towns and Townships.

29 "Public Land Survey System (PLSS)," Thomson Reuters Practical Law.

30 Austin Fernald, "The Difference Between a Town and a City; Plus Counties, Villages and More," *ZoningPoint* (blog).

31 Ballotpedia, s.v. "Township."

32 Ballotpedia, s.v. "Township."

providing jail services), townships are intertwined with towns and town government (which was treated in chapter 3, "City Government"). While mentioning towns and townships together, it is interesting to note that "the volunteer fire department is part of the living heritage of towns and townships."[33] The first one—the Union Fire Company in Philadelphia, Pennsylvania—was founded by Benjamin Franklin in 1736. Soon after its inception, more and more volunteer fire companies eventually spread across the country and still exist today.[34]

As the town/township model of local government moved west, it became more of a sub-parcel of the county rather than a geographic entity surrounding the town. The following states outside of New England engage in township government: Indiana, Kansas, Michigan, Missouri, Minnesota, New Jersey, North Dakota, Ohio, Pennsylvania, South Dakota, Wisconsin, and sometimes Illinois and Nebraska.[35] As such, they may share responsibilities with the county.[36] In recent years, providing municipal services such as water service, wastewater treatment, police protection, and zoning/building code enforcement has become the domain of some townships in the Midwest. This sort of service expansion occurs in states whose legislatures give townships flexible powers usually due to an increase in local population.[37] Funding for towns and townships primarily comes through property taxes but can also include state revenue, user/administrative fees, or special-assessment taxes. (A special-assessment is a tax levied on citizens to cover a specific project, usually infrastructure in

---

33 "Town and Township Government in the United States," National Association of Towns and Townships.

34 "Fire and Rescue History," City of Franklin, Virginia.

35 Ballotpedia, s.v. "Township."

36 "Townships in the U.S.," Michigan Townships Association.

37 "Townships in the U.S.," Michigan Townships Association.

nature such as roads or sewer lines.)[38] Lastly, as an example of linking the concept of townships to special districts, "some township volunteer fire departments have recently begun to combine personnel, equipment and property tax revenue to become official special district governments."[39]

REGIONAL GOVERNMENTS

Regional governments or councils extend beyond city boundaries but differ from county government. We have already covered the first two types of regional government in the previous chapter on the county because they fit closely within the context of a county equivalent. The first was the consolidated city-county model of government. The second was regional councils (also known as councils of governments, regional commissions, or planning regions). Recall that Connecticut has nine planning regions which serve as county equivalents. Within each region (much like a county), municipalities have formed together into a Regional Council of Governments.[40] Together, the municipalities can address common needs and interests in accordance with state plans/programs such as transportation or community development projects.

However, regional governments or regional councils can also extend across state lines to deliver projects and programs "such as Metropolitan Planning Organizations, Area Agencies on Aging, Economic Development Districts, 911 operators, and more."[41] An example is the Ohio-Kentucky-Indiana Regional Council of Governments (known as OKI) which in-

38 "Town and Township Government in the United States," National Association of Towns and Townships.

39 America Counts, "From Municipalities to Special Districts."

40 "Regional Councils of Governments," Office of the Secretary of State.

41 "What are Regional Councils?," National Association of Regional Councils (NARC).

cludes three states, eight counties, and many municipalities, business organizations, and community groups in the Cincinnati, Ohio area.[42] One of its projects is the evaluation of the multi-modal freight delivery systems in the region (goods delivered by such means as truck, rail, river, air, and so on).[43]

Regional governments are a complicated governance endeavor. They are not necessarily recommended as simple/local points of entry into the forgotten realm of civil government. However, for the purposes of this book, it is good to know that regional government endeavors exist and are complex.

Shared-Planning Resources

Many small communities contract with larger cities or counties to provide services they otherwise may be unable to afford, such as police or fire protection, solid waste management, water treatment, etc. "This type of arrangement is considered a regional government because it involves the shared planning of resources."[44]

Single-Purpose Entities

As the name implies, single-purpose entities are, in essence, special districts that can cross state lines. They address regional needs in a more particular manner than a governing entity with broader powers might be able to do. A well-known example of a single-purpose entity is the Port Authority of New York and New Jersey. Created in 1921 to settle bi-state harbor boundary disputes, its mission is to "meet the critical trans-

42 "What are Regional Councils?," NARC.

43 "Request for Qualifications Consultant Services for OKI Freight Plan," Ohio-Kentucky-Indiana Regional Council of Governments, 2022.

44 Ragone, *The Everything American Government Book*, 255.

portation infrastructure needs of the bi-state region's people, businesses, and visitors by providing the highest quality and most efficient transportation and port commerce facilities and the services to move people and goods within the region, provide access to the nation and the world, and promote the region's economic development."[45]

OTHER THINGS YOU SHOULD KNOW

Regarding special districts—there is always a financial cost to the citizen for the special district services. And it is not optional.

Regarding township governments in the Northeast and Midwest, these are typically small and approachable entry points into local government. There may be a township government that convenes very near your home.

THINGS YOU CAN DO

Find out what special districts are on your tax statement. For the districts that charge fees rather than collect taxes, if you are unable to locate them, ask your county election office or your state controller or your state legislators for assistance. They are elected to serve the people. Or you can see the document listed below.[46]

What are the special districts in your area? When do they meet? Are the board members elected or appointed? Find when and where each district meets and make it a project to go and visit each one. Another option may be to watch a live stream or recording of the meetings. Either way, watch for

45 "Port Authority of New York & New Jersey Mission Statement," Port Authority NY NJ, 2022.

46 U.S. Census Bureau, *Individual State Descriptions: 2022 Census of Governments*, (Washington, DC: U.S. Government Printing Office, 2019).

what engaged men and women sound like on boards. Are each of the members in attendance? Does each member appear to understand his or her duties? For example, if the district charges fees instead of collecting funds by taxation, do the board members understand what the fees are for?[47] This is yet another level of government where we can begin to scrutinize spending by looking at the budgets.

Note that in many districts, school bond measures can be voted on by renters as well as property owners. Because renters do not pay property taxes directly or even see a property tax statement, renters are more likely to vote for property tax hikes. That could be a potential point for voter education.

SO WHAT?

If special districts are unknown to most of us American Christians, that means we not only have much to learn, but we are not running these local governments. Thus, principles that are important to a significant part of the populace may not be upheld or honored.

Once, I had a conversation with a colleague who asked me if I thought that reforming public libraries was a hopeless endeavor. He wondered if there are state laws preventing libraries from circulating Christian books and materials. Absolutely not, was my reply. That would be against the First Amendment to the Constitution, and state law cannot supersede the Constitution. Further, there is great hope for public libraries, because their boards should be avail-

47 I watched a recording of the public health district for my region, and a board member did not understand a fee on the budget nor did it appear that he had invested any time in advance to understand the budget details. Public health districts played a significant role weighing in on local COVID-19 definitions and recommendations.

able for the public to sit on—either by election (on the local ballot) or by appointment.[48] *It is the board that directs the library, appoints its director, and holds that person accountable. This piece of information is something that many of us did not know. And so it goes with multiple other special districts across our locales.*

Sometimes special district elections do not even make the ballot because the races are uncontested (meaning that there is no opposing candidate to face the only individual who declared their candidacy for the office). If one individual, or in some cases a single political party, has held a monopoly on the elected special district seats in your area, it can be difficult to mobilize voters to actually vote or to see the need to vote. This topic will be addressed in chapter 8 regarding elections.

48 Here is an article giving further explanation: Tirzah Price, "Why You Should Sit on Your Library Board," October 5, 2021.

GOVERNANCE STRUCTURE IN THE UNITED STATES

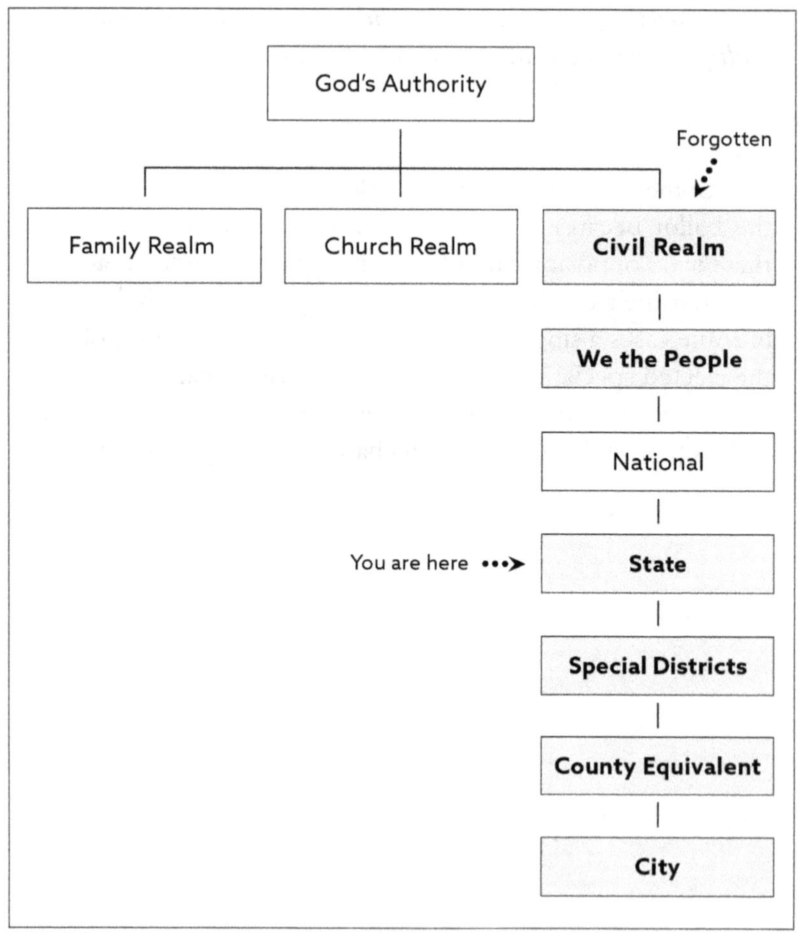

Figure 6.1

CHAPTER 6
State Government

For the last few years, Jeff has spent each day of the legislative session bringing pastors to his state capitol to minister individually to elected officeholders (regardless of their political affiliations or position). These meetings always include reading a passage of Scripture that either applies to each of them as a person or to the elected position, and the meetings conclude with an offer to pray with them. Several surprises have gripped Jeff as relationships between church leaders and legislators have developed.

First, pastors are shocked at how accessible and interested elected officeholders are in meeting with them, especially when they discover that Jeff is not lobbying them for anything. Second, the most successful meetings are generally with those legislators Jeff least expected, rebuking our temptation to treat people like political lepers. Third, sowing the Word into the lives and vocations of those elected to public office has not only taken root but is affecting policy decisions, political ideologies, and conduct among one another. Lastly, the relationships founded in Word and prayer are creating opportunities where churches and ministries can partner together with officeholders to tackle problems that are too much for the state to handle on its own—areas where God's institutions of church and state have a shared obligation.[1]

1 Pastor Jeff Evans, Director of Church Ambassador Network an Initiative of Minnesota Family Council & Institute. 🔗 I learned from Jeff that Philippians 1:27 (ESV)

LAW/FORMATION

Reserved Powers

In terms of the inverted model, we have reached the first level in this book which is not considered local government. When thinking about state government, consider that all fifty states must function in accordance with the U.S. Constitution. Article IV of the Constitution refers to the states directly, describing both their relationships with each other as well as each state's relationship to the federal government. Later in the document, the Tenth Amendment reserves powers for the states to exercise their regional differences (federalism). This reserved powers clause is so crucial to the American way of life that I will quote it directly here: "The powers not delegated to the United States by the Constitution, nor prohibited by it to the States, are reserved to the States respectively, or to the people." Because of this clause, the states have a wide scope of authority reserved for them (which is why states can do things like levy taxes) as long as they do not violate the U.S. Constitution (which is why states cannot coin their own money).

Prohibited Powers

So states cannot coin their own money. What else does the Constitution forbid states from doing? What are their prohibited powers? The list below is a summary taken directly from Article I, Section 10 of the U.S. Constitution. States may not do the following:

- Enter into treaties, alliances, or confederations

---

which reads "only let your manner of life be worthy of the gospel of Christ" actually means "only behave as citizens worthy of the gospel of Christ." See **biblegateway.com**.

- Grant letters of marque and reprisal[2]
- Coin money
- Emit bills of credit
- Make anything but gold and silver coin a tender in payment of debts
- Pass any bill of attainder[3] or *ex post facto* laws[4]
- Pass any law impairing the obligation of contract
- Grant any title of nobility

States may engage in the following activities **only** with the consent of Congress:

- Lay any duties[5] on imports/exports except what may be absolutely necessary for executing[6]
- Lay any duty of tonnage[7]
- Keep[8] troops or ships of war in time of peace
- Enter into any agreement or compact with another state
- Enter into any agreement or compact with a foreign power
- Engage in war only when actually invaded or in such imminent danger as will not admit of delay

---

2 "A letter of marque is permission to cross over the frontier into another country's territory in order to take a ship; a letter of reprisal authorizes taking the captured vessel to the home port of the capturer." Law Library—American Law and Legal Information, s.v. "Marque and Reprisal," 2023.

3 A bill of attainder is a punishment without proper legal proceedings.

4 An *ex post facto* law is passed after an action (which was legal at the time it occurred) takes place and then declares it illegal.

5 Duties are fees or taxes.

6 If there are any such that are absolutely necessary, the proceeds go to the federal treasury.

7 Duty of tonnage is fees charged for a ship to enter port based on its cargo capacity.

8 Keep as in *lodge*, *house*, *store*, or *dock*.

Another theme in American government is the separation of powers. Law is created or amended (updated/changed) in the legislative branch. At the state level, these are known as legislatures, and they act as mini-congresses. Law is executed or carried out in the executive branch—by the governor and a host of other elected officeholders like him, whom we will learn about in this chapter. Law is applied to real situations in the judicial branch—by the state supreme court and lesser state courts. Thus, the governance of our states mirrors the trifold separation outlined in the U.S. Constitution.

State government has jurisdiction over city- and county-level government, as well. We looked at city law in chapter 3 which deals with matters of local governance (such as parks, water usage, and waste issues). Also included would be any topics that We the People decide to address that are not otherwise prohibited by the U.S. Constitution or our state constitution.

In chapter 4, we learned that the county equivalents are political subdivisions of the state and carry out state business within their distinct boundaries, thus reaching people closer to their homes (which may be quite a long distance from the state capitol). In the county-equivalent chapter, we surveyed county law which often deals with its own land-use issues. Now we move to look at the laws that govern the state as a whole—laws that pertain to all state citizens—and that include topics such as homeschooling requirements or abortion regulation.

The states have rights that are recognized and protected in the U.S. Constitution (that's federalism, again). We will look at how the organization of state government mirrors the organization of national government, beginning with the state constitution, written statutory law, and administrative-agency law. Then, we will consider how the law is created with checks and balances in the executive and legislative branches and how it is interpreted in the state judicial branch.

State Constitutions

Our American system is founded upon what is written. A written contract has been essential to our nation since its earliest beginnings. For example, the Pilgrims would not disembark the *Mayflower* before drafting and signing the Mayflower Compact.[9] Our highest written American contract is the United States Constitution, which sets forth our federal government's form and function, and (as we have repeatedly noted) each state has its own constitution.[10] Just as the U.S. Constitution outlines the scope of the federal government, so state constitutions outline the scope of state government. These documents are crucial to the legal rights of each state and should be considered very seriously by the citizens who reside in the state. Although the state constitutions differ in length and detail (with no two state's documents being identical),[11] they follow the blueprint of the U.S. Constitution and possess common factors that will aid us in better understanding the

9 It was drafted and signed aboard the *Mayflower* on November 11, 1620.

10 Jesse M. Sumpter in his book, *A Short Introduction to Abraham Kuyper's Lectures on Calvinism* (Moscow, ID: Francis Drake Press, 2020), 27–28, notes an interesting conclusion based on prior works by Richard Hooker and C. S. Lewis as presented in Michael Ward's *Planet Narnia.* They describe our universe as a constitutional monarchy: "The constitution of our universe is Scripture, especially the law of God which he gave his people at Sinai." I refer to the law of God in chapter 2 as God's Universal Law. Thus, "a constitution, like the U.S. Constitution, is an important feature of a government system. A constitution is not just a necessity brought about by sin but it is actually a design supported by God's Word."

11 "State constitutions are also important to examine because they often mirror important political, economic and social changes occurring over time. As states have moved from reflecting rural economies characterized principally by natural resource extraction in the seventeenth and eighteenth centuries (mining, timber, fisheries and agriculture), to governing urbanizing industrial economies in the nineteenth and twentieth centuries (manufacturing), to providing guidance to post-industrial and knowledge-based economies in the late twentieth and early twenty-first centuries, citizens and their political representatives have made many revisions to their respective state constitutions—and even replaced them in their entirety when deemed necessary on rare occasion." Christopher A. Simon, Brent S. Steel, and Nicholas P. Lovrich, *State and Local Government and Politics: Prospects for Sustainability*, sec. 5.A.

structure of state government and their purpose.[12] And we cannot forget that the state constitutions actually served as the prototype for the U.S. Constitution.

In the same manner that the U.S. Constitution begins with the famous preamble, "We the People of the United States, in Order to form a more perfect Union," each state constitution also opens with a preamble. The preambulatory wording sets forth the document's purpose—the power to govern comes from the people, not from an elite ruling class nor a king nor a dictator.[13] That is why it is vital that We the People be well-educated citizens regarding the structure and operation of our government. That is why we can't merely affiliate with a political group and hope for the best. Standing in marked contrast to that attitude is the hard work of actually understanding the authority structure and operational structure of our systems of governance.

As mentioned above, each state constitution possesses a preamble explaining the document's purpose. Then, each constitution has a bill of rights or similar provision that outlines the state residents' fundamental freedoms, many of which are broader than those in the U.S. Constitution.[14] As described above, all state constitutions set forth the division of power among the executive, legislative, and judicial branches.[15] And just as our supreme law of the land reserves powers for the states in the Tenth Amendment, state constitutions make pro-

---

12 Another resource on state constitutions is G. Alan Tarr, *Understanding State Constitutions* (Princeton, NJ: Princeton University Press, 1998).

13 Sumpter, *A Short Introduction*, 27.

"I am not suggesting that this constitution is over God as a human constitution would be over a human king. Instead, we must understand that the law originates in God. This means that the law of God is not arbitrary rules, but that God's nature and the expression of his nature that we have in his Word are fixed and consistent. This does not mean that God is controlled by something outside of himself but rather that his nature is unchanging and eternal."

14 Herbert Sydney Duncombe and Robert Weisel, *State and Local Government in Idaho and in the Nation*, 22.

15 Duncombe and Weisel, *State and Local Government in Idaho and the Nation*, 22.

vision for the establishment and limitations of local governments (as we surveyed in the previous three chapters).[16]

Further, state constitutions contain sections establishing state agencies and departments (again, see chapter 2, "Layers of Law"), as well as state institutions, all of which also address practical issues such as voting, education, and finances.[17] Finally, each state constitution makes provision for future change: the amendment process.[18] Any amendments must bear in mind that the state constitution exists as the state's supreme law and must not violate the supreme law of the land (the U.S. Constitution). Take a moment and search the internet for your state's constitution. (Depending on where you live, the constitution will vary in length from other states and most likely has undergone many amendments.[19]) Note the sections it contains. Take the time to read through it. You will be of the rare people in your state who has done so.

---

16 Duncombe and Weisel, *State and Local Government in Idaho and the Nation*, 22.

17 "Other governmental institutions typically seen in state constitutions include the establishment of state offices and officials, including executive agencies and departments such as education, transportation, agriculture, fish and game, natural resources and the environment, attorney general, secretary of state, treasury, revenue, welfare (social services), health, civil service, various advisory boards, commissions, and governing boards for public colleges and universities. Typically, state constitutions also establish institutions such as state prisons, state mental health hospitals, state libraries, and state parks, and states provide for local school districts and other forms of local government-oriented entities to deal with such infrastructure matters as public utilities, irrigation, county roads and bridges, park and recreation facilities, local libraries and health clinics and hospitals." Simon, Steel, and Lovrich, *State and Local Government and Politics*, sec. 5.C.

18 "There are three major methods available to change or amend U.S. state constitutions. The methods include a legislative proposal, a popular initiative, and a constitutional convention. A fourth method, only available in Florida, involves a constitutional commission submitting a proposal directly to the state's voters for their consideration. Additionally, each state has the potential for a 'virtual' constitutional amendment through judicial re-interpretation of constitutional provisions. Of the four methods listed, only the constitutional convention provides elected officials an opportunity to collaborate in a deliberative setting on the entire constitution." Simon, Steel, and Lovrich, *State and Local Government and Politics*, sec. 5.D.

19 "The average state constitution has been amended about 115 times." Ballotpedia, s.v. "State constitution."

Interestingly, upon installment into office, newly elected representatives at the state, county, and city levels must solemnly swear to uphold the Constitution of the United States of America, the constitution of their state, and the duties of the local office. I wonder how many officeholders have actually read their state's constitution and know what it contains. I've encouraged you to read yours because knowledge is power. You never know when you may need to wield it.

Statutes (State Laws)

The beginning of recorded statutes (state codes of law) originated as state constitutions came to life with actual legislatures/general assemblies convening to make the laws that govern the state. That is why similar topics are covered in state constitutions and state codes of law.

If you look at your state government's website, there should be a link somewhere on the page to your state's code of laws. This version is the digital form of the hard-bound copies at your state capitol building. In my statehouse, these hard-bound copies reside in the Legislative Services Library—they should be housed in a similar area at your state's capitol building. As we learned in chapter 2, the librarians ensure that each law is recorded accurately both in the chronological volumes/compilations of laws (refer back to Figure 2.5) and in the topical volumes/compilations (Figure 2.6). In times past, attorneys needed to purchase these tomes volume by volume, thus amassing quite a collection of books over a lifetime to reference state law in their own offices. These bound statutes were stored in beautiful bookshelves (with glass fronts that lift upward and outward for dust control) known as lawyer's or barrister's bookcases. These bookcases have become antique collectors' items in the wake of the internet.

I invite you to pause this book and investigate your own state's laws. Choose a section or two that interests you and read the contents.[20] As you read, remember that this is the law of your entire state. It was placed there, over the course of time, by your state's legislature, each law having received the governor's stamp of approval. These laws can be reviewed by your state's courts, and if a state court rules that a law is in conflict with the state constitution, the court can declare the law unenforceable.

Before leaving the topic of state law itself, I would be remiss if I did not revisit another type of law mentioned in chapter 2, that of state-agency regulations. These rules exist in a category known as "having the power and effect of state law," even though the states' legislatures do not directly generate them. Instead, the legislatures enable these agencies to exist, delegating rule-making authority for the topics and activities relative to each agency's mission, and usually setting boundaries around that authority.[21] Because legislatures create these agencies, they generally live outside the checks and balances that the Founding Fathers placed within the U.S. Constitution. This situation can be concerning. In my state, the legislature reviews agency rules before it begins its annual legislative session. Check to see if there is a similar level of accountability in your state.

Many residents of each state do not know such rules exist. Thus, the people of the state are likely not acting as a check themselves. The primary check that bears on these agencies appears to be the power of the purse. The state budget is granted annually by each state's legislature (setting the

---

20 If your online state law organization appears too complex, try one of these websites which organize the laws in a very user-friendly fashion: **statelaws.findlaw.com** or **law.cornell.edu/states/listing**. 🔗 However, these websites are really no substitute for browsing around your own state's code. Remember that the laws are organized first by title, then sometimes by article, then by chapter, then by section (TiCS TACS).

21 See an explanatory example in Appendix D: Establishment and Enablement of State Agencies.

state budget is one of the duties of the state legislature). The judicial branch of each state should also act as a check on state agencies. I suggested a website in chapter 2 that lists agencies for each state,[22] but you can also find these on your own state government website (where you may have just looked at your state's code of statutory laws). There should be a link to a list of agencies for your state. Note that sometimes the branches of state government are counted in this list—which is rather strange—as if agencies were equal to the three branches in essential constitutional authority.

There is a continuum of opinion on how to consider these agencies ranging from specialized government enablement designed to solve citizens' (and the state's) problems to flagrant government overreach. For example, most people do not think of preserving state lands in the form of state parks (which are lovely to visit) as government overreach. Nor do we think of this when rooting for our favorite team during a state university football game on television at the holidays. Pleasant forms of state government do not tend to attract our attention; however, we might be tempted to cry, "Overreach!" or at least "Ouch!" if a state police officer stops us while on the state highway.[23]

In the days before state agencies, there was no uniform mechanism for solving problems like uncontrolled pollution, unsanitary restaurants, or inconsistent prescription drug ingredients. Today there is state regulation of business entities for the safety of others. The good side is that the United States is safer in many ways than it used to be. The downside is that it took the creation of agencies to accomplish this level of safety, and these agencies appear to have been enabled by

22 Found on The National Association of the Secretaries of State's Administrative Codes and Registers website.

23 Nick Ragone, *Everything American Government*, 241.

state legislatures not only to serve but to do so with largely unchecked and unbalanced power.[24]

Here is one example. In chapter 3, "City Government," I mentioned visiting the local wastewater treatment plant. The supervisor who gave the tour said that if a certain contaminant level is too high in the water, the state will substantially fine the city (the fine exists as the power and effect of law). I then inquired who "the state" was. The state, in this case, was the Idaho Department of Environmental Quality (IEQD). It was not the state legislature or an elected state executive but a state agency. The water reclamation supervisor explained that the city answers to the state (agency), which sets the Idaho water safety parameters. The state agency's standards are permitted to be more stringent than the national Environmental Protection Agency (EPA) standards, but they may not be more lenient than those of the EPA. This agency system mirrors federalism in general, as the city answers to the state, which then answers to the federal agency. The unanswered question is who does the EPA report to? That is a topic for the next chapter on national government.

SERVICES

In chapter 4, "County-Equivalent Government," we learned that counties provide services as an arm of state government. So most county-level services are often duplicated at the state level on a grander scale. Here are a few examples:

24 A resource designed to help citizens be more informed about legislation regarding state agencies is Ballotpedia's "Administrative State Legislation Tracker." Consider starting at the FAQ page. 🔗

Local/County Services	*State Services*
Parks	State parks
Sheriff's department	State police/troopers
Jail	State penitentiary
Election office	State election office
Highways	State highways
Hospital/home (behavioral/mental health)	State hospital
Fair (local, agricultural)	State fair
Trial courts	Appellate/supreme courts
Public education of children	State universities

GOVERNANCE STRUCTURE

Legislative Branch

Now, we will look at how lawmaking occurs at the state level. The complex reality is that lawmaking happens via citizen legislatures, some of which are part-time and some are year-round. Some have legislative staff and some don't. We will start by looking at the history and structure of the legislative branch followed by the lawmaking process.

Most Americans have heard of the U.S. House of Representatives and the Senate, which form our national legislature known as the United States Congress. We see clips of our national legislature meeting in the media, but we are not as familiar with how and when our state legislatures function. "There is almost nothing in popular culture to help voters understand [state] legislatures or lawmakers. Perhaps even more troubling, there are fewer and fewer stories from the state capitol printed in newspapers and broadcast on television and radio every year."[25]

Even though we, as Americans, are largely unfamiliar with our state legislatures, their existence actually predates the national legislature. In other words, state legislatures have been around long before Congress existed. Take for example, the Virginia General Assembly[26] founded in Jamestown, Virginia, in 1619, which was the first legislative assembly in the American colonies.[27] In 1643, it became a bicameral legislature consisting of the elected lower house (famously known as the House of Burgesses)[28] and an appointed upper house.[29] Following this early model, the U.S. Congress and all state legislatures (except one) are composed of two bodies or chambers in order to purposely complicate and slow the lawmaking process.[30] The exception is Nebraska, which has a single legislative body fittingly named the Unicameral.[31]

In the remaining forty-nine states, the upper house is called the Senate.[32] In most states, this is historically the small-

---

25 Gary F. Moncrief and Peverill Squire, *State Legislatures Today: Politics under the Domes*, 3rd. ed. (Lanham, MD: Rowman & Littlefield, 2015), 195.

26 "It became the General Assembly in 1776 with the ratification of the Virginia Constitution." Ballotpedia, s.v. "Virginia General Assembly."

27 USHistory.org, "The House of Burgesses," *U.S. History Online Textbook*, 2024.

28 A burgess is a citizen of a British borough or a representative of a borough, corporate town, or university in the British Parliament. *Merriam-Webster*, s.v. "burgess."

29 "The House of Burgesses," *U.S. History Online Textbook*.

30 Moncrief and Squire, *State Legislature Today*, 8.

31 "Vermont's unicameral assembly was transformed into a bicameral legislature in 1836" (Moncrief and Squire, *State Legislature Today*, 7). In contrast, Nebraska began as a bicameral legislature, and its state capitol actually had two chambers. However, an initiative passed by voters in 1934 changed its governance into a unicameral legislature with the goals of avoiding committee corruption and being more economically efficient (this was during the Great Depression). Interestingly, the Unicameral costs more per citizen to operate than its larger neighboring bicameral legislature in Iowa. Lastly, it should be noted that the legislature is elected in a nonpartisan fashion (similar to judges or candidates who run for city office having no party labels on the ballot) (Moncrief and Squire, *State Legislature Today*, 11–12).

32 "State and Local Government: Legislative Branch," The White House.

er and more prestigious chamber with its members often, but not always, serving longer four-year terms. The lower house is historically the larger and more populist/rowdy chamber, and its members typically serve shorter two-year terms. In many states, the larger lower chamber is called the House of Representatives, but other states use the following names: House of Delegates, State Assembly, or General Assembly.[33] The size of the state Senates varies: Alaska has the smallest Senate with twenty senators, and Minnesota has the largest with sixty-seven.[34] The lower chambers also vary, ranging from forty members (Alaska) to four hundred (New Hampshire).[35] Nevada holds one vacant seat in each chamber; otherwise, it would accompany Alaska in the smallest-of-both-chambers category.

The names of most of the forty-nine bicameral legislatures (referring to both houses together) fall into one of two basic categories: the Name-of-the-State State Legislature or Name-of-the-State General Assembly. There are some variations on these two themes, such as the North Dakota Legislative Assembly and the General Assembly of North Carolina. The two legislatures named quite differently from the rest are the General Court of the Commonwealth of Massachusetts[36] and the General Court of New Hampshire. One might think that they are courts in the judicial sense, and in colonial times they indeed served both judicial and legislative purposes. Today, however, they no longer perform judicial (court) purposes but only serve legislative (law-making) purposes as bicameral legislatures like the forty-nine others. Try looking up the name of your state's legislature by searching your state's name and the word *legislature* on the internet.

---

33 Ballotpedia, s.v. "State legislature."

34 Duncombe and Weisel, *State and Local Government in Idaho and the Nation*, 80.

35 Duncombe and Weisel, *State and Local Government in Idaho and the Nation*, 80.

36 There is more information here about Oliver Cromwell and the term *commonwealth* that is very interesting: Ryland Barton, "Curious Louisville: Why Is Kentucky A Commonwealth?," Louisville Public Media, published July 21, 2017.

When do state legislatures convene? Most state legislatures in the United States meet for only a portion of the year; their senators and representatives are considered citizen legislators because they typically have other careers. However, the following states have legislatures that meet year-round: Alaska, California, Hawaii, Illinois, Massachusetts, Michigan, New York, Ohio, Pennsylvania, and Wisconsin.[37] To quickly find when your state's legislature convenes and adjourns, check the National Conference of State Legislatures website on *The Forgotten Realm* links page.

Members of both houses are elected within legislative districts. This means that each state is divided into districts for the purpose of electing official representatives of the people to both chambers of the state's legislature. Most states have single-member districts where one officeholder is elected to a legislative body from one district.[38] For example, all states except Vermont and West Virginia elect one state senator per voting district.[39] Ten states have multi-member districts where two or more members are elected to their state legislative body from one district.[40] The **Ballotpedia** website in the footnote below is an excellent one-source stop for information on how each state's legislative districts are organized.[41] In the next section, we will learn about how they are shaped in terms of physical boundaries.

---

37 Ballotpedia, s.v. "States with a full-time legislature."

38 Ballotpedia, s.v. "Single-member district."

39 "The [Vermont] Senate consists of 30 members. Senate districting divides the 30 members into three single-member districts, six two-member districts, three three-member districts and one six-member district." Ballotpedia, s.v. "Vermont state legislative districts."

"There are 17 senatorial districts [in West Virginia]. Each district has two senators." Ballotpedia, s.v. "West Virginia state legislative districts."

40 These ten states are Arizona, Idaho, Maryland, New Hampshire, New Jersey, North Dakota, South Dakota, Vermont, Washington, and West Virginia. Ballotpedia, s.v. "Multi-member district."

41 Ballotpedia, s.v. "State Legislative Districts."

Redistricting or Reapportionment

My state of Idaho is one that operates under the commission model of redistricting or reapportionment.[42] *I attempted to view the local public hearing for my district remotely the evening that the commission was in town. Naively, I thought I could iron shirts while listening to the proceedings on my laptop. I knew nothing about redistricting/reapportionment except that civics books always connect it to the term gerrymandering. The meeting's visual content was very map-heavy, and that precluded ironing. Worse, I could not read the maps on my laptop. The remaining option was to dash over to City Hall, catch the commission members' presentation in person, and view the menu of potential maps there in person. The commissioners sat on the dais where the city councilors usually conduct business. However, the map-mounted posterboards were perpendicular to the audience—meaning not at a legible angle. Come to find out, the posterboards weren't readable either. Photocopied handouts, anyone? Or large PowerPoint maps? For the people to learn to govern, methodology reform is in order in such cases. Thankfully, we have the remainder of the decade for technology to improve and to learn about redistricting before the next round of meetings occurs.*

Redistricting, also called reapportionment, is redrawing the boundary lines of the geographic regions in which voters will elect state legislative representatives and the separate boundaries in which voters will elect federal legislative representatives for the next ten years. It is a hefty task that has been the source of much contention and strife.

42 "Reapportionment… had been the responsibility of the Legislature prior to 1994, when an amendment to the Idaho Constitution was adopted creating an independent commission to reapportion starting in 2001 and thereafter." "Idaho's Citizen Legislature—The Membership," Idaho State Legislature.

State legislative districts' boundaries do not correspond neatly to county boundaries. It seems like it would be simpler if they did. However, due to population distribution[43] within states, it is necessary to have district boundary lines that differ from county boundary lines. For this reason, state legislative districts are reconsidered every decade—usually the year following the U.S. Census—when the concentration of population is the most apparent. The goal is for districts to be relatively equal in terms of population. The boundary lines may have to move in response to shifts in population in order to achieve equal representation in the state legislature (and in Congress—even though those boundaries fall in different places).

The first question is how to draw the lines for these districts. Even though the population within districts may be equal, the decennial redistricting process can, in some ways, represent "politicians picking their voters as opposed to voters picking their politicians,"[44] and the districts might be shaped

---

43 "Redistricting and the Supreme Court: The Most Significant Cases," National Conference of State Legislatures (NCSL).

"*Reynolds v. Sims*, 377 U.S. 533 (1964)

Significance: Both houses of a bicameral state legislature must be apportioned substantially according to population. Legislative districts may deviate from strict population equality only as necessary to give representation to political subdivisions and provide for compact districts of contiguous territory. Legislative districts should be redrawn to reflect population shifts at least every 10 years. Once a constitutional violation has been shown, a court should take equitable action to correct it, bearing in mind the practical requirements of running an election.

Summary: Alabama Senate and House seats had not been reapportioned among the counties since 1903. 377 U.S. at 539–40. Each county had one or more senators and one or more representatives, regardless of population. According to the 1960 Census, the largest Senate district had about 41 times the population of the smallest Senate district, and the largest House district had about 16 times the population of the smallest House district. Id. at 545."

Alabama attempted to justify the disparity in the Senate by analogy to the federal system, but the Supreme Court found that comparison to not be pertinent. Id. at 571–75. Justice Earl Warren declared, "Legislators represent people, not trees or acres." Id. at 562.

The Court held that "the Equal Protection Clause requires that the seats in both houses of a bicameral state legislature must be apportioned on a population basis." Id. at 568.

44 "Since the U.S. Supreme Court handed down Reynolds v. Sims in 1964, all state legislative houses must be apportioned on the basis of population, meaning that

so as to give preference to a political party. This reshaping of districts in a highly irregular fashion to favor the majority party is termed *gerrymandering*.[45] You can learn a bit more about Gov. Elbridge Gerry and his salamander-shaped district in the following footnote.[46] In an effort to avoid majority-party politics, the Supreme Court has placed limits on districts, that they should not be "bizarrely shaped" and should be reasonably compact.[47] No salamanders.

---

all districts in a chamber in a state must have roughly the same population per legislator elected." Moncrief and Squire, *State Legislatures Today*, 22.

45 Thomas Hunter, a political science professor at the University of West Georgia as quoted in the following article: Becky Little, "How Gerrymandering Began in the US," History, updated August 7, 2023.

46 Elbridge Gerry was one of our nation's Founders, a signer of the Declaration of Independence, a member of the Second Continental Congress, a Framer of the Constitution, a Senator, a Representative, and the fifth Vice President. Funny. He did many noble (and eccentric) things, yet we know him for his mispronounced last name. Before Gerry, senatorial boundaries in Massachusetts did follow county boundaries. The senate-district map that he approved was all twisted and contorted. It was also successful to get Democratic-Republicans (Anti-Federalists) elected. Erick Trickey, "Where Did the Term 'Gerrymander' Come From?," *Smithsonian*, July 20, 2017.

47 "Redistricting and the Supreme Court," NCSL.
"*Bush v. Vera*, 517 U.S. 952 (1996)

Significance: If you want to argue that partisan politics, not race, was your dominant motive in drawing district lines, beware of using race as a proxy for political affiliation. To survive strict scrutiny under the Equal Protection Clause and avoid being struck down as a racial gerrymander, a district must be reasonably compact.

Summary: Under the 1990 reapportionment of seats in Congress, Texas was entitled to three additional congressional districts. The Texas Legislature decided to draw one new Hispanic-majority district in South Texas, one new African-American-majority district in Dallas County, and one new Hispanic-majority district in the Houston area. In addition, the legislature reconfigured a district in the Houston area to increase its percentage of African Americans. The legislature used sophisticated software that allowed it to redistrict with racial data at the census block level. Plaintiffs challenged 24 of the state's 30 congressional districts as racial gerrymanders. The Supreme Court struck down three districts, holding that race was the predominant factor in drawing the lines. In these districts, the court concluded that districts drawn to satisfy Section 2 of the VRA must not subordinate traditional redistricting principles more than reasonably necessary. The districts in question were in the courts words, 'bizarrely shaped and far from compact.' These characteristics were predominantly attributable to racially motivated gerrymandering."

Theoretically, redistricting should be based on the one-person, one-vote principle of equality.[48] This principle means that a person is a person—no matter how small, as Dr. Seuss quips,[49] and no matter what color.[50] It also means that the people rule with equal authority—their votes should carry the same weight regardless of their geographic residence.[51] The difficulty remains in how to categorize persons in terms of electing their representatives. Within the district, does the redistricting approach consider *the people* to mean all of the persons living there (including children, non-citizens, and convicted criminals)?[52] Or are *the people* all of the registered

48 "In *Reynolds v. Sims*, 377 U.S. 533 (1964), this Court held that the Equal Protection Clause of the Fourteenth Amendment includes a 'one-person, one-vote' principle. This principle requires that, 'when members of an elected body are chosen from separate districts, each district must be established on a basis that will insure, as far as is practicable, that equal numbers of voters can vote for proportionally equal numbers of officials.' *Hadley v. Junior Coll. Dist. Of Metro. Kansas City, Mo.*, 397 U.S. 50, 56 (1970)." QP Report for *Evenwel et al. v. Abbott, Governor of Texas, et al. (2016)*, United States Supreme Court.

49 Dr. Seuss, *Horton Hears a Who!* (New York: Random House, 1982).

50 As U.S. Const. amend. XIV, § 2 declares.

51 "Redistricting and the Supreme Court," NCSL.
"*Wesberry v. Sanders*, 376 U.S. 1 (1964)
Significance: The Court held that the constitutionality of congressional districts was a question that could be decided by the courts.
Summary: Voters in Georgia's Congressional District 5, which had three times the population of Congressional District 9, alleged that this imbalance denied them the full benefit of their right to vote. A three-judge federal district court held that drawing congressional districts was a task assigned by the Constitution to state legislatures, subject to guidance by Congress, and not assigned to the courts. The district court held that the complaint presented a "political question" the court had jurisdiction to decide, but should not. 376 U.S. at 2–3. The Supreme Court reversed, holding that congressional districts must be drawn so that "as nearly as is practicable one man's vote in a congressional election is worth as much as another's. Id. at 7–8."

52 "Redistricting and the Supreme Court," NCSL.
"*Evenwel v. Abbott*, 136 S. Ct. 1120 (2016)
Significance: Total population is a permissible metric for calculating compliance with 'one person, one vote.'
Summary: Since Reynolds and Wesberry, states have almost universally used total population as the unit for calculating population equality for districting plans. Plaintiffs in Evenwel challenged Texas's 2011 redistricting scheme, arguing that its use of total population violated the Equal Protection Clause by discriminating against voters in districts with low immigrant populations by giving voters in districts with significant immigrant populations a disproportionately weighted vote. The Supreme Court held that its past

voters who live there? Or are *the people* only those of voting age, whether they are registered to vote or not?[53] Who are *the people*? How are they to be equally divided among the districts?

In the past, the Supreme Court left this decision to the state, providing they did not discriminate by race[54] or other means. Currently, as a result of the 2016 Supreme Court case *Evenwel v. Abbott*, **total population** is the deciding factor for redrawing district boundaries (rather than taking into account voting age or citizenship of the residents).[55] Because of the principle of federalism, each state accomplishes the reapportionment of its districts' boundaries slightly differently. This leads us to yet another question: Who draws and approves the lines for those districts? The answer can *very generally* be grouped into five methods:[56]

- **Exclusively legislatively** passing the district-line plans like regular legislation is passed
- **Legislatively** with the advance assistance of an **advisory commission**

---

opinions confirmed that states may use total population in order to comply with one person, one vote. The court did not hold that other methods are impermissible."

53 Lyle Denniston, "Constitution Check: What does 'one-person, one-vote' mean now?" *Constitution Daily* (blog), National Constitution Center, April 5, 2016.

54 "Redistricting and the Supreme Court," NCSL.
"*Miller v. Johnson*, 515 U.S. 900 (1995)
Significance: A district becomes an unconstitutional racial gerrymander if race was the "predominant" factor in the drawing of its lines.
Summary: Following Shaw, it remained unclear what the standard of review was under the new racial gerrymandering doctrine. In Miller, the U.S. Department of Justice in 1991 refused preclearance to Georgia's initial congressional redistricting plan under § 5 of the Voting Rights Act, claiming the state needed to create an additional majority-minority district. Plaintiffs challenged the newly drawn districts as racial gerrymanders. The Supreme Court held for the plaintiffs, and established the rule for racial gerrymandering claims: if a district is drawn predominantly on the basis of race, it violates the Equal Protection Clause."

55 "Supreme Court Upholds 'One Person, One Vote,'" Brennan Center for Justice, April 4, 2016.

56 Credit for these five categories is given to the website **All About Redistricting** sponsored by Loyola Law School.

- **Legislatively** with a **backup commission's** assistance in case of legislative snags
- **Exclusively by a political commission** that contains elected officials
- **Exclusively by an independent commission** that contains no elected officials

This abundance of choices is due not only to the leeway that states have within federalism, but also to the contentions and strife referred to at the beginning of this section. Deciding who will vote where in order to be fairly represented in the legislature (and Congress—different districts, but the same principles) is a tall order. "Reformers often mistakenly assume that commissions will be less partisan than legislatures when conducting redistricting but that depends largely on the design of the board or commission."[57]

Granted, this information is a lot to process. However, you have ten years from the bookend of one census to another to figure it out. I can point you to an immensely helpful website, sponsored by Loyola Law School, entitled "All about Redistricting." This aptly named website explains the redistricting process, the challenges faced in state and federal courts regarding districts, and even some ideas for reform. The "FIND A STATE" button on the top toolbar directs visitors to extensive redistricting information about any state including its method used for redistricting and maps of congressional and legislative boundaries. When viewing maps by state on this website, there is a button for "STATE UPPER" and "STATE LOWER." States with enough population (excluding Nebraska) have separate district lines for their own upper chamber (senate) and lower chamber (house/assembly) districts. The separation of districts for the two chambers allows

---

57 "Redistricting Commissions: State Legislative Plans," National Conference of State Legislatures (NCSL).

for varied representation based on different criteria and ensures a diverse legislative body. The button for "CONGRESS" shows the national congressional districts for the U.S. House of Representatives, **not** those for the state level. We will briefly cover the national district in the next chapter. When the next census approaches, you now know that legislative redistricting should happen the following year. And because you will know how your state approaches the task, you should be in a fine position to participate as an informed citizen. That is part of recovering the forgotten realm.

Now, we return to the legislatures themselves. Each legislature has key leaders in both chambers. The state Senate's presiding leader is typically the lieutenant governor. As such, this person is the parliamentary chief of the Senate who maintains order and recognizes legislators who wish to speak. The lieutenant governor's assistant, replacement during an absence, and true majority party leader in the Senate is the president *pro tempore*[58] (Latin meaning "for the time being"). So, if the governor is absent, the lieutenant governor fills the governor's position, and the president *pro tem* fills the lieutenant's position presiding over the Senate for the time being. Thus, there is a sort of domino effect.

Regarding the office's powers, the lieutenant governor can only cast a tie-breaking vote. On recommendation of the president *pro tem*, the lieutenant governor also assigns bills to a committee. Those two leaders and the Senate minority leader appoint members to standing committees (we will learn about standing committees momentarily). Note that the minority leader refers to the senator chosen to represent the party that is not in control of the chamber floor. It follows, then, that the majority party holds the majority of seats in that chamber.

58 Or *pro tem* for short.

Both parties in the Senate also have leaders, assistant leaders, and caucus chairpersons.[59]

Similarly, the larger chamber (House or Assembly) has a speaker, a majority leader, and a minority leader. The Speaker of the House or Assembly, usually the most powerful person in the legislature, is selected by the chamber's members of the majority party and is confirmed by the entire chamber's vote. The speaker presides over the House/Assembly, recognizing representatives who would like to speak while maintaining parliamentary procedure. In addition to referring bills to committees and appointing committee chairpersons (committees will be explained soon), the speaker decides the order in which the bills will appear for debate and can personally participate in debating on and voting for/against bills because the speaker is also an elected representative to the House or Assembly.[60] Note that the speaker consults with the minority and majority leaders before appointing people or assigning bills. Like the Senate, the House or Assembly has assistant leaders and caucus chairpersons.

The process of making laws includes debating and voting on matters proposed by the governor (as mentioned above) or proposed by the elected members (which in turn may be brought to them by citizens, interest groups, or executive departments/agencies). The state legislatures have other tasks such as approving the state budget, appropriating funds,[61] setting tax rates,[62] confirming gubernatorial[63] appointments

59 A caucus is a convening of like-minded individuals in the state legislature (or in Congress). Duncombe and Weisel, *State and Local Government in Idaho and the Nation*, 86.

60 Duncombe and Weisel, *State and Local Government in Idaho and the Nation*, 85–86.

61 "Probably the most important function of the Legislature, appropriating money is carried out by passing bills which authorize units of government to spend money for specified purposes" Michigan Legislature, *A Student's Guide to the Legislative Process in Michigan*, April 2023.

62 Usually initiated by the state's larger body.

63 Meaning pertaining to the governor.

to state departments,[64] impeaching[65]/removing elected office-holders,[66] initiating amendments to the state constitution, and providing legislative oversight of agencies and administration.[67]

How a Bill Becomes a Law

Phase 1

Since the majority of what the state legislatures do is enact laws, let's look at how a bill (a piece of pre-law legislation written in a prescribed format) becomes law. Actually, an idea is where the process begins. The idea begins with a thought such as, "Hey, we should do this," or, "This is a problem, let's fix it." The process of doing something about it is called making a bill. The bill's trajectory is to pass both bodies of the state legislature without being vetoed by the governor.[68] Let's break that American process down and consider its steps.

Recall that at the local level of government, the parliamentary procedure manual is *Robert's Rules of Order*. Here, at the state level, the typical parliamentary tool of choice is *Mason's Manual of Legislative Procedure*. This explains why if you listen in on a legislature in session, the protocol will sound different than at the local level of government.

First, the bill must be written in a prescribed format. Legislatures have attorneys and staff on hand to turn ideas into properly written bills. The elected legislators themselves typically hand this step off to the professionals. Then the bill

64 Usually confirmed by the state's Senate.

65 To impeach is to charge an elected representative of the people with misconduct while in office.

66 Impeachment is usually initiated by the state's larger body and tried by the state's smaller body (Senate).

67 Duncombe and Weisel, *State and Local Government in Idaho and the Nation*, 82.

68 Except for Nebraska which has a one-chamber legislature. See "Lawmaking in Nebraska," Nebraska Legislature.

HOW A BILL BECOMES A LAW: PHASE 1

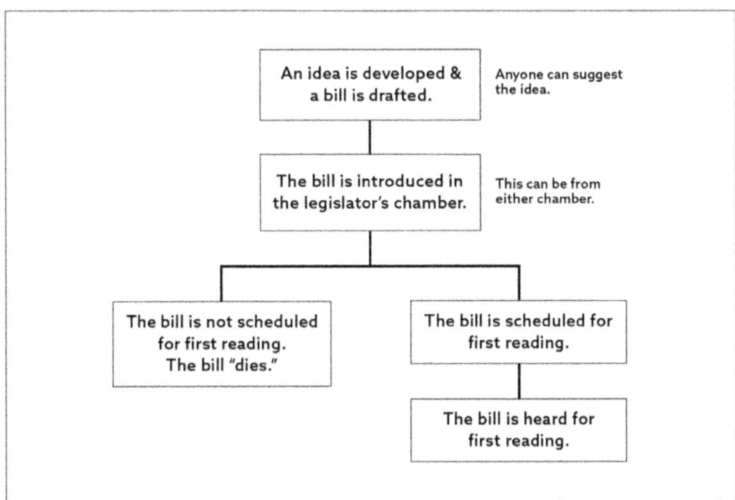

Figure 6.2

is filed with the clerk, after which it receives a bill number, is read by title, and double-checked for formatting errors. This process is known as the first reading.

The speaker then determines which committee the bill is assigned to. If the bill was sponsored by a committee rather than a single legislator, it is assigned to its committee of origin. The order of bill appearance is critical because bills that come later in the calendar have less time available to complete all of the required steps to become law.[69] Let's pause our bill's itinerary here to consider a significant yet somewhat shrouded procedure.

69 Duncombe and Weisel, *State and Local Government in Idaho and the Nation*, 93.

There are legislative staff members who then take that sponsored idea and craft it into the standard-issue-written format that all bills assume. Legislators are organized into committees with each committee focused on a particular area of law in order to research, report on, and debate bills pertaining to that topic. Each committee has between five to ten members and may form a subcommittee with three to five of those members. Assignments vary by state, but each legislator is appointed to between one and five committees based on one's knowledge and experience.[70] Most committees pertain to one chamber (senate and/or lower chamber) and are called standing committees.[71] Other committees pertain to both chambers and are called conference committees.[72] A few committees are for special investigative purposes and are (not surprisingly) called special committees. Sometimes, though, they are called ad hoc, investigative, select, or study committees.[73]

Here are some examples of the types of legislative committees that could occur in either chamber:

- Agricultural Affairs (agricultural issues)
- Appropriations (state budgets, revenue, appropriations)
- Business (banking, insurance issues, occupational licenses unrelated to healthcare)
- Commerce and Human Resources (wages/hours, unions, retirement plans)
- Education (public schools, colleges, and universities)

70 "Standing Committees," sec. 4.1 in *Inside the Legislative Process: A comprehensive survey by the American Society of Legislative Clerks and Secretaries in cooperation with the National Conference of State Legislatures*, National Conference of State Legislatures (NCSL), revised September 2009, Table 96-4.1, 4-6.

71 "Parliamentary Procedure: A Legislator's Guide," National Conference of State Legislatures (NCSL), November 4, 2022.

72 "Parliamentary Procedure," NCSL.

73 "Parliamentary Procedure," NCSL.

- Environment, Energy, and Technology (hazardous waste, sewage, recycling, cyber-security)
- Ethics (ethics complaints)
- Health and Welfare (health/child care, welfare, Medicaid, Medical occupational licensing)
- Judiciary, Rules, and Administration (courts, prisons, attorneys, juvenile justice, criminal justice)
- Local Government (city/county governance, taxing districts)
- Natural Resources (water quality/rights, fish & game, river restoration)
- Revenue and Taxation (sales/property/income taxes)
- State Affairs (statewide issues: elections, abortion, electric utility deregulation)
- Transportation (fuel taxes, state/local highways, motor vehicle issues)
- Ways and Means (for quickly introducing legislation, usually at the end of a session)

The above list of names indicates the type of work that takes place within committees. Each committee's potential bills (proposed laws) are considered by its members in much more detail than could take place by each chamber as a unit. Within committee meetings, there is an opportunity for citizen involvement (as paid lobbyists and as concerned individual citizens or loosely organized groups). This process occurs under the direction of a committee chairperson who formally presides and maintains order with parliamentary procedure.[74] The chairperson supervises and directs the administrative needs of the committee (including staff, records, custody of papers,

74 "Standing Committees," sec. 4.1 in *Inside the Legislative Process: A comprehensive survey by the American Society of Legislative Clerks and Secretaries in cooperation with the National Conference of State Legislatures,* NCSL, 4-2.

etc.).[75] Further, the committee's work, though essential to the law-making process, is purely advisory. The chamber reviews its work and may approve, amend, or reject it.

In theory, committees properly appropriate time and talent to form the advisory first step of a bill becoming law. In practice, committees may proceed with very little accountability or oversight. The chairperson can change the schedule (day and time) for a hearing that has already been posted. Similarly, the chairperson can propose amendments to the bill that drastically alter its form. If citizens plan to attend committee meetings, it can be a lot of work to prepare to give public input and demoralizing to find that the time, place, or bill's content has changed. It requires stalwart persistence on the part of concerned citizens to work with the committee system.

Phase 2

Now that we better understand the existence of committees, let's return to our bill that has been assigned a number and is waiting for us in its assigned committee. In the committee, there will be a public hearing where people either for or against the bill can testify. These are regular people—they may be concerned citizens or paid lobbyists. After the hearing and ensuing deliberation by legislators, the committee votes upon the bill. If it passes, the committee sends the bill to the chamber floor with an advisory recommendation to pass, not pass, amend, withdraw (in order to introduce another bill), refer to another standing committee, hold in this committee, or place on the floor with no recommendation.

75 "Standing Committees," NCSL, 4-2-4-3.

HOW A BILL BECOMES A LAW: PHASE 2

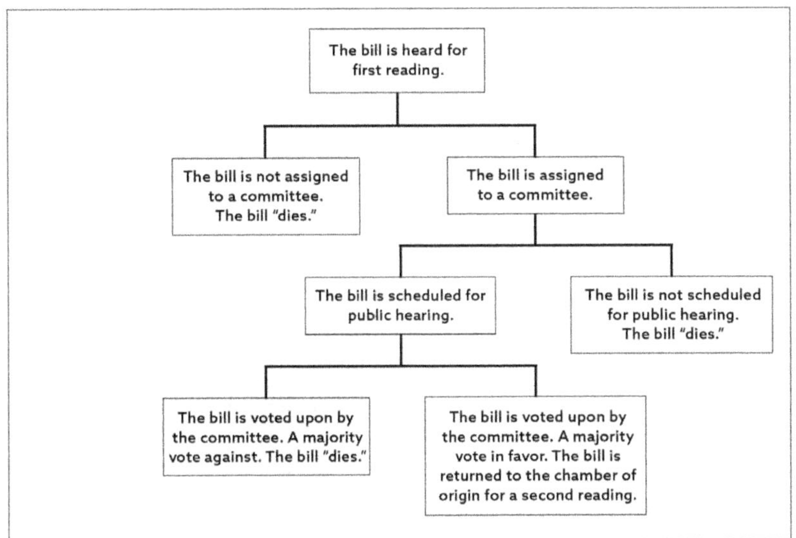

Figure 6.3

Phase 3

The standing committee's report for our bill is then read on the chamber floor, and the bill is placed on the agenda for a second reading. If there are no changes (amendments) proposed on the chamber floor, the bill passes the second reading and is placed on the agenda for a third reading. If there are amendments proposed on the chamber floor, the chamber becomes a committee of the whole (where the entire chamber operates under the rules for the committee) and considers arguments in favor of or against specific amendments. Each amendment must be voted on by the chamber individually. This process is designed to be lengthy so that bills are not passed in a lighthearted fashion. Each state has different chamber rules that govern the length of time and the number of times that a legislator is permitted to speak. After this process, all amendments that pass the floor are written into the bill before the third reading.

HOW A BILL BECOMES A LAW: PHASE 3

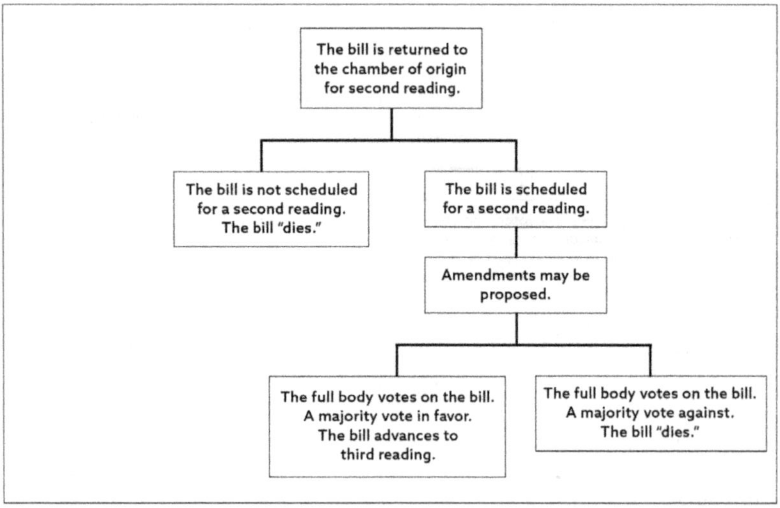

The bill is returned to the chamber of origin for second reading.

The bill is not scheduled for a second reading. The bill "dies."

The bill is scheduled for a second reading.

Amendments may be proposed.

The full body votes on the bill. A majority vote in favor. The bill advances to third reading.

The full body votes on the bill. A majority vote against. The bill "dies."

Figure 6.4

Phase 4

The legislators now reconsider our amended bill by debate beginning with the sponsor of the bill who hopes to sway the favor of the other legislators. At the conclusion of the debate, the bill's sponsor is given a final opportunity to speak, then a chamber vote is taken. If a bill does not receive a majority vote, it dies. If it does receive a majority vote in one chamber, it crosses over to the other chamber for the first reading and then to be referred to a committee (and is now known as a crossover bill).

HOW A BILL BECOMES A LAW: PHASE 4

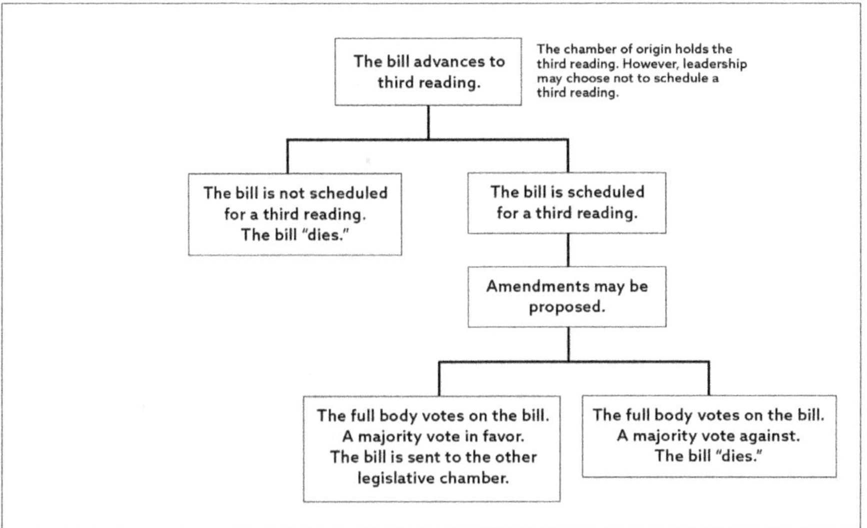

Figure 6.5

Phase 5

The legislative process begins again in the new chamber with a public hearing followed by a recommendation to pass, not pass, amend, withdraw (in order to introduce another bill), refer to another standing committee, hold in this committee, or place on the floor with no recommendation.

The decision on whether or not to amend the bill takes place on the second chamber's floor. Again, if no one calls for an amendment, the bill passes the second reading. If an amendment is desired, the second chamber considers arguments for and against amendments to the bill. Each amendment is voted on separately. If the bill passes the second reading, it is placed on the agenda for the third reading and sent to have any accepted amendments incorporated into the final copy.

HOW A BILL BECOMES A LAW: PHASE 5

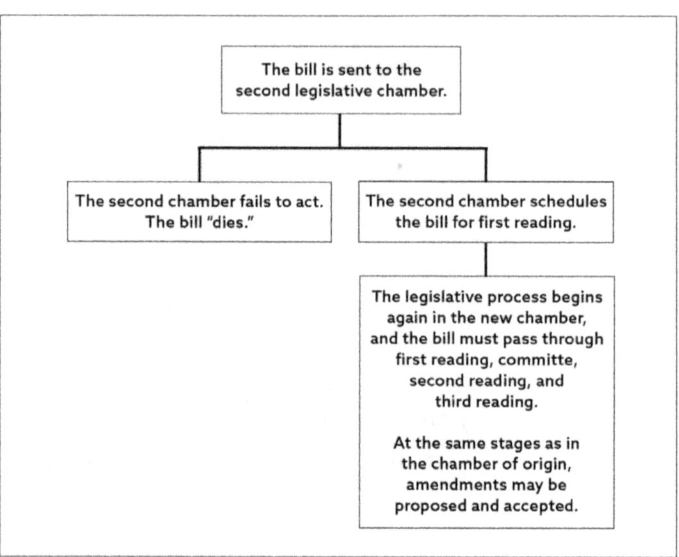

Figure 6.6

Phase 6

During the third reading, the leaders of the bill open the debate for the legislators to commence discussion of the bill: whether it should become law or not. Upon closing the debate, the speaker/lieutenant governor calls for a vote. If the bill does not receive a majority vote, it dies. If it does receive a majority vote, both chambers must then agree on their amendments to the bill. If they both agree (or if there are no amendments), then the bill advances to the governor. If they cannot agree on the amendments, the leadership of the two chambers calls a conference committee to mete out a compromise bill that must return to both chambers for a vote. Upon approval by both chambers, the bill then proceeds to the governor.

HOW A BILL BECOMES A LAW: PHASE 6

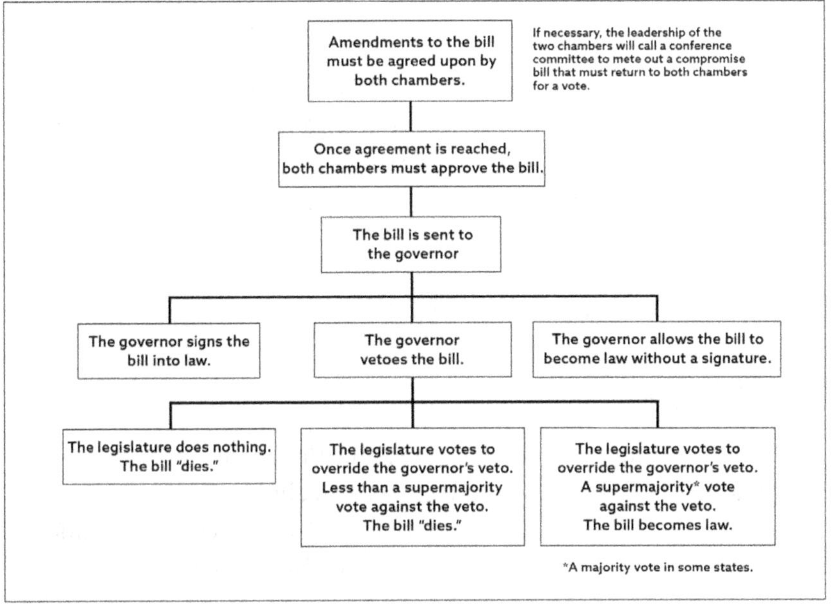

Figure 6.7

The governor (in all fifty states) has the power to veto the recently approved bill. Each state has either a specified number of days in which a bill will become law if not vetoed by the governor or a specified number of days in which a bill will die if not signed into law by the governor. Some states have the line-item veto available to the governor, which allows a particular portion to be stricken from the bill. A reduction veto may be available in some states which allows the governor to delete a budget item and then sign the bill. Or, the governor may have the power to amend or revise legislation with an amendatory veto. The state legislature may override the governor's veto, typically with a supermajority vote (majority means over 50% of the vote; supermajority means substantially more than 50%). This number is according to each state's law and may be 60% or 67% (the latter of which is a two-thirds majority vote).[76]

Note that if a bill dies, on rare occasions, it can come back from the dead. The contents of a dead bill can be resurrected to serve as an amendment to another bill which appears to have a fair chance of passing both chambers.

GOVERNANCE STRUCTURE

Executive Branch

Recall that at the national level, the President and the Vice President are the only two elected officeholders in the executive branch. At the state level, that template is expanded, and the elected members of the executive branch can consist of more than just the governor and/or lieutenant governor.[77] We the People may also elect the attorney general, the secretary of state, the state treasurer, the superintendent of public education, and the state comptroller, also called state controller or auditor. Though there are a host of other possible elected state executive offices across the states,[78] this book will focus

76 "Governor: Powers and Authority," National Governors Association.

77 New Jersey is the only state with one elected executive branch officeholder at the state level—the governor. G. Alan Tarr, *Understanding State Constitutions* (Princeton, NJ: Princeton University Press, 1998), 17.

78 According to Ballotpedia, this list could contain: Insurance Commissioner, Agriculture Commissioner, Natural Resources Commissioner, Labor Commissioner, Public Service Commissioner, State Board of Equalization, Public Utilities Commissioner, Industrial Commission Director, State Mine Inspector, Department of Revenue Commissioner, Commissioner of Energy and Environmental Protection, Chief Financial Officer, Director of the Department of Economic Opportunity, Director of Commerce and Consumer Affairs, State Examiner, Transportation Commission, Executive Director of Employment Security, Commissioner of Management and Budget, Tax Commissioner, Board of Elections. Across the states, some of these positions may be elected, some may be appointed by the governor, and some may not exist. Ballotpedia, s.v. "State Executive Offices."

on the list above. Later in the chapter, you will be prompted to look for any variations in your state.

Governor

Directly elected by the people in all fifty states, the governor is seen as the person who represents each entire state. As the President of the United States is to the nation, the governor is to the state. "No other state officeholder can attract media attention, influence national lawmakers, galvanize the public, and shape the national party like the governor."[79] The word *governor* actually means ruler and comes from the Latin word *gubernator.*[80] That's why the adjective used to describe things pertaining to the governor is gubernatorial.[81] Gubernatorial roles are many and varied. Let's take a quick look at them.[82]

First, the governor is the ceremonial head of state. As such, he or she welcomes special dignitaries at the state capitol, attends ceremonies and receptions, and recognizes the work of various groups across the state.

Second, the governor is the chief executive of a state's government and is the one to whom the other executive officers ordinarily report.[83] In this role, the governor performs the following duties:

- appointing and removing cabinet-level officials and members of boards/commissions (more in the "Ninth" point in this section)

79 Nick Ragone, *Everything American Government*, 237.

80 *Online Etymology Dictionary*, s.v. "governor (n.)."

81 Here is a short foray into the word gubernatorial: Anne Curzan and Rebecca Kruth, "Here's why we say 'gubernatorial' instead of 'governatorial,'" Michigan Public, June 10, 2018.

82 The following eight points are summarized from Duncombe and Weisel, *State and Local Government in Idaho and the Nation*, 61–63.

83 Ballotpedia, s.v. "State Executive Offices."

- issuing executive orders nearly as powerful as laws
- strongly influencing the annual budget
- conferencing with, influencing, and organizing state agencies

Third, though not a member of the legislature, the governor possesses some power in the legislative process through the annual State of the State Address, through the budget, and through influencing the agencies mentioned above. Additionally, the governor holds the power of veto. With the threat of veto in view, legislators can be influenced to make changes in a bill to shape it into a more governor-friendly form.

Fourth, the governor is the commander-in-chief of the state militia (the state unit of the National Guard when it is not employed in national service by the President).

Fifth, the governor has clemency power—the authority to exercise leniency toward individuals who have committed crimes. With this power, the governor can issue pardons (nullifying the legal consequences of a crime), commutations (shortening of a sentence), and reprieves (postponing the execution of a sentence).[84] Note that each state's constitution may have different limitations on the governor's clemency power.

Sixth, in some states, the governor is the leader of the state's political party. "Governors may use their role as party leaders to encourage support for legislative initiatives, and along with department heads and staff, may seek to influence the progress of legislation through regular meetings with legislators, legislative officials, and other stakeholders."[85] More on political parties in chapter 8 and stakeholdering in chapter 9.

Seventh, the governor can be the spokesperson for the people in events that significantly affect the state (or parts of it), such as extreme weather events, strikes, riots, or the

84 "Governors: Powers and Authority," National Governors Association.

85 "Governors: Powers and Authority," National Governors Association.

closing of a major industrial plant. The governor may declare an area a disaster area or lead a task force to secure help for a regional problem.

Eighth, the governor represents the state in dealings with national or international government. The governor may be a guest of the President at the White House or may meet with another country for purposes of selling the state's products abroad.

Ninth, the governor may be an *ex-officio* member of important state boards. Remember from chapter 3, that *ex-officio* means "because of the office." If a board has a permanent seat for whoever the current governor is, that is called an *ex-officio* position. This means that in addition to regular daily duties, the governor serves on specific boards or commissions that require a gubernatorial seat at their tables.

The governor not only sits on boards but also makes appointments to them, known as gubernatorial appointments. These individuals are chosen by the governor to fill cabinet-level executive roles on agencies/boards/commissions. As we learned in chapter 2, these boards are enabled by the state's legislature to exist. The appointees may or may not have some degree of qualification for the role. It is not unusual for a major donor to the governor's election campaign to be the recipient of one of these roles—and usually highly paid by the taxpayers. Of course, these agency directors lead their agencies with the particular political bent of the governor in mind as a condition of their appointment. Cabinet agencies report to the governor and convene in cabinet meetings to advise the governor as trusted allies.

Remember that gubernatorial authority is established by the executive powers listed in the state constitution. The same is true for the state's other executive officers which we will look at next. Because there are variations from state to state, some of the following offices are elected positions, and some are appointed positions. Nevertheless, they are all located at or near the state's capitol and are integral to running the state. These offices all have agencies, boards, and/or deputies (assistants) to help them carry out their duties. It is possible that they may be opposed to or work at odds with the governor within the scope of their individual offices. Though they are not generally obligated to support the governor's political vision, agenda, or will, they may not usurp the powers of the office of the governor.

Lieutenant Governor

The next elected executive office at the state level is the lieutenant governor. In many states, this office uniquely spans the executive and legislative branches of state government. In twenty-seven states, the lieutenant governor wears the hat of presiding over the state's Senate when it is in session (as mentioned earlier in our discussion of the legislative branch). Although not a legislator (and thus not permitted to vote in general), in many cases the lieutenant governor can testify on the Senate floor and cast a tie-breaking vote.[86] In Tennessee and West Virginia, the lieutenant governor is known as the president/speaker of the Senate and is elected to this dual role by the state legislature.[87] Texas's lieutenant governor is very powerful, making committee assignments for the House[88] and setting the agenda for the Senate.

The lieutenant governor also serves when the governor is temporarily absent. The word *lieutenant* makes sense if you are familiar with the French language. It can be broken into two parts: *lieu* which means "place," and *tenant* which means "holding." So, the lieutenant governor holds the place of the

86 "Roles in State Senates," National Lieutenant Governors Association, September 2022.

87 Ballotpedia, s.v. "Lieutenant Governor (state executive office)."

88 The House refers to the larger of the two bodies of the state legislature.

governor when needed. In some states, the governor and lieutenant are elected together, and in some states, they run separately on the ballot, meaning they can be from different political parties or different ideologies within the same party. In the latter case, the governor knows that it is not wise to be absent very long or very often; otherwise, his *lieu* will be *tenant*-ed by a member of the opposition. All but five states have this elected office—Arizona, Maine, New Hampshire, Oregon, and Wyoming do not.[89]

Attorney General

Another executive office is the state attorney general. The person who holds this office is considered the highest law enforcement official in the state.[90] As the chief legal officer of the state, the attorney general represents state agencies, offices, boards, and commissions, and provides legal opinions for state legislatures and other public officeholders.[91] Most attorneys general are elected, although some are appointed by the governor, the state legislature, or the state supreme court.[92]

Recall that in chapter 4, we learned that the county prosecutor is considered the county's highest law enforcement official and represents the county's people in criminal (and some civil) court cases. The attorney general serves in the same fashion but at the next level of government. As such, this elected executive represents the state in significant legal matters. Other state agencies may still have their own legal

---

89 Ballotpedia, s.v. "Lieutenant Governor (state executive office)."

90 Ballotpedia, s.v. "Attorney General (state executive office)."

91 "State Attorneys General," USAGov.

92 Forty-three states elect their attorney general; the governors of Alaska, Hawaii, New Hampshire, New Jersey, and Wyoming appoint the attorney general; the state legislature of Maine appoints its attorneys general, and the state supreme court of Tennessee appoints its attorney general. Ballotpedia, s.v. "Attorney General office comparison."

counsel for various functions. Some states delegate certain responsibilities, such as defending lawsuits against state emplyees, to specific divisions or appointed outside counsel.

If a case in a criminal suit that was handled at the county level by the county prosecutor is heard on appeal, the attorney general's office handles the appeal. If a county is sued, the state attorney general then represents the county. The office can also hear civil cases (such as when people owe money to the state) and can even handle situations of misconduct such as when an elected officeholder does something wrong in the state. Similarly, if local authorities request assistance for a specific case, the attorney general can step in. In the same way that the county prosecutor has deputy prosecutors to assist in the work, the state attorney general also has deputy attorneys general to assist in carrying out the prolific duties of this office.

Forty-four states have a type of appointed deputy attorney general whose task is to represent the state in federal cases (suits involving the federal government).[93] This position is known as the solicitor general and serves to help safeguard the state's interest against federal overreach. The solicitor general can also advise the attorney general to join other states in a suit against the federal government by filing an amicus brief—a friend of the court statewide brief. In short, the solicitor general represents state laws in state and federal courts.

Secretary of State

Like the attorney general, the secretary of state is elected in most states and appointed in others.[94] All states except for Alaska, Hawaii, and Utah have a secretary of state, although in

93 Dan Schweitzer et al., "The Constitutional Role of the State Solicitor General," March 24, 2023, produced by The National Constitution Center, video, 3:53.

94 Ballotpedia, s.v. "Secretary of State (state executive office)."

Massachusetts, Pennsylvania, and Virginia this office is called by another name—the secretary of the commonwealth.[95] Kentucky is also a commonwealth, but it has a secretary of state.[96] As the title implies, the secretary of state is the primary records keeper or secretary of each state.

What sort of records might the secretary of state maintain? For one, this office is the keeper of the state seal—the primary graphic emblem that represents the state. Another significant duty of this office in many states is to serve as the state's chief election official in charge of the election process and the official election results. In fact, for many states, the secretary of state's website is **the** place to go for election information both before (for voter registration, eligibility, and poll locations by county) and after (to find official election results) voting day. In chapter 4, we learned that one of the roles of the county clerk is to carry out local election duties as an arm of the state. Some states organize their election duties under other entities (see more information on this topic in chapter 8, Voting, Elections & Parties"). Other duties of the secretary of state's office may include recording official acts of the governor, registering businesses, and commissioning/regulating public notaries.[97]

Treasurer

This brings us to the office of the state treasurer which exists in forty-eight states.[98] It is an elected office in thirty-six of

95 Ballotpedia, s.v. "Secretary of State (state executive office)."

96 "There are four states in the United States that call themselves commonwealths: Kentucky, Massachusetts, Pennsylvania, and Virginia. The distinction is in name alone. The commonwealths are just like any other state in their politics and laws, and there is no difference in their relationship to the nation as a whole." *Merriam-Webster*, s.v. "What's the difference between a commonwealth and a state?."

97 Ballotpedia, s.v. "Secretary of State (state executive office)."

98 New York and Texas do not have the office of treasurer. Ballotpedia, s.v. "Treasurer (state executive office)."

those states.[99] This treasurer collects and invests state money, oversees state agency spending, and pays state bills.[100] Because this office oversees agency spending, it acts as a partial check/balance on state agency actions—at least in the financial sense. The treasurer serves, in essence, as the state's chief financial officer (CFO) and oversees the state's financial status, investments, and assets.[101] As such, this person works with state and local governments to manage their municipal bonds (which fund local infrastructure improvements) and to develop/deliver financial resources and programs (such as 529 college-savings plans). Further, the state treasurer invests and manages state funds (including employee pensions programs) and maintains unclaimed property programs to assist residents with lost/unclaimed funds or assets.[102]

Controller (Comptroller)

Often confused with the treasurer's office is the state controller, also called the comptroller (spelled with an *m* and a silent *p*) or the auditor. Nineteen states have a controller, with nine of those being elected and ten of those being appointed positions.[103] The position mainly involves "managing a statewide accounting system and providing internal controls for state agencies."[104] The controller somewhat invisibly works with the governor, lieutenant governor, and frequently the

99 "In the remaining twelve states, the position is appointed. In eight of those states the power of appointment is given to the governor, while in the remaining four the state legislature is empowered to select a treasurer." Ballotpedia, s.v. "Treasurer (state executive office)."

100 Ragone, *The Everything American Government Book*, 243.

101 "State Treasurers Count," National Association of State Treasurers, data compiled as of December 31, 2020.

102 "State Treasurers Count," National Association of State Treasurers.

103 Ballotpedia, s.v. "Controller (state executive office)."

104 "Government 101: What Does a State Comptroller Do?" MasterClass, September 12, 2022.

state treasurer to ensure that state funds are appropriately discharged. Similar to the treasurer, the controller functions as CFO/chief accountant for the state, hiring auditors to work alongside local governments or regional governments.[105] To find out if your state has a controller/comptroller, and to see what the position entails and whether it is an elected position or not, search the internet with these words: "state executive offices in the (your state's name here) constitution." That way, you'll at least know which name to settle upon. If your state does not have this executive position, the work may be done by the secretary of state or the treasurer. Whichever office does this work, check to see if it maintains a transparency website that makes public all governmental financial information from local budgets to salaries of all state and local government employees.[106]

Superintendent of Public Education

The last generally recognized statewide office is the superintendent of public education. Every state has an agency or department that oversees its system of public instruction. The superintendent of public education handles all of the individual city and county public school systems in the state as the chief state school officer who oversees public higher education, and works in concert with a state board of education.[107] The superintendent is elected in twelve states (as decreed either by the state constitution or the state code of statutes) and appointed in thirty-eight states. This executive office can go by many names, such as superintendent of schools, superintendent of education, superintendent of public instruction, secretary of education, or chief school administrator. Not only

105 "Government 101: What Does a State Comptroller Do?," MasterClass.

106 See *Transparent Idaho* (website), State of Idaho Controller's Office.

107 Ballotpedia, s.v. "Superintendent of Schools (state executive office)."

do the names vary from state to state, but the duties of this office also vary. Generally, the superintendent "hire[s] and supervise[s] all the schools' staff and principals and work[s] with school boards to make daily decisions about spending, facilities and educational programs."[108] The superintendent works with various constituencies and uses available funding in all state school districts to meet the needs of students and to meet educational goals while utilizing available funding.[109] Check to see where and when the state board of education convenes in your state for regional meetings, and try to attend in person or at least attend via live stream.

I hope that many of the readers of this book are part of a private Christian education enterprise or a homeschool venture. While such schools are not beholden to the department of public instruction (assuming they do not accept government funds), it is still good for these readers to know that this office exists. It is also good to know that each state legislature, along with the governor's approval, makes the laws that govern and fund public education within the state. It can be challenging to locate parental education rights within the state statutes. The state statute title dealing with the topic of education is a great place to look, but there may be other sections, such as parent-child relations. The Homeschool Legal Defense Association (HSLDA) website is an excellent resource to help parents locate and read their state laws. See the links page at **CivilRealm.com**.

Although typically outside the public system, homeschoolers and private schoolers who refuse all government funding yet give their children/students an excellent education are uniquely positioned to influence their state legislators. These people pay their taxes (which fund public education) but also privately fund the education of their own children. They

108 Danielle Smyth, "What Are the Duties of the Superintendent of Public Instruction?," *Houston Chronicle*, Chron., February 2, 2022.

109 Smyth, "What Are the Duties?"

are in a position to relate to their legislators without requesting or being desirous of state funding for education. They are free of the public education system and are free thinkers, yet they are interested in the well-being of the government. These are rare individuals in the eyes of our state legislators and state superintendent of public education. Learning about how the city, county, and state governance systems operate further places these individuals in a position of significant influence. One day, they may not be so rare. One day, they may set the state's educational bar higher.[110]

This section thus concludes an introduction to the most common executive branch offices at the state level. To look up the specific offices in your state, search for your state's constitution online. If you can find the table of contents, look for the executive branch. I encourage you to read that section because it is the foundational statement for the structure of your state's executive branch. You can find further details on this branch of state government in your state's code of laws (statutes).

GOVERNANCE STRUCTURE

The Judicial Branch

Within our nation's judicial branch, there is a federal court system and a state court system. The federal court system considers cases of a national nature, while the state court system considers cases of a local and state nature. Their design or form is very similar, but the content of the cases that they consider differs. On rare occasions, a person may be tried in

110 I work for New Saint Andrews College, a private Christian liberal arts college which does not accept any government money or federal financial aid including student loans and Pell Grants. The college is free of strings to the state and federal levels of government. It not only maintains an excellent relationship with state legislators and executives, but it also sets a high example of educational excellence.

both systems if both state and national laws are involved.[111] Both judicial systems serve the function of interpreting the law. Both systems are organized into geographic areas (usually called districts),[112] but the areas differ according to the system. There are state districts and federal districts.

Both systems possess the power of judicial review—the authority to assess the constitutionality of actions by the executive and legislative branches. Judicial review serves as a check on the other two branches, although it is not mentioned in the Constitution. It was instituted in 1803 as a result of the Supreme Court case *Marbury v. Madison*.[113] Because of this decision, the judicial branch set the precedent to give itself the ultimate authority to determine what is constitutional. At the state level, the state supreme court looks to its state constitution as the supreme law in order to determine what is and is not constitutional. At the federal level, the Supreme Court looks to the U.S. Constitution. This is a critical distinction. Remember, too, that lower courts must follow the precedent of higher courts. We will discuss the federal judicial system further in the next chapter.

Civil and Criminal Cases

Approximately ninety percent of cases heard in the American court system take place within the state (rather than the fed-

111 "A person who robs a bank may be tried and convicted in state court for robbery, then tried and convicted in federal court for the federal offense of robbery of a federally-chartered [F.D.I.C.] savings institution." Harvey Wallace, "Federal and State Jurisdiction." chap. 2.1 in *National Victim Assistance Academy*, ed. Anne Seymour, et al., Office for Victims of Crime, 2000.

112 The existence of judicial districts was also foreshadowed and differentiated from special districts in chapter 5, "Special Districts, Independent Cities, Townships & Regional Governments.

113 In this case, President Federalist John Adams made judicial appointments at the end of his term, but incoming President Jefferson's Secretary of State James Madison did not deliver the papers. Supreme Court Justice John Marshall decided the rather insignificant case in favor of Jefferson but much more importantly set the precedent for the judicial branch to have the final say on whether the other two branches' actions are constitutional or not.

eral) judicial system.[114] Because the U.S. Constitution reserves power to the states, each state's courts' names and processes vary greatly across the nation.[115] Each state court system is designed with the purpose of interpreting its own state constitution and code of laws. Interestingly, forty-nine of the states have a legal system based on common law. (Recall from chapter 2, that common law is law derived from the body of prior judicial decisions that helps interpret the meaning of legislative statutes.) Because of its history, Louisiana is the only state that is based upon French civil law rather than on British common law.[116]

In surveying the structure of the state court system, it is vital to understand the distinction between criminal and civil cases. A criminal case (a crime) represents a violation of state law such as robbery, assault, murder, drug-related crimes, rape, and so on. Crimes can be classified as felonies (grave crimes with long to lifetime sentences) and misdemeanors (less serious crimes with temporary penalties, fines, or punishments).[117] See footnote for an example of a misdemeanor becoming a felony.[118] Recall from earlier that the prosecutor brings a criminal case on behalf of the people of the state.

A civil case is a private dispute between two parties. Civil law deals with settling issues (usually in the form of payment) involving injury, harm, or loss such as divorce, custody, busi-

---

114 "State Courts vs. Federal Courts," Judicial Learning Center, 2019.

115 "The State Court Structures" charts at the **National Center for State Courts website** (mentioned in chapter 4, "County-Equivalent Government") are very helpful. Click on the desired state, and its court structure chart will appear. This website is also very convenient for comparing two or more states' judicial structure. Of course, you can search your own state, county, and city's government websites.

116 "Common law: Defining what it is and what you need to know," Thomson Reuters, November 15, 2022.

117 Felonies can result in loss of rights to vote, possess firearms, or hold public office and often involve a twelve-person jury. Misdemeanors are punishable by less than one year of incarceration and can involve a smaller (six-person) jury.

118 "You can be slightly over the limit during a DUI stop and get a misdemeanor, but if you have children in the car or are severely over the blood alcohol limit you can face a felony charge." "What's the Difference Between a Misdemeanor vs. Felony?" FindLaw, August 17, 2023.

ness disputes, vehicle accidents, medical malpractice, or personal injury. Civil law also covers probate cases involving wills and/or the disbursement of belongings of someone who dies. The plaintiff brings a civil case on his or her own behalf.

Judicial Districts

Each state is geographically divided into judicial districts to serve the legal needs of the citizens who live within those districts. Each state has a number of judges who preside in each specific district. Do not confuse these state districts with federal judicial districts—we will discuss them in chapter 7, "National Government."

Three Levels of Courts

The state court system follows this general process: The first or lowest level of courts are trial courts. This is the level where all cases begin (except for the states with municipal courts that we learned about in chapter 3). At the intermediate level, there are courts of appeal. In courts of appeal, a lower court's decision can be reviewed by a higher court. Appeals courts are next-resort courts for use (when it appears possible that the trial court's decision was made in error), and they serve as a check or balance within the judicial system. The court of last resort dealing with state-related laws is usually called the state supreme court. Let's look at each level in a little more detail.

First Tier: Trial Courts

The beginning level consists of first-tier courts or trial courts that hear cases regarding violation of state law. Note that there can be several types of these entry-level courts: criminal, civil, juvenile,[119] tax tribunal,[120] probate,[121] and so on. This specialization occurs primarily at the state and local entry-level courts rather than in federal courts.[122]

> In many states, courts of limited jurisdiction hear misdemeanor cases. Other state courts of general jurisdiction try felonies. Still other courts may be designated as juvenile courts and hear only matters involving juveniles. This process also occurs in certain civil courts that hear only family law matters, probate matters, housing matters, or civil cases involving damages.[123]

Knowing that the jury system exists only at the trial-court level is helpful. The state court system has two main juries: the grand jury and the petit jury. The grand jury customarily consists of eighteen citizens chosen by lottery from the judicial district in which a criminal case is potentially being tried. The grand jury's purpose is solely to decide whether there is sufficient evidence to warrant a trial or not. The petit jury (also just called the "jury") typically consists of twelve jurors chosen in the same manner—citizens chosen by lottery from the judicial district in which they live and in which the case will be tried. The petit jury can be used in both civil and criminal trials. In a civil suit, the petit jury decides questions of liability and compensation to the wronged (whether or not

---

119 A juvenile court handles criminal cases against children under eighteen years of age and operates under different (more flexible) parameters than a court for adults.

120 "A state tax tribunal is a means to resolve state tax appeal controversies prior to litigation, and in a forum outside the dominion and control of the state tax authority." "Chart of States with and without State Tax Tribunals (as of 6/2/20)," Association of International Certified Professional Accountants.

121 "A probate court is a court of limited jurisdiction that hears matters surrounding a person's death. For example, probate courts oversee the distribution of dead peoples' assets according to their wills and direct the distribution of dead peoples' assets if they die without a will." *Wex Legal Dictionary and Encyclopedia*, s.v. "Probate court," Legal Information Institute, Cornell Law School.

122 Wallace, "Federal and State Jurisdiction."

123 Wallace, "Federal and State Jurisdiction."

the defendant injured the plaintiff in a manner that requires restitution). In a criminal suit, the petit jury decides whether and of what offenses the defendant is guilty.

Second Tier: Appellate Courts

Second-tier courts are known as appellate courts and, like trial courts, are known by a variety of different names. These courts hear and review legal cases that have already received a ruling from a lower court. Because the jury system only exists at the trial-court level, appellate courts feature judges with no jury component.[124] They exist as specific courts in forty-two of the fifty states. The states of Delaware, Maine, Montana, New Hampshire, Rhode Island, South Dakota, Vermont, and Wyoming combine their appellate court duties with their state supreme courts. In other words, they combine the second- and third-tier courts.[125]

Third Tier: Supreme Courts

The third-tier court is the state supreme court. It is the final court of appeals, also known as the court of last resort. As such, this court holds final authority within the state court system. Like the other two levels in the state judicial branch, some states' supreme court names may differ slightly,[126] while one state (New York) completely deviates from the typical

---

124 *Wex Legal Dictionary and Encyclopedia*, s.v. "Appellate court," Legal Information Institute, Cornell Law School.

125 Ballotpedia, s.v. "Intermediate appellate courts."

126 For example: Maryland is Maryland Court of Appeals; Massachusetts is Massachusetts Supreme Judicial Court, New York is State of New York Court of Appeals, and West Virginia is Supreme Court of Appeals of West Virginia.

nomenclature for the three levels.[127] Most states, however, have chosen the simple title of Supreme Court. While most states have only one supreme court, the states of Oklahoma and Texas actually have two: one for criminal cases and one for civil cases.[128] For an authoritative description of how your state's judicial system functions, check your own state's **.gov** website for the judicial branch.

STATE JUDICIAL SYSTEM

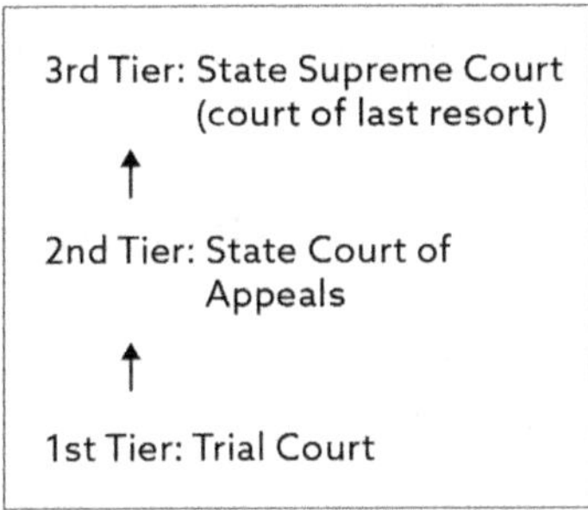

Figure 6.8

Names of Courts

As just mentioned, the names of the courts vary from state to state at all three levels, making it challenging to discuss the state court system as a whole. Do not be discouraged by the variety of names from state to state; knowing the three-tier system (combined into two tiers for some states) is the key to

127 New York's trial courts are known as New York Supreme Courts. Its appellate courts are known as New York Supreme Court, Appellate Division. The New York supreme court is known as State of New York Court of Appeals.

128 Texas has the Texas Court of Criminal Appeals and the Supreme Court of Texas for civil matters. Oklahoma has the Oklahoma Court of Criminal Appeals and the Oklahoma Supreme Court for civil matters.

understanding the system. Since most cases begin within the entry-level trial courts, it is helpful to know that they may be called by such varied names as district courts, circuit courts, superior courts, magistrate courts, common pleas courts, and so on.

Selection of Judges

Although federal judges are all appointed (as we will learn in the next chapter), state judges are selected in several different ways. Most state judges are elected.[129] Others are appointed for a given term, sometimes even for life. Still others are appointed for a time and then validated or removed by the electorate at the polls. This appointment process followed by election is known as the Missouri Plan because it originated in Missouri and was then applied by other states.[130] It is purported to allow a check on the judicial system by the public. However, election directly by We the People is a superior check to a judge who is first appointed by a commission or committee and then stands before the electorate at a later date. These procedures outlined above also hold true for state supreme court judges, who are called justices, with the presiding judge bearing the title of chief justice.[131]

---

129 *Encyclopedia Britannica*, s.v. "State and local government,"

130 "It involves the creation of a nominating commission that screens judicial candidates and submits to the appointing authority (such as the governor) a limited number of names of individuals considered to be qualified. The appointing authority chooses from the list, and any one so chosen assumes the judgeship for a probationary period. After this period the judge stands for popular election for a much longer term, not competing against other candidates but basing his candidacy on previous judgments." *Encyclopedia Britannica*, s.v. "Missouri Plan," September 18, 2019.

131 "Trial and intermediate appellate court judges in most states and in the federal judicial system are called judges, while those on the highest courts are justices. But that is not the case in New York, where some trial judges are known as justices, or in Texas, where intermediate appellate judges are called justices, and some of the highest court judges are judges." Jason Boatright, "The History, Meaning, and Use of the Words Justice and Judge," *St. Mary's Law Journal* 49, no. 4 (August 2018): 727.

OTHER THINGS YOU SHOULD KNOW

The Census Bureau produces a synopsis of the local governments within each state in a document titled *Individual State Descriptions: 2022 Census of Governments* (the web address is listed on the links page at **CivilRealm.com**).

Regarding the Legislative Branch

Legislators' jobs include much more than just the stated time that the legislature convenes: "For one thing, casework does not end when the session concludes. And the obligation to attend meetings in the district does not disappear. It is almost certainly the case that the general public overestimates the amount of money legislators are paid and underestimates the amount of work involved in their jobs. Lawmakers themselves recognize early on that the job is far more than it seems on the surface."[132]

Also, one of the things that the COVID-19 pandemic did was make remote testifying at the statehouse possible. This enables citizens to testify at the statehouse more easily or conveniently, but it is still not as effective as being there personally.

Regarding the Executive Branch

As mentioned earlier in the chapter, in addition to the governor, lieutenant governor, the attorney general, the secretary of state, the state treasurer, state comptroller/controller/auditor, and the superintendent of public education, there may be other elected (and appointed) executive-level offices in

132 Moncrief and Squire, *State Legislatures Today*, 203.

your state. This is a great time to go to your state's website and look at the complete list for your state.

Regarding the Judicial Branch

The "State Court Structures" charts at the **National Center for State Courts website** has detailed information for each state and a link leading to each state's supreme court website. Browsing there should lead you to the number of (state) judicial districts in your state. Another helpful website to uncover state judicial district information is **Ballotpedia.org** where you can search for courts and judges by state.

Search the internet for the names of courts within your specific state's judicial system.

- What are the first-tier courts called?
- What are the second-tier courts called?
- How is the third-tier (Supreme Court) structured?

THINGS YOU CAN DO

Hearkening back to the opening paragraph, if you are a pastor or in Christian ministry, you may want to connect with other like-minded people and begin a statehouse ministry. The staff at the Minnesota Family Council and Institute have put together an inspiring website to help you get started investing in your state-elected officeholders.[133]

If you are not a pastor or if you live far from the statehouse, praying regularly with state officeholders may not be feasible. However, it should give you pause whether you are

133 "Church Ambassador Network," Minnesota Family Council. See also "Pulpits & Politics," Minnesota Family Council.

STATE SYSTEMS

LEGISLATIVE

EXECUTIVE

JUDICIAL

State Voters

Legislature/General Assembly

Senate

House of ____ or ____ Assembly

Governor

State Judges**

**Some states' governors make judicial appointments

Other Voter-Elected Offices*

Lieutenant Governor
Attorney General
Secretary of State
Treasurer
Controller (Comptroller)
Superintendent of Public Education

Many Agency, Board & Commission Members

*Some states elect more or fewer offices than those listed here

Figure 6.9

KEY

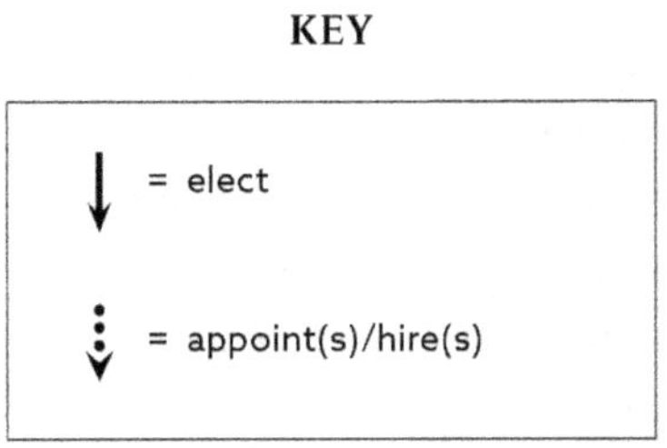

outside or inside of the statehouse. If you are on the outside, you can pray for those in all three branches of state government. You can research issues that are important factors in your state's future in order to be an aware citizen. You can email, handwrite, or type letters to your elected representatives in all three branches of government. (Or try Facebook Messenger or some other social media platform which sometimes connects the citizen to his or her legislator more efficiently than other avenues of communication.)

Spend time at your own state's website for each of the three branches of state government. There is an amazing civic education to be had there. Remember that you do not have to agree with or condone all that your state government does in order to be conversant with it. It is nearly impossible to effectively engage with a system that we do not understand let alone attempt to improve it.

Watch the local media outlets to be aware of times that these elected people are in town for community events such as those hosted by your local area chamber of commerce. Although the focus of this book is civic rather than partisan in nature, consider attending the Republican Party's annual Lincoln Day Dinner that takes place in your county each spring. This dinner is a fine opportunity to meet and chat with all levels of your elected representatives, and it is an exceptionally efficient way to connect with those who serve at the state level of government who may otherwise be quite far away geographically. Just be sure to do your homework in advance and research the individuals who will be there through their websites and look into some of their work and accomplishments. Even if you disagree with their positions on issues, find some common ground where you can agree. Often being in public office means receiving a heavy load of overly emotional verbal (often written) venting. Rise above base emotionalism by following Christ.

In the Legislative Branch

Pray for your Legislators.

Your state legislators are tasked with what is known as casework or constituent service which involves answering their constituents' emails, texts, or phone calls ranging from small issues to larger issues (such as assisting them in a dispute with a state agency).[134] State legislators need wisdom from God and input from those whom they represent in order to do their jobs well. Know those in your own district, as well as those in other districts. Pray for them by name.

Introduce yourself.

As just mentioned, state legislators often have legislative coffees hosted by the local chamber of commerce during legislative session (or livestreamed on Zoom) for the purpose of connecting with their constituents. I first met one of my state representatives at a meeting where many unhappy members of the public education system wanted more funding. After the meeting, I thanked my state representative for coming and presenting. Then, I introduced myself and kindly informed her that I am a homeschool parent who pays my taxes and asks nothing of the state for my children's education. Furthermore, I informed her that there is a very sizeable, quiet contingent of outstanding educators in the community who do likewise. I stressed that public money is not necessary to feed and educate the next generation. We have been friends ever since, in part, because I did not have my hand out for funds nor my mind darkened with ingratitude.

Have your children serve.

If you desire to experience the inside of the state capitol and you have children, consider enrolling them in the statehouse page program. Each state has different requirements, but it is an excellent opportunity for a young person to serve on the floor of the legislature.

---

134 Moncrief and Squire, *State Legislatures Today*, 23.

Likewise, for high schoolers, look into TeenPact Leadership Schools to experience four to five days of learning about the state legislature while at the capitol. I attended TeenPact as a parent, and the week presented opportunities to make appointments with leaders at the statehouse in addition to sitting in on classes. In the past, I have been able to shadow one of my state representatives and meet with the other two in addition to meeting the Speaker of the House and becoming acquainted with the staff at the legislative research library. (They showed me the volumes of state code and also have been willing to answer obscure questions that I have emailed them regarding information for this book.) Another year, I made appointments and visited with several members of my state executive branch and also met a supreme court justice. My friends who were at the capitol for TeenPact even met the governor.

Be a gracious observer.

Find out when your legislature is in session and go and observe both chambers in action (remember to remove any questionable items in advance from your handbag such as water bottles, utility knives, or multi-tools that you might normally carry before you enter). Schedule an appointment with your state legislators or other elected state officials in advance of your trip to the state house. Attend a committee meeting as well, if you are able. Be sure to follow up with a handwritten thank you note afterward to your elected officeholders and even to staff members who were helpful.

Be informed.

Locate your state's code of laws online and follow up on the topic of open-meeting or sunshine laws (first mentioned in chapter 3, "City Government"). A quick way to find your state law's interpretation of conducting open meetings is to search your state's name in your internet browser along with the words *open meeting laws* or *sunshine laws*. Simply browsing the state law itself takes longer but can be quite interesting. Try looking under the title *Government* and then under a section with a name such as *Meetings*.

Begin the process of locating, reading, and understanding your state's annual budget. Because this document is difficult to understand, I wonder if its complexity perpetuates state spending. Appropriations are based on the prior year's budget, and this encourages spending increases as well. Further, in the flurry of activity facing our legislators, I wonder if they pass appropriations bills because that is the simple way to move forward through their work. Imagine if they had a fiscally educated electorate who could keep them accountable and help guide them through the financial maze. Also, imagine if state programs (and funding increases) had to be proven effective before they were allowed to continue as a line item in the following year's budget.

Sign up to receive emails from the governor and elected representatives in order to follow their work. Also, sign up at your state legislature's website to follow your state's bill tracker in order to watch issues that come before the legislature. An excellent resource available to anyone is the Legiscan website which can be located at **legiscan.com**. Enter the name of your state, and Legiscan will show you the current legislation that is under consideration by both houses of your state's legislature.

Watch live coverage of your legislature as it is aired—most likely via your state legislature's website. Be well-informed enough to meet with representatives in a concerned-citizen-lobbyist role if necessary. In the process, avoid being combative; rather, be a gracious and well-informed constituent. Investing in our system of state governance is part of our dual inheritance. It is a tall order, but we are not without hope or guidance:

- "He who is faithful in what is least is faithful also in much" (Luke 16:10).
- "He who loves purity of heart / And has grace on his lips, / The king will be his friend" (Proverbs 22:11).
- "Do you see a man who excels in his work? / He will stand before kings; / He will not stand before unknown men" (Proverbs 22:29).

While at the statehouse on one of my visits, I had a conversation with a Christian gentleman state representative, and he expressed concern about a young man of his acquaintance who was especially interested in conspiracy theories and things politically extreme. He wondered how to guide a young person away from extremism and toward a reasoned approach to political involvement. I told him what we had discussed during one of our civics club meetings: "By long forbearance a ruler is persuaded, / And a gentle tongue breaks a bone." The representative's face lit up, and he was delighted. He requested the verse reference. It is Proverbs 25:15.

In the Executive Branch

- Watch the governor's State of the State Address at the outset of each year.
- Sign up to receive emails from each member of your state's executive branch.
- Look at each of their websites.
- Take any opportunity to meet an executive branch officeholder.

In the Judicial Branch

- Make a list of the judges at each tier of the judicial system for the district of the state in which you live including the state supreme court justices and pray for them by name.
- Pray that they would seek the Lord and be heirs of this promise as a result: "Evil men do not understand justice, / But those who seek the LORD understand all" (Proverbs 28:5).

Drug Court/Treatment Court Opportunities

For those readers who are not seeking further formal education, yet who are interested in the justice system and in ministering to others, take note of the possible existence of drug courts, also known as treatment courts. If they exist in your state, drug courts (similar, in a sense, to juvenile courts) are special court-instituted programs for individuals with alcohol or drug dependency problems. Participants have an opportunity for a second chance at life and for rehabilitation. "Treatment court participants who successfully complete the program can have their underlying criminal offenses dismissed or expunged. However, if a participant fails to complete the program, their case is processed through the traditional justice system."[135]

Typically across the nation, drug court programs present an opportunity for people suffering from addiction to find regularly scheduled help and encouragement from a team of people including the judge, prosecuting attorney, defense attorney, law-enforcement/parole officers, and members of the community in a way that differs from the normal criminal-jus-

135 "Treatment Courts: Special Feature," U.S. Department of Justice.

tice docket. It is an opportunity for the judge in a drug case to sit on the bench as a coach, providing an unusual occasion (within specific parameters) for justice and mercy to meet.

The judge and legal professionals take high-risk, high-need individuals and serve as coaches to direct them toward lifelong sobriety, rather than simply removing them from the streets and temporarily incarcerating them, which has little lasting benefit. Addiction offenders have frequently not tasted success and have never heard words such as, "Good job," or "Well done." This personal mentoring investment from a judge or legal professional can have life-changing results.

The drug court program also affords community members an opportunity to come alongside second-chance offenders and mentor them with personal touches such as offering tutoring in English, tutoring in preparation to take the GED (General Education Development) test, or donating such items as locally purchased and modestly priced gift cards as good-behavior incentives. Opportunities abound for gifts of toiletries, food, and clothing while these individuals make proactive steps toward sobriety and assimilation into a productive society. On a larger scale, local church groups can provide a home or apartment that serves as a haven dedicated to a drug-court individual's introductory steps toward rehabilitation. Understanding drug court is an example of how knowing the nuances in the structure of our government can lead to connecting with people to really make a difference in their lives and in our communities.

A Career in Law?

Before concluding this overview of the state judicial branch, I would like to encourage readers with opportunities for further education to consider exploring a vocation in law. There is a great need in our nation for attorneys to serve in many arenas, including as judges. Further, although it is not a requirement, many of our nation's state legislators are attorneys. Generally speaking, the individuals who understand our American system of governance the best are attorneys. Could God be calling you to invest your American inheritance in the legal profession? One place to look for more information is **Alliance Defending Freedom**'s website.

SO WHAT?

After having read this chapter, here are some questions to ask yourself:

- Do you understand that state government is monumental in our lives because much of the authority around us is granted by the state which is recognized and protected, in turn, by the U.S. Constitution?
- Do you understand the purpose of a state constitution?
- Do you understand the three branches of government at the state level?
- Do you understand how the state judicial branch works and differs from the federal judicial branch?
- Do you understand that state government agencies are enabled by the state legislature and exist under the executive branch?
- There is a risk that the Founding Fathers recognized: the government becoming the master of the people, rather than being a servant of the people. Is this book helping you think about the proper role of government?

GOVERNANCE STRUCTURE IN THE UNITED STATES

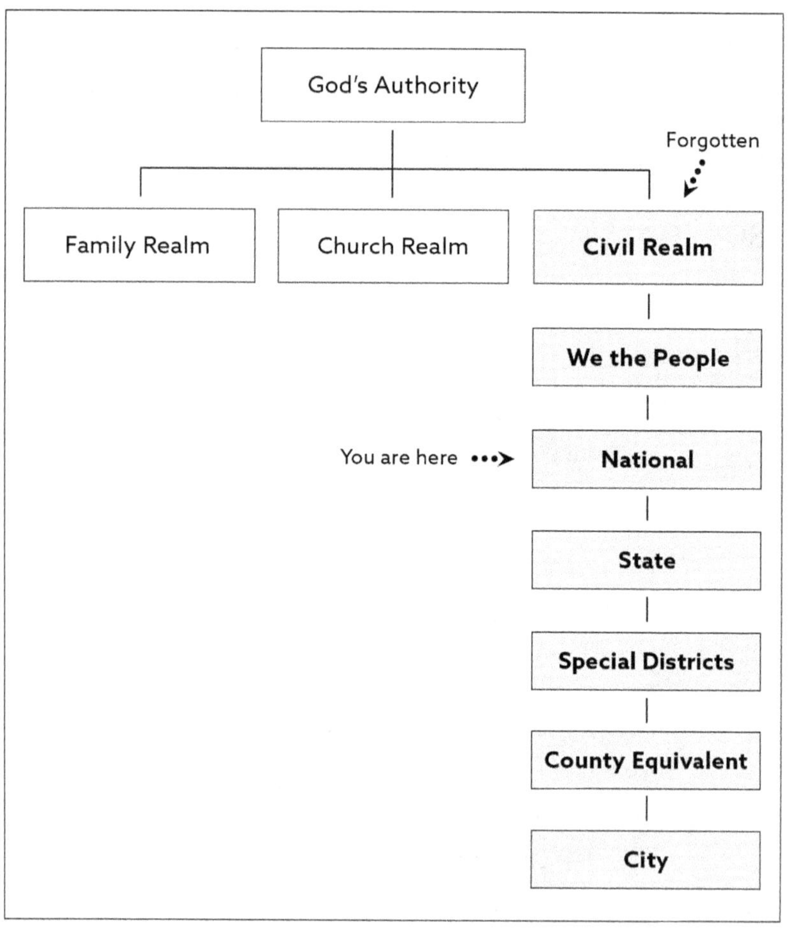

Figure 7.1

CHAPTER 7
National Government

By the end of his nearly decade-long stint working in politics in Washington, D.C., William was serving as a Deputy Assistant Secretary of Defense in the Pentagon, right down the hallway from the office of the Secretary of Defense himself. It was a higher-ranking position than he ever imagined he would have. William's job was to be the lead negotiator and liaison with the House of Representatives on behalf of the Office of the Secretary of Defense in defending the priorities and policies of the 2016 Trump Administration. This job came after spending a little over three years at the Department of State, doing similar legislative affairs work, including as the Director of House Affairs.

But how did William get there? As he would say—by God's grace. It was His hand of blessing. At the same time, William worked hard with his own hands while pursuing a path that just about anyone else could follow.

William moved to D.C. at the beginning of 2012 to join a church. He had just become a Christian and knew he needed to belong to a local church body. When he arrived in our nation's capital, William was essentially broke and had student loans hanging over his head. He needed a job—and fast. So he took work as a waiter at P. F. Chang's and then pursued getting a job in a Congressional office. Since he was new to town, he didn't know how things worked but wanted to take the initiative. So he printed his resume, put on a suit and tie, and walked around the Congressional office buildings, dropping his resume off with members of Congress from his home state of North Carolina. In a few weeks, he got a callback. It wasn't a job offer, but rather the chance to work as an unpaid intern for Rep. Virginia Foxx (R-NC). It was a chance to get his "foot in the door"—so he took it.

After interning for three months (and waiting tables on the side) William eventually got a full-time job as a Legislative Correspondent. In a couple of years, he became a Legislative Assistant, working for Rep. Dave Brat (R-VA), where he helped write bills that became law, passed amendments, wrote speeches, and met with constituents on the congressman's behalf. Next, William went on to be the Deputy Director of Government Relations for Heritage Action for America. In this role, he worked on critical pieces of legislation from the lobbying side, like the First Amendment Defense Act to protect those who believe in man-woman marriage. But after Trump won in 2016, he leaped at the chance to volunteer at the Presidential Transition Organization; again, he worked hard, and God blessed the effort. This opened the door for him to join the Department of State and work on foreign policy and international affairs. And William ended where he began this story: working at the Pentagon in the Senior Executive Service as a Deputy Assistant Secretary of Defense.

William lays out his path for you because he wants you to know that you can do it, too. He is from a small town in North Carolina. He loves his parents, but his family isn't politically connected—they weren't major donors or able to pull the strings for their son. They homeschooled him until high school when William began attending a Christian high school at a local Baptist church. He graduated from a small Christian college with a degree in history. Because William cares about our nation and its future, when he moved to D.C. he knew he had to do what he could and serve where he could to try to make a difference as a Christian in our federal government. The Lord was kind to bless his efforts—both his career and his wit-

ness to co-workers. During his time there, William was able to share the gospel with many co-workers and bring many to his church.

When he left D.C. in 2021, to pursue finishing his seminary degree and work at the intersection of faith and politics, he felt like David in Samuel 7:18 when he says to God, "Who am I, Sovereign Lord, and what is my family, that you have brought me this far?" William wants to inspire others like you, to let you know that you can pursue the same path that he did, seeking to make a difference on behalf of the Christian faith and the American people, even at some of the highest levels of our federal government.[1]

We now arrive at the national level. Often the most geographically distant and highest, this is yet the best-known layer of our government. As mentioned earlier, this national arena is where most civics books begin. From American government/history books to the media to educational materials to online and in-person courses, the content of national government is widely known and taught.

The preceding chapters have discussed our American government's formation, law, services, and structure at the city, county-equivalent, special district, and state levels. As such, they have done the heavy lifting for this chapter in manageable increments. This chapter could conceivably serve as the book's conclusion because a conclusion summarizes by briefly restating the main points. However, this is not just any American government book—it is an American government book for those who call themselves Christians. Therefore, we have a couple of chapters to explore in order to more fully uncover the forgotten realm.

1 This story is based on my personal correspondence with William Wolfe.

The continuing goal has been that you may understand the levels of American government better than you ever have so that you can engage in the public square to the glory of God. Apart from Christ, our study of government is rendered meaningless. If there is no absolute truth, why does the order and management of our nation matter? What makes one governmental system superior to another? Why not tear it all down and start over with an anti-gender, anti-colonial, anti-constitutional framework?

The answer is that the truth is written, transcribed, and recorded. It is written that in the beginning, God created the heavens and the earth. It is written that He created mankind, male and female. It is written that mankind fell (and falls) short of the glory of God. It is written that God did tear it all down (except for eight human beings on an ark full of animals). It is written that mankind continued through history in need of a Redeemer. The things written pointed forward to Him. The things written point back to Him. He is the center of all things, and all things hold together in Him. He is the Word who became flesh. His life, death, burial, resurrection, ascension, and glory were witnessed by thousands and recorded explicitly by direct eyewitnesses. The Word changed the Western world, and He continues in the process of remaking the rest of the world through the good news of His gospel.[2]

LAW & FORMATION

The fact that truth is written brings us back to God's universal law. The fact that our U.S. Constitution is written brings us back to national law. From the Constitution proceeds the

2 Aaron Earls, "10 Encouraging Trends of Global Christianity in 2020," Lifeway Research, June 10, 2020. See also "Status of Global Christianity, 2020, in the Context of 1900–2050," Center for the Study of Global Christianity, 2020.

basic structure of our nation's forms of governance (as described in chapter 2). Americans have historically been people of the written word. Even the early Puritan settlers, born out of the Protestant Reformation, which celebrated the rebirth of the holy Scriptures, highly valued codified thought. That precedent eventually led us first as colonies and then as states within a nation to form a constitution.

Prior to the founding of the United States, nations were governed by the laws that their monarchies had created. After its inception in ancient Greece, the concept of a constitution had fallen out of favor. Clarence B. Carson, in his book *Basic American Government*, states that "Americans may not have invented the written constitution, but they certainly made important innovations in the form, strengthened its image, and broadened its coverage."[3] The deep foundations of the U.S. Constitution have allowed it to be the oldest written constitution of government still in operation in the world.[4] Its longevity is in part because Congress did not create and cannot amend it. Due to Article V, the amendment process is not easy. In over two centuries of existence, the Constitution has only been amended twenty-seven times. There are two options for the amendment process, and they are as follows:

- Option 1: Two-thirds of both houses of Congress shall propose the amendment, and three-fourths of the state legislatures shall approve it.
- Option 2: Two-thirds of the states shall call a constitutional convention[5] to propose the amendment,

3 Clarence B. Carson, *Basic American Government*, 18.

4 "Introduction," Constitution of the United States, United States Senate.

5 Calling a constitutional convention raises a number of legal questions as outlined in this article: Brenda Erickson, "Amending the U.S. Constitution," National Conference of State Legislatures (NCSL).

> and three-fourths of the states in the convention shall approve it.[6]

All twenty-seven occasions of the Constitution being amended have occurred by the first option; there has never been a constitutional convention, after the origianl convention that created the Constitution.[7]

Although the U.S. Constitution is not a document inspired by God as the Scriptures are, it is a document drafted by men who believed in the principles of God's universal law. The Framers realized that man is not essentially good and that concentrated power corrupts the one who wields it. As James Madison states,

> But what is government itself but the greatest of all reflections on human nature? If men were angels, no government would be necessary. If angels were to govern men, neither external nor internal controls on government would be necessary. In framing a government which is to be administered by men over men, the great difficulty lies in this: you must first enable the government to control the governed; and in the next place oblige it to control itself.[8]

Therefore, power is spread between the federal and state governments and is further subdivided among three branches in order to check the power of one another.

---

6 Amanda Read, "The Article V Process Explained," July 16, 2017, produced by Matthew Perdie, published by Convention of States Project, video, 3:26.

7 The Twenty-First Amendment followed a slightly different path and was a unique process in the history of constitutional amendments. It was proposed by Congress then sent to the states where each state held a convention to debate and vote on the amendment's ratification. So, it was a variation of Option 1 because it originated in Congress but was approved not by state legislatures but by state-ratifying conventions.

8 James Madison, Alexander Hamilton, and John Jay, *The Federalist Papers*, no. 51, 320.

SERVICES

In the prior chapters, after covering how each level of government was formed, we considered the services offered at each of those levels. Recall from chapter 3 that accessibility to public services is one of the driving forces behind individuals organizing themselves into cities—the lowest level of government. Also in that chapter, we became familiar with the principle of subsidiarity which states that civil matters should be dealt with by the lowest level of government in relation to them. That means the level of government closest to an issue is the level most suited to address it.

Then, we saw in chapter 4 the two-tier relationship between the county (equivalent) and the state regarding many public services. We unveiled special districts in chapter 5 and learned that they are typically single-service providers. And as we've observed throughout this book, because of federalism, our nation was designed to have the limited powers belonging to the federal government with everything else reserved to the states. The original design was to have a limited federal government with services provided at the level of need—typically, the local level (and typically not provided by the realm of civil government but by the realms of family and church). That's just the opposite of what we have today. We have a heavy federal government, and it has become universally accepted to look to it to finance services at all levels. We need an inverted-model overhaul of the system where we, as Americans, who govern our cities, counties, special districts, and states begin to say, "No thank you" to federal government subsidies, grants, and loans.

In the upcoming section titled "Expressed or Enumerated Powers," we will look at that constitutional list of limited federal powers. That is where we find the constitutional mandate for federal services such as post offices and roads. So, when you get there, you might compare that list to this section, as it has much to do with the scope of federal services.

There are some services at the federal level that don't really have a state or local counterpart. A primary one is ensuring the nation's security. This includes maintaining the armed forces (Army, Navy, Air Force, Marine Corps, and Coast Guard) to defend against foreign threats and terrorism. The Department of Defense and the Department of Homeland Security are crucial in these efforts. As mentioned in chapter 6, "State Government," states do have their National Guard units, which can be called upon for domestic emergencies and support during national defense situations, under the authority of the state governor or the President. Note that there is no national police department. It is very important that America not have a gestapo. The FBI has uniforms, cars, equipment, and supplies, but it must ask permission to intervene in local affairs. This is a beautiful example of federalism.

Another area that doesn't seem to have a good state or local counterpart is control of the financial/monetary system. Entities like the Federal Reserve and the Federal Deposit Insurance Corporation (FDIC) manage the nation's monetary policy. This includes influencing interest rates, controlling inflation, and regulating banking institutions to ensure financial stability.

Here are some others that currently exist at the federal level and what they generally do:

- Social Security Administration (SSA) administers Social Security benefits and Medicare, providing financial support and healthcare coverage to eligible individuals. Medicaid is a joint federal and state program that provides financial support and healthcare coverage to eligible individuals at the state level.
- Federal Emergency Management Agency (FEMA) responds to disasters, provides disaster relief, and

coordinates recovery efforts nationwide. (Note that state emergency management agencies work closely with FEMA during disasters, implementing local response plans and coordinating resources.)

- The Environmental Protection Agency (EPA) regulates environmental standards at the national level, addressing air quality, water pollution, and hazardous waste. (Also as mentioned earlier in the book, state environmental agencies enforce EPA guidelines within their states and handle local environmental issues.)
- The Department of Education offers federal student aid programs (e.g., Pell Grants and student loans). We have seen an expansion of this role in recent years. (State governments have their own education departments which may provide direction to curriculum, as well as additional scholarships, grants, or tuition assistance for in-state students.)
- The Veterans Administration (VA) provides healthcare, benefits, and support to veterans.
- The Federal Aviation Administration (FAA) regulates air travel safety, manages airports, and controls airspace, while the Federal Railroad Administration regulates train travel. These agencies regulate standards to ensure safety standards and efficiency.
- Centers for Disease Control and Prevention (CDC) monitors public health, conducts research, and responds to health emergencies.
- And there are many, many more examples.

Depending on your life's journey, you may already have experience with one or more federal agencies. When thinking about how these agencies of the federal government operate, it is helpful to reflect on Figure 3.9, "The Types of People You

Will Meet in the Civil Realm," the tool created for interactions with bureaucrats. Depending on the moment, the leadership and culture of any agency can pass through seasons of incompetence, effectiveness, overreach, or abject failure. As we've been learning, in the end, the real question is what will we do to obtain different results? And will our frustration with bureaucratic agency overreach at the federal level paralyze us and prevent us from doing what we can where we are with what we have to reform our governmental systems at any and all levels?

In conclusion, while the design of federalism does limit the role of the federal government in providing services, it nonetheless fulfills some essential functions that are foundational to the nation's well-being and operational efficiency. These services complement the work done at the state and local levels, demonstrating the interconnectedness and balance of responsibilities within our federal system. Many books have been written and much thought has been given to services at the federal level (which ends up meaning federal executive agencies or federal bureaucracy—as will be explained in the sections just ahead). Meanwhile, perhaps this inverted view of services from the local level upwards will help American citizens approach federal governmental services in a more wholistic manner.

Local/County	***State***	***National***
County courthouse	State capitols	Capitol Hill
Parks	State parks	National parks
Highways	State highways	National highways (interstates)
	National Guard	U.S. Armed Forces
	State agencies	430+ federal agencies (including U.S. Postal Service)

GOVERNANCE STRUCTURE

Legislative Branch

Article I of the U.S. Constitution establishes the federal government's legislative branch. This branch makes policy (law) through one legislative body (Congress) consisting of two chambers (the House of Representatives and the Senate). Note that at the federal level, the two chambers are referred to as Congress; at the state level, they are typically known as one of the forty-nine bicameral legislatures. By constitutional design, Congress is to assemble at least once every year beginning at noon on the third day of January, having a majority of each chamber assembled in order to do business.[9] Each chamber "may determine the rules of its Proceedings, punish its Members for disorderly Behaviour, and, with the Concurrence of two thirds, expel a Member."[10] Except for cases of treason, felony, and breaches of the peace, the members are exempt from arrest during their term in service. (The Supreme Court has interpreted this statement to pertain to civil, not criminal offenses.)[11] The members shall not be appointed to any civil office nor hold any other office of the United States during their term of service.[12]

The process of passing a bill into law is nearly identical to the process described in chapter 6, "State Government." The differences are that both chambers of Congress have subcommittees as precursors to the committees, and after a bill passes both chambers separately, any resultant discrepancies must be equalized/streamlined in a joint conference committee (representing both chambers) as described in chapter 2.

---

9 U.S. Const. art. I, § 4.

10 U.S. Const. art. I, § 5.

11 "ArtI.S6.C1.2 Privilege from Arrest," Constitution Annotated.

12 U.S. Const. art. I, § 6.

Then, both chambers vote on the identical bill as the process continues. As in a state legislature, a bill requires a simple majority vote to pass. That's 218 out of 435 votes in the House, and 51 votes in the Senate.[13]

Each chamber keeps a journal of its proceedings and publishes it (except for secret sections).[14] This becomes the Statutes at Large which is then organized topically into the U.S. Code that we learned about in chapter 2.

Expressed or Enumerated Powers

Congress shall **only** have the following powers—called enumerated or expressed powers—according to Section 8 of Article I, which is summarized below (all other powers not listed here belong to the states):

- To lay and collect taxes, duties, imposts, and excises, which must be uniform throughout the United States
- To pay debts
- To provide for the common defense and general welfare of the United States
- To borrow money on the credit of the United States
- To regulate commerce with foreign nations, among several states, and with Indian Tribes

13 "The Legislative Process: How Are Laws Made?" U.S. House of Representatives.

"In a few instances, the Constitution requires a two-thirds vote of the Senate, including: expelling a senator; overriding a presidential veto; proposing a constitutional amendment for ratification by the states; convicting an impeached official; and consenting to ratification of a treaty. Under Senate debate rules, it takes a three-fifths majority of those duly chosen and sworn to invoke cloture and end debate on a piece of legislation. Senate rules also require a two-thirds vote to invoke cloture on a measure that would amend the Senate's rules though the measure itself requires only a simple majority vote for adoption." "About Voting," United States Senate.

14 U.S. Const. art. I, § 5.

- To establish a uniform rule of naturalization (citizenship)
- To develop consistent laws regarding bankruptcy throughout the United States[15]
- To coin money and regulate its value, and punish counterfeiters
- To fix the standard of weights and measures
- To establish post offices and roads
- To secure the copyright for scientists and authors
- To establish courts below the Supreme Court
- To define and punish piracy and felony committed at sea and offenses against nations
- To declare war
- To grant letters of marque and reprisal and make rules regarding captures on land and water
- To raise and support armies with money allotted for two years
- To provide and maintain a navy
- To make rules for the government and regulation of land and naval forces
- To call forth the militia for executing the nation's laws, suppressing insurrections, and repelling invasions[16]
- To provide for organizing, arming, and disciplining the militia and governing those in service to the United States
- To govern over the seat of the national government (Washington, D.C.) for the erection of forts, magazines, arsenals, dockyards, and other needful buildings

15 This is why bankruptcy must be filed in a federal court.

16 Overseen by the National Guard Bureau.

Implied Powers
(Necessary and Proper Clause or Elastic Clause)

This is the last power in the list from Article I, Section 8, above:

- To make all laws necessary and proper for carrying out the powers mentioned above vested by the Constitution in the government of the United States or any department or officer thereof.

Prohibited Powers

There are certain powers (called prohibited powers) that Congress shall **not** have. These prohibited powers are laid out in Section 9 of Article I, which is summarized below:

- Prohibits the importation of enslaved people after 1808
- Prohibits the suspension of the writ of *habeas corpus* (allowing a prisoner to challenge the imprisonment charges in court) except in the cases of rebellion or invasion
- Prohibits bills of attainder or *ex post facto* laws (laws declaring a person guilty after the fact)
- Prohibited the income tax until the Sixteenth Amendment was passed in 1913
- Prohibits interstate or interport taxing or favoritism
- Requires money withdrawn from the treasury to be appropriated by law
- Requires publishing of a statement and account of receipts and expenditures of public money
- Prohibits granting titles of nobility by the United States

- Prohibits granting titles of nobility on U.S. officeholders by foreign states (and U.S. officeholders cannot receive gifts from them without the consent of Congress)

House of Representatives

The method of composition of the two houses, however, does differ from that of state government. The composition of the 435-member lower chamber (the House of Representatives) is based upon each state's population. More populated states have more representatives and less populated states have fewer representatives with the combined total always equaling 435.[17] According to Article I of the Constitution, all states must have at least one representative,[18] and the number of representatives cannot be greater than one for every thirty thousand people. Because it is population-based, the House signifies a representative democracy. In other words, it is designed to represent the people. Because its representation is based on population, this lower chamber is elected from congressional districts. Recall from the previous chapter that the lines for these districts are updated each decade the year following the census. This process, called redistricting or reapportionment, varies from state to state.[19]

Of the two chambers of Congress, the House is known as the more rowdy and populist. These elected representatives of the people who serve in the House for short (two-year)

---

17 In 1929 the Permanent Apportionment Act became law, permanently setting the maximum number of representatives at 435. "How Your State Gets Its Seats: Congressional Apportionment," U.S. Capitol Visitor Center, 1. 🔗

18 Currently, seven states have one representative: Alaska, Wyoming, Montana, North Dakota, South Dakota, Vermont, and Delaware. "How Your State Gets Its Seats," 4.

19 Here, again, I recommend Loyola Law School's "All About Redistricting" website. Go to the "FIND A STATE" button on the top toolbar to enter your state. The button for "CONGRESS" shows the state's lines for equally distributing its population to be represented in the U.S. House of Representatives. 🔗

APPORTIONMENT OF THE U.S. HOUSE OF REPRESENTATIVES
(based on the 2020 Census)

Figure 7.2

Adapted from "2020 Census: Apportionment of the U.S. House of Representatives," U.S. Census Bureau.

terms can be as young as twenty-five years of age and must have been a U.S. citizen for seven years. They are led by the Speaker of the House who is chosen by House members of the party holding the majority of the seats. This chamber shall have the sole power to impeach[20]—to charge the President or other high officeholder with misconduct while in office. All revenue-related bills shall originate in the House.[21]

The Senate

The 100-member upper chamber, known as the Senate, affords the equal representation of two senators to each state. As such, in this chamber, small states are equally represented alongside large states. Thus, no legislative districts are necessary, as the two senators both represent and are elected by each state as a whole (in times past, they were chosen by the state legislatures). Senators elected to this more prestigious upper chamber serve longer (six-year) terms, must be a minimum of thirty years old, and must have been a U.S. citizen for nine years. Their terms are staggered into classes that expire every two years. If there are any vacancies before a senator's term expires, the state governor may make an appointment to the office.[22] This body is presided over ceremonially by the President of the Senate who is the Vice President of the United States. It is known as the upper and more distinguished of the two chambers of Congress due to its higher membership requirements, longer terms (with less turnover), smaller size (less than a fourth the size of the House of Representatives), and no limit on time allowed for verbal comment on proposed legislation. Along these lines, and with the intent of

20 U.S. Const. art. I, § 3.

21 U.S. Const. art. I, § 7.

22 U.S. Const. art. I, § 3. See also "ArtI.S3.C2.2 Senate Vacancies Clause," Constitution Annotated.

slowing the passage of legislation, the Senate has the ability to filibuster—to speak seemingly endlessly in order to delay the taking of a vote.

Whereas the House has the power to impeach (accuse), the Senate has the sole power to try all impeachments.[23] The chief justice of the Supreme Court presides over the impeachment trial, and two-thirds of the Senate members present must vote in favor of impeachment in order for the President (or any federal official) to be found guilty.[24] Further, a guilty impeachment verdict merely results in the President's removal from office.[25] Afterward, the President shall be liable and subject to further trial according to law. The Senate has never convicted anyone to date in U.S. history.[26] The Senate must also approve presidential appointments to the federal judiciary with a two-thirds vote.[27]

Parliamentary Procedure in the House and Senate

Readers may notice that parliamentary procedure becomes more complex between the local and state levels of government. *Robert's Rules of Order* is used at the local level of government. *Mason's Manual of Legislative Procedure* is typically used at the state level. As is typical at the federal level, the combination of parliamentary procedure manuals is quite complex. The House and Senate parliamentarians are highly specific professionals. Here is a list of some of the resources that

23 U.S. Const. art. I, § 3.

24 U.S. Const. art. I, § 3.

25 U.S. Const. art. I, § 3.

26 Richard Nixon resigned. See "ArtII.S4.4.7 President Richard Nixon and Impeachable Offenses," Constitution Annotated.

27 Meaning that when the President appoints a judge to a federal court or to the U.S. Supreme Court, the Senate must vote.

are employed in order to run each house of Congress by the book:[28]

House Rules and Manual (new editions are published each Congress)

- Constitution of the United States
- *A Manual of Parliamentary Practice for the Use of the Senate of the United States* (known as *Jefferson's Manual* by Thomas Jefferson)
- *Rules of the House of Representatives of the United States*
- *Hinds' and Cannon's Precedents of the House of Representatives*
- *Deschler-Brown Precedents of the United States House of Representatives*
- *Cannon's Procedure in the House of Representatives*
- *House Practice: A Guide to the Rules, Precedents and Procedures of the House*
- *Procedure in the U.S. House of Representatives*

Senate Manual (new editions are published each Congress)

- Contains the rules, orders, laws, and resolutions affecting the business of the Senate
- *Jefferson's Manual*
- Declaration of Independence
- Articles of Confederation
- Constitution of the United States, etc.
- *Senate Procedure*

---

28 "How Our Laws Are Made," Congress.gov.

GOVERNANCE STRUCTURE

Executive Branch

Article II of the U.S. Constitution establishes the executive branch of the federal government. This branch executes policy (law) through administration and regulations. At the state level, we learned that the executive branch consists of several elected offices in addition to the governor and lieutenant governor (the two of whom we would normally think of as representing the executive branch). At the federal level, there are only two: the President and the Vice President. Article II of the Constitution primarily refers to the President, who (along with the Vice President) shall hold office for a term of four years. For a quick review of the five different "hats" that the President wears in his role as chief executive, see the section titled "The Executive Branch" in chapter 2.

Electoral College

Every four years, the Electoral College captures our attention, but somehow that's not frequent enough for us to truly understand it. And unlike other parts of the Constitution, its principles are not reflected at lower layers of government. Although the term *electoral college* does not appear in the Constitution, the term *electors* is explained in Article II, Section 1 and in the Twelfth Amendment.

We don't have an electoral college to elect our governors or mayors—we elect them directly. Why is there a different method when it comes to electing our President and Vice President? And how does it work?

To answer the first question, the President and the Vice President are the only two elected officeholders who represent the entire nation. So there are a multitude of citizens who vote for them. All other elected members of our government represent certain geographical sectors of the nation.

The United States of America is not a pure democracy—nor was it ever intended to be. Ours is a federalist nation: the Constitution grants limited power to the federal government and recognizes all other powers as belonging to the states or to the people. Unlike a direct democratic election (which would result in millions of votes), the electoral college system operates through the states and simplifies the vote-counting process for the nation. Originally, it was a compromise between those who wanted Congress to elect the President and those who preferred a direct popular vote. It is designed to balance the influence of large and small states.

As for *how* the Electoral College works, let's look at the chronology leading up to the presidential election.

Nomination of Electors

A few months before the presidential election (also known as the general election), each political party in every state gathers to choose the electors for that party's presidential and vice presidential candidate. Each party's selection process can vary widely from state to state, but the overarching principles involve party loyalty, residency, and adherence to state and constitutional rules (such as not being an officeholder). These electors are the people whom the voters will actually vote for in the election (as described below). We will talk more about political parties in the next chapter, but for now, know that there are two main parties—Democratic and Republican.

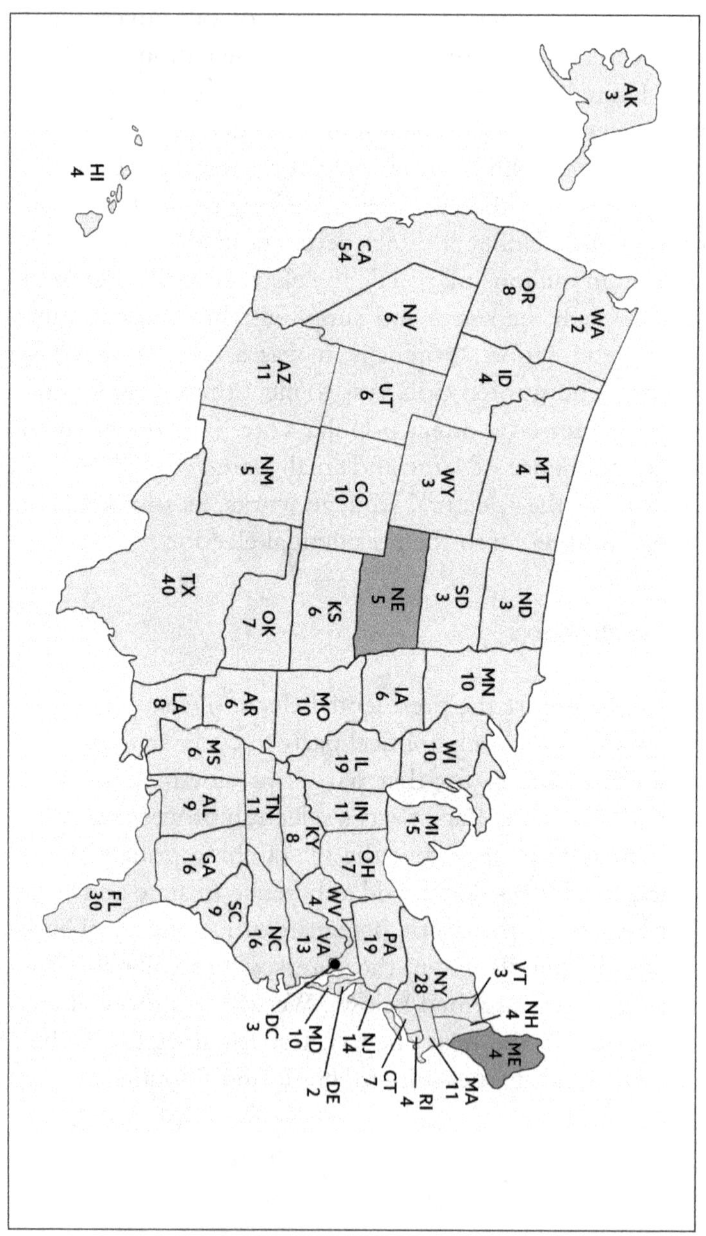
U.S ELECTORAL COLLEGE
AK 3
HI 4
WA 12
OR 8
CA 54
NV 6
ID 4
MT 4
WY 3
UT 6
AZ 11
CO 10
NM 5
ND 3
SD 3
NE 5
KS 6
OK 7
TX 40
MN 10
IA 6
MO 10
AR 6
LA 8
WI 10
IL 19
MS 6
MI 15
IN 11
KY 8
TN 11
AL 9
OH 17
WV 4
GA 16
FL 30
SC 9
NC 16
VA 13
PA 19
NY 28
VT 3
NH 4
ME 4
MA 11
RI 4
CT 7
NJ 14
DE 2
MD 10
DC 3

Figure 7.3

Appointment (election) of Electors at the General Election[29]

Each state shall appoint (elect) a number of electors equal to the number of representatives it has in Congress.[30] (For a quick reference, see Figure 7.3 to determine how many electors each state will appoint.) No elector is allowed to be a congressman (one who serves in the House) or a senator.[31] And the electors, presidential candidate, and vice presidential candidate should not all be from the same state otherwise the electors from that state may not vote in the Electoral College.[32]

Voter Experience (Presidential Election)

Presidential election day falls on the first Tuesday following the first Monday in November. It is actually the day that Americans vote for (appoint) the electors who will then **later** in December elect the President and the Vice President (see below). On this day in November, registered voters appear at the polls to vote for all of the offices on the ballot. Directly beneath the voter's instructions on the ballot, is a title such as:

CANDIDATES FOR UNITED STATES OFFICES

PRESIDENT
(Vote for One)

---

29 The Electoral College is the only system in American government where the word *appoint* actually means "elect."

30 The number of a state's representatives in the House of Representatives plus its two senators.

31 This paragraph is derived from U.S. Const. art II, § 1.

32 U.S. Const. amend. XII. See also Sarah Pruitt, "Can the President and Vice President Be From the Same State?," History, updated January 22, 2024.

Nested under that heading is the name of the political party and the presidential candidate's name with the vice presidential candidate's name tucked underneath because for the popular vote, these two individuals run together as one "ticket." **Some states list the electors' names under the candidates' names, and some do not. In the states that do not, it is very difficult for voters to understand that they are not actually casting their vote for the presidential ticket but for the slate of electors that should be listed under the candidates' names.** (See sample ballot available at **Ballotpedia'**s website listed at **CivilRealm.com**'s links page or check your state's election office website to view one.) The votes cast for all other offices on the ballot are directly for each candidate—not for electors.

Election Night

The night of the general election, all of the Electoral College votes for a state, with the exception of two states, go to the winner of the state's popular vote. This approach is called winner-take-all because the popular vote winner for the state takes all of the state's electoral votes. Maine and Nebraska, however, divide their electoral votes among their congressional districts and give two extra votes to the overall winner. Thus, their votes may be split among the candidates. "While it is rare for Maine or Nebraska to have a split vote, each has done so twice: Nebraska in 2008, Maine in 2016, and both Maine and Nebraska in 2020."[33]

The total number of possible electoral votes to be cast is 538:

33 "Distribution of Electoral Votes: Allocation among the States," U.S. National Archives and Records Administration.

	435 House of Representatives
	100 Senators
+	**3** D.C.
	538

The magic number of votes required for a candidate to become President is 270, which is a simple majority.[34]

	538		**269**
÷	**2**	+	**1**
	269		**270**

This means that the popular vote totals across the entire country are not directly decisive in determining the outcome of the presidential election. The result has occasionally been that a candidate wins the electoral vote who lost the popular vote.[35]

December

On the first Tuesday after the second Wednesday in December, the electors convene in their respective states, usually at the capitol, as directed by the legislature. Here, the electors cast their votes for President and for Vice President.[36] Note that in this part of the election, the Constitution specifies that electors must vote separately for the President and Vice President,[37] so the joint ticket for these offices no longer exists at this point. Each state's results are then sent to the President of the Senate (the current Vice President of the Unit-

34 "Electoral College Ties," 270 to Win.

35 Mindy Johnston, "list of U.S. presidential elections in which the winner lost the popular vote," *Encyclopedia Britannica.*

36 "Roles and Responsibilities in the Electoral College Process," U.S. National Archives and Records Administration, July 6, 2023.

37 U.S. Const. amend. XII.

ed States). For the most part, electors vote for the candidate representing their party. There are sometimes rogue electors (known as "faithless electors") who vote for the other party's candidate, but they have not, for the most part, influenced American elections.[38]

January 6[39]

On January 6, following every presidential election, the United States Congress meets in a joint session to count the electoral votes. The President of the Senate presides over this session and then announces who has been elected President and Vice President of the United States.[40]

A parting word regarding the Electoral College: Though this institution is a challenging concept for us to initially understand, like many other parts of our nation's founding, it has stood the test of time with very few wrinkles. It also becomes a topic of hot debate every four years—not just in our day but since its inception. However, unlike many other American voting procedures, it can only be changed by constitutional amendment, which (as we have learned) is designed to not be an easy process. We will continue the subject of voting, elections, and political parties in the next chapter.

---

38 Scott Bomboy, "The one election where Faithless Electors made a difference," *Constitution Daily* (blog), National Constitution Center, December 19, 2016.

Although I cannot endorse much on this site, this history is helpful: "Faithless Electors," Fair Vote, October 2022.

39 If January 6 falls on a Sunday, Congress may by law adjust the meeting day.

40 The best resource I have found for further information is Congressional Research Service's "Counting Electoral Votes: An Overview of Procedures at the Joint Session, Including Objections by Members of Congress" which is updated every four years in December after the General Election.

Presidential Cabinet

Although not mentioned by name in the Constitution, the presidential cabinet is based in Article 2, Section 2, and exists for the purpose of advising the President. There are no fewer than fifteen presidentially appointed department heads along with other executive-level agencies (in the list below, the traditional departments are listed first followed by the federal agencies). The total number of cabinet advisors can change over time, but each presidential appointee must be confirmed by the Senate. Filling the cabinet is one of the early tasks that a newly elected President undertakes, and meetings are held regularly. At the conference table, the President, by tradition, takes the center position with the oval table of advisors extending from his left and right sides. (Think something akin to an American King Arthur and the Knights of the Round Table.)

Cabinet Offices/Officers

The first fifteen members of the cabinet are the heads of the fifteen executive departments.

- Department of Agriculture, Secretary of Agriculture
- Department of Commerce, Secretary of Commerce
- Department of Defense, Secretary of Defense
- Department of Education, Secretary of Education
- Department of Energy, Secretary of Energy
- Department of Health and Human Services, Secretary of HHS

- Department of Homeland Security, Secretary of Homeland Security
- Department of Housing and Urban Development, Secretary of HUD
- Department of the Interior, Secretary of the Interior
- Department of Justice, Attorney General[41]
- Department of Labor, Secretary of Labor
- Department of State, Secretary of State
- Department of Transportation, Secretary of Transportation
- Department of Treasury, Secretary of the Treasury
- Department of Veterans Affairs, Secretary of Veterans Affairs

Offices/Officers with the Status of Cabinet-Rank

The President typically chooses to add other key federal officers to his cabinet. For example:

41 Do not confuse the Department of Justice with the U.S. Supreme Court which is a constitutional branch of government. It is a federal agency, not a court, and consists of more than forty organizations.

"These include the U.S. Attorneys (USAs) who prosecute offenders and represent the United States government in court; the major investigative agencies—the Federal Bureau of Investigation (FBI), the Drug Enforcement Administration (DEA), and the Bureau of Alcohol, Tobacco, Firearms and Explosives (ATF), which deter and investigate crimes and arrest criminal suspects; the U.S. Marshals Service (USMS), which protects the federal judiciary, apprehends fugitives, and detains persons in federal custody; the Bureau of Prisons (BOP), which confines convicted offenders; and the National Security Division (NSD), which brings together national security, counterterrorism, counterintelligence, and foreign intelligence surveillance operations under a single authority." "FY 2013 Annual Performance Report & FY 2015 Annual Performance Plan," U.S. Department of Justice, I-4.

- National Security, Director of National Intelligence
- Council on Environmental Quality (Environmental Protection Agency, Administrator of the EPA)
- United States Trade Representative
- Office of Management and the Budget, Director of the OMB
- U.S. Mission to the United Nations, The U.S. Ambassador (to the U.N.)
- Council of Economic Advisors, Chair of the Council of Economic Advisors
- Small Business Administration, Administrator of SBA
- White House Chief of Staff
- Office of Science and Technology Policy, Director of OSTP

Other Federally Appointed Offices/Officers[42]

The heads of these offices are filled by U.S. presidential appointment, but the offices are not cabinet-level. Federally appointed offices are the best examples of government entities that are the most difficult to hold accountable to the people. They are the federal parallel to special districts, however, while all of our local special districts relate to a geographic boundary, these offices span the entire nation.

- Federal Reserve System
- White House Press Secretary
- U.S. Postmaster General

42 Ballotpedia, s.v. "President of the United States."

- Central Intelligence Agency
- Federal Bureau of Investigation
- Internal Revenue Service
- Bureau of Alcohol, Tobacco, Firearms, and Explosives
- National Security Agency
- Congressional Budget Office
- Federal Election Commission
- Transportation Security Administration
- Drug Enforcement Administration
- Federal Communications Commission

Other Agencies, Boards, and Commissions

According to the *Federal Register* (the Daily Journal of the United States Government), there are a total of 434 federal agencies.[43] The three sections above (Cabinet, Offices with Status of Cabinet-Rank, and Federally Appointed Offices) are appointed by the President. They are known as the federal bureaucracy which exert tremendous overreach into the everyday lives of Americans. In fact, according to the White House website, the President makes over 4000 political appointments (meaning individuals or appointees) throughout the federal government.[44] Some are judges, but many are appointees to bureaucratic agencies that make rules indirectly (outside the constitutional legislative process). These rules have the force and effect of law and are listed in the Code of Federal Regulations (C.F.R.). As explained in chapter 2, the federal bureaucracy is sometimes erroneously referred to as

43 "Agencies," *Federal Register (Daily Journal of the United States Government)*, U.S. National Archives and Records Administration.

44 "Presidential Personnel Office," The White House.

the fourth branch of the U.S. government. Under the direction of We the People, it is the responsibility of the second and third branches to curb the overreach of the bureaucracy. This will require a decided approach by citizens to reject offers of government assistance both to us as individuals as well as to our state and local governments. Curbing federal overreach also involves electing a supermajority of members to Congress who are willing to cut the purse strings that finance bureaucratic agencies.

GOVERNANCE STRUCTURE

Judicial Branch

We surveyed the state court system in the previous chapter and learned that it pertains to cases involving violations of a state's constitution or laws. We also learned that the state and federal court systems hold an important power known as judicial review—the ability to declare laws unconstitutional—although that power is not described in the Constitution itself.

Like the state judicial system, the federal system operates in a three-tiered structure: trial courts (thankfully, always called district courts in this system), appellate courts (thankfully, always called Regional Circuit Courts of Appeal), and the Supreme Court of the United States. The first tier consists of the previously mentioned ninety-four district courts[45] where cases involving violations of federal law begin. The second tier includes the thirteen circuit courts[46] (the first level of appellate courts where cases can be tried a second time).

---

45 This number has increased over time.

46 This number has increased over time and includes a D.C. circuit and a federal circuit which hears special types of cases.

The third tier is the U.S. Supreme Court (where final federal decisions are made).[47]

FEDERAL JUDICIAL SYSTEM

3rd Tier: U.S. Supreme Court (court of last resort)
↑
2nd Tier: Regional Circuit Court of Appeals
↑
1st Tier: District Court

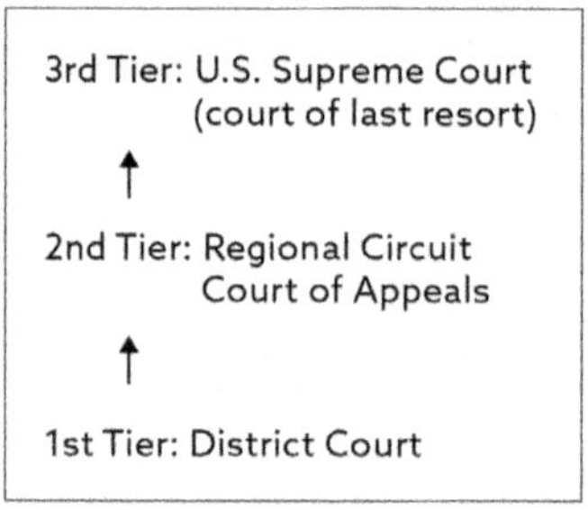

Figure 7.4

Because the federal system generally considers cases under national laws, federal courts have limited jurisdiction (the legal authority to hear a certain type of case). They only hear approximately ten percent of the cases in the nation. The specific type of cases that involve federal law can include business transactions across state lines (interstate commerce), certain drug cases, convicted felons who are found in possession of a firearm, monetary fraud involving federal agencies, robbery of an FDIC-insured bank, a crime committed on federal property, or civil rights/discrimination cases. Federal courts can also hear civil cases of limited jurisdiction when the plaintiff and defendant are from two different states with a dispute of $75,000 or more.[48] (If the amount is less, the case would be heard in state court, even though those involved in the dispute are from different states.)

---

47 "Introduction to the Federal Court System," U.S. Department of Justice.

48 "Comparing State and Federal Courts," Judicial Learning Center, December 30, 2020, video, 13:20. See also "A Conversation about the Courts: Judges Compare State and Federal Judicial Systems," Judicial Learning Center, 6.

Executive Branch Functioning Within the Judicial Branch

At the state level, recall that criminal cases are brought before a judge in the state judicial system by a county prosecutor or a state attorney general (or their deputies). In a similar fashion, criminal cases are typically brought before a judge in the federal judicial system by federal prosecutors called the United States attorneys, of which there are many.[49] Unlike the state- and county-level prosecutors who are elected, a federal prosecutor is appointed by the President in each of the 94 federal judicial districts to serve a term in office. As presidential appointees under the direction of the Attorney General, the U.S. attorneys represent the executive branch of government and can, in turn, appoint deputy prosecutors who are called assistant United States attorneys (AUSA). Cases are typically brought to them by executive-branch agencies such as the Drug Enforcement Agency (DEA) or the Bureau of Alcohol, Tobacco, and Firearms (ATF).[50] Note that the Attorney General, as the chief prosecutor for the entire nation, oversees each U.S. attorney as well as the U.S. Department of Justice.[51]

There is also the Office of the U.S. Solicitor General which supervises and conducts litigation in the U.S. Supreme Court where the United States is a party.[52] In the previous chapter, we learned of the state solicitor general who represents state laws in state and federal courts on behalf of the attorney general's office.[53] The U.S. solicitor general does similar work representing federal laws before the nation's highest court.[54]

49 "A Conversation about the Courts," 6.

50 "A Conversation about the Courts," 6.

51 Angela J. Davis, "The Power and Discretion of the American Prosecutor," *Droit et cultures* (online) 49, no. 1 (2005, online since March 2, 2010): 55–66.

52 "About the Office," Office of the Solicitor General, U.S. Department of Justice, last updated June 16, 2023.

53 "About the Office," U.S. Department of Justice.

54 "About the Office," U.S. Department of Justice.

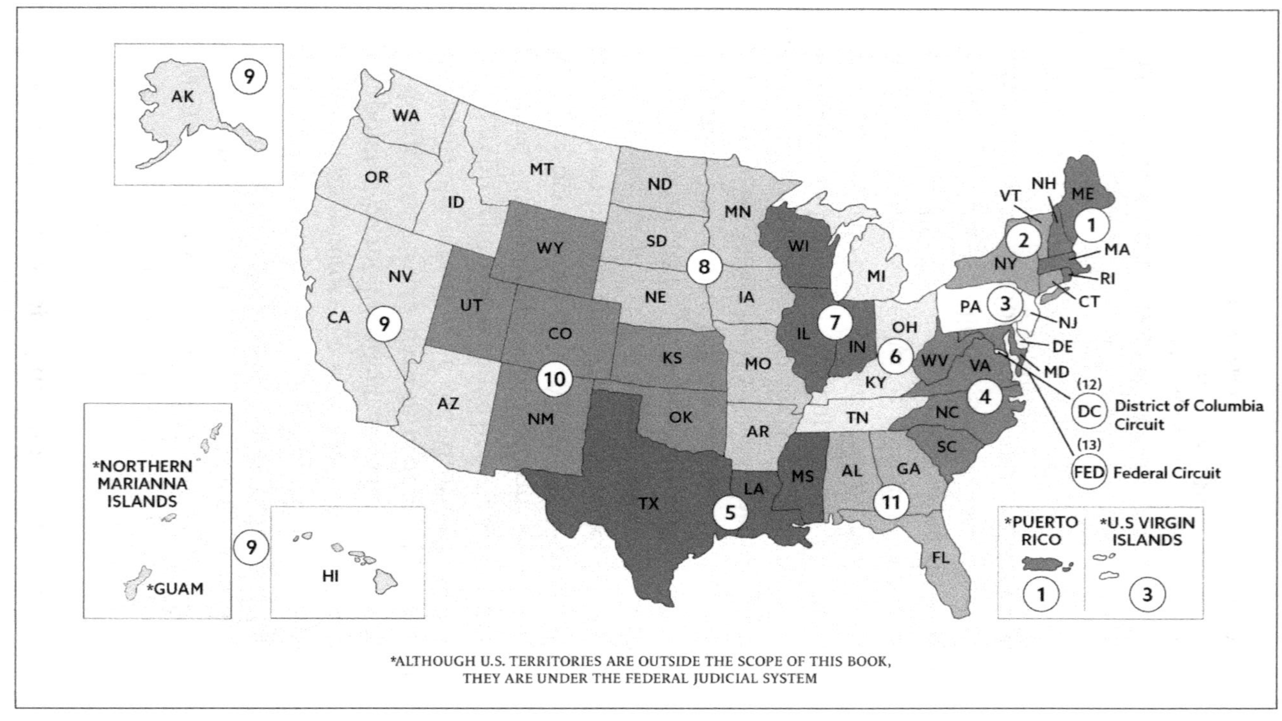
U.S. REGIONAL CIRCUIT COURTS OF APPEAL
AK
9
WA
OR
ID
MT
ND
SD
MN
WY
NV
UT
CA
9
CO
NE
IA
8
WI
MI
IL
7
IN
OH
6
KY
KS
MO
10
AZ
NM
OK
AR
TN
WV
VA
4
NC
SC
TX
LA
5
MS
AL
GA
11
FL
VT
NH
ME
1
2
NY
MA
RI
CT
PA
3
NJ
DE
MD
(12)
DC District of Columbia Circuit
(13)
FED Federal Circuit
*NORTHERN MARIANNA ISLANDS
*GUAM
9
HI
*PUERTO RICO
1
*U.S VIRGIN ISLANDS
3
*ALTHOUGH U.S. TERRITORIES ARE OUTSIDE THE SCOPE OF THIS BOOK, THEY ARE UNDER THE FEDERAL JUDICIAL SYSTEM

Figure 7.5

Both the federal "inferior"[55] judges and the Supreme Court justices are known as Article III judges because their job description is listed in the third article of the U.S. Constitution.[56] They are not elected by the people. Rather, their constitutionally ordained appointment by the President, listed in Article II, Section 2, must be confirmed by a majority vote of the U.S. Senate.[57] They serve for life terms or as long as they desire or until impeached by the House[58] and convicted by the Senate.[59] Thus, the presiding President holds far-reaching and significant sway over the direction of the judicial system. Inherent in this appointment process (i.e. appointment by the President plus confirmation by the Senate) is the collaboration of all three branches of the U.S. government, thus illustrating the system of checks and balances of power. Further, federally appointed judges/justices can do their work within the court system without needing to campaign for office or tailor their decisions to public opinion.

Federal Judicial Hierarchy

The highest court of the land, the Supreme Court, consists of one chief justice and eight associate justices who serve for life or as long as they desire—as Article III states, they "shall hold their Offices during good Behaviour, and shall, at stated Times, receive for their Services, a Compensation, which shall not be diminished during their Continuance in Office."[60]

55 Federal judges who are not supreme court justices as defined in Article III.

56 "A Conversation about the Courts," 3.

57 Majority vote = 51 votes. There are 100 members in the Senate. One more than half of the senators equals a majority vote.

58 U.S. Const. art. I, § 2.

59 U.S. Const. art. I, § 3.
See also "The Judicial Branch," The White House.

60 U.S. Const. art. III, § 1.

Because the federal American justice system is hierarchical, cases work their way up from the bottom, entry-level of the system (U.S. district courts) to the middle (U.S. regional circuit courts of appeal) where a case that previously lost could be heard again on appeal to the top (U.S. Supreme Court). This process requires lower courts to follow the previous decisions of higher courts in this system and also to take into account decisions in similar courts across the nation.

Let's look at a practical example of the court system in action. Say you want to challenge a federal law (like the airport mask mandate that was challenged). You would start in district court in a state that would be favorable to your cause. You would ask the district court judge to enjoin or stop enforcement of the law. (The district court has the power to do that.) However, the administration then has the ability to challenge the ruling and appeal to the appropriate regional circuit court of appeal, and then to the Supreme Court. The case is not done until both parties choose to stop appealing, or until the appeals process is exhausted (i.e. you ask the Supreme Court to hear it, and they choose whether or not to do so).

There can be a lot of confusion and uncertainty when a law is first challenged. Different district courts can reach different decisions, or even different regional circuit courts of appeal can reach different decisions (this is called a circuit split). Courts at the same level do not have to follow each other; they only have to follow the courts at the higher levels. As a result, it is possible for one interpretation to apply in one region and another interpretation to apply in another region. It can get messy. If there is a circuit split, it is more likely the Supreme Court will want to take up the case. (Also, don't forget that in the previous chapter, we learned that each state has its own state court system and the same messiness among state districts can take place with each having its own interpretations of similar, overlapping laws.)

NATIONAL SYSTEM

LEGISLATIVE

EXECUTIVE

JUDICIAL

U.S. Voters

Congress

Senate &
House of Representatives

President (VP)

Federal Judges

434 Agencies, Offices & Departments
(over 4,000 Presidential appointees)

Figure 7.6

KEY

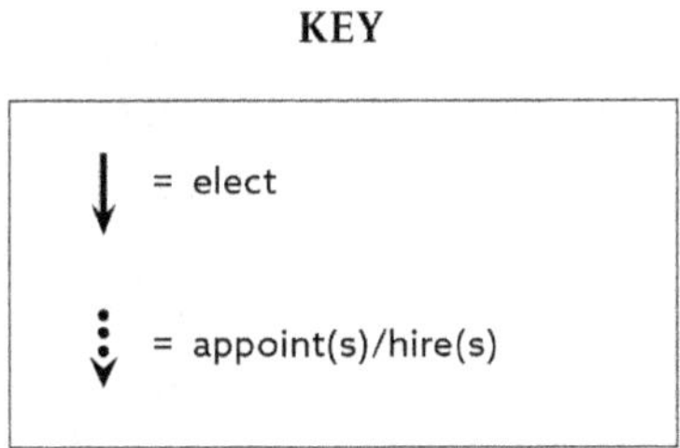

OTHER THINGS YOU SHOULD KNOW

As Americans, we live under a federalist system, where the federal government can only do what is permitted in the Constitution. We also reside in states which can do anything not forbidden by the Constitution. Our Framers intended states to be free to conduct their own business. Despite this design, federal funding works its way not only into the states but also into local county and municipal governments quite regularly,[61] and federal funding comes with strings attached. These strings cause states and localities to be dependent upon the federal government.

You may have noticed certain associations appearing in footnotes across this book as readily available sources of information. But they do not exist simply to provide accessible governmental data. They monitor federal government programs and seek to secure federal funding for themselves whether at the state or local level. Some of these organizations known as the "Big Seven" are located in the nation's capital: The National Governors Association, The Council of State Governments, The National Association of Counties, The National Conference of State Legislatures, The National League of Cities, The U.S. Conference of Mayors, and the International City/County Management Association.[62]

Federal grants (money) given to cities allow cities to sidestep the state and obtain "necessary" funding directly from the national government in order to implement local programs or projects. Similarly, states often have open palms, ready to accept federal funding, adeptly using lobbyists to help do so. Occasionally, and on the bright side, "political as well as philosophical considerations have prompted governors not only to turn down the opportunity to secure this aid but to actively criticize and oppose the federal programs."[63] For example, several governors opposed the federal Affordable Care Act's expansion of Medicaid (a.k.a. Obamacare) despite the fact that their states would have received federal funds for it.[64]

---

61 A history of the development of this phenomenon can be found in David R. Berman's book, *Local Government and the States: Autonomy, Politics, and Policy*, 27–42.

62 Berman, *Local Government and the States*, 26.

63 Berman, *Local Government and the States*, 27.

64 Berman, *Local Government and the States*, 27.

THINGS YOU CAN DO

- Read the U.S. Constitution if you have not already done so. Most people can only talk about it; be someone who can locate principles and quotes within it.
- Spend time perusing the (federal) Government Publishing Office's website: **govinfo.gov**. If there is one useful website pertaining to the federal government, **govinfo.gov** is it. From "Cornerstone Documents" (in the "Other Resources" tab) to federal agency reports to an A-Z topical index (which literally covers everything from **A:** Americans with Disabilities Act of 1990 to **almost Z:** George Washington's Farewell Address and, of course, Watergate) this website is highly instructive. Current bills before the House or Senate can also be located there. The website even tells the reader where to locate information that is not housed within **govinfo.gov**.
- Consider taking a Constitution class such as Homeschool Legal Defense's Constitutional Law class or Hillsdale College's Introduction to the Constitution or Constitution 101. Links can be found on *The Forgotten Realm* website: **CivilRealm.com**.
- Be in contact with the local offices of your senators and representatives to set up an appointment with one of the legislative assistants there.
- Pray for the President, Vice President, your two senators, your one or more U.S. representatives, the Supreme Court justices, and the inferior court judges in your district by name.
- Consider planning a visit to Washington, D.C., to see how our capital city works. Although it is an experience of a lifetime, visiting does not automatically make you an involved citizen. Visitors to Washington, D.C., are typically closer to the role of

tourists than concerned citizens, but there is much to be learned and gleaned from a historical, architectural, political, judicial, legislative, and executive perspective. Our nation's capital is a remarkable place and very much worth visiting. Contact the office of your congressional representative (from the House or Senate) to schedule a tour of the U.S. Capitol building. Consider planning a visit to the Supreme Court and the White House, as well, to cover all three branches of the government. Don't forget to see our nation's founding documents at the National Archives and Thomas Jefferson's personal library on display at The Library of Congress.

- Or, you may be inclined, as William was, to make your way in Washington, D.C., buy a suit, make copies of your résumé, and start networking. Who knows the good that you might do? But, you don't need to do it alone like William did. American Moment is an organization that exists in Washington, D.C., created with the express purpose of training and placing young people into policy-making positions on Capitol Hill.[65]

SO WHAT?

- Have you seen across this book and in this chapter that our nation has an exceptional founding and that the Framers of the Constitution wrote an exceptional document that actually set out to limit the federal government—to prevent the type of government overreach that we are witnessing today?

65 Capitol Hill is the location of the legislative and judicial branches of the federal government.

As we near the end of this book, here are some questions to ask yourself:

- Is it clear that Article I of the Constitution describes Congress? That Article II describes the presidency? And that Article III describes the federal judiciary?
- Is it clear that not only does Congress create laws, but the federal agencies (enabled by Congress) create rules with the force and effect of law?
- Is it clear that the President is not elected by popular vote of the people but by the Electoral College? And that a strong power of the presidency is making appointments to federal offices? Did you notice that the President makes appointments within both the executive and judicial branches of government?
- Is it clear that the federal court system handles cases that deal with federal laws? And that federal judges/ justices are appointed for life? Does it make sense that there are federal judges located across the nation to fill the district court and circuit court positions (in addition to the Supreme Court positions)?

CHAPTER 8
Voting, Elections & Parties

When Colton first started looking at elections and politics in his county, he telephoned the county clerk and said, "I see that there is going to be an election in May for the highway district and the library district. Tell me about those: Who is going to be on the ballot? Who is running, and what's the deal?"

To Colton's astonishment, the clerk answered, "Well, there might not even be an election."

"What do you mean there might not even be an election?"

"These races are often uncontested. People don't even file to run."

Colton was amazed to hear that somebody could complete the paperwork and get the job. He had previously come across individuals who didn't embrace the American dream of all sorts of people running for the same office. He described it this way: "They see the dream, and they despise it. These are the people filing the papers and getting the seats. And we don't even get to vote on it. And we should. We should because it is our property tax money that goes to this."

From our contemporary headlines, many are aware that libraries are not the most family-friendly in their agenda anymore. That is tragic because taxpayers on both sides of the aisle are paying for them. So one of the things that Colton wanted to do as a library-trustee candidate was to give a voice to conservatives. He described the library board this way:

There are five trustees—a board of five members. Not one of them is conservative. Not one. There has not been a contested library district election in this county for ten years. During that time, the left has stacked the board. The board seats consist of four- and six-year terms. This election will determine who gets a voice on that board for the next close-to-a-decade. Think about that. It's important. So I go around the county, and I talk to people, and I knock on their doors and say, "Hey, I'm running for library trustee. I want your vote."

They say, "We have a library district? We get to vote for that?"

"Yes, you do, and you pay $1.7 million in property tax. Which is 1.7 million reasons why you ought to be voting."[1]

Though much of this book does not emphasize voting, the process is crucial. Colton refers to it as the "American dream." It can also be referred to as one of the four pillars of citizenship, though it is the one that is not required by law. (The other three are serving for jury duty, paying taxes, and registering for the Selective Service.)

In terms of logic, if we don't vote, conservative Christian people will not be elected to public office. Without voting, the entire system of government by We the People collapses. My concern is that the election process has become so complex that many of us have opted out of it altogether and are not exercising our dual citizenship to shape the public square and thus to shape the entire nation. I hope to change that.

Because of federalism (limited powers of the federal government and wide powers to the state governments), each state conducts elections differently. Keeping this patchwork quilt of election processes in mind, there are six big questions that require answers:

1 This contribution is based on a local civics club presentation by Colton Bennett.

- **What?**
- **Who?**
- **When?**
- **Where?**
- **Why?**
- **How?**

WHAT are elections about?

In elections, Americans choose from among ourselves who will represent us to uphold the U.S. Constitution and the laws of the land. You have learned that the United States of America is a constitutional republic designed to govern a pluralistic people. Thus, We the People elect our representatives to do their designated jobs on our behalf for the stated amount of time.

Once elected, it is easy for individuals to forget that they have been placed in office to serve our interests and instead be lured away from their obligation by the seduction of power. The process of reelection serves as a check on this potential abuse of power by providing a public review of their on-the-job performance.

Further, as citizens, elections allow us to elect representatives from among ourselves to create, revise, and enforce the law in all three branches of government.[2] This definition reinforces the idea (from chapter 2, "Layers of Law") that law is the cornerstone of the American system of governance. Before reading this book, I am not sure that most of us would initially align elections so closely with creating, revising, and enforcing the law. It's all about the law.

---

2 Ballotpedia, s.v. "Election."

Take heart that as you have waded through the previous chapters, you have simultaneously gained a familiarity with the job description of virtually all public offices[3] that appear on the ballot. That is a sizable accomplishment—a level of knowledge that most Americans (even those already in public office) do not necessarily possess.

To be conversant with the election process, it helps to know a few vocabulary words that recur. The word *voting* goes by various names. In order to define our terms, let's take a quick look at their distinctions but note that in day-to-day usage, they are generally treated as synonyms.

- *Suffrage* comes from the Latin word *suffragium* which means "support, ballot, vote; right of voting; a voting tablet."[4] If you have watched the classic Disney movie *Mary Poppins*, you may remember Mrs. Banks seeking the right to vote for British women and campaigning with other suffragettes.
- *Enfranchisement* and the *franchise* come from the twelfth-century Old French word *franchise* which means "freedom, exemption; right, or privilege" which comes from a variant stem of *franc* meaning "free."[5] Someone who has gained a right is enfranchised, while someone who has lost a right is disenfranchised.
- *Ballot* (mentioned above) is a much more intuitive word to us Americans. It often is used in conjunction with the word *secret*, which makes sense be-

3 Duxbury, Vermont is the only place in the country that had an elected dogcatcher. Turns out, though, that Duxbury was in violation of the Vermont constitution. There is no elected position of dogcatcher. So the position is now appointed. Scott Detrow, "'You Couldn't Get Elected Dogcatcher!' No, Seriously," April 7, 2018, in *Weekend Edition Saturday*, produced by NPR. 🔗 (The topic of elected and appointed positions is addressed in chapter 3, "City Government," as is the relationship between city and state.)

4 *Online Etymology Dictionary*, s.v. "suffrage (n.)."

5 *Online Etymology Dictionary*, s.v. "franchise (n)."

cause since the 1540s, ballot has meant "a small ball used in voting" and also "a secret vote taken by ballots." In ancient times, votes were cast by placing pebbles into an urn; in the Middle Ages, pebbles were no longer used, having been replaced by small balls. By 1776, *ballot* had also come to include pieces of paper used in secret voting.[6]

- *Poll* is an archaic word referring to hairs of the head and later came to mean "[the act of] counting heads." Today the poll is the local location where we can go to cast our votes—and therefore where voters' heads are counted, if you will. A polling location typically transmits to its county election organizer a count or tally of the number of the following:
  - registered voters who showed up to vote and proved their identity
  - individuals who registered to vote that day because the individuals met the legal qualification (if same-day registration is legal in the state)
  - ballots that were completed
  - ballots that were spoiled, which means cast, but (for some reason) the voter did not wish to correct a problem on his or her ballot such as choosing more candidates than the instructions direct

These counts are typically verified and reconciled back at the local election office. As you can imagine, one of the reasons such counts are important is to prevent illegal votes from being cast. For example, if there are 300 voters in a precinct (lo-

6 *Online Etymology Dictionary*, s.v. "ballot (n.)." See also *Merriam-Webster*, s.v. "History of 'Ballot: Where Your Vote Comes From.'"

cal voting area) but 413 votes are cast, then there is a problem because the law (as stated earlier) is one person, one vote.

As an aside, any election in which 100% of the registered voters cast votes is extremely unlikely. For example, a count of 300 ballots cast when there are only 300 eligible voters existing on the voter roll would raise questions in most jurisdictions. Why? People are busy with life—away on business trips, taking care of a loved one, having a baby, and so on. Thus, not everyone shows up to vote. It would be the exceedingly rare exception for every single registered voter to cast a vote—and certainly not the rule. In summary, counting the heads and the votes is important to sustain untainted election results.

Initiative and Referendum

In twenty-six of the fifty states, citizen-initiated measures, such as the initiative and the referendum,[7] can show up on the ballot to the surprise of many voters. The initiative initiates new legislation after having received a certain number of voting citizens' signatures. The referendum takes an existing law and places it on the ballot for the people to decide if it should continue to exist or be removed. Sometimes this process is called a veto referendum.[8] Citizen groups can drive an initiative if the state legislature or city officeholders refuse to respond to an issue in the face of opposing public opinion. If the initiative and referendum exist in your state, rules for creating, campaigning, and voting for them should be available in local and state election offices. The original authority, boundaries, and limitations for these rules reside in state law.

With the exception of the New England town meeting, the initiative and the referendum are the closest mechanisms

7 Ballotpedia, s.v. "States with initiative or referendum."

8 Ballotpedia, s.v. "Initiative and referendum."

that Americans have to direct democracy. Because our nation is based upon representative democracy, we should weigh an initiative or a referendum carefully. Ours is not a nation of **direct** democracy; the United States is a republic that relies on **representative** democracy. Recall that the U.S. Constitution establishes a system of representative democracy where citizens elect officeholders to represent us as We the People. Direct democracy—the people voting directly for ourselves on issues—is not the constitutionally described manner of governance. While not prohibited, direct democracy must be approached cautiously. The Framers of the Constitution attempted to protect the nation from impulsive mob rule which is where direct democracy could potentially lead.

Recall Election

If you don't like the results that you are getting from your elected representative, you can wait until the next election. Or, you can try to fix it right now with the recall which is the procedure of removing an elected representative from office by a vote of the people. Check your state laws to see how the recall works.

WHO votes, and WHO campaigns for office?

Voters and candidates come from the same pool—We the People. And whether voting or campaigning, it is a legal qualification that an individual be registered to vote. For this book's purpose, we will distinguish the two groups as voters and candidates (knowing that both are registered voters).

Candidates

Because this book is an introductory handbook, it focuses on voters. However, a few words regarding candidates are in order. Candidates are Americans who apply for specific jobs typically on the public payroll. If they are elected to a volunteer position—such as a library trustee—they still wield the public's dollars for the government services and supplies that they are elected to oversee. They put their résumés (themselves/their experience) before the voters to determine if they will be "hired" to serve in the desired office. Depending upon the state of residence, there are candidacy filing deadlines. And in some cases, there are job qualifications such as age, residency, place of birth, or professional requirements that must be met in order to campaign for a specific public office.[9]

Winning an election for a public service office means beginning to do the actual work of that job. Of course, this is America, and individuals are free to run for office without ever having attended routine public meetings associated with the office being sought. But, as you have worked through the previous chapters of this book, you can see how that tactic is not efficient, productive, or sensible. A more informed approach is to quietly observe the political landscape, then campaign and then govern effectively.[10] This type of leadership includes knowing the structure of the governance model (how it works and the authority structure), knowing parliamentary procedure, and knowing how to dig into the minutes of prior meetings to understand the issues. At all costs, avoid coming to the office uninformed and expecting objective on-the-job

9 To file for candidacy at the federal level, see the Federal Election Commission website. 🔗

10 Aaron Renn, "Conservatives Need to Learn How to Govern," *The Aaron Renn Show*, streamed live on May 8, 2023, YouTube video, 26:04. 🔗

training. There is beauty and blessing in the thought-out approach to the long game.

Lastly, the moment that candidates begin fundraising, they encounter state or national campaign finance laws relative to the office being sought.[11] These laws are regulatory in nature, but they also provide the public with the opportunity to look at the rolls and discover which organizations fund which candidates.

Voters

The U.S. Constitution and the Bill of Rights assume that American citizens age eighteen or older[12] have the right to vote.[13] American citizenship is granted by birth or through naturalization (the process of becoming a citizen).[14] Non-citizens do not vote (except in very few local elections allowed by certain municipalities).[15] The law is one citizen, one vote with the voting process under the control of each state. As a result, and as a surprise to many Americans, each state has its own voter requirements for residents. For a national state-by-state

11 On the internet, search Federal Elections Commission campaign finance disclosure and filing declarations for information on laws regulating your ability to run for office.

12 Amendment 26.

13 Article 2, Section 1 discusses electors meeting in their respective states; Article 3, Section 4 guarantees every state a republican form of government; Amendment 10 gives powers not delegated to the United States by the Constitution nor prohibited by it to the States, or to the people; Amendment 15, Section 1 guarantees the right to vote regardless of race, color, or previous condition of servitude; Amendment 19 guarantees the right to vote regardless of sex; Amendment 24 guarantees the right to vote regardless of whether a citizen's taxes are paid; Amendment 26, Section 1 guarantees the right to vote to persons eighteen years of age and older.

14 "U.S. Citizen Definition," U.S. Immigration Glossary.
See also "4 Ways to Become a U.S. Citizen," *Fileright Immigration* (blog), FileRight.

15 The debate over whether non-citizens should vote has been going on for over two hundred years. One party wants everyone to vote in order to advance a progressive agenda. The other party wants only citizens to vote in order to maintain a conservative agenda.

summary of requirements, look at **Ballotpedia**'s state voter identification laws.[16] Note that no state's requirements may conflict with the U.S. Constitution.

The first point is to **register** to vote: All states offer in-person voter registration at the local election office (which is a branch of the state election office functioning under the laws of the state). Note that the name each state gives this office varies (see Figure 8.1), and the department under which it exists varies. Additionally, most states offer online registration which makes the process more streamlined. Lastly, The National Voter Registration Act of 1993 (also known as the Motor Voter Act) requires states to offer voter registration at state motor vehicle agencies.[17] Be sure to sign the voter registration application.

The next point is to **remain registered** to vote: Submit a change of address form whenever you move within your state and re-register to vote whenever you make an out-of-state move so that you are eligible to vote. If your address is not current, you may be turned away at the polls because your provable identity is not secure. If you can afford to, keep the address on your driver's license or photo identification updated. It costs to replace the card. However, because of the Motor Voter Act, the roster at the polls will show your correct address if you update it at the local motor vehicle office even if your photo ID doesn't. This is good news for college students who move frequently. (Be sure to see your state's requirements for how to prove your place of residence.)

If you do not drive, you can obtain a state-issued photo identification card through the driver's license office. Again, keep the address on the card current or at least keep it updated at the licensing office. Note that in some states, you can

---

16 Ballotpedia, s.v. "Voter identification laws by state."

17 "The National Voter Registration Act Of 1993 (NVRA)," U.S. Department of Justice—Civil Rights Division, updated July 20, 2022.

register on the day of the election at the polls with the proper state-required identification. The assumption is that the address on your driver's license is up-to-date. Further, if you do not drive, it is assumed that you have a photo ID. Some states require a state-issued photo ID for college students (rather than a college-issued photo ID) as a measure to ensure voter accuracy and prevent fraud.

You may have to declare your political party affiliation when you register to vote, though not all states require this step. Ask when you register whether or not this step is a state voter eligibility requirement for certain elections.

WHEN do we vote?

Is there some secret to knowing when elections take place? Don't most of us just follow the prophetic cues that colorful yard signs give us? When we begin to see signs, the time must be drawing nigh. But prophetic signs aren't the best answer.

The best answer I have found is that, in most places, **every year is an election year**—and up to four elections may occur in some years. Let's un-invert our approach and consider elections from the top (Constitution) down (state then local).

According to the U.S. Constitution, federal elections take place every two years, during even-numbered years. They alternate between a presidential cycle when both the President and members of Congress are elected and a midterm cycle when only Congress is elected.[18] And they come in two parts: the primary or first election and the general or second election. The rule is one vote per voter per election. The other rule is that,

18 Recall that members of the House of Representatives serve two-year terms, and senators serve six-year terms, with one-third of the Senate elected every two years. Hence, there must be a federal election every two years.

for voters, the primary is not a prerequisite for the general. All registered voters are eligible to vote in the general election.

Many people stop thinking about elections at this point because they define the civil realm by who the President of the United States is. We will begin on this well-known path, but we won't stop there. We have an entire civil realm to uncover, and knowing when elections are scheduled helps us gauge what is going on, how long it should last, and what we can do about it. Knowing the **when** enables us to plan ahead and act rather than procrastinate and react. So why two elections? Let's consider them one at a time.

Primary & General Elections

Primary Election

The purpose of the primary election is to determine each party's nominee for the general election in November. The primary narrows the field of candidates for a particular party and can appear in one of three forms: open, closed, and semi-closed. (Third-party candidates may have to wait for the second election to appear on the ballot—each state does it differently.) We typically think of primaries in terms of the presidency, but all levels of officeholders (that are elected in even years) can be on the ballot.

Open Primaries

In a state with an open primary, a voter of any political affiliation is eligible to vote in any party's primary (but may only vote once). A registered Republican, for example, may vote in the Democratic primary. Absentee voting rules may vary.

Closed Primaries

In a state with a closed primary, a voter is only eligible to vote in the party declared during the voter registration process. A registered Republican, for example, can only vote in the Republican primary (which really means that the voter must vote on a Republican ballot because the Democratic and Republican elections occur at the same time and location). Typically, absentee voters must vote in accordance with their declared party at registration.

Semi-Closed Primaries

In a state with a semi-closed primary, a voter who is not affiliated with a party may vote in either party's primary. For example, a voter who registered as an Independent may vote in either the Democratic or Republican primary. However, if a voter registered as a Democrat or a Republican, the primary ballot must match that registration. For example, if a person registered to vote as a Republican, he or she is only eligible to vote in the Republican primary.

Presidential Caucus

Instead of holding a primary election, a presidential caucus is conducted sometimes in some states. A caucus is a private meeting for members inside one political party to discuss and nominate a presidential candidate to be on the ballot for the general election. The party caucus takes place less than a year before the presidential election, and may be held simultaneously at many locations within the state so that all eligible voters may attend and cast a vote. It may be the state law, or it may be a political party's state headquarters, that chooses to conduct a statewide caucus for presidential candidates. Because each party may conduct its own caucus affairs within certain guidelines, there will be different emphases and presentations at the various locations.

National Convention

At different times and in different cities, the Republican National Convention and the Democratic National Convention take place. These conventions are really just a formality because the nominee has been known well in advance based on the results of the primary elections and caucuses. These two events happen in even-numbered years, on a four-year cycle (e.g. 2020, 2024, 2028, and so on), between March and September before the general election. Each party's purpose for convening is to choose its party's official candidate for the presidential ballot. Delegates from each state (based on the results of the primaries) are sent by their respective party to cast votes for the candidates. (Independent candidates do not have a convention, but they may be required to secure a certain number of signatures in order to appear on the general election ballot.) Each party's candidate who secures the nomination to run for President then chooses a vice-presidential running mate of his or her own selection, usually in close strategic conversation with the national party and frequently with partisan members of Congress.

General Elections

The general election for President of the United States is accompanied by other offices which are on each state and

local election calendar and takes place in November every four years in even years.[19]

Special Elections (to Congress)

Occasionally, states may choose to hold a special election when one of its members of Congress prematurely leaves office. Each state's laws determine the time frame in which these elections are eligible to take place.

State Election Offices

State election offices are known by a variety of different names (see Figure 8.1). Browse your state election office website to find your calendar of elections. Do not be discouraged if you cannot find it—not all state governments value transparency and clarity on their websites. Try calling the state office and seeking help over the phone. You can also look for the website's link to your local election office. Don't forget that the local county-equivalent election office is an arm of the state government. You should be able to find answers there or by phone or by visiting the office in person. Ask what elections take place this year and when. Remember that the local election office is the place that conducts the actual elections—even presidential ones. The staff there should be able to guide you toward other deadlines such as the last day to register to vote, the last day to submit an absentee ballot (if available in your state), and the dates that early in-person voting might take place. Absentee ballots typically must be requested, and some states require a stated reason why the voter cannot vote at the polls. Most states have a mail-in voting option, and a

---

19 Although it sounds awkward, presidential election day is always described as taking place on the first Tuesday after the first Monday in November.

STATE ELECTION OFFICES
WHAT IS YOURS CALLED?

Board of Elections

- New York

Department of Elections

- Delaware
- Virginia

Department of State

- Florida
- Pennsylvania

Division of Elections

- Alaska

Election Commission

- South Carolina

Elections Division

- Wisconsin

Lt. Gov. Elections

- Utah

Office of Elections

- Hawaii

Secretary of State

- Alabama
- Arizona
- Arkansas
- California
- Colorado
- Georgia
- Idaho
- Indiana
- Iowa
- Kansas
- Louisiana
- Maine
- Michigan
- Minnesota
- Mississippi
- Missouri
- Montana
- Nebraska
- Nevada
- New Hampshire
- New Jersey
- New Mexico
- North Dakota
- Ohio
- Oregon
- Rhode Island
- South Dakota
- Tennessee
- Texas
- Vermont
- Washington
- West Virginia
- Wyoming

Secretary of the Commonwealth

- Massachusetts

Secretary of *the* State

- Connecticut

State Board of Elections

- Illinois
- Kentucky
- Maryland
- North Carolina

State Election Board

- Oklahoma

Figure 8.1

The information in this figure is from **usa.gov**.

few states conduct voting exclusively by mail-in ballot, sending to every registered voter.

If we can learn when to expect elections to occur, then we won't be surprised by them. Surprise has often been our reaction when we discover that, yes, today is election day. Surprise was also the reaction that Colton experienced in our opening story when he discovered that in the absence of challengers, smaller elections may not be publicized or even take place. Lastly, chagrin ensues when you are away on vacation, didn't vote absentee, and didn't realize your mistake until a loved one sends you a remember-to-vote-today text. Put the voting dates on your calendar as if they were birthdays or anniversaries.

WHERE do elections take place?

While you are at the website for your state's office of elections, see if you can locate where you should vote and the hours that the polls are open. The website may redirect you to the local county-equivalent election office. If you cannot find a place to enter your address to find your voting location, try checking **vote.org** and searching for your polling place by state.[20] That website should then take you to the appropriate page of your state's election division's website where you should be able to enter your address and find your polling location. You have to vote at the proper location on election day for two reasons:

1. To verify your identity by providing a driver's license or photo identification card that must match the registered voter roster of names at that location

20 Note that websites such as **vote.org** should redirect you to your state or local elections website.

(for your precinct). State laws vary considerably regarding proof of address.

2. There is a ballot prepared for you and your neighbors (in your precinct) that may differ from ballots for other nearby neighborhoods.

So people vote within their precinct, but what does that mean? A precinct is a synonym for a voting district. (Not to be confused with a police precinct which is a geographical area where police patrol in large metropolitan areas.) The whole nation is broken down into these geographical voting districts. They are the smallest geographic subset or political division related to elections. Their purpose is to organize voter locations for manageable units of the population and also to promote citizen awareness and involvement in political civic affairs.

Each precinct (think of it as your neighborhood) has a publicly elected representative from each legally qualified political party (in most places, just Democratic and Republican parties). This precinct committee person may go by various names in various parts of the country.[21] The job of precinct leaders is to get to know their neighbors, help inform those neighbors on civic issues, and promote voting on behalf of the party with which the precinct leader is affiliated.

Also, note that in certain elections there may be occasions when you may show up to vote (at the correct location), and there is nothing/no one to vote for. As an example, in many city elections, the process is still conducted by the local county-equivalent election office. Therefore, if you live outside the city limits, you most likely cannot vote for those candidates. There may also be another race on the ballot, such as school board positions. Note that rarely do all of the seats for boards expire at the same time. Only a portion of a board or council

21 Among the other names are precinct captain, precinct chairman, precinct committee officer, precinct committeeman, or precinct delegate.

is typically eligible for reelection each election cycle. Thus, it is possible that there may be no school board members whose terms have expired in your district/zone/precinct. You may show up at the polls only to be told that there is nothing/no one on your ballot to vote for this election. Understanding these nuances can also help us to comprehend that there can be different ballots for different precincts within a local voting area. These different ballots are called ballot faces. Understanding the concept of ballot faces aids voters to appreciate the complex preparations that the local election office must complete in order to be ready for voters. It also helps explain the importance of where we vote—we can't simply show up at any polling location to vote just because we are Americans.

WHY vote?

This entire book describes the larger picture of dual citizenship, our American inheritance of the constitutional system of governance, the privilege of electing our leaders who then represent us, and the importance of creating, revising, and enforcing the law. It all surrounds the why of voting. We vote so that our voice is heard. Voting is also the means that God uses in the United States to remove kings and raise up kings (or in this case, Presidents, congressmen, governors, legislators, and all other local officeholders).

HOW do I vote? HOW do I find election results?

After you know the what, who, when, where, and why of voting, you are ready to do it. Armed with knowledge from your state and local election offices, you know what you need to have with you. Remember your voter guide and the indentification that your state requires (usually your driver's license, if it is current and your address is correct). Go to your precinct location. Follow the poll worker's instructions once you arrive. I cannot accurately describe the process further because it varies from state to state.

As a general rule, for state-level or federal-level race election results, check your state election office's website. To check results for local races, see your local election office's website. Note that some districts (as in a state legislative race, for example) may be composed of parts of various counties (or county equivalents). Therefore, be sure to watch the results on the state website rather than the local website where you live. The results will be different for your district depending upon which county's results you check. It is an interesting exercise to compare the website results from the local election office to those of the state office.

POLITICAL PARTIES

Although not mentioned in the Constitution, our nation currently works within a two-party system that has been in use since the early days of our nation. Today these two parties are the Democratic Party and the Republican Party,[22] also known as the Grand Old Party or G.O.P.[23] Political parties are simply structures made by people to represent the principles and values of a particular group. The document which catalogs and memorializes the principles and values of the party is called the party platform. Each topic or stated position within the

---

22 For more information on the history of the party system, see "About Parties and Leadership: Historical Overview," United States Senate.

23 "As early as the 1870s, politicians and newspapers began to refer to the Republican Party as both the 'grand old party' and the 'gallant old party' to emphasize its role in preserving the Union during the Civil War." Christopher Klein, "Why Is the Republican Party Known as the GOP?," History, updated June 1, 2023.

platform is called a plank. If you consider yourself an adherent of, or you are officially a member of, or you are a candidate representing a political party, you essentially stand on the platform in order to speak about the principles and values of the party.

For practical purposes, I am directing your focus to the existing two-party structure because we have so much to recover in the civil realm. Although third parties offer an alternative for voters, third-party candidates rarely win, and voting for them often results in a loss of votes for a more viable candidate. Further, the three branches of our government at the national level are designed to function within the two-party system. Think, at the federal level, of the largely winner-take-all approach of the Electoral College in addition to the House and Senate's organization along party lines. Or at the local level think of the precinct committee person who volunteers in your area. At this time in history, it doesn't seem to make sense to invest in raising a third party to the functional level of the existing two. There is so much other priority work to do in the forgotten realm.

At the state and county-equivalent level, the party organizations support a greenhouse farming operation—growing candidates to run for statewide offices (in addition to U.S. Congressional representatives for each state). Individuals are being identified, brought into the political fold, nurtured, and given opportunities and training on local boards and commissions—all within the context of preparing leaders who can step into higher offices and promote the party's agenda. This preparation includes developing an awareness of relevant existing laws, relationships with others in the party or in office, public speaking ability, decorum, and a political résumé.

Regular meetings of each party are often at the county-equivalent level, held in a location at the county seat, and are open to anyone who is interested. Look online to find out when your party of choice is meeting. You should also search online for each party's version of the platform for the national level and then for your specific state. In all, you should be able to locate four documents:

- The National Democratic Party Platform
- The State Democratic Party Platform
- The National Republican Party Platform
- The State Republican Party Platform

Include in your search the name of your state, the party name, and the words *current platform*. Enter, for example, "Ohio Republican Party current platform." You will most likely have to poke around within the party website for your state. When you locate the platform, read it. Do the same thing for the other party, and find which platform most aligns with what you value and believe. Often, one platform or the other will largely describe what you hold to. Just as it is with your family and friends, you won't likely agree on every point all the time. But, just as with your family and friends, you can lobby to change opinions… and platforms.

In former times, the parties each had a spectrum within them ranging from liberal to conservative. First, to define our terms, according to *Merriam-Webster* online dictionary *liberal* means holding to "a political philosophy based on belief in progress, the essential goodness of the human race, and the autonomy of the individual and standing for the protection of political and civil liberties specifically: such a philosophy that considers government as a crucial instrument for amelioration of social inequities (such as those involving race, gender, or class)."[24] *Conservative* means adherence to "a political philosophy based on tradition and social stability, stressing

24 *Merriam-Webster*, s.v. "liberal."

established institutions, and preferring gradual development to abrupt change specifically: such a philosophy calling for lower taxes, limited government regulation of business and investing, a strong national defense, and individual financial responsibility for personal needs (such as retirement income or health-care coverage)."[25]

Although it is possible that a conservative Democrat could have quite a bit of overlap with a liberal Republican, it is much more common that the parties are completely different ideological camps. In politics, the left is now considered liberal (supporting progressive reforms), and the right is considered conservative (supporting conservative reforms).[26] The left typically progresses, and the right typically conserves. This contrast can even be detected when comparing the robustness of the Democratic Party's national website to the less-vibrant Republican Party's national website. Search the two national websites and compare their robustness and functionality.

Of course, within the context described above, on the extremes, you can find members of the far left espousing Marxist[27] ideology and those on the far right embracing fascist[28] dogma. And here's one more terminology detail: States that are characterized by progressivism/liberalism are called blue states. And states that generally hold conservative values are known as red states. What follows is a general description of each party.

---

25 *Merriam-Webster*, s.v. "conservative."

26 The political terms *left* and *right* originated in the 1789 pre-revolutionary French National Assembly relative to the seating of Assembly delegates in relation to the king. Those seated in the center were moderates, holding the middle. Those on the king's left were revolutionary commoners. Those to his right were the aristocratic traditionalists.

27 Karl Marx's theory of the superiority of collective ownership in the form of socialism and its purer form of communism as opposed to free-market capitalism and private ownership of goods, services, and property.

28 Benito Mussolini's theory of centralized national government under a strong militaristic, dictatorial leader.

Lefty-Loosey: The Democratic Party

The Democratic Party Platform[29] favors economically liberal policies where the government provides for Americans' needs collectively through economic policies such as universal health care and shared prosperity (expanding unemployment benefits, minimum wage level, government food programs, affordable housing programs, and taxes to fund such concepts). Socially, the party is in favor of human rights but is ardently against human rights for the unborn. It supports concepts such as government-funded daycare and universal early childhood education. The party refers to climate change as a global emergency. The essence of the party platform indicates that We the People are not able to think for ourselves, take care of ourselves, or accept the consequences of our own decisions. Rather, American citizens are in need of government protection and advocacy on every front of our lives from cradle to grave.

Righty-Tighty: The Republican Party

The Republican Party Platform[30] emphasizes the centrality of the U.S. Constitution which returns decision-making control to the people and to the states. The essence of the party platform indicates that We the People are actually able to take care of ourselves and accept the consequences of our own decisions. Therefore, American citizens are not in need of government protection and advocacy on every front of our lives from cradle to grave. Rather, Republicans cherish individual liberty and freedom from overreaching governmental control.

29 "Party Platform," Democratic National Committee.

30 "Our Platform," Republican National Committee.

Lefty-Loosey, Righty-Tighty

It depends on which way you turn the civic screw. Turning to the right conserves the constitutional system that is in place. Turning to the left progresses beyond the constitutional system to implement more social and economic governmental programs. I find the following quote from the 1959 book *American Voting Behavior* to still be a reasonable assessment of the two parties:

> The *conservative* party… has broadly an interest in quieting things down politically, in damping the urgency of demands for specific and positive action. The *liberal* party, on the other hand, has an interest in arousing the public to the urgencies of action and tends to stress such action issues whenever they seem to be politically opportune.[31]

This quote helps explain why conservative Christians have generally not been on the front lines politically but rather posit a reactionary stance and fight against proposed ideas and legislation. In concert with the tradition of greenhouse farming explained earlier, it also helps explain why leftist groups have a better understanding of civics than their conservative counterparts and why their political websites offer comprehensive help to the seeker. After all, in order to play the game well, one must know the rules. Liberals know the rules, and they typically win the game.

I say, typically, with its two implications: liberals are generally used to winning in politics (of course, not every single race and not every single piece of legislation) and exude an

31 Eugene Burdick and Arthur J. Brodbeck, eds., *American Voting Behavior*, 109. This quote is from chapter 4, "'Voting' and the Equilibrium of the American Political System" by Talcott Parsons, which, in turn, is a critique of a 1952 study conducted by Bernard R. Berelson, Paul F. Lazarsfeld, and William N. McPhee entitled *Voting* (Chicago, IL: University of Chicago Press, 1954). Thus this quote stems from interdisciplinary study that spans the 1950s.

affinity for the process of helping move the country progressively toward liberalism. There is a reason that liberals are known as progressives. It also explains why liberals tend to take it so hard when they do not progress. They are collectively, vocally reactive against conservative victories.

Conservatives, generally speaking, do not know how to regularly engage in a plethora of action issues. We know how to engage on single issues that are dear to our way of life (rights for the unborn, heterosexual marriage, liberty in education), but we do not typically involve ourselves holistically in the civic realm.[32] Hearkening back to this book's opening reference to our dual citizenship, I hope to inspire us to change that. Not through anger, frustration, or hatred, but through a deep appreciation of what we have been given as Christians who are Americans and through a recognition of our duty to invest our talents in this gift.

You do not need to be an evangelist for said party, but you should be cognizant of the party's platform and the extent of your alignment with it. Also, be aware that there is a hierarchy structure within the party system. While that is not the subject of this book, it is important for you to know that it exists and is called by different names in different states.

Finally, it should go without saying, but I find it necessary to insert here, that having varying partisan persuasions from others should not preclude us from being friendly with them. There is a strange misconception afoot in our nation that differences equal hate. Of course, Scripture asks in Amos 3:3, "Can two walk together, unless they are agreed?" But in Luke 6:32–36, Jesus also asks the following questions:

> But if you love those who love you, what credit is that to you? For even sinners love those who love them. And if

32 The above quote also helps explain why conservatives do not typically teach their children civics beyond the U.S. Constitution and the Founding Fathers.

> you do good to those who do good to you, what credit is that to you? For even sinners do the same. And if you lend to those from whom you hope to receive back, what credit is that to you? For even sinners lend to sinners to receive as much back. But love your enemies, do good, and lend, hoping for nothing in return; and your reward will be great, and you will be sons of the Most High. For He is kind to the unthankful and evil. Therefore be merciful, just as your Father also is merciful.

Nonpartisan

The public offices that require candidates to declare their political party affiliation are considered partisan. The individuals who campaign and are listed on the ballot for these offices do so under their party affiliation. However, some offices do not require the candidate to declare a political party affiliation, in which case the office is considered nonpartisan. Typically, these elections are for judges and for local positions—mayor or councilors/commissioners in addition to school board members. Because Nebraska is unicameral, it is the only state legislature that is nonpartisan.

Knowing which public offices are partisan or nonpartisan is part of the patchwork quilt across each jurisdiction. It is a reflection of We the People—right where we live. What is important to one region may be less of a priority to another, thus the people of one geographic locale will decide they want partisan candidates for an office, while another group of people in another locale will have determined that they want nonpartisan candidates for the very same elected role.

When individuals campaign for a nonpartisan office, they do not check their political beliefs and values at the door. Rather, these beliefs inform their views and decisions within the nonpartisan office should they win the election.

In many jurisdictions, nonpartisan candidates are recipients of campaign contributions from political parties or partisan special interest groups who want to see their preferred-partisan candidate elected to the nonpartisan office in question. In other words, partisans hold nonpartisan offices. The first time I went to a Republican party dinner, I was shocked to see two local elected representatives who were nonpartisan officeholders in attendance there. Based on having observed their words and actions in office, I would have expected them to be registered Democrats.

Regarding judges, we discussed in the county and state chapters that they can be appointed or elected. Here, we take that concept a step further and consider political party as well. Judgeships are an interesting topic when it comes to being partisan or nonpartisan. It is done differently throughout the country, so you will need to check to see how your state conducts its judicial elections.[33] Special interest groups rate and score the nonpartisan judges. They are scored for the likelihood that they will issue decisions that appeal to the special interest groups.

OTHER THINGS YOU SHOULD KNOW

There is nothing wrong with voting for a candidate who is not a Christian or who does not share all of your values. It is not a sin to vote for a non-Christian. In fact, thinking that one must only vote for Christians is a sign of not having labored much in the civil realm. Think of the prophet Daniel who was able to serve God faithfully alongside other high-level, pagan appointees in Babylon under several administrations.

Further, have you voted for someone and not known anything about that person? Or, have you skipped names on

33 Ballotpedia, s.v. "Partisan election of judges."

the ballot because you didn't know them? Most likely, when you feel the guilt, you do not have the time to solve the problem. That is why you are reading this book.

Voter Guides

Within the boundaries of each state, there are special interest groups who inform their members with a list of candidates that they endorse. For example, friends of the library have memberships that inform their constituents. Or the American Association of Retired People (AARP) publishes a magazine with inserts customized for each state. College alumni associations can educate within their circles. These examples may quite likely have a liberal bent to them. And liberal voter guides are prevalent because progressives know how to mobilize their voter base.

To obtain a conservative voter guide check with local churches. Sometimes churches feature voter guides in their emails or on their information tables located near an entrance. Look online for one as well. Go to the internet and search for a voter guide on your local party's website. Guides are especially helpful for nonpartisan races such as judges, school boards, and city offices.

THINGS YOU CAN DO

- Don't use the excuses in Figure 8.2 on the following page that the U.S. Census Bureau documented.[34]
- Keep your photo ID (driver's license) address current.

34 Adapted from Jacob Fabina and Zachary Scherer, "Voting and Registration in the Election of November 2020," *Current Population Survey Reports*, U.S. Census Bureau, Washington, DC, 2022.

REASONS FOR NOT VOTING: PRESIDENTIAL ELECTIONS, 2004–2020
(in percent)

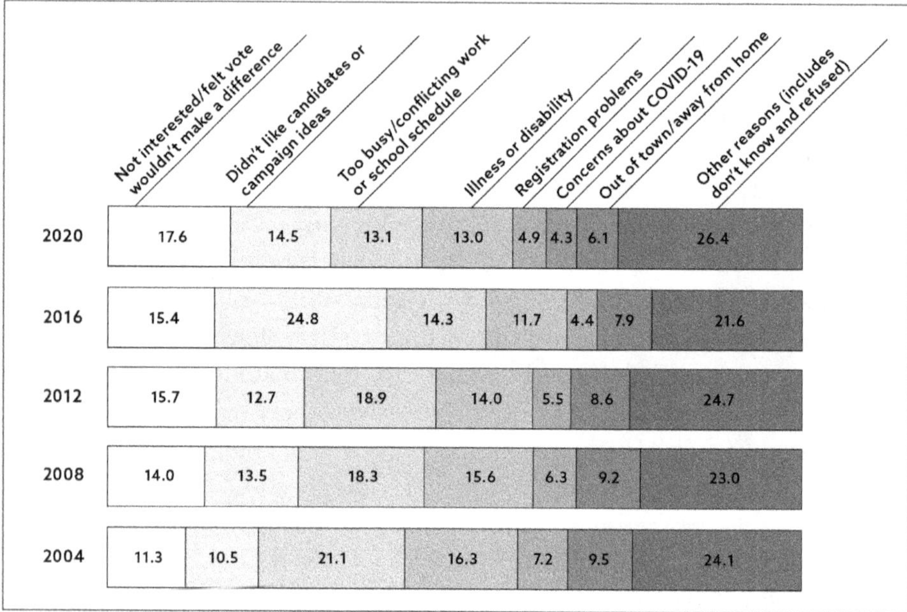

Figure 8.2

- Contact your state's election office (see Figure 8.1). Look online for the location, website, and phone number of your local election office. Call or visit the office or search your state's election website to find answers to the following questions:
    - What are the dates of the election cycle in my area?
    - What offices are up for election in each of those months?
    - What do I need to do to register to vote?

- When does voter registration close before an election?
- Is there early voting?
- Is there registration at the polls on election day?
  - What is needed to do that?
- How does absentee voting work in my state?
- Can you help me with which districts I live in?
  - What is my precinct?
  - For city elections, do we have districts?
  - For county (equivalent) elections, do we have districts?
  - What special districts are elected when for my address?
  - What is my state legislative district?
  - What is my state judicial district?
  - What is my U.S. congressional district?
- Where can I see a ballot in advance of the election?
- Where do I look to see who the candidates are?
- Where do I look to watch voting results?
  - What results for my area should I look for on the state site versus the local site?
- How do I sign up to be a poll worker for the next election? This is a great opportunity to learn more about the election process while serving the community. Prepare to take a several-hour training class

and work a long (thirteen-or-more-hour) day. Serving as a poll worker is a paid position. A compendium of federal laws by state governing the role of poll worker is available online.[35]

- Consider collaborating with others to put together a voter guide for your community.
- Keep the position of precinct committee person in mind as an entry point into the forgotten realm for yourself or for any of your extroverted friends or acquaintances. It is a position that already exists—you do not have to create or define it. Some counties (or equivalents) even have a specific job description for it. You can find a list of the open precinct seats at your party's local website. If a position is not open, you can run as a candidate for one in the next election. I think that the precinct job is a strategic position that should be filled by an enthusiastic person for every single precinct within a county. When serving in this role, a person can go door-to-door and do whatever is needed to promote civic awareness such as
    - offering surveys
    - encouraging voting
    - talking to shut-ins and helping them with any civic problems that they are having
    - raising awareness of emerging issues
    - arranging for the party to transport people to the polls to vote

35 United States Election Assistance Commission, "Poll Worker Resources for Voters," Help America Vote, February 1, 2024. 🔗 You may want to search online for the newest version of *The Compendium of State Poll Worker Requirements* by the United States Election Assistance Commission.

    - encouraging neighbors in general

- Make friends with other Christians outside your circles in the community.
    - give them this book
    - encourage them to vote[36]

SO WHAT?

After having read this chapter, do you understand that the voting process has gotten away from conservatives and that there are certain proactive steps that you can take to change that? Let's review answers to our initial big questions in terms of action points.

Who should vote?

You! (If you are 18 years of age or older and an American citizen.) **You can register to vote in most states with a photo ID and proof of address.** Typically, state laws presuppose that the two addresses match, so keep your driver's license address up to date or seek an approved photo ID. It is best to register now. You may still be able to vote if you register later, but don't count on it. Be sure to familiarize yourself with the hurdles involved in registering to vote and voting. Complications in the process (like states that have the option to register at the polls) generally serve as hurdles to conservatives and enablement to progressives.

---

36 For an excellent set of reasons to vote, see Minnesota Family Council's Biblical Basis for Voting infographic on the links page at **CivilRealm.com**.

Who do you vote for?

Do your research. In both a nonpartisan election (city, judge, special districts) and a primary/general election, it is hard to know who you should cast your vote for. Seek the help of voter guides and try to attend candidate forums to hear from the candidates themselves.

When do you vote?

Again, do your research! Like we know holidays or birthdays or seasons of the year, we need to know the election calendar schedule. If a race is uncontested, we might not even know that there could be an election. Therefore, find out what all of the possible races are within the even years and the odd years.

Where do you vote? Where do you live? What is your civic address for each possible race?

Know your place within the system—your civic address across the voting spectrum. The first part of your civic address is your precinct, and that is where you report to vote on election day. If you live in one town and work in another, you must vote in the precinct of your hometown.

Early voting and absentee voting may be viable options in your state. Early voting may take place at a different location (and that complicates the task). If you vote absentee, find out the deadlines and drop off or mail your ballot in plenty of time for it to be counted. (Note that early voting and absentee voting have the possibility of letting the other party know what is transpiring.)

How to mobilize others to vote?

Encouragement. Conservatives can be jaded, having given up on the idea of effecting change in our nation. We can encourage others to care, to know the inheritance we have been given. Liberals do run virtually every institution in America except for the church, but it doesn't have to be this way.

Taking initiative with collaboration. When I turn on the radio and listen to National Public Radio, I wonder, "If it is National *and* Public, why do the voices so confidently (need I say, arrogantly?) portray only one liberal point of view? Why are conservative voices relegated to private talk radio programs and Christian radio stations? What is *public* (as in *We the People*) about National *Public* Radio?" I would like to see a new America where the conservative voice incrementally emerges. That would involve learning to get along among our conservative groups/constituencies and appreciating one another. We can hold to our distinctives while valuing others.

Compare your local Democratic party website to your local Republican party website. Which party makes the registration and voting steps clear? Which party appeals to and attempts to mobilize young people?

Here are some mobilization suggestions from my county's Democratic party's website:

- Register here (local election office's registration link).
- Vote early here (local election office's early voter location link).
- Vote absentee here (local election office's absentee voter link).
- Vote on election day here (local election office's poll location link).

- Knock on your neighbors' doors and encourage them to vote.
- Hold signs at the street corners.
- Take friends with you to vote.

The approach of the two parties in your area of the nation may differ from mine. But, generally, the left mobilizes young people, and the right does not. Consequently, the right probably does not utilize social media platforms to motivate people to vote. Many of the college-age young people that I know are either disengaged or desire to be engaged but need help and resources. Start by giving them this book. (See Appendix F: All Sorts of Districts to complete your Civic Roster and Civic Address worksheets.)

CHAPTER 9
Christian Diplomacy

"You have two minutes to speak, Mrs. Landis."

"Thank you, Mr. Chairman. While my two assistants hand out copies of the study that I will address, let me preface by saying that I am not paid for my work on this issue. You have heard from the paid lobbyists representing the other side. Now you are hearing from regular citizens."

This presentation took place at a legislative sub-session at my state capitol. In exactly two minutes, I walked the senators and representatives constituting this committee through their own copies of a study that a paid lobbyist named Erin (who, incidentally, had been granted unlimited time to speak) had just referenced. My state representative responded to Erin's presentation by requesting a copy of said study from her, which she could not provide. Moments later, it was my turn to present. Providentially, I had my two children distribute fourteen copies of that exact study—one to each legislator.

At the end of my allotted time to speak, the chairman surprisingly offered me more time to comment. I declined, stating that I could talk on this issue for another couple of hours and should stop now.

Later that week, I met personally with my state legislator at a local Starbucks for two hours and provided him with article after article to support each point that I was in the process of making. As a result of this newfound knowledge, he became sympathetic to my viewpoint and was glad to be presented with facts rather than emotional arguments.

Without a Christian grounding and without a secure idea of both who God is and what our role is in the public square, I would be doing you a disservice to simply teach you the mechanics of the various levels of government. If you were to attend public meetings without a clear idea of how to navigate them, you would run a very real risk of getting angry or overreacting to the business at hand or just giving up altogether. Therefore, I have coined the term *Christian diplomacy*[1]—skill in handling civil affairs guided by the principles of God's Word. It's a subtle, winsome, and powerful mustard-seed approach of entering the forgotten realm. An informed approach based on an educated faith. Rather than entering the public arena with sleeves pushed up and temples pulsating, rather than determining to set things right in one fell swoop, rather than publicly rebuking the powers that be, I suggest entering as an ambassador or diplomat who employs the skill of Christian diplomacy.

Being a Christian diplomat takes time; it requires patience and investment in our leaders. It requires overcoming our own complacency and desire for comfort that we discussed at the beginning of the book. It is almost always a temptation (at least for me) to find a reason, any reason, not to attend a public meeting. I caved to this temptation one time during COVID: I just threw up my hands and went grocery shopping instead of following all of the imposed rules requiring sitting six feet away from the nearest person while being masked

1 At least I thought that I had coined the term. It was used in 1903 by William Armstead Haggerty in his thesis, *The Triumph of Christian Diplomacy* (Boston, MA: Boston University Libraries, 1903), and by Godfrey John in his article, "Christian Diplomacy," *Christian Science Sentinel* 88, no. 3 (January 20, 1986).

while watching the councilors on a Zoom screen while the total number of people in the chamber was strictly limited for the entire meeting. I just couldn't take it that night. Sometimes that sort of thing overcomes a person.

Here's a question for Christians to ask ourselves: Where is it darkest in our country? What area of our nation needs the light of Christ the most? Of course, I think it is the civil realm. The people operating it think that they are the enlightened ones. After all, they are, by and large, the children of the Enlightenment and its luminescent public education system. And they are running things. So what are we to do? We are to shine the light of Christ in the civil realm without much ado, regardless of campaign signs, regardless of strong party affiliation. The first part of that is simply being present—being salt and light in the room. In general, Christians have been absent regarding our systems of governance. That means we haven't gotten to know the people in governance positions. How can we befriend them or minister to them if we don't get to know them, even in a distant sense?

It is difficult to put words to these concepts, but if Christ is the answer, if He is the nexus of all things, and if He came to save the world, then why do we shy away from applying that truth in the civil realm? Why has the gospel not been the answer there? Does it lose its efficacy in the civil realm? I contend that we have forgotten to believe it there. Maybe because we have forgotten to be there. Even though conventional wisdom mistakenly tells us that the civil realm and people of faith are separated by a wall, they really do belong together. Let's take each of these facets of Christian diplomacy one at a time: subtlety, winsomeness, a mustard-seed approach, and an educated faith.

Subtlety

First, this approach is subtle—at least in its inception. Typically, there is no rounding up of fellow concerned citizens into an action group, no gathering of the troops. The subtle approach doesn't start with handing the minutemen arms. No, the subtle approach looks daily into the Scriptures. This quiet course of action surveys the political situation of our nation and asks questions such as:

- What am I to believe and do in the place where God has put me?
- How can I invest in my community instead of complaining against dignitaries? (2 Peter 2:10).
- How can I believe in the power of God and in His goodness that extends to all three realms of governance?
- How can I be an agent of change right where I live?
- How can I have the courage to step into the civil realm?
- In what ways can I bring my family along with me (whatever my age)?

The subtle approach finds out when local governmental entities meet and slips in to attend such meetings in an unassuming fashion. Its general demeanor should be discreet and peaceable. Take, for example, the following passage from 1 Timothy 2:1–5:

> Therefore I exhort first of all that supplications, prayers, intercessions, and giving of thanks be made for all men, for kings and all who are in authority, that we may lead a quiet and peaceable life in all godliness and reverence. For this is

> good and acceptable in the sight of God our Savior, who desires all men to be saved and to come to the knowledge of the truth. For there is one God and one Mediator between God and men, the Man Christ Jesus.

If you have the boldness to actually attend local governing meetings, you may find yourself in deep waters that you don't understand. In such a case, it is wise to assume the quiet/subtle approach. Take heart. Proverbs 17:28 tells us that "Even a fool is counted wise when he holds his peace; / When he shuts his lips, he is considered perceptive," and Proverbs 21:23 says, "whoever guards his mouth and tongue / Keeps his soul from troubles." If someone inquires of you, kindly introduce yourself. If he or she presses you for information, refer to yourself as a "concerned citizen." If you must add more, "a concerned citizen learning more about our government" is a good answer. After all, it is the truth. You are there on the hunt for knowledge of how our system of government works. We can't recover even a fraction of influence in the civil realm if we don't know what our system of government is. There is so much to learn. If, of course, you happen to have your child or children in attendance with you, a simple "we're on a local government field trip" response works nicely.

In order to stay on the subtle, quiet front, you might refrain from entering a governmental meeting too early. That way, you can avoid unnecessary chit-chat—especially while trying to determine who's who and how the system works. Likewise, a general guideline is to leave promptly when the meeting is over, especially in the early stages of attendance. I have been attending city council for over five years now, and I have just recently begun to visit with a few people afterward. But because of the regularity of council meetings, one of the ladies who also attends (from the other side of the aisle—meaning that she is not conservative) has allowed me to drive her home after the meetings. I look forward to spending time with her, and I count her friendship as a privilege.

There is a time to be loud within the subtle approach. There is a time to cry out. Proverbs 2:3–6 encourages us that if we cry out for discernment, if we lift up our voice for understanding, if we seek her as silver and search for her as we would for hidden treasure, then we will understand the fear of the Lord and will find the knowledge of God. Here, we are promised that the Lord gives wisdom—He gives it to those who cry out for it—and from His mouth come knowledge and understanding. This loud quietness, this crying out for wisdom, is so desperately necessary as we enter the forgotten realm of the public square. Crying out to God for insight on how to fix our governmental woes is far superior to complaining about them.

Winsomeness

Next, this approach is winsome. Granted, the word *winsome* has fallen on hard times. But, frankly, I can't find a suitable synonym. The word has come to imply abandoning one's commitments in order to please men. I don't ascribe to that. Proverbs 25:26–28 has a few things to say about such flip-flopping:

> A righteous man who falters before the wicked
> Is like a murky spring and a polluted well.
>
> It is not good to eat much honey;
> So to seek one's own glory is not glory.
>
> Whoever has no rule over his own spirit
> Is like a city broken down, without walls.

So what do I mean by the term *winsome*? *Merriam-Webster* defines it to mean generally pleasing and engaging often because of a childlike charm and innocence or having/showing a good mood or disposition. Perhaps after having observed people in the civil realm behave in a politically frustrated manner, it would be refreshing to observe a manner characterized by a dash of sunny disposition. An interest in governing affairs laced with kindness toward others—whichever side of the aisle those others may occupy—goes a long way.

Granted, it is clear that men may revile and persecute and speak evil against us. And we are told to rejoice when they do. But we don't have to provoke others to do so. Nor do we seek, on the other hand, to have all men speak well of us. Scripture pronounces a woe on that kind of behavior—something which should cause us to think, "Yikes!" Yet God does allow His servants to grow in favor with both Himself and with men. Within the books of Luke, Proverbs, and 1 Corinthians (particularly 1 Corinthians 13), He tells us how to do so. Entering our systems of governance quietly while asking for wisdom as we proceed really is winsome in the long run. Otherwise, what are we to do with a truth such as "He who earnestly seeks good finds favor" (Proverbs 11:27)?

Winsomeness is not an end in itself, but "when a man's ways please the Lord, / He makes even his enemies to be at peace with him" (Proverbs 16:7). We see that principle here in the book of Proverbs. We see it in Psalm 1 where the man who meditates in God's Word brings forth fruit, and whatever he does prospers. We see it in the life of Solomon, Joseph, Daniel, Stephen, and, of course, in Jesus.

It is critical, when we attend government meetings, that we hold onto the Word of God. I consider the Book of Proverbs to be **the** handbook for Christian diplomacy. The following is a group of verses regarding the winsomeness that can accompany us in the forgotten realm of the public square. It is a reminder that should be ever-present with us as we go:

> Let not mercy and truth forsake you;
> Bind them around your neck,

> Write them on the tablet of your heart,
> And so find favor and high esteem
> In the sight of God and man (Proverbs 3:3–5).
>
> He who loves purity of heart
> And has grace on his lips,
> The king will be his friend (Proverbs 22:11).
>
> There is gold and a multitude of rubies (think paid lobbyists),
> But the lips of knowledge are a precious jewel (think unpaid lobbyists) (Proverbs 20:15).
>
> What is desired in a man is kindness,
> And a poor man is better than a liar (Proverbs 19:22).

You can find more verses like this in the online resource at **CivilRealm.com**.

Winsomeness is different from a worrisome approach to politics and government. This winsomeness has its confidence grounded squarely in the Lord, knowing that our true citizenship is in heaven (Philippians 3:20). Yet, our American citizenship is here on earth, and there still remains governing work appointed for us to do in this life. (Remember dual citizenship from the beginning of the book?) That work, to enter the civil realm with an understanding of the structure of government, can be challenging, as we have seen in the preceding chapters. However, we are told in Proverbs 13:15 that good understanding gains favor and that the real hardship belongs to the unfaithful.

I remember meeting for lunch with one of my district's state representatives—a moderate Republican who was censured by the county's Republican party for her voting record in the legislature. Her claim is that she was elected to represent the people of her district, not the Republican party. She described the unpleasantness of being a moderate in a strongly conservative statehouse and trying to work with her colleagues there. She mentioned one very conservative representative who is an exception to the rule. She referred to him as a gentleman and a statesman. He also happens to be a friend of mine. How does he exemplify winsomeness in the civil realm (something that few have the skill to do)? I decided to ask him, and here is his answer:

> Winsomeness—most of my thoughts lean toward speaking truth with humility and grace. It is not a manipulative rhetorical technique but is instead a proclaiming of truth which resonates with all created beings and draws them in. Winsomeness allows for conflicting views without conflict. It is contradiction without condemnation—not belittling or sarcastic but noble and confident. It challenges thoughts without assumption or accusation (without attacking the thinker).[2]

Mustard-Seed Approach

And now, back to the other qualities of Christian diplomacy. It is not only subtle and winsome, but it is a powerful mustard-seed approach. Jesus likened the kingdom of heaven to a mustard seed, "the least of all the seeds; but when it is grown it is greater than the herbs and becomes a tree" (Matthew 13:32). We should be accustomed to seeing very small things grow into very powerful things. Think of infants becoming adults. Or the skill of learning phonics blossoming into the skill of reading and writing novels. Or minuscule floating snowflakes becoming snowbanks. Think, as this verse tells us, of mustard seeds becoming trees.

In light of this principle, we should be enamored with the idea of a small interest in government at the local, state, or national level by concerned Christians here, there, and everywhere eventually growing into a grand recovering of one of the realms of government that God has set over us. "What?"

2 Idaho District 1 State Representative, Sage Dixon.

you say, "I merely attend city council meetings twice a month on Monday nights." Precisely. That's a mustard-seed approach. And it becomes powerful. Initially, Christian diplomacy is not about getting out the vote (GOTV).[3] It is not about the next election (at least not yet). It is about learning how our government functions. It is about discovering our role within that function. It is about reading and memorizing God's Word and allowing Him to guide us by wisdom into all truth.

That truth is not just in the Bible, it is in the authority that He has put over people within the realm of the family, the realm of the church, and the realm of the civil government. It's about loving the people in each of those realms. Not always easy with family. Not always easy with church members. And guess what? Not always easy with those in civil government. We the People are quite a motley crew. We need to pray for and be kind to the people in our homes and in our churches. In a similar fashion, we need to pray for and be kind to the people in our government. After all, we live in a constitutional republic, not a dictatorship. Civility matters.

We do have a part to play. When we pick up that role, it can look particularly small in the grand scheme of things. That can be pretty discouraging. Week after week, month after month, we pray for our leaders. We meet with them. We attend government meetings. We invest in the system—in the people. As we sow, we trust God to bring the fruit.

An Educated Faith

Lastly, Christian diplomacy is based on an educated faith—a faith that is firmly rooted in the person and work of God the Son, Jesus Christ, as our intermediary to God the Father through the ministry of God the Holy Spirit. These three Per-

3 Ballotpedia, s.v. "Get out the Vote."

sons are one God—the perfect Triune God—the Trinity revealed to us mortals in His holy Word, which we know as the Bible. This theology all seems pretty heavy, but it is the bedrock that stabilizes us as we enter the civil realm. This foundation prevents us from being "tossed to and fro and carried about with every wind of doctrine" (Ephesians 4:14). As followers of Christ, we do not merely hope that the things we believe are true. We know that they are true because they are written (John 20:31). What sorts of things do we know? We know that

> by Him all things were created that are in heaven and that are on earth, visible and invisible, whether thrones or dominions or principalities or powers [or Democrats or Republicans]. All things were created through Him and for Him. And He is before all things, and in Him all things consist (Colossians 1:16–17).
>
> Moreover, it is written to us that "all things are yours: whether… the world or life or death, or things present or things to come—all are yours. And you *are* Christ's, and Christ *is* God's (1 Corinthians 3:21–23).

Not only do we have an American right to enter this civil realm, but more importantly, we have a biblical right. We are heirs of the world that Christ redeemed through His great sacrifice on the cross. He suffered for our sakes, died, and rose again from the dead to remake the world—to make it His new creation. He did so as the second Adam—the Man who would do it right this time.

We could certainly use some parameters like this in the public square: "And be kind to one another, tenderhearted, forgiving one another, even as God in Christ forgave you" (Ephesians 4:32). Do these verses mean that we should be milquetoasts, predictably caving beneath those with whom we disagree? On the contrary, these verses describe our forbearance with others, not our agreement with them. And nowhere are we called to be hypocrites or compromisers, embracing things that we do not believe to be true.

Suppose we apply similar verses to our endeavors at Christian diplomacy. In such cases, we can be more patient with legislators who may not understand the nuances of the issues we intend to explain. We continue to work within the system's rules, but we do it endowed with wisdom from the God of the system. Again, as we are told in Proverbs 28:5, "Evil men do not understand justice, / But those who seek the LORD understand all." It is not our job to single out who the evil men (or women) may be. Instead, we are given a fantastic blessing that flows from seeking the Lord—understanding all. This promise does not transform us into walking know-it-alls or, even worse, social media know-it-alls who vent on hot topics. Instead, this promise endears us to seek the Lord and endows us with an uncanny understanding of the events surrounding us in the public square. I have experienced the blessing of this God-given understanding time and again.

I am not unique, though. You can walk by faith into the public square and into your government meetings. Go. Listen. Learn. It will most likely be quite confusing at first. You will need to process the regular flow of meetings, consent and action agendas, requirements for motions, executive sessions, preliminary committees, appointed commissions, annual budgets, and comprehensive plans—all this along with new faces and the formal terms of speech that we use to address these officeholders (who are elected representatives of the people) as well as the attendant hired/appointed staff (who are the people really running the place). In the process of frequenting meetings to observe how government works, don't be surprised if you eventually become fond of the elected and appointed members despite their quirks or different beliefs. Don't be surprised if you become concerned about their souls. Don't be surprised if you begin to cease looking at them as the adversary or the enemy (though you very frequently may not agree with their position). Don't be surprised if you come to terms with the idea that God has placed each of them in their office—because "He removes kings and raises up kings" (Daniel 2:21).

In all of this, we remember that God has given us the truth, and the truth has set us free. We know that He is the Savior of the world. And, at some point, while observing governing meetings, don't be surprised when you sense that many of our leaders need to be saved. Realizing all of this, we recall that it is the "God who commanded light to shine out of darkness who has shone in our hearts to give the light of the knowledge of the glory of God in the face of Jesus Christ" (2 Corinthians 4:6). And we begin to piece together the kingdoms that God has placed over mankind. We begin to see the Venn diagram merging its lobes together. We begin to see that we attend governing meetings so that God's light can shine there. We learn to respect our governing leaders and learn to enjoy them, but we also press them toward the truth. This requires being wise as serpents and gentle as doves. Because, as Proverbs 21:22 states, "A wise man scales the city of the mighty, / And brings down the trusted stronghold."

What does all of this Christian diplomacy talk have to do with the story that opened this chapter about speaking as an unpaid lobbyist at my state capitol? Everything. Because it is a quiet, winsome, and powerful mustard-seed approach to entering the forgotten realm which is based on an educated faith. If I had entered the statehouse floor loudly or in a manner that boldly proclaimed my certain unalienable rights, that approach would have neither granted me admittance nor an audience. At least not the audience whom I was seeking. Nor the long-lasting help that God provided not only through my presentation but also through the speeches and presentations of others that day. Let me tell you a bit of backstory in order to illuminate some of the principles of Christian diplomacy:

Months before that statehouse day, I had heard of this interim study committee. I contacted several state representatives providing them with a list of potential speakers to present their expertise that day. Of course, these speakers were unpaid lobbyists, but they knew their material.

As the date approached, I met with a regional group, and we realized that the statehouse had invited its own speakers, and our two lists of names were not in alignment. The invited speakers were paid lobbyists. I had heard them before. They each had a pre-set-party line. The regional rag-tag group I was affiliated with were unpaid lobbyists who cared about the issue from the heart rather than from the pocketbook. We each were assigned a topic. The group leader asked me to speak on a none-too-simple study conducted by researchers at Lawrence Berkeley National Laboratory.

Granted, I had looked over that study for months, but the mathematical principles behind it were quite advanced. I sought help to understand the study's mechanics but was unable to find someone who had the time or understanding to assist me. The long night before my statehouse presentation, I struggled for wisdom. While I worked, I simultaneously dealt with an attendant migraine. But, as the night wore on, providentially, I began to see a design problem embedded in the study. Then, it came into focus, as did my presentation.

I had wrestled with God the long night before, claiming Proverbs 2:3–9:

> *Yes, if you cry out for discernment,*
> *And lift up your voice for understanding,*
> *If you seek her as silver,*
> *And search for her as for hidden treasures;*
> *Then you will understand the fear of the* LORD,
> *And find the knowledge of God.*
> *For the* LORD *gives wisdom;*
> *From His mouth come knowledge and understanding;*
> *He stores up sound wisdom for the upright;*

He is a shield to those who walk uprightly;
He guards the paths of justice,
And preserves the way of His saints.
Then you will understand righteousness and justice,
Equity and every good path.

In the morning, He gave wisdom, knowledge, and understanding regarding the significant flaw in the Berkeley study and how to uncover it for a group of legislators in a two-minute presentation. True to Psalm 30:5, joy did indeed come in the morning.

After that sleepless stretch, accompanied by my two youngest children, I hydroplaned our minivan for an hour to Indianapolis in a driving rainstorm. Arriving none too soon at the statehouse, I parked at a hard-to-find yet somewhat nearby meter, not knowing that it would have been far simpler to park in a parking garage. (Statehouses are in big cities which can present challenges for country folk.)

Having passed through security, the three of us found a nearby empty table and began to color-code sections of the fourteen copies of said Berkeley study. Did I mention that we unpaid lobbyists had agreed to wear the color red so that we at least stood together as an identifiable block? My daughter wore my red cardigan sweater—she didn't own a red shirt. And my son wore a red bow tie with his black suit. So there we were, present and accounted for with the stack of requisite studies in tow. After finding the senate chamber, we made our way to a table of familiar faces also clad in red garb, and we sat down. The stack of Berkeley studies was on my lap under the table, and my two children (glad to have a day off regular homeschool) were at my side.

Before the presentation began, a state representative approached me at our regional group's table and announced that we concerned citizens (We the People) would not be allowed to speak today. There simply would not be time.

Previous to this new declaration, We the People had been told that we would each have two minutes to present. My study was col-

or-coded specifically so that I could walk the listeners through it in exactly two minutes. A feat that is not a personal strength—I have a knack for going overtime or being late for almost everything.

This new pronouncement simply would not do. It was unjust. Recalling the migraine headache, the frightful early-morning hydroplaning drive, the missed day of homeschool, the revelation of the study's weak link, and the extended table of allies to my left, I firmly and slowly replied, "We will speak." This message was reported to the chairman of the study committee. Marvelously, all of us red-clad people were granted permission to speak with what time was remaining after the block of paid lobbyists had presented, taking as long as they desired, of course.

This was an informed approach based on an educated faith. And it was quiet. The only loud part of our presentations was our bright red clothes. By God's grace, all of our presentations were winsome and effective (I can't vouch for the clothing). Happy children passing out papers on cue at their parent's request to senators and representatives is winsome. Especially by today's standards. A group of concerned citizens who intentionally yet respectfully present data is equally winsome.

God's grace brought us citizens there, sustained us, and took us home. It also allowed us to network with allies and friends that day, which is another story. Allies and friends are the providential fruit of serving our God in faith. Further, by God's grace, we spoke on behalf of others from our rural counties who could not speak publicly. Our group kept the frame of the legislators in mind. We did not lash out at them. We did not talk down to them.

There is no way that legislators can be experts on every subject that comes to them. That is why they hold interim study committees in the first place. Likewise, I could not hate the paid lobbyists (although their presentations were quite frustrating). They probably haven't been on the other side of the issue. They are paid to think one way. It is not my job to change their minds—only to do a better job for free than they are paid to do. And by God's grace, that is possible.

———·———

The background components of Christian diplomacy may not be easily seen at first. They are subtle, winsome, mustard-seedy, and grounded in an informed faith. Despite weaknesses common to mankind, our Savior is strong, and He shows Himself strong on our behalf. We are His people. He is our God. This is His kingdom, His civil realm, and we serve Him in it. We are His diplomats, His ambassadors or representatives, as described in 2 Corinthians 5:20: "Now then, we are ambassadors for Christ, as though God were pleading through us: we implore you on Christ's behalf, be reconciled to God."

OTHER THINGS YOU SHOULD KNOW

A significant tool worth mentioning in the civil realm that we may eventually be called upon to employ, or that we can observe being employed by others, is stakeholdering. A stakeholder is anyone who is involved in or affected by a course of action. In some cases, just having a strong opinion and a lot of name recognition can catapult a person into stakeholder status—just so that they can be used to influence others.

Stakeholdering consists of first determining who all of the people or groups (stakeholders) are who have a positive or negative interest in a proposed project, developing a plan to communicate with them, then actually doing so to influence them favorably toward your perspective relative to the endeavor. More simply, stakeholdering is finding all of the various people or groups involved in a proposed project and talking with each of them. This networking activity takes place very frequently in the civil realm. It can be done well (which requires time, patience, and seeing the big picture) or poorly (inconsistently or incompletely). Perhaps, I can say that it can be done winsomely or coarsely. Public works projects at virtually any level of government require stakeholdering by those in public office. For example, if a state plans to build a new highway, there are many stakeholders to consult (and to convince that it is a good and/or profitable endeavor). If a city envisions a new downtown streetscape, again, there are many stakeholders to consult.

If this advance-communication work is done well, the project is more likely to succeed. A potential, though not exhaustive, list of stakeholders who could or should be consulted in advance of a proposal is as follows:

- business owners
- private property owners
- the medical community
- the police department or sheriff
- the city's public works (water, sewer, stormwater)
- the electrical company (not part of the city, county, or state)
- contractors
- subcontractors
- consumers
- federal, state, or local grant money authorities
- government licensing agencies (state or federal)
- community groups that may or may not approve of the project
- engineering companies
- consulting companies
- vendors/suppliers

As an ambassador or diplomat who enters the civil realm and begins attending public meetings, your initial job is to observe how business is being done. Refer to the stakeholdering list above while you listen to a proposal to ascertain how the council, commission, board, or legislature considers the stakeholders involved. Listen to determine who presents ideas for change clearly and succinctly. In the course of business, try to determine what the problem statement is—what core dilemma is being discussed? A good rule of thumb when observing an issue on the floor at public meetings is to ask yourself, "What is the problem statement that they are talking about?" You will notice that sometimes those who are leading voices in the meeting do not know what is going on. Sometimes some of them do. Sometimes most or all of them do. Also, recall Figure 3.9, "The Types of People You Will Meet in the Civil Realm" from chapter 3, "City Government." Use that as an aid to help you determine what you are observing. And remember to extend grace to others—none of us gets everything right all of the time.

THINGS YOU CAN DO

Read the Book of Proverbs daily.

For the most part, each chapter corresponds numerically with the day of the month, which makes it easy to read the Book of Proverbs continuously on a cycle throughout the whole year. The contents of that book are priceless in the civil realm.

Subscribe to the local newspaper. (I know I said that before.)

More than likely, the articles will be slanted. Good guys may be portrayed as bad guys, and vice versa. So beware and don't accept the slant as the truth. Today, journalism focuses on reasons or causes behind events rather than on the facts surrounding the events. In his book *Antifragile*, Nassim Nicholas

Taleb refers to the notion of *cause* as suspect because the cause of an event is typically neither easily detectable nor definable. He considers this situation to be a "reason to ignore newspapers."[4] I consider it a reason to provide a cleaner form of journalism. Just as Christians have been absent from the civil realm, we have also been absent from journalism. Our nation's journalism schools are filled with young people who follow the lead of professors who have forgotten God. As the academy goes, so goes the culture. Therefore, consider studying journalism or encouraging young people who have a penchant for writing to do so. The need for objective reporting is great.[5] Far-left and far-right "journalism" perform similar gigs; their lenses are simply pointed in opposite directions. There is a large middle contingent in America that would be refreshed with just the facts.[6]

Subscribe to or produce an evenhanded review of local happenings.

If no one produces such a review, consider starting one.[7] Recovering true journalism is one way to assist the trek back into the civil realm.

Be leery of social media posts.

Obviously, the platforms of social media are ubiquitous and cannot be ignored. However prevalent it may be, social me-

4 Nassim Nicholas Taleb, *Antifragile* (New York: Random House Trade, 2012), 56.

5 Dan Carlin, "A Recipe for Caesar," March 31, 2020, in *Common Sense with Dan Carlin*, produced by Dan Carlin, Apple Podcast, 1:26:19.

6 For more on this, see Tony Woodlief's *I, Citizen: A Blueprint for Reclaiming American Self-Governance* (New York: Encounter Books, 2017).

7 For an example of how this could be done, visit Moscow Report's web page at **moscowidaho.news**.

dia typically tends toward a form of interaction that sharply differs from what I pursue in the course of this book. Thus, be aware of one of the drawbacks of social media: it can be a hotbed of tempers. Usually, people do not possess the wherewithal to verbally seethe in real life as they do via the written word on social media. Because God's law is fulfilled in the command, "You shall love your neighbor as yourself" (Galatians 5:14), be very careful about posting political comments online. A wayward post can really unravel productive efforts spent in person.[8] Scripture warns us, "If you bite and devour one another, beware lest you be consumed by one another!" (Galatians 5:15). My hope is that readers will see how much true work there is to be done in the civil realm and such realization will limit or govern our social media interactions. If you absolutely must post, maintain self-control and know when **not** to have the last word.

Scour your government websites.

Watch recordings of meetings. See what meetings are up and coming. Learn your leaders' names. Read your city, county, state, and national codes of law and constitutions. Sign up at each website to be notified when the meeting agendas and minutes are posted. Or give yourself reminders to check the agenda ahead of time. The law dictates how far in advance of a meeting the agenda must be posted. Thus, you can check, for example, on Friday afternoon to see the agenda for the following Monday's meeting. Print it out, if you are able, and take it along on Monday for writing notes, jotting down your own comments, and recording quotes of what was said. Then

8 This podcast is an excellent resource regarding the productivity of investing in real people in real time as opposed to venting one's thoughts online: Rosaria Butterfield, "Christians, the LGBTQ Community, and the Call to Hospitality," interview by Matt Tully, *Crossway Podcast*, May 13, 2019, 59:07.

keep a stack of these agendas at home. Refer to them as needed. They contain a lot of valuable information.

Take others along with you.

Moms and dads, take your kids. Teachers and professors, take your students. Neighbors, take your friends. Husbands, take your wives. You get the idea. It really helps to attend government meetings with a companion. Afterward, you can compare notes. You have someone to lean on as you reel from what may have transpired during the meetings. You have someone to encourage you to persevere, to forge onward.

Start a civic renewal prayer meeting.

Pray for your governing leaders by name and by the office they hold as elected representatives of the people. Our churches tend to pray for the big offices; suggest that we pray for the county commissioners or the county prosecutor or the local judges by name. In fact, start a weekly civic prayer meeting and pray through each person's name listed on the civic roster that you developed in the previous chapter. It may be the most important action that you take in the civil realm.

Meet with your leaders for coffee.

Inform and educate them on issues that you know and care about. They represent you as your elected representative, and you can offer them feedback that they are unlikely to hear otherwise. This service to them is especially helpful if it is of an informative rather than an emotional nature. Rather than criticizing their work, offer them a powerful alternative viewpoint, keeping in mind the principles of Christian diplomacy.

Send your leaders thank-you notes.

Or Christmas cards or congratulations cards. They usually only hear from their constituents when there are problems. Turn the tables and communicate with them over something positive. Email is great. Handwritten is superb. Everyone knows that a handwritten card or note is a lost art. As such, taking the time to write and send or hand deliver one communicates a deeper level of sincerity.

Remember to network with those who helped you.

Send a follow-up report or message of thanks to all colleagues (or cobelligerents) who have offered their assistance to you. A quick phone call, text, or email should suffice here. Communication keeps your allies on the same page: they appreciate the feedback and are quite willing to help again as needed if you take the time to keep them in the loop.

Consider starting a civics club.

This could take place at your local Christian college, homeschool co-op, private Christian school, library, or church with the purpose of teaching the structure of the various levels of government. My club's format is quite simple:

1. Open with prayer
2. Sing a hymn[9] or Psalm
3. Have a lecture explaining the mechanics of government. These are the topics I recommend covering when beginning a civics club:

9 The civics club that I attend is partial to singing "O God of Earth and Altar."

- The Christian and Community Involvement
- City Government
- County Government
- Special Districts
- State Government
- National Government

Subsequent meetings could feature guest speakers or field trips for each level of government. Personally, I have not affiliated my civics club members with activist groups or political parties, because there is so much work to be done in simply educating the members on how the mechanics of each level of government work. As my friend and editor Aiden Anderson states, "We must keep preaching structure to those who only want to think about issues." Activism complicates that process and places our focus on issues, and that tends to whip up our emotions rather than inform our minds. However, affiliating with a political party or becoming a citizen activist can be a natural next step for individuals to take if they so desire.

SO WHAT?

Within this call to Christian diplomacy, there is much from the Scriptures to guide and steady us. As we enter the civil realm, we must claim God's promises to us. Depending upon what you are called to do, the public square can be an unsettling place. Remember this proverb: "Whoever listens to me will dwell safely, / And will be secure, without fear of evil" (Proverbs 1:33). That good news settles the heart of a newcomer stepping into the unknown arenas of governance. It also helps to remember that "the king's heart is in the hand of the LORD, / Like the rivers of water; / He turns it wherever He wishes" (Proverbs 21:1). Knowing that the king's heart is right where God has placed it also musters one's resolve. Think of Pharaoh. As we read Exodus, there is the story from God's perspective and the story that man sees. We must trust God in the midst of what we don't understand. We walk by faith not by sight. Understanding this truth removes much of the pain from politics. The hard part is remembering and believing it in the heat of arduous political moments when all appears to be crushed.

Within Christian diplomacy, there are various ways to uphold the truth, but hatred for our fellow man is not one of them. While observing governmental meetings or reviewing the results of those meetings, recall that "he who is devoid of wisdom despises his neighbor, / But a man of understanding holds his peace" (Proverbs 11:12). Also, "he who despises his neighbor sins; / But he who has mercy on the poor, happy is he" (Proverbs 14:21). Conducting ourselves in this manner is hard work. Living by faith is not always easy. There have been many times when I come home after attending a public meeting, fall into a chair, bemoan the state of our government's affairs, and question the value of my efforts. I have friends who are citizen legislators who leave their families right after Christmas to serve six and nine hours away at our statehouse from January through March. I have a friend who attends every county commissioner meeting in my county while holding down a full-time job and wearing a couple of part-time hats simultaneously. Another has a distinguished law degree and recently enlisted in the armed forces in order to become a better statesman. All of these are situations that make me think of Tony Woodlief's assessment, "It's no easy thing, saving a country."[10]

10 Tony Woodlief, *I, Citizen*, 207.

Whatever your part within Christian diplomacy, as you learn the structures of how our government should operate, continue to steady yourself between the ditches of hatred of your fellow man on the one hand and abandonment of the mission on the other. Rather than fall into one of those ditches, try uniting your civic knowledge with faith and love. The Apostle Paul himself reminds us of this most important mission stating that "though I have the gift of prophecy, and understand all mysteries and all knowledge, and though I have all faith, so that I could remove mountains, but have not love, I am nothing" (1 Corinthians 13:2).

In light of all of this, do you see areas of government that need to be run better? Do you see injustice? Do you want to make a difference in this nation? Do you see that the salt has lost its savor and is being trodden underfoot by men? Go forth with Christian diplomacy and shine the light of Christ in the civil realm without loud verbal protest. Quietly enter. Respect your fellow man. Be a student of your surroundings. Be patient. Be kind. Walk in faith. Research your topics. Deal shrewdly. In essence, as you follow Christ within the family realm and within the church realm, do likewise within this previously forgotten realm. And begin to see the salvation of the Lord there.

CONCLUSION

Many years ago, my young family took regular walks around the block in our neighborhood. During those walks, we became acquainted with a neighbor lady who would step outside for fresh air. Actually, she stepped outside to smoke, away from her ailing ninety-something-year-old mother's oxygen tank. I suspect that smoking provided a convenient reason to go outdoors because after her mother passed away, Miss Knell gave up the habit.

It was a delight to get to know our senior citizen friend. We attended Miss Knell's mother's calling hours (wake) after she passed. We shared the gospel with Miss Knell. We invited her to church. She was high church; we were low church. But she attended with us once anyway and joined us for dinner afterward. We loved talking sports and cooking and yard work and daily life with her.

But I have a regret: I never asked Miss Knell about her civic involvement. Sometimes her neighbor would stop by while we were visiting and casually ask if she was planning to attend city council that week. I wondered what city council was. I wondered why Miss Knell went. I never asked. I was busy hunting down an educational philosophy, remodeling an old house, and raising little people. Our family eventually moved away from Miss Knell's stately neighborhood to the other side of the nation. We kept in touch with her over the years. Eventually, her life here on earth came to a close.

Somewhere in that time frame, I began attending city council. And I thought of Miss Knell. She had attended city council. She went in order to be informed. That's the extent of what I knew about her involvement. If only I had asked her more. I know that her memory inspires me on the nights when I would rather do anything else than attend a local government meeting. I can remember Miss Knell asking her neighbor, "Are you going to council tomorrow night?" Recently, I texted a former mutual neighbor and inquired if she knew more about Miss Knell's civic motives. I discovered that Miss Knell was the millionaire next door: she left her town's community foundation over a million dollars. The Knell family had lived in their home for a century, and she was the last of the clan. Miss Knell had invested not only her time but also her money in her community, her church, and the lives of those around her. She never ran for office. She just paid attention, held others accountable, and knew where to invest her resources for those who would carry on after her.

So here we are at the end of our journey through *The Forgotten Realm*. We have covered much territory. At the outset, we learned about the three realms of government—family, church, and civil. God is the Lord over all three realms, and He calls us to exercise self-control within each of them. In the flesh, we have trouble with self-control, or any other virtue, which is why He sent His Son as our Redeemer. And one of the many fruits of His Spirit is self-control.

We discovered our possession of citizenship in two places at once: our dual citizenship on earth and in heaven. It is the glue that connects our faith and our government. That leads us to Thomas Jefferson's famous separation-of-church-and-state letter that referred to the protection of the church realm from government overreach. Just the reverse of how the story is retold today. A wall of separation does exist, and it is there to protect the church from the state—from national control over religion in America. After having read this book, it should be clear that many of us Christians have been conducting our lives as if there were, indeed, a wall of separation—separating us from the civil realm. Many of us have either felt excluded from going there or have simply stayed away because it was such an unknown place to us. Whatever the reasons, it has become the forgotten realm.

We've looked at the layers of law that we live under. Then, by inverting the normal model of describing American government, we have been able to survey the governance landscape from the bottom up. We've distilled election and voting information into a manageable, personalized format. Finally, we have learned some principles of Christian diplomacy to guide our steps within the civil realm.

All along the way, the goal has been twofold: to piece together the structure of our American governmental system and to learn how to wisely engage within it. Each chapter has offered concrete suggestions for engagement within the civil realm—things that you and I can do today and tomorrow, things that we can continue to do next week, and things that will eventually become normal in our lives, our friends' lives, and our children's lives.

It is time to recover the forgotten realm—God's plan of civil government for man. In America, He has blessed us with a constitutional republic. There is a plan for our governing process. The Founding Fathers prayerfully formed it. The Framers prayerfully crafted it into a written Constitution. They expected us to understand the process, operate within it, and act to preserve it. We, on the other hand, have assumed that it can operate without us. It can, and it has, but the results are not pretty.

This book has been a call to begin with the mustard-seed approach: starting very small. Small beginnings are nothing to be ashamed of. Rather, they are things to embrace as starting points. Everything has to start somewhere. An outstanding way to begin is to crown Jesus as the center of our lives. If He is the center, the Sun of our solar system, then these three realms all exist in harmony as they orbit around Him (Malachi 4:2). Recognizing the existence and call of the civil realm means that I am asking you to add more to your already-busy days. But that addition may quite possibly introduce a much-needed balance. Bringing the civil realm to bear on our lives will allow us to tap into the Scriptures and especially the book of Proverbs in a poignant way. God's Word will spring into our lives with fresh meaning.

At the beginning of this book, I said that our plight in the civil realm is a problem of knowledge. Here, at the book's conclusion, the reverse is true. After having read this book, you can see the civil realm, and you possess the knowledge of governance. You are holding the key that unlocks the door. Reflect for a moment: What caught your attention as you read through this book? Given your skill set and gifts, where can you enter the civil realm today as an engaged citizen?

And don't fear that you will be alone. It might feel lonely at first, but think of Thomas, Susan, Cody, Jeff, William, and Colton. They are just some of the wonderful people I have met on this journey. You will meet many new friends along the way and learn things about your neighbors and relatives, too. And encompassing you all around is Jesus who promised never to leave you nor forsake you.

Further, consider the generations to come. Our children and their children and their children will understand this American inheritance better than we did. Often people are discouraged about the prospects of the next generation, but I am hopeful. Quite hopeful. We can give our young people a powerful combination—the gift of civic knowledge along with the love of Christ because "knowledge [alone] puffs up, but love edifies" (1 Corinthians 8:1).

This book is the plan.

In conversation after conversation, I have heard Christian thinkers express that we American Christian conservatives need a plan.

"What's the plan?" they ask.

"This book," I reply.

Conservatives conserve by nature; we are not driven to progress like progressives. That quality causes conservatives to be on the defensive. *The Forgotten Realm*, however, unlocks the structure of the entire system of American governance and demonstrates how we can proactively engage in it with wisdom. We can shoulder our duties rather than brandish our rights.[1] My hope and prayer is that this engagement will usher in the beginning of a new civic revival in our nation.

May others meet Jesus through His Word in this book. May we become His ambassadors in our cities, counties (and equivalents), special districts, states, and nation in order to minister to others who have not known Him in those places. May we become and also raise future statesmen, leaders, journalists, lawyers, attorneys, judges, and justices. May we become people who help heal our nation and our communities. People who pray with those going in and out of the courthouse. People who host statehouse ministries and lodge others who travel on a shoestring to the statehouse. People who begin to teach civics with Christian diplomacy in our Christian schools, homeschool co-ops, and Christian colleges. People who host Bible studies in Washington, D.C. People who thank our elected representatives. People who invite them for coffee or dinner. People who pray with them and show them the love

1 "But Jesus called them to Himself and said to them, "You know that those who are considered rulers over the Gentiles Lord it over them, and their great ones exercise authority over them. Yet it shall not be so among you; but whoever desires to become great among you shall be your servant. And whoever of you desires to be first shall be slave of all" (Mark 10:42–44).

of Christ. People who share this book with college students on campuses all over the nation and encourage them to stand firm in their faith. People who take field trips to our city buildings, our county buildings, our special district buildings, our statehouse, our nation's capitol, and to the public meetings that occur inside those halls.

In his 1961 inaugural address, former President John F. Kennedy (a liberal for his day) implored the American public to "ask not what your country can do for you—ask what you can do for your country." Before reading this book, JFK's summons may have seemed like a tall order, but now you know a litany of things that you can do for your country—at any level of government. Now you can engage. You can be in the *civil* realm (no longer the *forgotten* realm). Take heart, step inside, and know that "the future belongs to those who show up."[2]

---

2 Mark Steyn, "The Future Is Showing up," Steyn Online, October 18, 2021.

GOVERNANCE STRUCTURE IN THE UNITED STATES

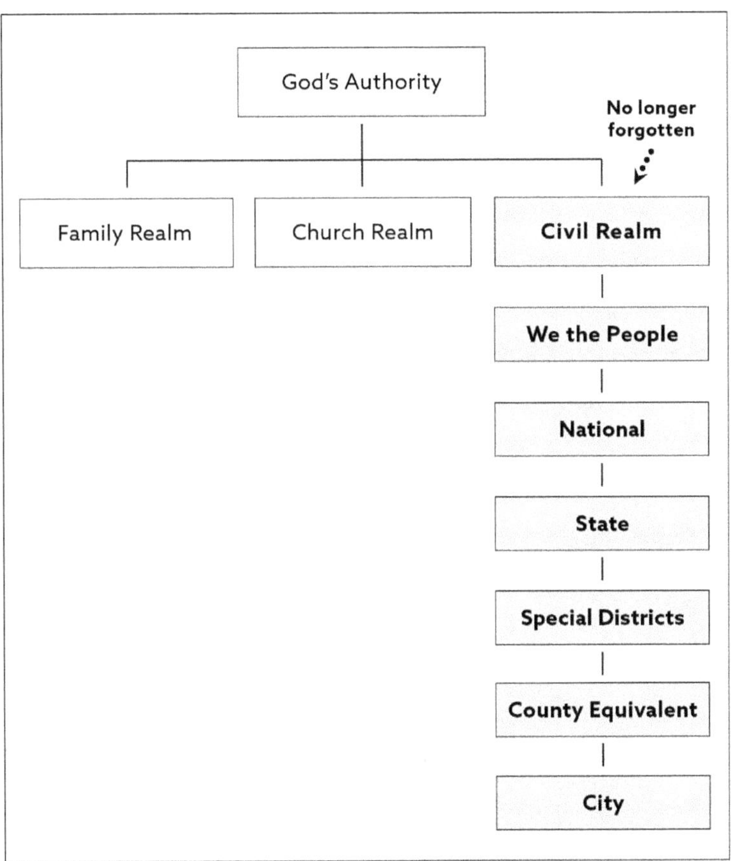

Figure C.1

APPENDICES

APPENDIX A
The Declaration of Independence

When in the Course of human events, it becomes necessary for one people to dissolve the political bands which have connected them with another, and to assume among the powers of the earth, the separate and equal station to which the Laws of Nature and of Nature's God entitle them, a decent respect to the opinions of mankind requires that they should declare the causes which impel them to the separation.

We hold these truths to be self-evident, that all men are created equal, that they are endowed by their Creator with certain unalienable Rights, that among these are Life, Liberty and the pursuit of Happiness.—That to secure these rights, Governments are instituted among Men, deriving their just powers from the consent of the governed,—That whenever any Form of Government becomes destructive of these ends, it is the Right of the People to alter or to abolish it, and to institute new Government, laying its foundation on such principles and organizing its powers in such form, as to them shall seem most likely to effect their Safety and Happiness. Prudence, indeed, will dictate that Governments long established should not be changed for light and transient causes; and accordingly all experience hath shewn, that mankind are more disposed to suffer, while evils are sufferable, than to right themselves by abolishing the forms to which they are accustomed. But when a long train of abuses and usurpations, pursuing invariably the same Object evinces a design to reduce them under absolute Despotism, it is their right, it is their duty, to throw off such Government, and to provide new Guards for their future security.—Such has been the patient sufferance of these Colonies; and such is now the necessity which constrains them to alter their former Systems of Government. The history of the present King of Great Britain is a history of repeated injuries and usurpations, all having in direct object the establishment of an absolute Tyranny over these States. To prove this, let Facts be submitted to a candid world.

He has refused his Assent to Laws, the most wholesome and necessary for the public good.

He has forbidden his Governors to pass Laws of immediate and pressing importance, unless suspended in their operation till his Assent should be obtained; and when so suspended, he has utterly neglected to attend to them.

He has refused to pass other Laws for the accommodation of large districts of people, unless those people would relinquish the right of Representation in the Legislature, a right inestimable to them and formidable to tyrants only.

He has called together legislative bodies at places unusual, uncomfortable, and distant from the depository of their public Records, for the sole purpose of fatiguing them into compliance with his measures.

He has dissolved Representative Houses repeatedly, for opposing with manly firmness his invasions on the rights of the people.

He has refused for a long time, after such dissolutions, to cause others to be elected; whereby the Legislative powers, incapable of Annihilation, have returned to the People at large for their exercise; the State remaining in the mean time exposed to all the dangers of invasion from without, and convulsions within.

He has endeavoured to prevent the population of these States; for that purpose obstructing the Laws for Naturalization of

Foreigners; refusing to pass others to encourage their migrations hither, and raising the conditions of new Appropriations of Lands.

He has obstructed the Administration of Justice, by refusing his Assent to Laws for establishing Judiciary powers.

He has made Judges dependent on his Will alone, for the tenure of their offices, and the amount and payment of their salaries.

He has erected a multitude of New Offices, and sent hither swarms of Officers to harass our people, and eat out their substance.

He has kept among us, in times of peace, Standing Armies without the Consent of our legislatures.

He has affected to render the Military independent of and superior to the Civil power.

He has combined with others to subject us to a jurisdiction foreign to our constitution, and unacknowledged by our laws; giving his Assent to their Acts of pretended Legislation:

For Quartering large bodies of armed troops among us:

For protecting them, by a mock Trial, from punishment for any Murders which they should commit on the Inhabitants of these States:

For cutting off our Trade with all parts of the world:

For imposing Taxes on us without our Consent:

For depriving us in many cases, of the benefits of Trial by Jury:

For transporting us beyond Seas to be tried for pretended offenses:

For abolishing the free System of English Laws in a neighbouring Province, establishing therein an Arbitrary government, and enlarging its Boundaries so as to render it at once an example and fit instrument for introducing the same absolute rule into these Colonies:

For taking away our Charters, abolishing our most valuable Laws, and altering fundamentally the Forms of our Governments:

For suspending our own Legislatures, and declaring themselves invested with power to legislate for us in all cases whatsoever.

He has abdicated Government here, by declaring us out of his Protection and waging War against us.

He has plundered our seas, ravaged our Coasts, burnt our towns, and destroyed the lives of our people.

He is at this time transporting large Armies of foreign Mercenaries to compleat the works of death, desolation and tyranny, already begun with circumstances of Cruelty & perfidy scarcely paralleled in the most barbarous ages, and totally unworthy the Head of a civilized nation.

He has constrained our fellow Citizens taken Captive on the high Seas to bear Arms against their Country, to become the executioners of their friends and Brethren, or to fall themselves by their Hands.

He has excited domestic insurrections amongst us, and has endeavoured to bring on the inhabitants of our frontiers, the merciless Indian Savages, whose known rule of warfare, is an undistinguished destruction of all ages, sexes and conditions.

In every stage of these Oppressions We have Petitioned for Redress in the most humble terms: Our repeated Petitions have been answered only by repeated injury. A Prince whose character is thus marked by every act which may define a Tyrant, is unfit to be the ruler of a free people.

Nor have We been wanting in attentions to our Brittish brethren. We have warned them from time to time of attempts by their legislature to extend an unwarrantable jurisdiction over us. We have reminded them of the circumstances of our emigration and settlement here. We have appealed to their native justice and magnanimity, and we have conjured them by the ties of our common kindred to disavow these usurpations, which, would inevitably interrupt our connections and correspondence. They too have been deaf to the voice of justice and of consanguinity. We must, therefore, acquiesce in the necessity, which denounces our Separation, and hold them, as we hold the rest of mankind, Enemies in War, in Peace Friends.

We, therefore, the Representatives of the united States of America, in General Congress, Assembled, appealing to the Supreme Judge of the world for the rectitude of our intentions, do, in the Name, and by Authority of the good People of these Colonies, solemnly publish and declare, That these United Colonies are, and of Right ought to be Free and Independent States; that they are Absolved from all Allegiance to the British Crown, and that all political connection between them and the State of Great Britain, is and ought to be totally dissolved; and that as Free and Independent States, they have full Power to levy War, conclude Peace, contract Alliances, establish Commerce, and to do all other Acts and Things which Independent States may of right do. And for the support of this Declaration, with a firm reliance on the protection of divine Providence, we mutually pledge to each other our Lives, our Fortunes and our sacred Honor.

Georgia

Button Gwinnett
Lyman Hall
George Walton

North Carolina

William Hooper
Joseph Hewes
John Penn

South Carolina

Edward Rutledge
Thomas Heyward, Jr.
Thomas Lynch, Jr.
Arthur Middleton

Maryland

Samuel Chase
William Paca
Thomas Stone
Charles Carroll of Carrollton

Delaware

Caesar Rodney
George Read
Thomas McKean

Virginia

George Wythe
Richard Henry Lee
Thomas Jefferson
Benjamin Harrison
Thomas Nelson, Jr.
Francis Lightfoot Lee
Carter Braxton

Pennsylvania

Robert Morris
Benjamin Rush
Benjamin Franklin
John Morton
George Clymer
James Smith
George Taylor
James Wilson
George Ross

New York

William Floyd
Philip Livingston
Francis Lewis
Lewis Morris

New Jersey

Richard Stockton
John Witherspooon
Francis Hopkinson
John Hart
Abraham Clark

New Hampshire

Josiah Bartlett
William Whipple

Massachusetts

John Hancock
Samuel Adams
John Adams
Robert Treat Paine
Elbridge Gerry

Rhode Island

Stephen Hopkins
William Ellery

Connecticut

Roger Sherman
Samuel Huntington
William Williams
Oliver Wolcott

New Hampshire

Matthew Thornton

APPENDIX B
The United States Constitution

Note: The sections that are crossed out are what have been stricken from the original text due to amendment.

Preamble

We the People of the United States, in Order to form a more perfect Union, establish Justice, insure domestic Tranquility, provide for the common defence, promote the general Welfare, and secure the Blessings of Liberty to ourselves and our Posterity, do ordain and establish this Constitution for the United States of America.

Article I

Section. 1.

All legislative Powers herein granted shall be vested in a Congress of the United States, which shall consist of a Senate and House of Representatives.

Section. 2.

The House of Representatives shall be composed of Members chosen every second Year by the People of the several States, and the Electors in each State shall have the Qualifications requisite for Electors of the most numerous Branch of the State Legislature.

No Person shall be a Representative who shall not have attained to the Age of twenty five Years, and been seven Years a Citizen of the United States, and who shall not, when elected, be an Inhabitant of that State in which he shall be chosen.

~~Representatives and direct Taxes shall be apportioned among the several States which may be included within this Union, according to their respective Numbers, which shall be determined by adding to the whole Number of free Persons, including those bound to Service for a Term of Years, and excluding Indians not taxed, three fifths of all other Persons.~~ The actual Enumeration shall be made within three Years after the first Meeting of the Congress of the United States, and within every subsequent Term of ten Years, in such Manner as they shall by Law direct. The Number of Representatives shall not exceed one for every thirty Thousand, but each State shall have at Least one Representative; and until such enumeration shall be made, the State of New Hampshire shall be entitled to chuse three, Massachusetts eight, Rhode-Island and Providence Plantations one, Connecticut five, New-York six, New Jersey four, Pennsylvania eight, Delaware one, Maryland six, Virginia ten, North Carolina five, South Carolina five, and Georgia three.

When vacancies happen in the Representation from any State, the Executive Authority thereof shall issue Writs of Election to fill such Vacancies.

The House of Representatives shall chuse their Speaker and other Officers; and shall have the sole Power of Impeachment.

Section. 3.

The Senate of the United States shall be composed of two Senators from each State, ~~chosen by the Legislature~~ thereof, for six Years; and each Senator shall have one Vote.

Immediately after they shall be assembled in Consequence of the first Election, they shall be divided as equally as may be into three Classes. The Seats of the Senators of the first Class shall be vacated at the Expiration of the second Year, of the second Class at the Expiration of the fourth Year, and of the third

Class at the Expiration of the sixth Year, so that one third may be chosen every second Year; ~~and if Vacancies happen by Resignation, or otherwise, during the Recess of the Legislature of any State, the Executive thereof may make temporary Appointments until the next Meeting of the Legislature, which shall then fill such Vacancies.~~

No Person shall be a Senator who shall not have attained to the Age of thirty Years, and been nine Years a Citizen of the United States, and who shall not, when elected, be an Inhabitant of that State for which he shall be chosen.

The Vice President of the United States shall be President of the Senate, but shall have no Vote, unless they be equally divided.

The Senate shall chuse their other Officers, and also a President *pro tempore*, in the Absence of the Vice President, or when he shall exercise the Office of President of the United States.

The Senate shall have the sole Power to try all Impeachments. When sitting for that Purpose, they shall be on Oath or Affirmation. When the President of the United States is tried, the Chief Justice shall preside: And no Person shall be convicted without the Concurrence of two thirds of the Members present.

Judgment in Cases of Impeachment shall not extend further than to removal from Office, and disqualification to hold and enjoy any Office of honor, Trust or Profit under the United States: but the Party convicted shall nevertheless be liable and subject to Indictment, Trial, Judgment and Punishment, according to Law.

Section. 4.

The Times, Places and Manner of holding Elections for Senators and Representatives, shall be prescribed in each State by the Legislature thereof; but the Congress may at any time by Law make or alter such Regulations, except as to the Places of chusing Senators.

The Congress shall assemble at least once in every Year, and such Meeting shall be on ~~the first Monday in December~~, unless they shall by Law appoint a different Day.

Section. 5.

Each House shall be the Judge of the Elections, Returns and Qualifications of its own Members, and a Majority of each shall constitute a Quorum to do Business; but a smaller Number may adjourn from day to day, and may be authorized to compel the Attendance of absent Members, in such Manner, and under such Penalties as each House may provide.

Each House may determine the Rules of its Proceedings, punish its Members for disorderly Behaviour, and, with the Concurrence of two thirds, expel a Member.

Each House shall keep a Journal of its Proceedings, and from time to time publish the same, excepting such Parts as may in their Judgment require Secrecy; and the Yeas and Nays of the Members of either House on any question shall, at the Desire of one fifth of those Present, be entered on the Journal.

Neither House, during the Session of Congress, shall, without the Consent of the other, adjourn for more than three days, nor to any other Place than that in which the two Houses shall be sitting.

Section. 6.

The Senators and Representatives shall receive a Compensation for their Services, to be ascertained by Law, and paid out of the Treasury of the United States. They shall in all Cases, except Treason, Felony and Breach of the Peace, be privileged from Arrest during their Attendance at the Session of their respective Houses, and in going to and returning from the same; and for any Speech or Debate in either House, they shall not be questioned in any other Place.

No Senator or Representative shall, during the Time for which he was elected, be appointed to any civil Office under the Authority of the United States, which shall have been created, or the Emoluments whereof shall have been encreased during such time; and no Person holding any Office under the United States, shall be a Member of either House during his Continuance in Office.

Section. 7.

All Bills for raising Revenue shall originate in the House of Representatives; but the Senate may propose or concur with Amendments as on other Bills.

Every Bill which shall have passed the House of Representatives and the Senate, shall, before it become a Law, be presented to the President of the United States; If he approve he shall sign it, but if not he shall return it, with his Objections to that House in which it shall have originated, who shall enter the Objections at large on their Journal, and proceed to reconsider it. If after such Reconsideration two thirds of that House shall agree to pass the Bill, it shall be sent, together with the Objections, to the other House, by which it shall likewise be reconsidered, and if approved by two thirds of that House, it shall become a Law. But in all such Cases the Votes of both Houses shall be determined by yeas and Nays, and the Names of the Persons voting for and against the Bill shall be entered on the Journal of each House respectively. If any Bill shall not be returned by the President within ten Days (Sundays excepted) after it shall have been presented to him, the Same shall be a Law, in like Manner as if he had signed it, unless the Congress by their Adjournment prevent its Return, in which Case it shall not be a Law.

Every Order, Resolution, or Vote to which the Concurrence of the Senate and House of Representatives may be necessary (except on a question of Adjournment) shall be presented to the President of the United States; and before the Same shall take Effect, shall be approved by him, or being disapproved by him, shall be repassed by two thirds of the Senate and House of Representatives, according to the Rules and Limitations prescribed in the Case of a Bill.

Section. 8.

The Congress shall have Power

- To lay and collect Taxes, Duties, Imposts and Excises, to pay the Debts and provide for the common Defence and general Welfare of the United States; but all Duties, Imposts and Excises shall be uniform throughout the United States;
- To borrow Money on the credit of the United States;
- To regulate Commerce with foreign Nations, and among the several States, and with the Indian Tribes;
- To establish an uniform Rule of Naturalization, and uniform Laws on the subject of Bankruptcies throughout the United States;
- To coin Money, regulate the Value thereof, and of foreign Coin, and fix the Standard of Weights and Measures;
- To provide for the Punishment of counterfeiting the Securities and current Coin of the United States;
- To establish Post Offices and post Roads;
- To promote the Progress of Science and useful Arts, by securing for limited Times to Authors and Inventors the exclusive Right to their respective Writings and Discoveries;
- To constitute Tribunals inferior to the supreme Court;
- To define and punish Piracies and Felonies committed on the high Seas, and Offences against the Law of Nations;
- To declare War, grant Letters of Marque and Reprisal, and make Rules concerning Captures on Land and Water;
- To raise and support Armies, but no Appropriation of Money to that Use shall be for a longer Term than two Years;
- To provide and maintain a Navy;

- To make Rules for the Government and Regulation of the land and naval Forces;
- To provide for calling forth the Militia to execute the Laws of the Union, suppress Insurrections and repel Invasions;
- To provide for organizing, arming, and disciplining, the Militia, and for governing such Part of them as may be employed in the Service of the United States, reserving to the States respectively, the Appointment of the Officers, and the Authority of training the Militia according to the discipline prescribed by Congress;
- To exercise exclusive Legislation in all Cases whatsoever, over such District (not exceeding ten Miles square) as may, by Cession of particular States, and the Acceptance of Congress, become the Seat of the Government of the United States, and to exercise like Authority over all Places purchased by the Consent of the Legislature of the State in which the Same shall be, for the Erection of Forts, Magazines, Arsenals, dock-Yards, and other needful Buildings;—And
- To make all Laws which shall be necessary and proper for carrying into Execution the foregoing Powers, and all other Powers vested by this Constitution in the Government of the United States, or in any Department or Officer thereof.

Section. 9.

The Migration or Importation of such Persons as any of the States now existing shall think proper to admit, shall not be prohibited by the Congress prior to the Year one thousand eight hundred and eight, but a Tax or duty may be imposed on such Importation, not exceeding ten dollars for each Person.

The Privilege of the Writ of Habeas Corpus shall not be suspended, unless when in Cases of Rebellion or Invasion the public Safety may require it.

No Bill of Attainder or ex post facto Law shall be passed.

No Capitation, or other direct, Tax shall be laid, ~~unless in Proportion to the Census or enumeration herein before directed to be taken~~.

No Tax or Duty shall be laid on Articles exported from any State.

No Preference shall be given by any Regulation of Commerce or Revenue to the Ports of one State over those of another: nor shall Vessels bound to, or from, one State, be obliged to enter, clear, or pay Duties in another.

No Money shall be drawn from the Treasury, but in Consequence of Appropriations made by Law; and a regular Statement and Account of the Receipts and Expenditures of all public Money shall be published from time to time.

No Title of Nobility shall be granted by the United States: And no Person holding any Office of Profit or Trust under them, shall, without the Consent of the Congress, accept of any present, Emolument, Office, or Title, of any kind whatever, from any King, Prince, or foreign State.

Section. 10.

No State shall enter into any Treaty, Alliance, or Confederation; grant Letters of Marque and Reprisal; coin Money; emit Bills of Credit; make any Thing but gold and silver Coin a Tender in Payment of Debts; pass any Bill of Attainder, ex post facto Law, or Law impairing the Obligation of Contracts, or grant any Title of Nobility.

No State shall, without the Consent of the Congress, lay any Imposts or Duties on Imports or Exports, except what may be absolutely necessary for executing it's inspection Laws: and the net Produce of all Duties and Imposts, laid by any State on Imports or Exports, shall be for the Use of the Treasury of the United States; and all such Laws shall be subject to the Revision and Controul of the Congress.

No State shall, without the Consent of Congress, lay any Duty of Tonnage, keep Troops, or Ships of War in time of Peace, enter into any Agreement or Compact with another State, or with a foreign Power, or engage in War, unless actually invaded, or in such imminent Danger as will not admit of delay.

Article II

Section. 1.

The executive Power shall be vested in a President of the United States of America. He shall hold his Office during the Term of four Years, and, together with the Vice President, chosen for the same Term, be elected, as follows.

Each State shall appoint, in such Manner as the Legislature thereof may direct, a Number of Electors, equal to the whole Number of Senators and Representatives to which the State may be entitled in the Congress: but no Senator or Representative, or Person holding an Office of Trust or Profit under the United States, shall be appointed an Elector.

~~The Electors shall meet in their respective States, and vote by Ballot for two Persons, of whom one at least shall not be an Inhabitant of the same State with themselves. And they shall make a List of all the Persons voted for, and of the Number of Votes for each; which List they shall sign and certify, and transmit sealed to the Seat of the Government of the United States, directed to the President of the Senate. The President of the Senate shall, in the Presence of the Senate and House of Representatives, open all the Certificates, and the Votes shall then be counted. The Person having the greatest Number of Votes shall be the President, if such Number be a Majority of the whole Number of Electors appointed; and if there be more than one who have such Majority, and have an equal Number of Votes, then the House of Representatives shall immediately chuse by Ballot one of them for President; and if no Person have a Majority, then from the five highest on the List the said House shall in like Manner chuse the President. But in chusing the President, the Votes shall be taken by States, the Representation from each~~

~~State having one Vote; A quorum for this Purpose shall consist of a Member or Members from two thirds of the States, and a Majority of all the States shall be necessary to a Choice. In every Case, after the Choice of the President, the Person having the greatest Number of Votes of the Electors shall be the Vice President. But if there should remain two or more who have equal Votes, the Senate shall chuse from them by Ballot the Vice President.~~

The Congress may determine the Time of chusing the Electors, and the Day on which they shall give their Votes; which Day shall be the same throughout the United States.

No Person except a natural born Citizen, or a Citizen of the United States, at the time of the Adoption of this Constitution, shall be eligible to the Office of President; neither shall any Person be eligible to that Office who shall not have attained to the Age of thirty five Years, and been fourteen Years a Resident within the United States.

~~In Case of the Removal of the President from Office, or of his Death, Resignation, or Inability to discharge the Powers and Duties of the said Office, the Same shall devolve on the Vice President, and the Congress may by Law provide for the Case of Removal, Death, Resignation or Inability, both of the President and Vice President, declaring what Officer shall then act as President, and such Officer shall act accordingly, until the Disability be removed, or a President shall be elected.~~

The President shall, at stated Times, receive for his Services, a Compensation, which shall neither be encreased nor diminished during the Period for which he shall have been elected, and he shall not receive within that Period any other Emolument from the United States, or any of them.

Before he enter on the Execution of his Office, he shall take the following Oath or Affirmation:—"I do solemnly swear (or affirm) that I will faithfully execute the Office of President of the United States, and will to the best of my Ability, preserve, protect and defend the Constitution of the United States."

Section. 2.

The President shall be Commander in Chief of the Army and Navy of the United States, and of the Militia of the several States, when called into the actual Service of the United States; he may require the Opinion, in writing, of the principal Officer in each of the executive Departments, upon any Subject relating to the Duties of their respective Offices, and he shall have Power to grant Reprieves and Pardons for Offences against the United States, except in Cases of Impeachment.

He shall have Power, by and with the Advice and Consent of the Senate, to make Treaties, provided two thirds of the Senators present concur; and he shall nominate, and by and with the Advice and Consent of the Senate, shall appoint Ambassadors, other public Ministers and Consuls, Judges of the supreme Court, and all other Officers of the United States, whose Appointments are not herein otherwise provided for, and which shall be established by Law: but the Congress may by Law vest the Appointment of such inferior Officers, as they think proper, in the President alone, in the Courts of Law, or in the Heads of Departments.

The President shall have Power to fill up all Vacancies that may happen during the Recess of the Senate, by granting Commissions which shall expire at the End of their next Session.

Section. 3.

He shall from time to time give to the Congress Information of the State of the Union, and recommend to their Consideration such Measures as he shall judge necessary and expedient; he may, on extraordinary Occasions, convene both Houses, or either of them, and in Case of Disagreement between them, with Respect to the Time of Adjournment, he may adjourn them to such Time as he shall think proper; he shall receive Ambassadors and other public Ministers; he shall take Care that the Laws be faithfully executed, and shall Commission all the Officers of the United States.

Section. 4.

The President, Vice President and all civil Officers of the United States, shall be removed from Office on Impeachment for, and Conviction of, Treason, Bribery, or other high Crimes and Misdemeanors.

Article III

Section. 1.

The judicial Power of the United States, shall be vested in one supreme Court, and in such inferior Courts as the Congress may from time to time ordain and establish. The Judges, both of the supreme and inferior Courts, shall hold their Offices during good Behaviour, and shall, at stated Times, receive for their Services, a Compensation, which shall not be diminished during their Continuance in Office.

Section. 2.

The judicial Power shall extend to all Cases, in Law and Equity, arising under this Constitution, the Laws of the United States, and Treaties made, or which shall be made, under their Authority;—to all Cases affecting Ambassadors, other public Ministers and Consuls;—to all Cases of admiralty and maritime Jurisdiction;—to Controversies to which the United States shall be a Party;—to Controversies between two or more States;~~—between a State and Citizens of another State,—~~between Citizens of different States,—between Citizens of the same State claiming Lands under Grants of different States, and between a State, or the Citizens thereof, and foreign States, Citizens or Subjects.

In all Cases affecting Ambassadors, other public Ministers and Consuls, and those in which a State shall be Party, the supreme Court shall have original Jurisdiction. In all the other Cases before mentioned, the supreme Court shall have appellate Jurisdiction, both as to Law and Fact, with such Exceptions, and under such Regulations as the Congress shall make.

The Trial of all Crimes, except in Cases of Impeachment, shall be by Jury; and such Trial shall be held in the State where the said Crimes shall have been committed; but when not committed within any State, the Trial shall be at such Place or Places as the Congress may by Law have directed.

Section. 3.

Treason against the United States, shall consist only in levying War against them, or in adhering to their Enemies, giving them Aid and Comfort. No Person shall be convicted of Treason unless on the Testimony of two Witnesses to the same overt Act, or on Confession in open Court.

The Congress shall have Power to declare the Punishment of Treason, but no Attainder of Treason shall work Corruption of Blood, or Forfeiture except during the Life of the Person attainted.

Article IV

Section. 1.

Full Faith and Credit shall be given in each State to the public Acts, Records, and judicial Proceedings of every other State. And the Congress may by general Laws prescribe the Manner in which such Acts, Records and Proceedings shall be proved, and the Effect thereof.

Section. 2.

The Citizens of each State shall be entitled to all Privileges and Immunities of Citizens in the several States.

A Person charged in any State with Treason, Felony, or other Crime, who shall flee from Justice, and be found in another State, shall on Demand of the executive Authority of the State from which he fled, be delivered up, to be removed to the State having Jurisdiction of the Crime.

~~No Person held to Service or Labour in one State, under the Laws thereof, escaping into another, shall, in Consequence of any Law or Regulation therein, be discharged from such Service or Labour, but shall be delivered up on Claim of the Party to whom such Service or Labour may be due.~~

Section. 3.

New States may be admitted by the Congress into this Union; but no new State shall be formed or erected within the Jurisdiction of any other State; nor any State be formed by the Junction of two or more States, or Parts of States, without the Consent of the Legislatures of the States concerned as well as of the Congress.

The Congress shall have Power to dispose of and make all needful Rules and Regulations respecting the Territory or other Property belonging to the United States; and nothing in this Constitution shall be so construed as to Prejudice any Claims of the United States, or of any particular State.

Section. 4.

The United States shall guarantee to every State in this Union a Republican Form of Government, and shall protect each of them against Invasion; and on Application of the Legislature, or of the Executive (when the Legislature cannot be convened) against domestic Violence.

Article V

The Congress, whenever two thirds of both Houses shall deem it necessary, shall propose Amendments to this Constitution, or, on the Application of the Legislatures of two thirds of the several States, shall call a Convention for proposing Amendments, which, in either Case, shall be valid to all Intents and Purposes, as Part of this Constitution, when ratified by the Legislatures of three fourths of the several States, or by Conventions in three fourths thereof, as the one or the other Mode of Ratification may be proposed by the Congress; Provided that no Amendment which may be made prior to the Year One thousand eight hundred and eight shall in any Manner affect the first and fourth Clauses in the Ninth Section of the first Article; and that no State, without its Consent, shall be deprived of its equal Suffrage in the Senate.

Article VI

All Debts contracted and Engagements entered into, before the Adoption of this Constitution, shall be as valid against the United States under this Constitution, as under the Confederation.

This Constitution, and the Laws of the United States which shall be made in Pursuance thereof; and all Treaties made, or which shall be made, under the Authority of the United States, shall be the supreme Law of the Land; and the Judges in every State shall be bound thereby, any Thing in the Constitution or Laws of any State to the Contrary notwithstanding.

The Senators and Representatives before mentioned, and the Members of the several State Legislatures, and all executive and judicial Officers, both of the United States and of the several States, shall be bound by Oath or Affirmation, to support this Constitution; but no religious Test shall ever be required as a Qualification to any Office or public Trust under the United States.

Article VII

The Ratification of the Conventions of nine States, shall be sufficient for the Establishment of this Constitution between the States so ratifying the Same.

George Washington
President and deputy from Virginia

Delaware

George Read
Gunning Bedford, Jr.
John Dickinson
Richard Bassett
Jacob Broom

Maryland

James McHenry
Daniel of St. Thomas Jenifer
Daniel Carroll

Virginia

John Blair
James Madison, Jr.

North Carolina

William Blount
Richard Dobbs Spaight, Sr.
Hugh Williamson

South Carolina

John Rutledge
Charles Cotesworth
Charles Pinckney
Pierce Butler

Georgia

William Few
Abraham Baldwin

New Hampshire

John Langdon
Nicholas Gilman

Massachusetts

Nathaniel Gorham
Rufus King

Connecticut

William Samuel Johnson
Roger Sherman

New York

Alexander Hamilton

New Jersey

William Livingston
David Brearly
William Paterson
Jonathan Dayton

Pennsylvania

Benjamin Franklin
Thomas Mifflin
Robert Morris
George Clymer
Thomas FitzSimons
Jared Ingersoll
James Wilson
Gouverneur Morris

BILL OF RIGHTS

Preamble

Congress of the United States begun and held at the City of New York, on Wednesday the fourth of March, one thousand seven hundred and eighty-nine.

The Conventions of a number of the States, having at the time of their adopting the Constitution expressed a desire in order to prevent misconstruction or abuse of its powers, that further declaratory and restrictive clauses should be added: And as extending the ground of public confidence in the Government will best ensure the beneficent ends of its institution.

Resolved by the Senate and House of Representatives of the United States of America in Congress assembled, two thirds of both Houses concurring that the following Articles be proposed to the Legislatures of the several states as Amendments to the Constitution of the United States, all or any of which articles, when ratified by three fourths of the said Legislatures to be valid to all intents and purposes as part of the said Constitution.

Articles in addition to, and Amendment of the Constitution of the United States of America, proposed by Congress and Ratified by the Legislatures of the several States, pursuant to the fifth Article of the original Constitution.

Article the first... After the first enumeration required by the first article of the Constitution, there shall be one Representative for every thirty thousand, until the number shall amount to one hundred, after which the proportion shall be so regulated by Congress, that there shall be not less than one hundred Representatives, nor less than one Representative for every forty thousand persons, until the number of Representatives shall amount to two hundred; after which the proportion shall be so regulated by Congress, that there shall not be less than two hundred Representatives, nor more than one Representative for every fifty thousand persons.

Article the second... No law, varying the compensation for the services of the Senators and Representatives, shall take effect, until an election of Representatives shall have intervened.

Article the third... Congress shall make no law respecting an establishment of religion, or prohibiting the free exercise thereof; or abridging the freedom of speech, or of the press; or the right of the people peaceably to assemble, and to petition the Government for a redress of grievances.

Article the fourth... A well regulated Militia, being necessary to the security of a free State, the right of the people to keep and bear Arms, shall not be infringed.

Article the fifth... No Soldier shall, in time of peace be quartered in any house, without the consent of the Owner, nor in time of war, but in a manner to be prescribed by law.

Article the sixth... The right of the people to be secure in their persons, houses, papers, and effects, against unreasonable searches and seizures, shall not be violated, and no Warrants shall issue, but upon probable cause, supported by Oath or affirmation, and particularly describing the place to be searched, and the persons or things to be seized.

Article the seventh... No person shall be held to answer for a capital, or otherwise infamous crime, unless on a presentment or indictment of a Grand Jury, except in cases arising in the land or naval forces, or in the Militia, when in actual service in time of War or public danger; nor shall any person be subject for the same offence to be twice put in jeopardy of life or limb; nor shall be compelled in any criminal case to be a witness against himself, nor be deprived of life, liberty, or property, without due process of law; nor shall private property be taken for public use, without just compensation.

Article the eighth... In all criminal prosecutions, the accused shall enjoy the right to a speedy and public trial, by an impartial jury of the State and district wherein the crime shall have been committed, which district shall have been previously ascertained by law, and to be informed of the nature and cause of the accusation; to be confronted with the witnesses against him; to have compulsory process for obtaining witnesses in his favor, and to have the Assistance of Counsel for his defence.

Article the ninth... In suits at common law, where the value in controversy shall exceed twenty dollars, the right of trial by jury shall be preserved, and no fact tried by a jury, shall be otherwise re-examined in any Court of the United States, than according to the rules of the common law.

Article the tenth... Excessive bail shall not be required, nor excessive fines imposed, nor cruel and unusual punishments inflicted.

Article the eleventh... The enumeration in the Constitution, of certain rights, shall not be construed to deny or disparage others retained by the people.

Article the twelfth... The powers not delegated to the United States by the Constitution, nor prohibited by it to the States, are reserved to the States respectively, or to the people.

ATTEST,

Frederick Augustus Muhlenberg, Speaker of the House of Representatives

John Adams, Vice-President of the United States, and President of the Senate
John Beckley, Clerk of the House of Representatives.
Sam. A Otis, Secretary of the Senate

Amendment I (1791)

Congress shall make no law respecting an establishment of religion, or prohibiting the free exercise thereof; or abridging the freedom of speech, or of the press; or the right of the people peaceably to assemble, and to petition the Government for a redress of grievances.

Amendment II (1791)

A well regulated Militia, being necessary to the security of a free State, the right of the people to keep and bear Arms, shall not be infringed.

Amendment III (1791)

No Soldier shall, in time of peace be quartered in any house, without the consent of the Owner, nor in time of war, but in a manner to be prescribed by law.

Amendment IV (1791)

The right of the people to be secure in their persons, houses, papers, and effects, against unreasonable searches and seizures, shall not be violated, and no Warrants shall issue, but upon probable cause, supported by Oath or affirmation, and particularly describing the place to be searched, and the persons or things to be seized.

Amendment V (1791)

No person shall be held to answer for a capital, or otherwise infamous crime, unless on a presentment or indictment of a Grand Jury, except in cases arising in the land or naval forces, or in the Militia, when in actual service in time of War or public danger; nor shall any person be subject for the same offence to be twice put in jeopardy of life or limb; nor shall be compelled in any criminal case to be a witness against himself, nor be deprived of life, liberty, or property, without due process of law; nor shall private property be taken for public use, without just compensation.

Amendment VI (1791)

In all criminal prosecutions, the accused shall enjoy the right to a speedy and public trial, by an impartial jury of the State and district wherein the crime shall have been committed, which district shall have been previously ascertained by law, and to be informed of the nature and cause of the accusation; to be confronted with the witnesses against him; to have compulsory process for obtaining witnesses in his favor, and to have the Assistance of Counsel for his defence.

Amendment VII (1791)

In Suits at common law, where the value in controversy shall exceed twenty dollars, the right of trial by jury shall be preserved, and no fact tried by a jury, shall be otherwise reexamined in any Court of the United States, than according to the rules of the common law.

Amendment VIII (1791)

Excessive bail shall not be required, nor excessive fines imposed, nor cruel and unusual punishments inflicted.

Amendment IX (1791)

The enumeration in the Constitution, of certain rights, shall not be construed to deny or disparage others retained by the people.

Amendment X (1791)

The powers not delegated to the United States by the Constitution, nor prohibited by it to the States, are reserved to the States respectively, or to the people.

Subsequent Amendments

Amendment XI (1795/1798)

The Judicial power of the United States shall not be construed to extend to any suit in law or equity, commenced or prosecuted against one of the United States by Citizens of another State, or by Citizens or Subjects of any Foreign State.

Amendment XII (1804)

The Electors shall meet in their respective states and vote by ballot for President and Vice-President, one of whom, at least, shall not be an inhabitant of the same state with themselves; they shall name in their ballots the person voted for as President, and in distinct ballots the person voted for as Vice-President, and they shall make distinct lists of all persons voted for as President, and of all persons voted for as Vice-President, and of the number of votes for each, which lists they shall sign and certify, and transmit sealed to the seat of the government of the United States, directed to the President of the Senate;—The President of the Senate shall, in the presence of the Senate and House of Representatives, open all the certificates and the votes shall then be counted;—The person having the greatest Number of votes for President, shall be the President, if such number be a majority of the whole number of Electors appointed; and if no person have such majority, then from the persons having the highest numbers not exceeding three on the list of those voted for as President, the House of Representatives shall choose immediately, by ballot, the President. But in choosing the President, the votes shall be taken by states, the representation from each state having one vote; a quorum for this purpose shall consist of a member or members from two-thirds of the states, and a majority of all the states shall be necessary to a choice. *And if the House of Representatives shall not choose a President whenever the right of choice shall devolve upon them, before the fourth day of March next following, then the Vice-President shall act as President, as in the case of the death or other constitutional disability of the President*—The person having the greatest number of votes as Vice-President, shall be the Vice-President, if such number be a majority of the whole number of Electors appointed, and if no person have a majority, then from the two highest numbers on the list, the Senate shall choose the Vice-President; a quorum for the purpose shall consist of two-thirds of the whole number of Senators, and a majority of the whole number shall be necessary to a choice. But no person constitutionally ineligible to the office of President shall be eligible to that of Vice-President of the United States.

Amendment XIII (1865)

Section 1.

Neither slavery nor involuntary servitude, except as a punishment for crime whereof the party shall have been duly convicted, shall exist within the United States, or any place subject to their jurisdiction.

Section 2.

Congress shall have power to enforce this article by appropriate legislation

Amendment XIV (1868)

Section 1.

All persons born or naturalized in the United States, and subject to the jurisdiction thereof, are citizens of the United States and of the State wherein they reside. No State shall make or enforce any law which shall abridge the privileges or immunities of citizens of the United States; nor shall any State deprive any person of life, liberty, or property, without due process of law; nor deny to any person within its jurisdiction the equal protection of the laws.

Section 2.

Representatives shall be apportioned among the several States according to their respective numbers, counting the whole number of persons in each State, excluding Indians not taxed. But when the right to vote at any election for the choice of electors for President and Vice President of the United States, Representatives in Congress, the Executive and Judicial officers of a State, or the members of the Legislature thereof, is denied to any of the male inhabitants of such State, being twenty-one years of age, and citizens of the United States, or in any way abridged, except for participation in rebellion, or other crime, the basis of representation therein shall be reduced in the proportion which the number of such male citizens shall bear to the whole number of male citizens twenty-one years of age in such State.

Section 3.

No person shall be a Senator or Representative in Congress, or elector of President and Vice President, or hold any office, civil or military, under the United States, or under any State, who, having previously taken an oath, as a member of Congress, or as an officer of the United States, or as a member of any State legislature, or as an executive or judicial officer of any State, to support the Constitution of the United States, shall have engaged in insurrection or rebellion against the same, or given aid or comfort to the enemies thereof. But Congress may by a vote of two-thirds of each House, remove such disability.

Section 4.

The validity of the public debt of the United States, authorized by law, including debts incurred for payment of pensions and bounties for services in suppressing insurrection or rebellion, shall not be questioned. But neither the United States nor any

State shall assume or pay any debt or obligation incurred in aid of insurrection or rebellion against the United States, or any claim for the loss or emancipation of any slave; but all such debts, obligations and claims shall be held illegal and void.

Section 5.

The Congress shall have power to enforce, by appropriate legislation, the provisions of this article.

Amendment XV (1870)

Section 1.

The right of citizens of the United States to vote shall not be denied or abridged by the United States or by any State on account of race, color, or previous condition of servitude.

Section 2.

The Congress shall have power to enforce this article by appropriate legislation.

Amendment XVI (1913)

The Congress shall have power to lay and collect taxes on incomes, from whatever source derived, without apportionment among the several States, and without regard to any census or enumeration.

Amendment XVII (1913)

The Senate of the United States shall be composed of two Senators from each State, elected by the people thereof, for six years; and each Senator shall have one vote. The electors in each State shall have the qualifications requisite for electors of the most numerous branch of the State legislatures.

When vacancies happen in the representation of any State in the Senate, the executive authority of such State shall issue writs of election to fill such vacancies: Provided, That the legislature of any State may empower the executive thereof to make temporary appointments until the people fill the vacancies by election as the legislature may direct.

This amendment shall not be so construed as to affect the election or term of any Senator chosen before it becomes valid as part of the Constitution.

Amendment XVIII (1919)

~~Section 1.~~

~~After one year from the ratification of this article the manufacture, sale, or transportation of intoxicating liquors within, the importation thereof into, or the exportation thereof from the United States and all territory subject to the jurisdiction thereof for beverage purposes is hereby prohibited.~~

~~Section 2.~~

~~The Congress and the several States shall have concurrent power to enforce this article by appropriate legislation.~~

~~Section 3.~~

~~This article shall be inoperative unless it shall have been ratified as an amendment to the Constitution by the legislatures of the several States, as provided in the Constitution, within seven years from the date of the submission hereof to the States by the Congress.~~

Amendment XIX (1920)

The right of citizens of the United States to vote shall not be denied or abridged by the United States or by any State on account of sex.

Congress shall have power to enforce this article by appropriate legislation.

Amendment XX (1933)

Section 1.

The terms of the President and Vice President shall end at noon on the 20th day of January, and the terms of Senators and Representatives at noon on the 3d day of January, of the years in which such terms would have ended if this article had not been ratified; and the terms of their successors shall then begin.

Section 2.

The Congress shall assemble at least once in every year, and such meeting shall begin at noon on the 3d day of January, unless they shall by law appoint a different day.

Section 3.

If, at the time fixed for the beginning of the term of the President, the President elect shall have died, the Vice President elect shall become President. If a President shall not have been chosen before the time fixed for the beginning of his term, or if the President elect shall have failed to qualify, then the Vice President elect shall act as President until a President shall have qualified; and the Congress may by law provide for the case wherein neither a President elect nor a Vice President elect shall have qualified, declaring who shall then act as President, or the manner in which one who is to act shall be selected, and such person shall act accordingly until a President or Vice President shall have qualified.

Section 4.

The Congress may by law provide for the case of the death of any of the persons from whom the House of Representatives may choose a President whenever the right of choice shall have devolved upon them, and for the case of the death of any of the persons from whom the Senate may choose a Vice President whenever the right of choice shall have devolved upon them.

Section 5.

Sections 1 and 2 shall take effect on the 15th day of October following the ratification of this article.

Section 6.

This article shall be inoperative unless it shall have been ratified as an amendment to the Constitution by the legislatures of three-fourths of the several States within seven years from the date of its submission.

Amendment XXI (1933)

Section 1.

The eighteenth article of amendment to the Constitution of the United States is hereby repealed.

Section 2.

The transportation or importation into any State, Territory, or possession of the United States for delivery or use therein of intoxicating liquors, in violation of the laws thereof, is hereby prohibited.

Section 3.

This article shall be inoperative unless it shall have been ratified as an amendment to the Constitution by conventions in the several States, as provided in the Constitution, within seven years from the date of the submission hereof to the States by the Congress.

Amendment XXII (1951)

Section 1.

No person shall be elected to the office of the President more than twice, and no person who has held the office of President, or acted as President, for more than two years of a term to which some other person was elected President shall be elected to the office of the President more than once. But this Article shall not apply to any person holding the office of President, when this Article was proposed by the Congress, and shall not prevent any person who may be holding the office of President, or acting as President, during the term within which this Article becomes operative from holding the office of President or acting as President during the remainder of such term.

Section 2.

This article shall be inoperative unless it shall have been ratified as an amendment to the Constitution by the legislatures of three-fourths of the several States within seven years from the date of its submission to the States by the Congress.

Amendment XXIII (1961)

Section 1.

The District constituting the seat of Government of the United States shall appoint in such manner as the Congress may direct: A number of electors of President and Vice President equal to the whole number of Senators and Representatives in Congress to which the District would be entitled if it were a State, but in no event more than the least populous State; they shall be in addition to those appointed by the States, but they shall be considered, for the purposes of the election of President and Vice President, to be electors appointed by a State; and they shall meet in the District and perform such duties as provided by the twelfth article of amendment.

Section 2.

The Congress shall have power to enforce this article by appropriate legislation.

Amendment XXIV (1964)

Section 1.

The right of citizens of the United States to vote in any primary or other election for President or Vice President for electors for President or Vice President, or for Senator or Representative in Congress, shall not be denied or abridged by the United States or any State by reason of failure to pay any poll tax or other tax.

Section 2.

The Congress shall have power to enforce this article by appropriate legislation.

Amendment XXV (1967)

Section 1.

In case of the removal of the President from office or of his death or resignation, the Vice President shall become President.

Section 2.

Whenever there is a vacancy in the office of the Vice President, the President shall nominate a Vice President who shall take office upon confirmation by a majority vote of both Houses of Congress.

Section 3.

Whenever the President transmits to the President pro tempore of the Senate and the Speaker of the House of Representatives his written declaration that he is unable to discharge the powers and duties of his office, and until he transmits to them a written declaration to the contrary, such powers and duties shall be discharged by the Vice President as Acting President.

Section 4.

Whenever the Vice President and a majority of either the principal officers of the executive departments or of such other body as Congress may by law provide, transmit to the President pro tempore of the Senate and the Speaker of the House of Representatives their written declaration that the President is unable to discharge the powers and duties of his office, the Vice President shall immediately assume the powers and duties of the office as Acting President.

Thereafter, when the President transmits to the President pro tempore of the Senate and the Speaker of the House of Representatives his written declaration that no inability exists, he shall resume the powers and duties of his office unless the Vice President and a majority of either the principal officers of the executive department or of such other body as Congress may by law provide, transmit within four days to the President pro tempore of the Senate and the Speaker of the House of Representatives their written declaration that the President is unable to discharge the powers and duties of his office. Thereupon Congress shall decide the issue, assembling within forty-eight hours for that purpose if not in session. If the Congress, within twenty-one days after receipt of the latter written declaration, or, if Congress is not in session, within twenty-one days after Congress is required to assemble, determines by two-thirds vote of both Houses that the President is unable to discharge the powers and duties of his office, the Vice President shall continue to discharge the same as Acting President; otherwise, the President shall resume the powers and duties of his office.

Amendment XXVI (1971)

Section 1.

The right of citizens of the United States, who are eighteen years of age or older, to vote shall not be denied or abridged by the United States or by any State on account of age.

Section 2.

The Congress shall have power to enforce this article by appropriate legislation.

Amendment XXVII (1992)

No law varying the compensation for the services of the Senators and Representatives shall take effect, until an election of Representatives shall have intervened.

APPENDIX C
Thomas Jefferson's Letter to the Danbury Baptists

THE FINAL LETTER, AS SENT

To messers. Nehemiah Dodge, Ephraim Robbins, & Stephen S. Nelson, a committee of the Danbury Baptist association in the state of Connecticut.

Gentlemen

The affectionate sentiments of esteem and approbation which you are so good as to express towards me, on behalf of the Danbury Baptist association, give me the highest satisfaction. My duties dictate a faithful and zealous pursuit of the interests of my constituents, & in proportion as they are persuaded of my fidelity to those duties, the discharge of them becomes more and more pleasing.

Believing with you that religion is a matter which lies solely between Man & his God, that he owes account to none other for his faith or his worship, that the legitimate powers of government reach actions only, & not opinions, I contemplate with sovereign reverence that act of the whole American people which declared that their legislature should "make no law respecting an establishment of religion, or prohibiting the free exercise thereof," thus building a wall of separation between Church & State. Adhering to this expression of the supreme will of the nation in behalf of the rights of conscience, I shall see with sincere satisfaction the progress of those sentiments which tend to restore to man all his natural rights, convinced he has no natural right in opposition to his social duties.

I reciprocate your kind prayers for the protection & blessing of the common father and creator of man, and tender you for yourselves & your religious association, assurances of my high respect & esteem.

Th Jefferson
Jan. 1. 1802.

THE DRAFT AND RECENTLY DISCOVERED TEXT

To messers Nehemiah Dodge, Ephraim Robbins, & Stephen S. Nelson, a committee of the Danbury Baptist association in the state of Connecticut.

Gentlemen

The affectionate sentiments of esteem & approbation which you are so good as to express towards me, on behalf of the Danbury Baptist association, give me the highest satisfaction. My duties dictate a faithful & zealous pursuit of the interests of my constituents, and, in proportion as they are persuaded of my fidelity to those duties, the discharge of them becomes more & more pleasing.

Believing with you that religion is a matter which lies solely between man & his god, that he owes account to none other for his faith or his worship, that the legitimate powers of government reach actions only and not opinions, I contemplate with sovereign reverence that act of the whole American people which declared that their legislature should "make no law respecting an establishment of religion, or prohibiting the free exercise thereof;" thus building a wall of eternal separation between Church

& State. Congress thus inhibited from acts respecting religion, and the Executive authorised only to execute their acts, I have refrained from prescribing even those occasional performances of devotion, practiced indeed by the Executive of another nation as the legal head of its church, but subject here, as religious exercises only to the voluntary regulations and discipline of each respective sect,

[Jefferson first wrote: *"confining myself therefore to the duties of my station, which are merely temporal, be assured that your religious rights shall never be infringed by any act of mine and that."* These lines he crossed out and then wrote: *"concurring with"*; having crossed out these two words, he wrote: *"Adhering to this great act of national legislation in behalf of the rights of conscience"*; next he crossed out these words and wrote: *"Adhering to this expression of the supreme will of the nation in behalf of the rights of conscience I shall see with friendly dispositions the progress of those sentiments which tend to restore to man all his natural rights, convinced that he has no natural rights in opposition to his social duties."*]

I reciprocate your kind prayers for the protection & blessing of the common father and creator of man, and tender you for yourselves & the Danbury Baptist [your religious] association assurances of my high respect & esteem.

Th Jefferson
Jan. 1. 1802.

APPENDIX D
Establishment & Enablement of State Agencies

At the state level, you will have a state constitution, state legislative statutes, and state agency administrative rules. There may also be state agency policies, procedures, and guidelines, but this appendix only focuses on the first three.

In Idaho, the state constitution is the Idaho Constitution, the state legislative statutes are the Idaho Code, and the state agency administrative rules are the Idaho Administrative Code also known as the Idaho Administrative Procedures Act (IDAPA).

Again, in Idaho, there are state legislative statutes that direct state agencies to promulgate administrative rules for a specific purpose. This statute is often referred to as an "enabling statute." During each legislative session, the legislature may review the state agency administrative rules for compliance with the enabling statute and either approve or reject the rules. Below is an example that will hopefully clarify all of this information.

The Idaho Constitution directing the legislature to establish a state agency:

> Idaho Constitution, Article X Public Institutions, Section 5. The state legislature shall establish a nonpartisan board to be known as the state board of correction… This board shall have the control, direction and management of the penitentiaries of the state, their employees and properties,

> and of adult felony probation and parole, with such compensation, powers, and duties as may be prescribed by law.

The legislature establishing the agency as directed:

> Idaho Code § 20-201A. (1) There is hereby created a nonpartisan board of three (3) members to be known as the state board of correction... The board shall be the Constitutional Board of Correction prescribed by Section 5, Article X, of the Constitution of the State of Idaho.

The legislature directing the state agency to promulgate certain rules, the "enabling statute," and that such rules are subject to review by the legislature for compliance with the enabling statute:

> Idaho Code § 20-209... (4) The state board of correction shall have the authority to promulgate rules required by law or necessary or desirable to carry out all duties assigned to the department of correction pursuant to the provisions of Chapter 8, Title 20, Idaho Code, which authority shall include the power and duties to prescribe standards, rules, and procedures for licensure of private prison contractors, to develop and provide, in conjunction with the department of administration, a uniform contract for use by local contracting authorities in contracting with private prison contractors, to review records and historical information of all prisoners proposed to be housed in private prison facilities and to approve or reject the housing of all prisoners, to monitor the status of insurance of private prison contractors, to approve suitable training programs for firearm certification for employees of private prison contractors, and to approve suitable drug testing programs for prisoners housed with private prison contractors. All final decisions by the board shall be subject to review pursuant to the provisions and procedures of the Administrative Procedure Act, Chapter 52, Title 67, Idaho Code.

The legislature cautioning the state agency that it must only make rules that are consistent with the enabling statute or Idaho Constitution:

> Idaho Code § 20-212. (1) The state board of correction shall make all necessary rules to carry out the provisions of this chapter not inconsistent with express statutes or the state constitution and to carry out those duties assigned to the department of correction pursuant to the provisions of Chapter 8, Title 20, Idaho Code.

The legislature's process of reviewing administrative rules for compliance with the enabling statute:

> Idaho Code § 67-5291. (1) The standing committees of the legislature may review temporary, pending and final rules which have been published in the bulletin or in the administrative code. If reviewed, the standing committee which reviewed the rules shall report to the membership of the body its findings and recommendations concerning its review of the rules… A concurrent resolution may be adopted approving the rule, in whole or in part, or rejecting the rule where it is determined that the rule, or part of the rule, is not consistent with the legislative intent of the statute that the rule was written to interpret, prescribe, implement or enforce, or where it is determined that any rule, or part of a rule, previously promulgated and reviewed by the legislature shall be deemed not to be consistent with the legislative intent of the statute the rule was written to interpret, prescribe, implement or enforce. The rejection of a rule, or part of a rule, by the legislature via concurrent resolution shall prevent the agency's intended action from remaining in effect beyond the date of the legislative action.[1]

---

1 Thank you to Eric R. Glover for providing Appendix D.

APPENDIX E
Civic Parenting

Civic parenting—what's that? It's not far from Christian diplomacy, really. Civic parenting means raising our children to care about more than themselves, their family, their friends, and their church friends. In essence, it is a call to parents to walk with our children into our communities and into the civil realm.

Like most of us, our children would prefer to keep to the well-worn paths—to what is comfortable. However, as we parent them, we can help to enlarge their understanding of the world. If they are familiar with the realms of family and church, we can introduce them to the civil realm and the larger community around them.

Of course, we have to exercise wisdom because it is not our goal to show them the ways of the world. Just to step out of their own little world and learn about others' worlds. What do I mean? Well, it depends upon what age of children we are considering.

So let's start pretty young. When our children were very young, my husband and I taught them to be kind to others. To refrain from being rude. To look people in the eye and speak to them politely. No turning the head away feigning shyness. No ignoring others who were present and accounted for.

As they grew into toddlers and young children, this continued. We took them out into the community. We went to the zoo, to historic homes, to museums, to classical and sacred music concerts. They learned to conduct themselves in public without becoming a public nuisance. I reminded them that when we went out in public, we represented our Triune God, their dad, and homeschooling. So, they needed to look presentable and act presentable, even if they didn't feel like it.

As grade schoolers and junior highers, we made them participate in an activity that was outside their comfort zone. Based upon where we lived (rather rural), we chose 4-H. The 4-Hers went to public school and had different interests from my children. But we became 4-Hers anyway. It helped us understand extension offices at land-grant universities, and it helped us understand people a little better. We picked up practical skills along the way and became very fond of our 4-H leader.

Also, we frequented the public library pretty heavily. After all, there were art and theater programs there, not to mention a lot of books to check out. The art and theater programs enabled us to rub shoulders with a variety of people—young and old. And to exercise some theatrical chutzpah along the way.

We learned that we could cooperate, and even flourish, around a variety of people who were not just like us. We learned to do what we could with what we had where we were. And God blessed those years.

I had not yet learned to attend public meetings like Susan did with her children. And the thought always flashed through my mind to stop in at the fire station and ask for a tour, but I never did it. But we did go see the mayor one day. My daughter was in a local youth theater play, cast as the Artful Dodger in *Oliver Twist.* We actually had made an appointment at his office some time in advance, and when we called to confirm it, the secretary seemed to have made a mistake. The mayor was out for the morning. I decided that we should go anyway and leave him a pair of free tickets for the performance. So the Artful Dodger walked into the mayor's office and visited with the secretary. Then, who walked in, but the mayor himself! The mayor invited the Dodger into his office for a chat. As they rounded the corner, I heard a "Thank you, Governor," announced in cockney. The two tickets were put to good use that weekend—sitting in the audience was a young American mayor accompanied by his lovely new wife.

Families who are raising happy, obedient, alert children who are schooled in the things of the Lord and who can sit with their parents in the gate can play a significant role in the future of taking back our local, state, and even national governmental processes. It is just another realm of life that we can presently participate in together to glorify God. And when our children grow older, the public square (or gate as Solomon calls it) will not be unfamiliar to them. As young adults, they will have logged much experience in local government. They will be leaders in their own right and will be like young Timothy who was "an example to the believers in word, in conduct, in love, in spirit, in faith, in purity" (1 Timothy 4:12).

When my own family was called into the public square, my children were older than Susan's. Mine ranged from ten years old to college age. I remember preparing for a county meeting presentation scheduled to take place that evening (after a long day of homeschooling), and the clock was ticking. The meeting was in an hour. First, I couldn't find a particular journal article I had been looking for, so I asked my high-school-aged daughter to pray with me. And, lo, continuing the online search process, I found just the perfect article. However, this low-tech mom couldn't get the printer to work. Something was wrong. Again, I asked my daughter to pray with me and then assist. She came to my aid, coaxed the printer into submission, and produced hard copies of that article—enough for everyone on the board of the county plan commission, which was to be shortly convening in the next town over which was the county seat (a term that we learn about in this book). That article made a difference in the outcome of the evening's meeting. I couldn't have done it alone. It was Providence working through generational collaboration. Talk about taking the humdrum out of life—and just under the wire. A few years later, during her last year of college, that daughter decided to apply for an appointed position within one of our local city government commissions.

By participating with us in these sorts of endeavors, our children not only witness the importance of civic engagement, but they become already civically engaged themselves. They have begun the journey; they have come to the party; they have entered the public square earlier than we did. And they didn't do it alone. They did it within their family, if not also in the community. And they did it in a family with parents who read the Scriptures to them. The children take it all in—the Old Testament, the New Testament sprinkled with soft rains, then downpours from the book of Proverbs.

Here's a quick story about our then-ten-year-old son: all of our children were brought up on the Book of Proverbs. But the dosage increased with the passage of time, and we progressed from years of a proverb a day (as in a verse) to a chapter a day. One Saturday morning, I took our younger two children to a legislative breakfast (we were hoping for some donuts there). Sadly, when we arrived, the donuts were gone. No donuts. Just watching and listening to the legislative part without the breakfast part. Various regular people stood up and spoke their minds on governmental issues. One gentleman, in a rugby-striped T-shirt, talked and talked and talked. He was not of our family's political persuasion. Later that evening, after my husband had arrived home from work, he read us a chapter of Proverbs and asked us more about our day. Our son recounted the affairs of the day, telling of the legislative "breakfast." He described a man there who "ha[d] no delight in understanding, / But in expressing his own heart" (Proverbs 18:2). It is amazing what children pick up and internalize both concerning the Scriptures and daily life.

As I presently write about civic engagement, my son, the used-to-be-ten-year-old child, is accompanying me to observe the city council tonight. He is also on the meeting's agenda to be appointed by the mayor as a non-voting high school member of our city's parks and recreation commission. I write this to show the natural progression of generational blessing on the heads of God's people when they walk in His ways in faith. Even if you don't generally hold parks and rec departments in high esteem, the appointment serves as an entry-level position to begin understanding the machinations of local government. The takeaway can simultaneously be "how to do it" and "how not to do it." We don't have to buy entirely into the process to learn from it. Humility must accompany us into the public square. If we are simply philosophically above the way things are done, then we remain spectators rather than informed agents for change.

In this sort of intergenerational civic investment, God blesses us and our children after us with wisdom. When we engage in the civil realm ordained by God, why should we doubt that He will bless our cities and counties? Why should we doubt that He will bless our states? Our nation? Remember Daniel, Hananiah, Mishael, and Azariah. Think about Psalm 8:2: "Out of the mouth of babes and nursing infants / You have ordained strength, / Because of Your enemies, / That You may silence the enemy and the avenger." Children represent small beginnings of strength and influence. That is why raising children is such a noble calling. That is why one day, they will stand on our shoulders and see farther into the work ahead than we can currently see.

Here are two applications for readers who have children:

First, bringing your children into the civil realm (after having taught them public niceties such as looking people in the eye, shaking hands, answering politely, and not demanding constant attention) is quite winsome. I genuinely believe that if we merely re-entered the public square with our modestly well-behaved children, the world would be taken aback. Of course, we don't parade our children about as a show, and we must always be at war with pridefulness, and we must teach them not to trust strangers. But, honestly, no one ever apprised me of how much attention well-behaved, polite children garner. Almost always, I took my children shopping with me when they were young, and I was astounded at how often people stopped me to compliment them and comment on how encouraged they were to see pleasant children. It gives a soul hope for the future.

And second, a classical Christian education is not a prerequisite for their lives, and neither is homeschooling, but please consider giving your children the gift of one or both.[1] And remember to teach them actual civics[2] in addition to the classics and the Founding Fathers. You never know when they will need to put their knowledge into action or come to your aid with it.

---

1 Dennis Prager, "The Single Best Thing Americans Can Do to Retake America," *Epoch Times*, June 14, 2021.

2 Throughout this book, I encourage parents to expose their children to the workings of government by attending meetings at the city, county, state, and national levels.

APPENDIX F
All Sorts of Districts

My Civic Address:

In the same manner that each of us knows our physical mailing address, we can also know our civic address. This address is not for the purpose of receiving mail at our homes, rather it is for understanding where each of us is situated as a member of We the People for the purposes of elections, voting, and connecting with our elected representatives. Fill in any district numbers that you already know. Leave those districts that you cannot yet identify blank and seek help from your local election office to complete them.

My Civic Roster:

Once you know your civic address (meaning what district you live in for each level of the three branches of government), then you can determine who represents your district. In essence—who represents your voice in our American system of representative government. Note that the judicial branch can be quite a mystery to the average citizen. Make an appointment with your local (county-equivalent) clerk of courts or county prosecutor to assist you with completing and understanding who represents you in the judicial districts if you are unable to find those people's names online.

U.S. Postal Service Address:

Street: ____________________________
City: ______________________________
State: _____________________________
Nation: ____________________________

My Civic Address:

My Precinct No. _____
(local voting precinct)

City (Council) District No. _____
(optional, varies by city)

County (Commissioner) District No. _____
(optional, varies by county)

Special Districts (unnumbered)

School District No. _____

My Civic Roster:

My Precinct Leader: ______________________________
(the one who comes to my door with voting information)

My City Councilors/Commissioners: ______________________________

____

____

____

____

My Mayor: ______________________________

My County Commissioners/Councilors: ______________________________

____

____

____

____

My Special District Board Members: ______________________________

____

____

____

____

My School Board Members: ______________________________

____

____

____

State Legislative District No. _____

State Judicial District No. _____

U.S. Congressional District No. _____

U.S. Judicial District No. _____

My State Legislators: ________________________________

____

____

____

My State Judges: ___________________________________

____

____

____

My U.S. Congressional Representatives: _______________

____

____

____

My Federal Judges (appointed by the President): _________

____

____

____

My Supreme Court Chief Justice: ____________________

My Supreme Court Justices: ________________________

____

____

____

Who Is on My Ballot?

You should be able to see your ballot in advance at your state elections website. Often you can write in the name of someone who is not listed on the ballot.

Federal Legislative: ______________________________

Federal Executive: ______________________________

Federal Judicial: N/A (appointed by President)

State Legislative: ______________________________

State Executive: ______________________________

State Judicial: ______________________________

State Electoral College Delegates: ____________________

Local City Legislative: ______________________________

Local County Legislative: ____________________________

Local Special Districts (Legislative/Executive?): _______

____

Local School Board: ______________________________

Local City Executive: ______________________________

Local County Executive: ___________________________

Local Judicial: ______________________________

Local Precinct Leader: ____________________________

Who Was Just Elected?

Federal Legislative: ______________________________

Federal Executive: ______________________________

Federal Judicial: ______________________________

State Legislative: ______________________________

State Executive: ______________________________

State Judicial: ______________________________

Local City Legislative: ______________________________

Local County Legislative: ______________________________

Local Special Districts: ______________________________

Local School Board: ______________________________

Local City Executive: ______________________________

Local County Executive: ______________________________

Local Judicial: ______________________________

Local Precinct Leader: ______________________________

What Is on My Ballot?

Initiative: ______________________________

Referendum: ______________________________

Tax Levy: ______________________________

State or National Constitutional Amendment: __________

____

____

My Election Cycles:

How many elections are there in my area per year? Another way to phrase this question is: How many election cycles are there annually where I live? List the months of those cycles here:

1.
2.
3.
4.

Does my state have open or closed or semi-closed presidential primary elections? ___________________________

The Election Cycle Reflected by Branch

When are elections for districts for all three branches of government? ______________________________

Legislative

US: ______________________________

State: ______________________________

Special District: ______________________________

County-Equivalent: ______________________________

City: ______________________________

Executive

US: ______________________________

State: ______________________________

County-Equivalent: ______________________________

City: ______________________________

Judicial

Federal: ______________________________

State: ______________________________

Local (usually appointed?): ______________________________

My State's Voting Laws

GLOSSARY

absentee voting or ballot—a voting-by-mail option offered by some states instead of voting in person when a ballot is requested in advance

activist—one who works to bring about social or political change

ad hoc committee—see *special committee*

ad hoc districts—see *special districts*

Administrative Procedure Act—the 1946 act passed by Congress that governs the process by which federal agencies develop and issue regulations

administrative-agency law—the rules of administrative agencies that have the force and effect of law

Affordable Care Act (ACA)—2010 act passed by Congress, also known as Obamacare and the Patient Protection and Affordable Care Act (PPACA)

agency—a group which is authorized to act for or in place of another

agenda—upcoming order of business of a public meeting usually posted in advance of the meeting

agent—one who is authorized to act for or in place of another

ambassador—an official or unofficial representative or messenger

amendatory veto—a chief executive's power to amend or revise legislation before signing it into law

amendments—changes to a governing document

American Federalism—see *federalism, American*

American Revolution—the thirteen colonies' war for independence from Great Britain; also know as the American War for Independence

***amicus* brief**—a brief filed by a third party to advise a court, literally a *friend of the court* brief

annexation—the process of urban expansion where some suburban areas become legally attached to or joined with existing municipalities

annual budget—document that shows all of the incoming revenue and outgoing expenditures for the year

appellate court—second-tier court where a case is reviewed after having been tried in a first-tier court

appropriation—authorization (usually by the legislature) to allocate and spend government funds

article—a paragraph division within a code of law

Articles of Confederation—the nation's first constitution

assistant United States attorneys—federal deputy prosecutors for each federal judicial district

associate justice—one of the justices of the U.S. or state Supreme Court who is not the chief justice

at large—elected across the entire region, not elected by districts

attorney general—an elected executive office (state or national) held by the chief law officer who serves as legal counsel for that level of government

attorney, city—appointed legal counsel on staff for the city who attends public meetings, reviews documents, and represents the city in court cases

attorney, county—appointed legal counsel on staff for the county who attends public meetings, reviews documents, and represents the county in court cases; in some states, this is the title of the county's prosecutor who represents the state in court cases, and those states may distinguish their appointed staff attorney with a title such as county counsel

auditor, county—see *clerk/auditor/recorder, county*

auditor, state—see *controller, state*

authoritarian—having power concentrated in an elite individual or group apart from constitutional representation

ballot—the right to vote; a small ball or piece of paper used for voting

ballot face—the sheet (ballot) tailored to each specific voting precinct

ballot initiative—see *initiative*

bicameral—a two-chamber legislature

bill—a written document proposed to become a law

Bill of Rights/bill of rights—the first ten amendments to the Constitution or the list of rights in each state's constitution and even in some city constitutions/charters

blue state—a state whose voters tend to support liberal policies and candidates

board—see *commission*

borough—county equivalent in Alaska; also see *town*

Brown v. Board of Education of Topeka—the 1953 Supreme Court case declaring that the separation of children by race in public schools is unconstitutional

bureaucracy—the non-elected government employees of administrative agencies

bureaucrat—a member of a bureaucracy

bureaucratic—possessing the characteristics of a bureaucracy (following rules, generating or requiring paperwork, etc.)

cabinet—the advisors of the President of the United States

candidate—an American who applies (by election) for a specific job on the public payroll

capital, city—the chief administrative city of a level of government

capitol—the building itself at the capital city

case law—see *common law*

casework—service by a legislator to those he or she represents

caucus—a convening of like-minded individuals in Congress or the state legislature to discuss strategy and whip the vote

caucus chairperson—the person who presides over the meetings held by a party's parliamentary caucus

caucus, presidential—a private meeting for members inside one political party to discuss and nominate a candidate to be on the ballot (may be held simultaneously at many locations within the state)

ceremonial law—Old Testament law that governed religious ceremonies and was fulfilled in Christ

chair/chairman/chairperson—the individual appointed to supervise and direct the administrative needs of a board, commission, or committee

chamber—the house of a legislative body, literally a *room*

chamber of commerce—a membership-based group of businesses joining together for mutual benefit to promote the local community's economic/business interest

charter—founding document that sets forth the rights of the governed

checks and balances—each of the three branches of government (legislative, executive, and judicial) has some degree of oversight to exercise in relation to the other two branches

Chevron U.S.A., Inc. v. Natural Resources Defense Council, Inc.—the 1984 case that had required courts to defer to an administrative agency's interpretation of its own regulation(s)

chief executive—an individual who heads the division of government that executes or carries out the law

chief justice—the principle justice of the Supreme Court of the United States or of the highest state court

Christendom—the dominion that Christ purchased with His blood, often known as the parts of the world where Christianity prevails

Christian diplomacy—skill in handling civil affairs guided by the principles of God's Word

circuit court, federal—appellate court that reviews decisions from a U.S. district court

circuit court, state—general-jurisdiction trial court

circuit courts of appeal—second-tier appellate courts in the federal judicial system

circuit split—a situation where different circuit courts of appeal reach different decisions

citizen—a native-born or naturalized member of a nation

citizenship—the position or status of being a citizen; see also *dual citizenship*

city—a voluntary association of people who gather together and decide to form a municipal corporation under the laws of the state in which they reside

city charter—a constitution for a city (not all cities have charters; some have their rights embedded in state law)

city code of laws (ordinances)—a systematic grouping of laws for a city

city council—see *council, city*

city manager/administrator/supervisor—a staff member who serves as the chief administrative officer of the city

civic—relating to citizens from a city or town (and state or nation)

civics—a social science dealing with the rights and duties of citizens

civil—relating to citizenship regarding the law

civil case—a private dispute between two parties

civil realm—all levels of American government

civil township—a type of local government in a grey area between counties and municipalities that can serve as a political subdivision of the county

classified charter—a charter that classifies cities by population and sometimes by form of government (mayor-council or council-manager)

clemency power—the authority to exercise leniency toward individuals who have committed crimes

clerk/auditor/recorder, county—an appointed or elected constitutional row officer who maintains county records from cradle to grave; may oversee courts and elections

closed meeting—meetings closed to the public for a specific list of reasons

closed meeting laws—laws declaring which meetings the public may not access for specific legal reasons

closed primary—an election having different ballots each tailored to voters registered with one of the two major parties; also see *primary election*

cobelligerent—a nation, state, or individual that allies with another against a common enemy

Code of Federal Regulations—the Federal Register rearranged topically in a manner useful for referencing

code of laws—a systematic grouping of laws for a specified level of government

Code of Laws of the United States of America (U.S. Code)—the Statutes at Large rearranged topically in a manner useful for referencing

codify—to compile a group of laws topically in a manner useful for referencing

commander-in-chief—chief executive who holds supreme command of the armed forces (without the power to declare war)

commission—a board consisting of appointed rather than elected officials who often serve in a volunteer capacity

commission, redistricting—a board of members appointed to reset the boundaries of electoral districts after the census

commission system—form of local government where the commission sits collectively as the legislative body

committee—a group of legislators assigned to a topic of law who research, report on, and debate bills pertaining to the topic

committee of the whole (House/Assembly or Senate)—a process where the entire chamber operates under the rules for the committee

common law—American law, also called *case law*, that has its roots in British law and is derived from the body of prior judicial decisions instead of from legislative status

common pleas court—the name for trial courts in certain states

communal society—a society based upon communal ownership and use of goods/property

community improvement district—see *special districts*

commutation—the shortening of a judicial sentence

comprehensive plan—general plan or master plan showing the goals of a city and serves as the foundational land-use planning and zoning document required by state statute

compromise—the art of finding common ground without discarding one's principles

comptroller, state—see *controller, state*

confederation—a league or group of allies

conference committee—a committee for both chambers of the legislature

Congress—the name of the legislature at the national level in the United States consisting of the House of Representatives and the Senate

conservative—having a political philosophy based on tradition and social stability, stressing established institutions, and preferring gradual development to abrupt change because mankind is not inherently good

consolidated city-council system—a merger resulting in a unified city-county governance system with a single chief executive and a multi-district council with a few at-large seats

constable—a town or township's officer responsible for peace-keeping and minor judicial duties

constituent—one who is represented by an elected officeholder or other head of a group or organization

constituent service—service by a legislator to those he or she represents

constitution—the primary written governance document of a group of people

Constitution of the United States of America—the supreme law of the land of the United States, also known as the *U.S. Constitution*

constitutional convention—a proposal to amend the Constitution requiring three-fourths of the states in the convention to approve it

constitutional democracy—government by the people based on a written constitution

constitutional law—written law that embodies the rules of a political or social organization (a city, state, or nation)

constitutional officers—elected executive members of county government whose origin of power is anchored in the state constitution; see *row officers*

constitutional-representative democracy—government by elected representatives of the people based on a written constitution

constitutional republic—a form of government that exists under the rules of a written constitution where the governing members temporarily serve as representatives of the people

controller, sate—an appointed or elected state executive office with varying financial duties such as managing a statewide accounting system and providing internal controls for agencies; also called the *comptroller*

coroner—a typically elected county-equivalent-level office for the purpose of determining an otherwise uncertain cause of death

corporation—a body (from the Latin word *corpus*) of people formed, authorized, and recognized by (state) law to act as a single person and be legally endowed with various rights and duties

council—legislative body of a local government

council, city—the legislative body of a municipal government

council, county—the fiscal body of county government

council, regional—a county-equivalent region; also see *regional governments/councils*

council-administrator system—a form of local (county) government consisting of an elected council and a county administrator hired by the council

council-elected executive system—a form of local (county) government consisting of an elected council and a separately elected chief executive

council-manager system—a form of local (municipal) government consisting of an elected council, an appointed (sometimes elected) weak mayor, and a city manager hired by the council

councils of governments—see *regional governments/councils*

county—a mid-sized unit of local government that administers functions delegated to it by the state

county engineer—typically appointed officer who is responsible for designing and constructing county infrastructure

county equivalent—a region such as a parish, borough, or regional council that is recognized by the U.S. Census Bureau as equivalent to a county

county prosecutor—an appointed or elected constitutional row officer (attorney) who decides what offenses should be charged against whom and presents the case in court representing the government

county seat—the city which is the administrative center of the county where services such as the county courthouse are located

county surveyor—an officer (typically appointed) who maintains county land survey records including property boundary lines

county treasurer—see *treasurer, county*

court—an institution authorized to administer justice in civil and criminal matters in accordance with the rule of law

criminal case—a violation of state law such as robbery, assault, murder, drug-related crimes, rape, etc.

crossover bill—a bill approved by the chamber in which it was introduced that moves forward for consideration in the opposite chamber

Declaration of Independence—the founding document of America's separation and independence from Great Britain

defendant—the party or person against whom a lawsuit is brought before a court

democracy—government either purely by the people or representationally by those they elect

democratic—of, by, or for the people

Democratic National Convention—the Democratic party's national gathering for the purpose of selecting its official candidate for the November presidential ballot

Democratic party—one of the two major political parties in the United States

dependent districts—types of special districts that rely upon another existing local government to govern them (such as the local board of county commissioners)

deputy—a person given full power of an officer without holding the office (i.e. deputy sheriff, deputy prosecutor, deputy attorney general)

despot—a ruler who exercises absolute power in a tyrannical fashion

dictator—a ruler who exercises absolute control

diplomat—one skilled in conducting negotiations between potentially adversarial groups

discretionary power—the power or authority granted by the state to municipalities to conduct their own affairs

district—geographic region with boundaries for election and representation purposes

district attorney (DA)—see *county prosecutor*

district court, federal—trial court

district court, state—varies by state from general trial court to limited-jurisdiction court

District of Columbia—Washington D.C., the capital of the United States; a district which is not one of the fifty states

double jeopardy—being tried twice for the same offense in a court of law

drug court—special court-instituted programs for individuals with alcohol or drug dependency problems that provide an opportunity for a second chance and rehabilitation; also called *treatment court*

dual citizenship—citizenship in one's nation and in the kingdom of heaven

dual-court system—the American judicial system that exists in two tracks: the *federal track* and the *state track*

due process of law—principle from the Fourteenth Amendment that the government must follow lawful procedures before depriving a person of life, liberty, or property

duty—fee or tax

elastic clause—also known as *necessary and proper clause*; see *implied powers*

elected representative—any person elected (not appointed) to public office

election cycle—the number of elections that take place in a year in a county-equivalent geographical area

Electoral College—the group of electors who choose the President and Vice President of the United States

electorate—the voters

enabling statutes—laws passed by state legislators that direct agencies to make administrative rules that serve their purposes

enfranchisement—the act of endowing with a privilege, particularly the right to vote

enjoin—to stop enforcement of law

enumerated/expressed powers—powers that Congress possesses according to Article I, Section 8 of the U.S. Constitution

Evenwel v. Abbott—the 2016 Supreme Court case which upheld that total population could be used when considering redistricting

ex officio—literally *because of the office*; one who serves in a position because of the office held in another position

ex post facto—literally *out of a thing done afterward*; a law that retroactively declares an act that was legal at the time it was committed to be illegal

executive branch/power—the division of government that executes or carries out the law, often led by an individual, an executive head; see *chief executive*

executive order—a rule or order issued by the head of the executive branch of government that has the force and effect of law

executive session—a meeting that is closed to the public for specific legal reasons

extra-territorial powers—powers that extend beyond a local government's territorial limits/boundaries

fascist—based on Benito Mussolini's theory of centralized national government under a strong militaristic, dictatorial leader

federal law—law that governs across the United States

Federal Register—the chronological list of federal agency rules and regulations having the effect of law; also known as the *Daily Journal of the United States Government*

federal regulatory agencies—agencies that create regulations, rules, procedures, orders, and decisions at the federal level which possess legal effect

federalism—an organizational system where power is distributed between a central authority and constituent (subordinate) units

federalism, American—the principle that the Constitution gives our national government limited powers while recognizing the powers of the states and the people; governmental powers are shared between federal government and state governments

felony—a serious crime with a potentially long sentence that can result in the loss of the right to vote, possess firearms, or hold public office

filibuster—the act of speaking endlessly to delay the vote on a bill in the Senate (to filibuster)

first reading—the process of filing a bill with the clerk, assigning it a bill number, reading it by title, and double-checking it for formatting errors

first-tier court—the court where a case enters the judicial system; also known as *trial court*

fiscal authority—the power for a municipality or county to set tax rates, determine revenue sources, borrow funds, etc.

Founders—the men who founded or established the United States of America

Framers—the men who wrote the Constitution of the United States of America

franchise—the right (to vote)

functional authority—the power to govern locally in a narrow or broad manner regarding the functions a city or county performs

General Assembly, state—another name for the House of Representatives at the state level; in several states, the name of two chambers of the state legislature meeting together, see *House of Representatives, some states/national*

general election—the second of two elections during the presidential election cycle purposed with choosing officeholders

gerrymandering—reshaping districts in a highly irregular fashion to favor the majority party

gospel—the good news of faith in Jesus Christ for the forgiveness of sin

governance—exercising the core functions of the government entity within the boundaries of delegated authority

government—the governing authority structure for each of the realms of life

government-subsidized services—public control or oversight of local services

governor—the chief executive of a state's government and the one to whom the other executive officers ordinarily report

grand jury—eighteen citizens chosen by lottery from the judicial district in which they live and in which a criminal case is potentially being tried

Grand Old Party (G.O.P)—another name for the *Republican Party*

grassroots—meaning at the most basic level, usually involving ordinary people

Great Depression—the decade from 1929 to 1939 during which America experienced the worst economic downturn in its history

gubernatorial—meaning pertaining to the governor

hamlet—a small community often within a town

home-rule charter—charter that grants power to a local government to exercise self-government under the authority of the state constitution and state laws

House of Delegates—another name for the House of Representatives at the state level; see *House of Representatives, some states/national*

House of Representatives, some states/national—the lower, larger, and more populist chamber of a legislative body

House Rules and Manual—the combined methods used by the parliamentarian of the U.S. House of Representatives

impeach—to charge the President, Vice President, or other high officeholder with misconduct while in office

implied powers—powers possessed by Congress that are implied in Article I, Section 8 and are useful to implement the enumerated/expressed powers

independent city—a city that is independent of (legally separated from) a county or replaces a county that altogether ceased to exist

independent districts—special districts that have board members who are typically elected by the people but can also include board members who are appointed by another local government's representative to serve for fixed terms

infrastructure—the basic physical systems that undergird a community such as water and sewer works, stormwater drainage, bridges, roads, etc.

initiative—the procedure of initiating (introducing) a piece of proposed legislation directly on the ballot

investigative committee—see *special committee*

judge—elected or appointed officeholder who presides over a court of law

judicial branch/power—the division of government that judges or interprets the law

judicial district, state—the division of a state into geographic areas over which the state court system has jurisdiction

judicial review—the authority to assess the constitutionality of actions by the executive and legislative branches

judiciary—a jurisdiction's system of courts, synonymous with the judicial branch

jurisdiction—the legal authority to hear a certain type of case or the geographic boundary surrounding a law

jury duty—the summons to serve as a juror in a legal proceeding

justice—a judge who serves on the highest court of appeals

justice of the peace—a local public servant who in some states can act as a municipal court judge, officiate at marriage ceremonies, and witness signatures or oaths

juvenile court—a court that has special jurisdiction over those under eighteen years of age

law—rules passed by a legislative body for the purpose of governance

legislation—law(s) passed by a governing body (typically a legislature)

legislative branch/power—the division of government that creates or enacts the law

legislative districts, state (single-member/multi-member)—geographical districts based on population for the purpose of electing official representatives of the people to both chambers of a state's legislature; single-member is one representative per district, multi-member is two or more representatives per district

legislator—an individual who is elected to serve in the legislature

legislature—the governing body which convenes and passes laws

letter of marque—permission to cross over the frontier into another country's territory in order to take a vessel on the seas

letter of reprisal—permission to take a captured vessel to the home port of the capturer

levy—a financial assessment imposed upon those who are governed within a jurisdiction or the act of imposing such assessment

liberal—having the belief in the essential goodness of the human race and the autonomy of the individual's political and civil liberties while requiring the government's superintending care from cradle to grave

libertarian—one who values liberty from government oversight

lieutenant governor—the vice chief executive officer of the state who serves while the governor is temporarily absent

limited town meeting—see *representative town meeting*

line-item veto—a chief executive's power to strike a particular line or section from a bill before signing it into law

lobbying—the act of persuading those in authority of a certain position

lobbyist—one who seeks to persuade those in authority of a certain position

local government—the levels of American government existing below the level of the state

magistrate court—a trial-level state court

Magna Carta—the Great Charter of 1215 when King John of England granted certain rights to the English people

mail-in voting—voting conducted exclusively by mail-in ballots which are sent to every registered voter

majority vote—a vote passing by more than half the total of the group, meaning more than 50%

Marbury v. Madison—the 1803 Supreme Court case that set the precedent for the judicial branch to have the final say on whether the other two branches' actions are constitutional or not

Marxist—referring to Karl Marx's theory of the superiority of collective ownership in the form of socialism and its purer form of communism as opposed to free-market capitalism and private ownership of goods, services, and property

Mason's Manual of Legislative Procedure—the book of parliamentary procedure for public meetings at the state level

Mayflower Compact—the first governing document of the first permanent English settlement in the New World, the Plymouth Colony

mayor—the executive (or ceremonial) head of a city

mayor-council system—a form of municipal government with a strong full-time executive mayor elected at large and council members elected either at large or by district who comprise the legislative body

minority leader of Senate, national and state—the Senator chosen to represent the party not in control of the chamber floor

minutes—a record of business completed at the prior public meeting

misdemeanor—a less serious offence than a felony, punishable by less than one year of incarceration

mission statement—current purpose and current key objectives needed to accomplish a vision statement

monarch—one who reigns over a kingdom or empire

moral law—Old Testament law that continues to be applicable in post-New Testament times

Motor Voter Act—see *National Voter Registration Act*

multi-member district—a district that elects two or more members to its legislative body

municipal—pertaining to the city

municipal corporation—a body (from the Latin word *corpus*) of people representing a city that is formed, authorized, and recognized by (state) law to act as a single person and legally endowed with various rights and duties such as the ability to enter into contracts, to sue and be sued, and to own property

municipal court—a type of court which is created and operated by a city or town and is not always subject to the state judicial system

municipality—a city

nation—a group of people residing within specified borders governed by overarching law

national law—law that governs a nation (consisting of a national constitution, statutes, and agency rules)

National Voter Registration Act—1993 act passed by Congress requiring states to offer voter registration at state motor vehicle agencies; also known as *Motor Voter Act*

naturalization—the process of becoming a citizen

necessary and proper clause—also known as *elastic clause*; see *implied powers*

New Deal—executive agencies and programs instituted by Franklin Delano Roosevelt during the Great Depression

nonpartisan—not affiliated with a political party

open-meeting laws—laws declaring that the public must have access to public/open meetings

open meeting—public meeting to conduct government business

open primary—a primary election ballot open to all voters regardless of party affiliation

open town meeting—see *town meeting*

optional charter—offers a selection of charter options written by the state

ordinance—a local law

orthodoxy—true belief (what to believe)

orthopraxy—true practice (what to do)

pardon—the excusing of an offense without exacting a penalty

parish—county-equivalent regions in Louisiana; see also *county* and *county equivalent*

parliament—a legislative body that governs

parliamentary procedure—a series of formal rules that define the structure and order of business for a public meeting

partisan—affiliated with or biased toward a political party

party—a political organization that runs candidates for office

party platform—the document which catalogs and memorializes the principles and values of a party

personnel authority—the power to govern the number of municipal employees, their pay, rules, and employment conditions

petit jury—also known as the "jury"; consists of twelve jurors chosen by lottery from the judicial district in which they live and in which a civil or criminal case will be tried

Pilgrims—the English colonists who first landed at Provincetown, Massachusetts, and settled at Plymouth, Massachusetts, in 1620

plaintiff—the party or person who brings a lawsuit before a court

plank—each topic or state position within the party platform

Planned Parenthood v. Carey—1992 Supreme Court case generally upholding *Roe v. Wade*

planning board/commission—an appointed board/commission that reviews and recommends changes to the comprehensive plan and the land-use ordinance

planning region—county equivalent in Connecticut; also called *Regional Councils of Government (COG)*

Plessy v. Ferguson—1896 Supreme Court case declaring that facilities could be racially separate as long as they were equal

pocket veto—a bill not signed by the chief executive within ten days of receipt (excluding Sundays)

police power—the authority of a government to regulate control over people or property within its jurisdiction to accomplish a public goal usually regarding the protection of the public's health, safety, and welfare

policy—procedure for a governing body

politburo—policy-making body of the Communist party

poll—the act of counting heads for voting or tallying purposes

polls—the place where voting takes place

popular vote—the vote for U.S. President (and Vice President) counted by percentage of the population

preamble—the introductory text of a governing document that states the intention of what will follow

precinct—the smallest geographic subset or political division relating to elections; a voting district

precinct captain/chairman/committee officer/committee person/committeeman/delegate—the person who is elected to serve the party's constituents in a precinct

President of the United States (POTUS)—the chief executive officer of the United States

president *pro tempore* of Senate, state—the assistant to the president of the state Senate who steps in to substitute for the governor if the lieutenant governor steps out, and the true majority party leader

presidential election cycle—election for the President of the United States that occurs every four years on the first Tuesday after the first Monday in November

primary election—the first of two elections during the presidential election cycle; its purpose is to narrow the field of candidates from a political party

principle of subsidiarity—the principle that civil matters should be dealt with by the lowest level of government in relation to them

privatization—the change from public to private oversight

probate court—a special jurisdiction court that oversees the execution of wills, estates, and such

progressive—having the belief in progress, the essential goodness of the human race, and the autonomy of the individual's political and civil liberties while requiring the government's superintending care from cradle to grave; see *liberal*

prohibited powers—powers forbidden to Congress by the U.S. Constitution

promulgate—to make laws known publicly and to put them into force

prosecuting attorney—see *county prosecutor*

public defender—a typically appointed attorney who defends clients otherwise unable to afford their own legal assistance

public meeting—any meeting open to the public where elected or appointed individuals within the civil realm make decisions about policy, spending, or priorities

public office—typically an elected position of government leadership involving responsibility to the public characterized by both authority and service

public servant—a person who is employed by the government or serves in a volunteer capacity

public square—the literal space where people gather locally to govern or the theoretical space that conveys public opinion

public works—the ways that a city tends to its infrastructure

pure democracy—a form of government where the people govern themselves directly through the will of the majority

quasi-corporation—an unincorporated public entity enabled by state law to act independently of the state with legal status to perform certain functions rather than full corporate functions

quasi-judicial—declaring judgments but not as part of the judicial branch of government

quorum—the minimum number of members of an assembly that must be present to make a meeting valid

ratify—to formally confirm or adopt (as in the original states ratifying the Constitution)

realm—sphere or domain

reapportionment—see *redistricting*

recall—the procedure of removing an elected representative from office by a vote of the people

recorder—see *clerk/auditor/recorder, county*

red state—a state whose voters tend to support conservative policies and candidates

redistricting—the decennial redrawing of the geographic boundary lines of legislative districts based on U.S. Census results to equalize population; also known as *reapportionment*

reduction veto—a chief executive's power to delete a budget item from a bill before signing it into law

referendum—the process of placing an existing law on the ballot for voters to decide whether it should continue to exist; sometimes called a *veto referendum*

regional commission/council/government—a form of government that can extend beyond city or state boundaries to provide regional projects or programs

Regional Councils of Government (COG)—county-equivalent planning regions for the state of Connecticut

representative democracy—a form of government where the people elect representatives to govern them

representative town meeting—a form of government where eligible voters elect residents to represent them to vote as a board; see *representative democracy*

reprieve—a cancellation or postponement of punishment

republic—a nation with a form of government where power resides in the voting citizens who elect representatives to govern for them according to written law

republican (form of) government—a form of government where power resides in the voting citizens who elect representatives to govern for them according to written law

Republican National Convention—the Republican party's national gathering for the purpose of selecting its official candidate for the November presidential ballot

Republican Party (G.O.P.)—one of the two major political parties in the United States; also known as the *Grand Old Party*

reserved powers clause—the Tenth Amendment to the U.S. Constitution stating that the powers not delegated to the United States by the Constitution, nor prohibited by it to the States are reserved to the States respectively, or to the people

resolution—a formal expression of intent drafted by a governing body not having the force of law

revolution—the overthrowing of one government in favor of another

Robert's Rules of Order—the book of parliamentary procedure for public meetings at the local level

Roe v. Wade—1973 Supreme Court decision declaring that the Constitution protects a woman's right to abortion

rolls—official list of voters' names

row officers—elected executive members of county government whose origin of power is anchored in the state constitution; usually listed in a row on the ballot; also known as *constitutional officers*

school district—a special kind of special district that receives state funding to oversee local public education

second reading—presentation of a bill on the chamber floor to be considered, amended, passed, or to die

second-tier court—court where a case is reviewed after having been tried in a first-tier court; also known as *appellate court*

secretary of commonwealth/state—an elected (sometimes appointed) executive office that is the primary records keeper for a state often including elections records

section—a subdivision of law below an article

select board/selectmen—the chief executive body of town government

select committee—see *special committee*

Selective Service—mandatory military draft for men instituted in 1917 by the Selective Service Act

self-government—self-control

semi-closed primary—characterized by two primary election ballots each tailored to voters registered with one of the two major political parties; unaffiliated voters are free to vote on either ballot

Senate, state/national—the upper, typically smaller, and more prestigious chamber of a legislative body

Senate Manual—the combined methods used by the parliamentarian of the U.S. Senate

separation of powers—the constitutional separation of American government into three powers: the legislative branch in Article I, the executive branch in Article II, and the judicial branch in Article III

shared-planning resources—a type of regional government contract between smaller communities and larger communities to provide resources to the smaller

sheriff—a typically elected (but sometimes appointed) constitutional row officer who provides law enforcement to areas of the county that are outside incorporated towns

single-member district—a district that elects one member to its legislative body

single-purpose entities—special districts that can cross state lines

solicitor general—appointed deputy attorney general whose task is to represent the state in federal cases (suits involving the federal government)

Speaker of the House of Representatives, national—most powerful member of the House; chosen by majority party members

Speaker of the House or Assembly, state—most powerful member of the House/Assembly; chosen by majority party members

special-assessment tax—a tax levied on citizens to cover a special project, usually infrastructure

special charter—a charter offering the least local control because it is obtained through an act of the state legislature; it is the oldest form of charter

special committee—a committee for special investigative purposes

special districts—local governments formed by communities in order to provide some public service within defined boundaries

special services areas—see *special districts*

stakeholdering—finding all of the various people or groups involved in a proposed project and talking with each of them

standing committee—a committee for only one chamber of the legislature

stare decisis—Latin for *to stand by things decided*, the policy of not overturning prior court decisions

state—synonym for civil government; also refers to the constitutional (subordinate) governing entities that make up the fifty United States

state-agency regulations—see *administrative-agency law*

State Assembly—another name for the House of Representatives at the state level; see *House of Representatives, some states/national*

state law—law that governs a state, consisting of state constitutions, statutes, and agency rules

State of the City Address—annual speech delivered by the mayor to the city on the current condition of the city; usually given early in the calendar year

State of the State Address—annual speech delivered by the governor to the state legislature on the current condition of the state; usually given early in the calendar year

State of the Union Address—annual speech delivered by the President of the United States to Congress on the current condition of the nation; usually given early in the calendar year

state seal—the primary graphic emblem that represents the state

state treasurer—see *treasurer, state*

statute—a law passed by a legislative body

Statutes at Large—the chronological list of laws enacted by Congress

statutory law—state law established by an act of the legislature or federal law established by Congress

strategic plan—the shorter-term implementation of the comprehensive plan

structural authority—the power of a local government to choose its own organizational system of government

study committee—see *special committee*

subcommittee—subdivision of a congressional/legislative committee

subpoena—a written document instructing a person's mandatory attendance at a trial for the purpose of providing evidence

suffrage—the right of voting

summons—a written document instructing a person's mandatory attendance at a trial

sunshine laws—laws declaring that the public must have access to public/open meetings; also called open-meeting laws

superior court—a trial-level court in many states

superintendent of public education—elected or appointed state-level officeholder who handles all of the individual city and county public school systems in the state as the chief state school officer, overseeing public higher education and working in concert with a state board of education; also known as the superintendent of schools, superintendent of education, superintendent of public instruction, secretary of education, or chief school administrator

supermajority vote—substantially more than 50% of a vote by a group; this number changes according to each state's laws and may be two-thirds (66.66%) or three-fifths (60%) of the group's vote

Supreme Court of the United States (SCOTUS)—the highest court in the federal judicial track, also known as the U.S. Supreme Court

supreme court, state—the highest court in the state judicial track (except in the state of New York)

survey township—a six-mile by six-mile square plot of land that is referred to by a number based on the Public Land Survey System (PLSS)

tax assessor—an appointed or elected constitutional row officer who assesses the value of properties in the county to determine the property tax for each

tax tribunal—a special jurisdiction court that hears tax-related issues

taxing districts—see *special districts*

third reading—presentation of a bill on the chamber floor to be further amended, passed, and sent to the second chamber, or to die

third-tier court—final court of appeals; see also *supreme court, state*

title—the heading of a topic of law

town—used interchangeably with the term *city* in this book; in specific state codes, a town, borough, hamlet, or village may represent a certain population

town meeting—a New England form of government referring to the meeting itself of the voters of a town for the transaction of town business or the legislative body; an example of pure democracy

treasurer, county—an appointed or elected constitutional row officer vested with the authority to collect all money due to the county treasury

treasurer, state—an appointed or elected executive who serves as the state's chief financial officer collecting/investing state money, overseeing state agency spending, and paying state bills

treatment court—see *drug court*

trial court—first-tier court where a case enters the judicial system

Unicameral—one-chamber legislature (only found in Nebraska)

unincorporated—not having the powers granted to a corporation

United States Attorneys—chief federal-level prosecutors for each federal judicial district

universal law—God's law as understood before the written Scriptures or as recorded in the Old and New Testaments of the Bible

U.S. Code—see *Code of Laws of the United States of America*

U.S. Constitution—see *Constitution of the United States*

U.S. Supreme Court—see *Supreme Court of the United States*

veto—a chief executive's power to decline or request amendment to measures passed by the legislative body; see *amendatory veto*, *line-item veto*, and *reduction veto*

veto referendum—see *referendum*

Vice President—the vice chief executive of the United States

village—see *town*

vision statement—future ambition of what a city wants to be

vote—to cast a decision; see also *majority vote* and *supermajority vote*

warrant—a written document authorizing a person's arrest

We the People—the first three words of the Constitution referring to government by the people; self-government

whip the vote—to enforce the party platform

winsomeness—speaking the truth with humility and grace in a generally pleasing and engaging manner

writ of *habeas corpus*—an inquiry into whether a person is detained in custody lawfully or not

zoning board/commission—an appointed board that conducts public hearings often requesting variances under the land use ordinance

BIBLIOGRAPHY

270 to Win. "Electoral College Ties." www.270towin.com.

Adkins, Lenore T. "What does a public defender do in the U.S.?" ShareAmerica. September 17, 2020. archive-share.america.gov.

Adrian, Charles R. *State and Local Governments*. 2nd ed. New York: McGraw-Hill, 1967.

Ahrens, Lynn, vocalist, composer, and writer. "The Preamble." *Schoolhouse Rock!: Special 30th Anniversary Edition*. DVD. Directed by Tom Warburton. 1975; Burbank, CA: Buena Vista Home Entertainment, 2002. Available on YouTube.

America Counts. "From Municipalities to Special Districts, Official Count of Every Type of Local Government in 2017 Census of Governments." U.S. Census Bureau. October 29, 2019. www.census.gov.

American Bar Association. "How Courts Work." September 9, 2019. www.americanbar.org.

Ang, Carmen. "Animated Map: The History of U.S. Counties." Visual Capitalist. Published July 31, 2020. www.visualcapitalist.com.

Annenberg Classroom. "Fifth Amendment—Right Against Self-Incrimination." May 5, 2017. www.annenbergclassroom.org.

Anthony, Clarence E. Foreword to "Principles of Home Rule for the 21st Century" by National League of Cities. 2020. Accessed September 2, 2023. www.nlc.org.

Ashcroft, John R. "The Missouri Roster 2021–2022: A Directory of State, District, County and Federal Officials." Missouri Secretary of State. Jefferson City, MO: 2021. www.sos.mo.gov.

AskTheLawyers. "What Kind of Offenses Are Handled in Municipal Court?" Accessed April 26, 2020. www.askthelawyers.com.

Association of International Certified Professional Accountants. "Chart of States with and without State Tax Tribunals." June 2, 2020. us.aicpa.org.

Assumption Parish Police Jury, Louisiana. "What is a Police Jury and its Duties?" www.assumptionla.com.

Bacon, Francis. *The Works of Francis Bacon, Lord Chancellor of England: A New Edition with a Life of the Author by Basil Montagu*. Vol. 1, compiled by Basil Montagu. Philadelphia, PA: Carey & Hart, 1852.

Barton, Ryland. "Curious Louisville: Why Is Kentucky A Commonwealth?" Louisville Public Media, published July 21, 2017. wfpl.org.

Beier, Anne. *The Importance of Being an Active Citizen*. 1st ed. A Primary Source Library of American Citizenship. New York: Rosen Central Primary Source, 2004.

Berman, David R. *Local Government and the States: Autonomy, Politics, and Policy*. 2nd ed. New York: Routledge, 2020.

———, ed. *Local Governments in an Era of Change*. Westport, CT: Greenwood Press, 1993.

Bledsoe, Richard. *Metropolitan Manifesto: On Being the Counselor to the King in a Pluralistic Empire.* Monroe, LA: Theopolis Books, 2015.

Boardman, Andy. "Here's How Much Money Rhode Island Is Getting from the American Rescue Plan." Uprise RI. May 11, 2021. upriseri.com.

Boatright, Jason. "The History, Meaning, and Use of the Words Justice and Judge." *St. Mary's Law Journal* 49, no. 4 (August 2018). commons.stmarytx.edu.

Boersma, Hans. "Sphere Sovereignty." *Clarion* 36, no. 21 (October 23, 1987): 462. clarionmagazine.ca.

Bomboy, Scott. "The one election where Faithless Electors made a difference." *Constitution Daily* (blog), National Constitution Center. December 19, 2016. constitutioncenter.org.

Bratt, James D., ed. *Abraham Kuyper: A Centennial Reader.* Grand Rapids, MI: Eerdmans, 1998.

Brennan Center for Justice. "Supreme Court Upholds 'One Person, One Vote.'" April 14, 2016. www.brennancenter.org.

Burdick, Eugene and Arthur J. Brodbeck, eds. *American Voting Behavior.* New York: Free Press, 1959.

Butterfield, Rosaria. "Christians, the LGBTQ Community, and the Call to Hospitality." By Matt Tully. *The Crossway Podcast,* May 13, 2019. www.crossway.org.

———. *The Gospel Comes with a House Key: Practicing Radically Ordinary Hospitality in Our Post-Christian World.* Wheaton, IL: Crossway, 2018.

Byers, Jacqueline J. "County Treasurer: Keeper of the Dollar$." National Association of Counties Research Brief. November 2008. www.naco.org.

———. "Role of the County Clerk." National Association of Counties Research Brief. November 2008. www.naco.org.

CDC. "Coroner Training Requirements." Public Health Professionals Gateway. Last reviewed February 8, 2023. www.cdc.gov.

CT.gov. "Governor Lamont Announces U.S. Census Bureau Approves Proposal for Connecticut's Planning Regions To Become County Equivalents." The Office of Governor Ned Lamont. June 6, 2022. portal.ct.gov.

——— "Marshal Commission, State: FAQs." portal.ct.gov.

California Senate Local Government Committee. *What's So Special about Special Districts? A Citizen's Guide to Special Districts in California.* 4th ed., October 2010. santaclaralafco.org.

Carey, Maeve C. "An Overview of Federal Regulations and the Rulemaking Process." Congressional Research Service. Updated March 19, 2021. sgp.fas.org.

Carlin, Dan. "A Recipe for Caesar." Produced by Dan Carlin. *Common Sense with Dan Carlin.* March 31, 2020. Podcast, 1:26:19. podcasts.apple.com.us.

Carson, Clarence B. *Basic American Government.* Wadley, AL: American Textbook Committee, 1993.

Carson City, Nevada. "City Facts." Last updated July 26, 2016. www.carson.org.

Casetext. "California Gov. Code § 82048.5." casetext.com.

Center for the Study of Global Christianity. "Status of Global Christianity, 2020, in the Context of 1900–2050." 2020. www.gordonconwell.edu.

Charter of Alaska. "Art. II, § 5." Municode. library. municode.com.

City and County of Honolulu. "Revised Charter of the City & County of Honolulu 1973 (2017 Edition)." January 4, 2021. www.honolulu.gov.

City of Franklin, Virginia. "Fire and Rescue History." www.franklinva.com.

City of Portland. "Portland Voters Approve Charter Reform, City Launches Transition." November 9, 2022. www.portland.gov.

Clark County, Washington. "Article 3 The Executive Branch." Clark City Council, 2024. clark.wa.gov.

Columbia Law Review, Harvard Law Review, University of Pennsylvania Law Review, and Yale Law Journal. *The Bluebook: A Uniform System of Citation.* 21st ed. Cambridge, MA: Harvard Law Review Association, 2020.

Congress.gov. "Counting Electoral Votes: An Overview of Procedures at the Join Session, Including Objections by Members of Congress." Congressional Research Service Updated December 8, 2020. sgp.fas.org.

———. "How Our Laws Are Made." Revised and updated by John V. Sullivan. July 24, 2097. www.congress.gov.

Congressional Research Service. "Counting Electoral Votes: An Overview of Procedures at the Joint Session, Including Objections by Memberes of Congress." crsreports.congress.gov.

Constitution Annotated. "ArtI.S3.C2.2 Senate Vacancies Clause." constitution.congress.gov.

———. "ArtI.S6.C1.2 Privilege from Arrest." constitution .congress.gov.

———. "ArtII.S4.4.7 President Richard Nixon and Impeachable Offenses." constitution.congress.gov.

———. "Constitution of the United States." Accessed October 13, 2021. constitution.congress.gov.

———. "Intro.7.3 Federalism and the Constitution." constitution .congress.gov.

———. "Table of Supreme Court Decisions Overruled by Subsequent Decisions." Accessed August 28, 2023. constitution.congress.gov.

Coppa, Frank J. *County Government: A Guide to Efficient and Accountable Government.* Westport, CT: Praeger, 2000.

Corbett, Steve, and Brian Fikkert. *When Helping Hurts: How to Alleviate Poverty without Hurting the Poor—and Yourself.* Chicago, IL: Moody Publishers, 2009.

Cornell Law School. "Listing by Jurisdiction." Legal Information Institute. www.law.cornell.edu.

Corwin, Edward S. *The "Higher Law" Background Of American Constitutional Law.* Indianapolis, IN: Liberty Fund, 2008.

Curzan, Anne and Rebecca Kruth. "Here's why we say 'gubernatorial' instead of 'governatorial.' *Michigan Public.* June 10, 2018. www.michiganradio.org.

Davidson, Nestor M. "Local Constitutions." *Texas Law Review* 99, no. 5 (April 2021). texaslawreview.org.

Davis, Angela J. "The Powers and Discretion of the American Prosecutor." *Droit et Cultures* (online) 40, no. 1 (2005): 55–66. Online since March 2, 2010. journals.openedition.org.

———. "Prosecutors as the Most Powerful Actor in the Criminal Justice System." Race, Racism and the Law. February 7, 2014. racism.org.

Democratic National Committee. "Party Platform." democrats.org.

Denniston, Lyle. "Constitution Check: What does 'one-person, one-vote' mean now?" *Constitution Daily* (blog). National Constitution Center. April 5, 2016. constitutioncenter.org.

Detrow, Scott. "'You Couldn't Get Elected Dogcatcher!' No, Seriously." Produced by NPR. *Weekend Edition Saturday*. April 7, 2018. www.npr.org.

Diligent. "How to Report Corruption in Local Government." *Diligent Blog*. March 19, 2019. www.diligent.com.

Disney in Florida. "Reedy Creek: The Facts You Need in 2024." February 1, 2024. disneyconnect.com.

Douglas, Joshua A. "The Right to Vote under Local Law." *George Washington Law Review* 85, no. 4 (September 12, 2017). www.gwlr.org.

Drutman, Lee. *The Business of America is Lobbying: How Corporations Became Politicized and Politics Became More Corporate*. New York: Oxford University Press, 2015.

Duane, James J. *You Have the Right to Remain Innocent: What Police Officers Tell Their Children about the Fifth Amendment*. New York: Little A, 2016.

Dudley, Susan E. "Milestones in the Evolution of the Administrative State." *Daedalus*. Summer 2021. www.amacad.org.

Duncombe, Herbert Sydney, and Robert Weisel. *State and Local Government in Idaho and in the Nation*. Moscow, ID: University Press of Idaho, 1984.

Earls, Aaron. "10 Encouraging Trends of Global Christianity in 2020." Lifeway Research. June 10, 2020. research.lifeway.com.

Egoshin, Alex. "The Oldest Cities in the U.S. Mapped." *Vivid Maps*. March 23, 2022. vividmaps.com.

Eichner, James A., and Linda M. Shields. *Local Government*. 2nd rev. ed. New York: F. Watts, 1983.

Elazar, Daniel Judah. *Exploring Federalism*. Tuscaloosa: University of Alabama Press, 1987.

Elias, Stephen R. *Legal Research: How to Find & Understand the Law*. 19th ed. Nolo, 2021.

Ellul, Jacques. *The Meaning of the City*. Grand Rapids, MI: William B. Eerdmans, 1993.

Erb, Kelly Phillips. "Disney Sues Florida Gov. Ron DeSantis Over Control Of Special District, Alleging Retaliation." *Forbes*. April 26, 2023. www.forbes.com.

Erickson, Brenda. "Amending the U.S. Constitution." National Conference of State Legislatures (NCSL). Updated August 1, 2017. www.ncsl.org.

Fabina, Jacob, and Zachary Scherer. "Voting and Registration in the Election of November 2020." Current Population Reports, U.S. Census Bureau. January 2022. www.census.gov.

Fair Vote. "Faithless Electors." October 2022. fairvote.org.

Federal Bureau of Investigation. "Public Corruption." www.fbi.gov.

Federal Election Commission. "Registering a Candidate." www.fec.gov.

Fernald, Austin. "The Difference Between a Town and a City; Plus Counties, Villages and More." *ZoningPoint Blog*. zoningpoint.com.

FileRight. "4 Ways to Become a U.S. Citizen." Last updated October 17, 2021. www.fileright.com.

FindLaw. "Bush v. Vera, 517 U.S. 952 (1996)." caselaw.findlaw.com.

———. "Evenwel v. Abbott, 578 U.S. ___ (2016)." caselaw.findlaw.com.

———. "Miller v. Johnson, 515 U.S. 900 (1995)." caselaw.findlaw.com.

———. "Reynolds v. Sims, 377 U.S. 533 (1964)." caselaw.findlaw.com.

———. "Wesberry v. Sanders, 376 U.S. 1 (1964)." caselaw.findlaw.com.

———. "What's the Difference Between a Misdemeanor vs. Felony?" Last reviewed August 17, 2023. www.findlaw.com.

Franklin County Forensic Science Center. "What Is a Coroner?" coroner.franklincountyohio.gov.

Gideon at 50. "Nebraska." perma.cc/U4QE-WUJA.

Global Site Plans—The Grid. "Connecticut Since the Abolition of County Government in 1959." Smart Cities Dive. Accessed October 26, 2021. www.smartcitiesdive.com.

The Great State of Alaska—Department of Commerce, Community, and Economic Development. "Municipal Govern ment Structure in Alaska." Revised October 2, 2018. www.commerce.alaska.gov.

The Great State of Alaska—Department of Public Safety. "Alaska State Troopers—Recruitment." dps.alaska.gov.

Hadley, Debbie. "7 New Deal Programs That Still Exist Today." *ThoughtCo.* Updated September , 2024. www.thoughtco.com. 🔗

Haggerty, William Armstead. *The Triumph of Christian Diplomacy.* Boston, MA: Boston University Libraries, 1903. open.bu.edu. 🔗

Hall, Jeremy L and Michael W. Hail. "Special Districts." Center for the Study of Federalism—Encyclopedia. Last updated 2006. encyclopedia.federalism.org. 🔗

Hayward, Steven F. "The Threat to Liberty: The administrative state and the end of constitutional government." *Claremont Review of Books.* Winter 2016/17. claremontreviewofbooks.com. 🔗

Hess, Stephen, David Riordan, and John Oram. "Not All Counties Are Equal." *Mapzen* (blog). March 23, 2016. www.mapzen.com. 🔗

Hobbes, Thomas. *Leviathan.* Edited with introduction by Christopher Brooke. UK: Penguin Random House, 2017.

Home School Legal Defense Association. "Homeschool Laws by State." hslda.org. 🔗

Howard, Andrew. "The Public's Defender: Analyzing the Impact of Electing Public Defenders." *Columbia Human Rights Law Review Online* (April 15, 2020.) hrlr.law.columbia.edu. 🔗

Idaho County. "Assessor." idahocounty.org. 🔗

Idaho Secretary of State. *Idaho Blue Book.* Caldwell, ID: Caxton Printers, 2021.

Idaho State Legislature. "Idaho's Citizen Legislature—The Membership." legislature.idaho.gov. 🔗

IndyStar. "Unravelling local government: County commissioners vs. county council." *IndyStar.* April 22, 2016. wwwindystar.com. 🔗

International County-City Management Association (ICMA). "Municipal Form of Government (2018–19)." icma.org.

Jackson, Robert H. "The Federal Prosecutor." *Journal of Criminal Law and Criminology* 31, no. 1 (Summer 1940). scholarlycommons.law.northwestern.edu.

Jefferson, Thomas. *A Manual of Parliamentary Practice.* Philadelphia, PA: Parrish, Dunning & Mears, 1853.

———. "Letter to the Danbury Baptists." Library of Congress Information Bulletin. June 1998. www.loc.gov.

John, Godfrey. "Christian Diplomacy." *Christian Science Sentinel* 88, no. 3 (January 20, 1986). sentinel.christianscience.com.

Johnston, Mindy. "list of U.S. presidential elections in which the winner lost the popular vote." *Encyclopedia Britannica*, April 3, 2024. www.britannica.com.

Judicial Learning Center. "Comparing State and Federal Courts." 2019. Video. judicallearningcenter.org.

——— "A Conversation about the Courts: Judges Compare State and Federal Judicial Systems." 2019. Transcript. judiciallearningcenter.org.

———. "State Courts vs. Federal Courts." judiciallearningcenter.org.

Justia. "Delegation of Legislative Power." Accessed August 29, 2023. law.justia.com.

———. "Evenwel v. Abbott, 578 U.S. ___ (2016)." supreme.justia.com.

———. "MO Rev Stat § 81.020 (2022)." law.justia.com.

Kamin, Sam and Zachary Shiffler. "Obvious But Not Clear: The Right to Refuse to Cooperate with the Police during a Terry Stop." *American University Law Review* 69, no. 3 (2020). aulawreview.org.

Katz, Eric. "Supreme Court ends judicial deference to federal agency expertise." Government Executive. June 28, 2024. www.govexec.com.

Kaufman, Herbert. *Politics and Policies in State and Local Governments.* Foundations of Modern Political Science Series. Englewood Cliffs, NJ: Prentice-Hall, 1963.

Kentucky League of Cities. "Form of Government." Accessed September 2, 2023. www.klc.org.

Kiernan, John S. "Property Taxes by State (2024)." WalletHub. February 20, 2024. wallethub.com.

Klein, Christopher. "Why Is the Republican Party Known as the GOP?" History. Updated June 1, 2023. www.history.com.

Krutz, Glen. *American Government 3e.* Rice University, 2021. assets.openstax.org.

Kuyper, Abraham. *Lectures on Calvinism.* Grand Rapids, MI: Eerdmans, 1987.

Latah County, Idaho. "Commissioners." 2024. www.latah.id.us.

Law Library—American Law and Legal Information. "Marque and Reprisal." 2023. law.jrank.org.

Linn, Jan. *Evangelicalism and the Decline of American Politics.* Eugene, OR: Cascade Books, 2017.

Little, Becky. "How Gerrymandering Began in the US." *History.* Last updated August 7, 2023. www.history.com.

Lo, Lydia. "Who Zones? Mapping Land-Use Authority across the US." *Urban Wire* (blog). Urban Institute. December 9, 2019. www.urban.org.

Loyola Law School. "All About Redistricting." redistricting.lls.edu.

MacDonald, William. "Thou Shalt Not Revile the Gods Nor Curse the Ruler of Thy People (Exodus 22:28)—Truths to Live By One Day at a Time." *Bible Portal.* August 19, 2023. bibleportal.com.

Madison, James, Alexander Hamilton, and John Jay. *The Federalist Papers*. Edited by Isaac Kramnick. London: Penguin Books, 1987.

Marquette University Law School. "Marquette Law School Supreme Court Survey." Marquette University Law School Poll: A Comprehensive Look at the Wisconsin Vote. law.marquette.edu.

Marquette University News Center. "New Nationwide Marquette Law School Poll Finds Confidence in U.S. Supreme Court Overall, Though More Pronounced Among Conservatives." October 21, 2019. www.marquette.edu.

Martin, Paul. *A Christian in Local Politics*. Rotherham, England: Paul Martin, 2021.

Marx, Herbert L. *State and Local Government.* Reference Shelf Series, vol. 34, no 3. New York: Hw Wilson, 1962.

Maryland State Archives. "Baltimore City, Maryland." Maryland Manual On-Line: A Guide to Maryland & Its Government. Accessed July 17, 2023. msa.maryland.gov.

Mason, Paul. *Mason's Manual of Legislative Procedure*. Aurora, CO: Frederic Printing, 2020.

Massachusetts Court System. "John Adams & the Massachusetts Constitution." Accessed August 28, 2023. www.mass.gov.

MasterClass. "Government 101: What Does a State Comptroller Do?" September 12, 2022. www.masterclass.com.

Matthews, Byron S. *Local Government: How to Get into It, How to Administer it Effectively*. Chicago, IL: Nelson-Hall, 1970.

McCarthy, Jean. "Why Become a City?" *City and Town*. Massachusetts Department of Revenue Division of Local Services (MDR) 12, no. 9 (November 1999). www.mass.gov.

McCurley, John. "Police Jurisdiction: Where Can Officers Make Arrests?" Lawyers.com. Last updated November 3, 2020. www.lawyers.com.

McDurmon, Joel. *Restoring America One County at a Time*. Dallas, GA: Devoted Books, 2012.

Michigan Legislature. *A Student's Guide to the Legislative Process in Michigan*. Revised April 2023. www.legislature.mi.gov.

Michigan Townships Association. "Townships in the U.S." 2023. michigantownships.org.

Mike Crapo U.S. Senator for Idaho. "Crapo Honors Latah County Sheriff With Spirit of Idaho Award." September 5, 2019. www.crapo.senate.gov.

Mills, Joel. "Lewiston Votes for Strong Mayor." *Lewiston Tribune*. November 3, 2021. lmtribune.com.

Minnesota Family Council. "Biblical Basis for Voting." www.mfc.org.

———. "Church Ambassador Network." www.mfc.org.

———. "Pulpits & Politics." www.mfc.org.

Montgomery County | PA. "Row Officers." www.montcopa.org.

Morlan, Robert L. "Local Governments—The Cities." In *The Fifty States and Their Local Governments*, edited by James W. Fesler, 494. New York: Alfred A. Knopf, 1967.

Moscow Report. moscowidaho.news.

Mosvick, Nicholas. "How the Supreme Court Created Agency Deference." *Constitution Daily* (blog). National Constitution Center. Last modified June 25, 2021. constitutioncenter.org.

Municipal Research and Services Center (MRSC). "City and Town Classification." Last modified February 23, 2024. mrsc.org.

———. "County Elected and Appointed Officials." Last modified December 12, 2022. mrsc.org.

———. "County Forms of Government: Commission Form." Last modified May 6, 2024. mrsc.org.

———. "Knowing Your Roles: City and Town Governments." *Insight* (blog). January 10, 2024. mrsc.org.

Municode. "St. Augustine Beach, Florida—Code of Ordinances/Charter Laws." Accessed September 2, 2023. library.municode.com.

Natapoff, Alexandra. "Criminal Municipal Courts." *Harvard Law Review* 134, no. 3. January 2021. harvardlawreview.org.

National Association of Counties (NACo). "2017 County Authority." County Explorer. ce.naco.org.

———. "Counties Matter: Stronger Counties. Stronger America." February 20, 2023. naco.org.

———. "Federal Policies Matter to County Government." September 22, 2015. YouTube video, 5:57. www.youtube.com.

National Association of Regional Councils. "What are Regional Councils?" narc.org.

National Association of Secretaries of State. "Administrative Rules—United States of America." Administrative Codes and Registers (ACR). Accessed August 28, 2023. www.administrativerules.org.

National Association of State Treasurers. "State Treasurers Count." December 31, 2020. nast.org.

National Association of Towns and Townships. "Town and Township Government in the United States." www.toi.org.

National Center for State Courts. "State Court Structures." 2024. cspbr.azurewebsites.net.

National Civic League. *Model City Charter.* 8th Edition, Second Printing. Denver, CO: National Civic League, 2011. www.nationalcivicleague.org.

———. *Model County Charter.* Revised Edition. Denver, CO: National Civic League, 1990. www.miamidade.gov.

National Conference of State Legislatures (NCSL). "2022 State Legislative Session Calendar." Last modified December 12, 2022. ncsl.org.

———. *Inside the Legislative Process: A comprehensive survey by the American Society of Legislative Clerks and Secretaries in cooperation with the National Conference of State Legislatures.* Revised September 2009. www.ncsl.org.

———. "Parliamentary Procedure: A Legislator's Guide." Updated November 4, 2022. www.ncsl.org.

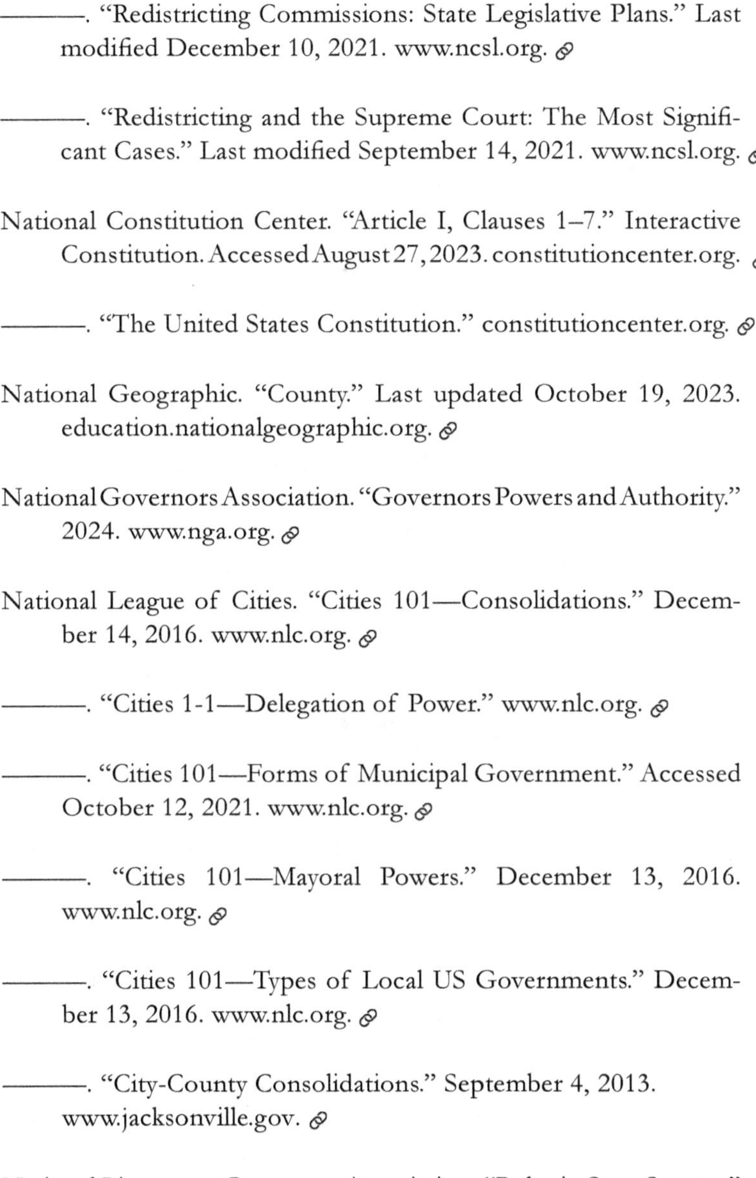

———. "Redistricting Commissions: State Legislative Plans." Last modified December 10, 2021. www.ncsl.org.

———. "Redistricting and the Supreme Court: The Most Significant Cases." Last modified September 14, 2021. www.ncsl.org.

National Constitution Center. "Article I, Clauses 1–7." Interactive Constitution. Accessed August 27, 2023. constitutioncenter.org.

———. "The United States Constitution." constitutioncenter.org.

National Geographic. "County." Last updated October 19, 2023. education.nationalgeographic.org.

National Governors Association. "Governors Powers and Authority." 2024. www.nga.org.

National League of Cities. "Cities 101—Consolidations." December 14, 2016. www.nlc.org.

———. "Cities 1-1—Delegation of Power." www.nlc.org.

———. "Cities 101—Forms of Municipal Government." Accessed October 12, 2021. www.nlc.org.

———. "Cities 101—Mayoral Powers." December 13, 2016. www.nlc.org.

———. "Cities 101—Types of Local US Governments." December 13, 2016. www.nlc.org.

———. "City-County Consolidations." September 4, 2013. www.jacksonville.gov.

National Lieutenant Governors Association. "Roles in State Senates." September 2022. nlga.us.

National Park Service. "The First Residents of Jamestown." Last modified February 26, 2015. www.nps.gov.

National Sheriffs' Association. "FAQ: Question 6." Last modified 2021. www.sheriffs.org.

———. "Office of Sheriff State-by-State Elections Information." www.sheriffs.org.

Nebraska Legislature. "Lawmaking in Nebraska." nebraskalegislature.gov.

New Jersey Department of Community Affairs. *Optional Municipal Charter Law*. January 2017. www.nj.gov.

New Jersey Legislative District Data Book. "Inventory of Municipal Forms of Government in New Jersey." July 1, 2011. njdatabook.rutgers.edu.

New Saint Andrews College. *Thirty-Three Theses on Culture Shaping*. 2nd revised edition. Moscow, ID: Canon Press, 2021.

New York State. "New York Counties." www.ny.gov.

Office of the Secretary of State. "Regional Councils of Governments." portal.ct.gov.

Ohio-Kentucky-Indiana Regional Council of Governments. "Request for Qualifications Consultant Services for OKI Freight Plan." 2022. www.oki.org.

Ouellette, John. "Local Government 101." Massachusetts Municipal Association. Last updated September 19, 2023. www.mma.org.

Planetizen. "What Are Comprehensive Plans?" *Planopedia*, June 23, 2021. www.planetizen.com.

Pope Benedict XVI. *Compendium of the Catechism of the Catholic Church.* Vatican City: Libreria Editrice Vaticana, 2005. www.vatican.va.

Port Authority of New York & New Jersey. "Mission Statement." 2022. www.panynj.gov.

Prager, Dennis. "The Single Best Thing Americans Can Do to Retake America." *Epoch Times.* June 14, 2021. www.theepochtimes.com.

Price, Tirzah. "Why You Should Sit on Your Library Board." October 5, 2021. bookriot.com.

Pruitt, Sarah. "Can the President and Vice President Be From the Same State?" History. Last modified September 21, 2023. www.history.com.

Ragone, Nick. *The Everything American Government Book: From the Constitution to Present-Day Elections, All You Need to Understand Our Democratic System.* The Everything Series. Avon, MA: Adams Media, 2004.

Rassier, Dylan G., Melissa J. Braybrooks, Jason W. Chute, and Howard I. Krakower. "Quasi-Corporations and Institutional Sectors in the U.S. National Accounts." Bureau of Economic Analysis and United States Department of Commerce. July 2016. www.bea.gov.

Read, Amanda. "The Article V Process Explained." Produced by Matthew Perdie. Convention Of States Project. July 16, 2017. conventionofstates.com.

The Recorder. "A New England Tradition." May 3, 2015. YouTube video, 1:29. www.youtube.com.

Renn, Aaron. "Conservatives Need to Learn How to Govern." *The Aaron Renn Show.* May 8, 2023. YouTube video, 26:05. www.youtube.com.

———. "A Field Guide to Chambers of Commerce." *The Aaron Renn Show*. January 31, 2022. YouTube video, 26:59. www.youtu.be.

Republican National Committee. "Our Platform." 2016. gop.com.

Rhodes, Ron. *The Complete Guide to Christian Denominations*. Eugene, OR: Harvest House Publishers, 2005.

Rice, Bradley R. "Commission Form of City Government." *Handbook of Texas Online*, 1952. Updated June 1, 1995. www.tshaonline.org.

Robert, Henry M., III, Daniel H. Honemann, and Thomas J. Balch. *Robert's Rules of Order Newly Revised.* 12th ed. New York: PublicAffairs, 2020.

———. *Robert's Rules of Order Newly Revised in Brief.* 3rd ed. New York: PublicAffairs, 2020.

Robertson, David Brian. *The Original Compromise: What the Constitution's Framers Were Really Thinking*. New York: Oxford University Press, 2013.

Rosen, Jill. "Americans don't know much about state government, survey finds." Hub at Johns Hopkins University, December 14, 2018. hub.jhu.edu.

Roth Davies Trial Lawyers. "What Is the Difference Between Municipal Court, District Court and Federal Court?" 2024. www.rothdavies.com.

Rowling, J. K. *Harry Potter and the Goblet of Fire*. New York: Arthur A. Levine Books, 2000.

Sanford, William R. and Carl R. Green. B*asic Principles of American Government.* New York: Amsco School Publications, 1986.

Schaeffer, Francis A. *How Should We Then Live? The Rise and Decline of Western Thought and Culture*. Old Tappan, NJ: F. H. Revell, 1976.

Schweitzer, Dan, Lindsay See, Barbara Underwood, and Jeffrey Rosen. "The Constitutional Role of the State Solicitor General." Produced by The National Constitution Center. March 24, 2023. Video, 55:35. constitutioncenter.org.

Seuss, Dr. *Horton Hears a Who!* New York: Random House, 1982.

Sheldon, Jack, vocalist. "I'm Just a Bill." By David Frishberg. *Schoolhouse Rock!: Special 30th Anniversary Edition*. DVD. Directed by Tom Warburton. 1975; Burbank, CA: Buena Vista Home Entertainment, 2002. Available on YouTube.

Simmons, Raymond. *The Confessional County: Realizing the Kingdom through Local Christendom*. 1st ed. Edinburgh, Scotland: New Dunedin Press, 2021.

Simon, Christopher A., Brent S. Steel, and Nicholas P. Lovrich. *State and Local Government and Politics: Prospects for Sustainability*. Corvallis: Oregon State University, 2019. open.oregonstate.education.

Sklansky, David Alan. "The Nature and Function of Prosecutorial Power." *Journal of Criminal Law and Criminology* 106, no. 3 (2017). scholarlycommons.law.northwestern.edu.

Smyth, Danielle. "What Are the Duties of the Superintendent of Public Instruction?" *Chron*. February 2, 2022. work.chron.com.

State of Florida—Fourteenth Judicial Circuit. "Public Defender." www.jud14.flcourts.org.

State of Hawaii. "Department of Law Enforcement." law.hawaii.gov.

State of Idaho Controller's Office. *Transparent Idaho* (website). transparent.idaho.gov.

State of New Jersey. "Governor Murphy Signs Legislation to Eliminate the Title of 'Freeholder' from Public Office." Office of Governor Phil Murphy. August 21, 2020. www.nj.gov.

Stevenson, Sandra M. *Understanding Local Government.* 2nd ed. The Understanding Series. Newark, NJ: LexisNexis, 2009.

Steyn, Mark. "The Future Is Showing Up." *Steyn Online.* October 18, 2021. www.steynonline.com.

STLOUIS-MO.GOV. "A Brief History of Saint Louis." www.stlouis-mo.gov.

Sunshine, Glenn S. *Slaying Leviathan: Limited Government and Resistance in the Christian Tradition.* Moscow, ID: Canon Press, 2020.

Supreme Court of the United States. "The Court and Constitutional Interpretation." www.supremecourt.gov.

Taleb, Nassim Nicholas. *Antifragile.* New York: Random House Trade, 2012.

Tarr, G. Alan. *Understanding State Constitutions.* Princeton, NJ: Princeton University Press, 1998.

Tazein, Almas. "Vision and Mission of Award-Winning Cities, Municipalities, and Local Governments around the World." BPIR.com. November 23, 2021. www.bpir.com.

TeenPact Leadership Schools. "Changing Lives to Change the World." teenpact.com.

Texas Association of Counties. "County Tax Assessor-Collector." texascountiesdeliver.org.

Texas Judicial Branch. "Criminal Court of Appeals." www.txcourts.gov.

Thomson Reuters. "Common law: Defining what it is and what you need to know." Last modified November 15, 2022. legal.thomsonreuters.com.

Thomson Reuters Practical Law. "Public Land Survey System (PLSS)." content.next.westlaw.com.

Townsend, Rebecca and Carmin C. Reiss. "An Enduring System of Local Deliberative Democracy: The 21st Century Legal and Normative Structure of Massachusetts Town Meeting." *Journal of Deliberative Democracy* 18, no 1 (June 1, 2022). doi.org/10.16997/jdd.1136.

Trewhella, Matthew J. *The Doctrine of the Lesser Magistrates: A Proper Resistance to Tyranny and a Repudiation of Unlimited Obedience to Civil Government.* North Charleston, SC: CreateSpace Independent Publishing Platform, 2013.

Trickey, Erick. "Where Did the Term 'Gerrymander' Come From?" *Smithsonian.* Last updated July 20, 2017. www.smithsonianmag.com.

U.S. Capitol Visitor Center. "How Your State Gets Its Seats: Congressional Apportionment." www.visitthecapitol.gov.

U.S. Census Bureau."2020 Census: Apportionment of the U.S. House of Representatives." April 26, 2021. www.census.gov.

———. "Connecticut." Last modified October 8, 2021. www.census.gov.

———. "Independent City Definition." www.census.gov.

———. *Individual State Descriptions: 2017.* Released 2019. www.census.gov.

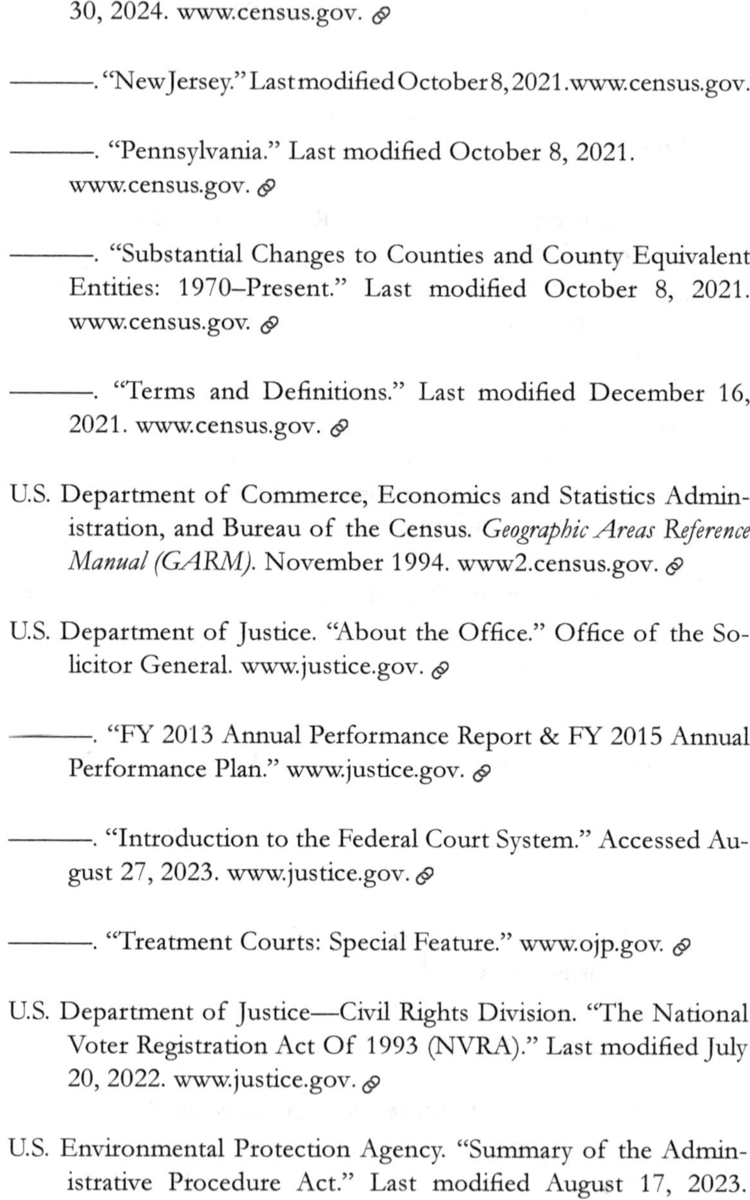

———. *Individual State Descriptions: 2022 Census of Governments*. April 30, 2024. www.census.gov.

———. "New Jersey." Last modified October 8, 2021. www.census.gov.

———. "Pennsylvania." Last modified October 8, 2021. www.census.gov.

———. "Substantial Changes to Counties and County Equivalent Entities: 1970–Present." Last modified October 8, 2021. www.census.gov.

———. "Terms and Definitions." Last modified December 16, 2021. www.census.gov.

U.S. Department of Commerce, Economics and Statistics Administration, and Bureau of the Census. *Geographic Areas Reference Manual (GARM)*. November 1994. www2.census.gov.

U.S. Department of Justice. "About the Office." Office of the Solicitor General. www.justice.gov.

———. "FY 2013 Annual Performance Report & FY 2015 Annual Performance Plan." www.justice.gov.

———. "Introduction to the Federal Court System." Accessed August 27, 2023. www.justice.gov.

———. "Treatment Courts: Special Feature." www.ojp.gov.

U.S. Department of Justice—Civil Rights Division. "The National Voter Registration Act Of 1993 (NVRA)." Last modified July 20, 2022. www.justice.gov.

U.S. Environmental Protection Agency. "Summary of the Administrative Procedure Act." Last modified August 17, 2023. www.epa.gov.

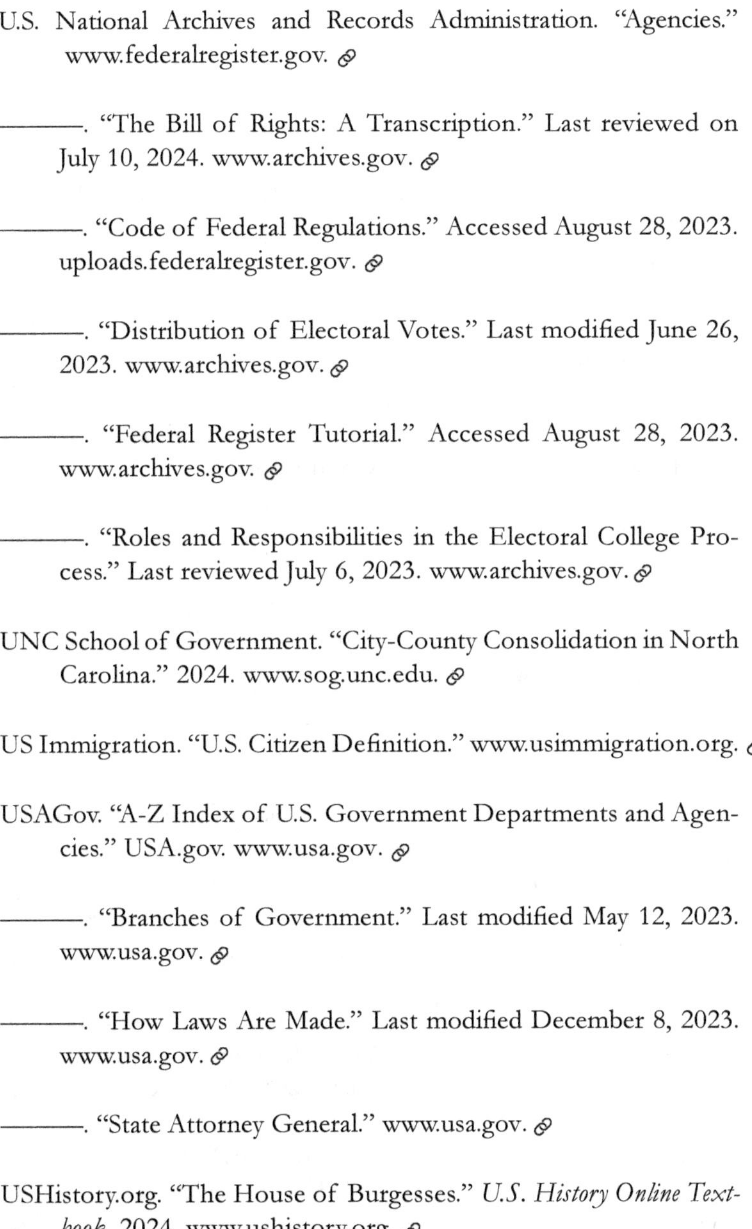

U.S. National Archives and Records Administration. "Agencies." www.federalregister.gov.

———. "The Bill of Rights: A Transcription." Last reviewed on July 10, 2024. www.archives.gov.

———. "Code of Federal Regulations." Accessed August 28, 2023. uploads.federalregister.gov.

———. "Distribution of Electoral Votes." Last modified June 26, 2023. www.archives.gov.

———. "Federal Register Tutorial." Accessed August 28, 2023. www.archives.gov.

———. "Roles and Responsibilities in the Electoral College Process." Last reviewed July 6, 2023. www.archives.gov.

UNC School of Government. "City-County Consolidation in North Carolina." 2024. www.sog.unc.edu.

US Immigration. "U.S. Citizen Definition." www.usimmigration.org.

USAGov. "A-Z Index of U.S. Government Departments and Agencies." USA.gov. www.usa.gov.

———. "Branches of Government." Last modified May 12, 2023. www.usa.gov.

———. "How Laws Are Made." Last modified December 8, 2023. www.usa.gov.

———. "State Attorney General." www.usa.gov.

USHistory.org. "The House of Burgesses." *U.S. History Online Textbook*. 2024. www.ushistory.org.

USLegal. "State-by-State Summary of Judicial Selection." courts.uslegal.com.

———. "State Constitutions." system.uslegal.com.

United States Attorney's Office—Middle District of Alabama. "Former School Superintendent Pleads Guilty in Virtual Education Fraud Case," December 17, 2021. www.justice.gov.

United States Election Assistance Commission. "Poll Worker Resources for Voters." Help America Vote. www.eac.gov.

United States House of Representatives. "The Legislative Process: How Are Laws Made?" www.house.gov.

———. "United States Code." Office of the Law Revision Counsel. uscode.house.gov.

United States Senate. "About Parties and Leadership: Historical Overview." www.senate.gov.

———. "About Voting." www.senate.gov.

———. "Introduction" to the Constitution of the United States. www.senate.gov.

United States Supreme Court. "QP Report for Evenwel et al. v. Abbott, Governor of Texas, et al. (2016)." www.supremecourt.gov.

University of Georgia School of Law. "How Laws Are Made: The Administrative Agencies." Alexander Campbell King Law Library. Last modified September 1, 2021. libguides.law.uga.edu.

University of Tennessee Municipal Technical Advisory Service (MTAS). "Types of Charters." Last reviewed December 20, 2021. www.mtas.tennessee.edu.

Vermilion Parish Tourist Commission,"Why Is Louisiana the Only State to Have Parishes and Not Counties?" vermilion.org.

Virginia Humanities. "Virginia Counties 1634–1640." Encyclopedia Virginia, 2020. encyclopediavirginia.org.

Virginia Law. "Code of Virginia, Article 2: Consolidation of Certain Counties, Citites, and Towns. § 15.2–3534: Optional provisions of consolidation agreement." Legislative Information System. law.lis.virginia.gov.

———. "Constitution of Virginia, Article VII, § 1." Legislative Information System. law.lis.virginia.gov.

Virginia Places. "Virginia Cities That Have 'Disappeared'—and Why." www.virginiaplaces.org.

Vivid Maps. "The Oldest Cities in the U.S. Mapped." March 23, 2022. vividmaps.com.

Wainwright, Paul. "A Space for Faith: The Colonial Meeting Houses of New England." Posted by 4x5guy, February 22, 2010. YouTube video, 3:35. www.youtu.be.

Wallace, Harvey. "Federal and State Jurisdiction." In *National Victim Assistance Academy*, edited by Anne Seymour, Morna Murray, Jane Sigmon, Melissa Hook, Christine Edmonds, Mario Gaboury, and Grace Coleman. Office for Victims of Crime, 2000. ncjrs.gov.

The White House. "The Executive Branch." www.whitehouse.gov.

———. "The Judicial Branch." www.whitehouse.gov.

———. "Presidential Personnel Office." www.whitehouse.gov.

———. "State and Local Government: Legislative Branch." www.whitehouse.gov.

Wolfe, Stephen. *The Case for Christian Nationalism.* Moscow, ID: Canon Press, 2022.

Woodlief, Tony. *I, Citizen: A Blueprint for Reclaiming American Self-Governance.* New York: Encounter Books, 2017.

World Population Review. "States with the Most Counties 2024." worldpopulationreview.com.

Wormuth, Francis D. *Origins of Modern Constitutionalism.* New York: Harper and Brothers, 1949.

Your Missouri Judges. "How the Missouri Plan Works." yourmissourijudges.org.

Zale, Kellen. "Compensating City Councils." *Stanford Law Review* 70 (March 26, 2018). papers.ssrn.com.

Zambito, Thomas C. "NY created an agency to OK wind and solar projects quickly. Upstate towns aren't happy." *Journal News.* LoHud. October 12, 2022. www.lohud.com.

Zhorov, Irina. "Explainer: Cities, boroughs, and townships, oh my! Pa. municipalities clarified." WHYY. April 4, 2016. whyy.org.

www.ingramcontent.com/pod-product-compliance
Lightning Source LLC
Chambersburg PA
CBHW062109020426
42335CB00013B/901

* 9 7 8 1 9 6 3 5 0 5 0 8 5 *